Embodiment and Eating Disorders

This is an insightful and essential new volume for academics and professionals interested in the lived experience of those who struggle with disordered eating. *Embodiment and Eating Disorders* situates the complicated – and increasingly prevalent – topic of disordered eating at the crossroads of many academic disciplines, articulating a notion of embodied selfhood that rejects the separation of mind and body and calls for a feminist, existential, and sociopolitically aware approach to eating disorder treatment. Experts from a variety of backgrounds and specializations examine theories of embodiment, current empirical research, and practical examples and strategies for prevention and treatment.

Hillary L. McBride, MA, RCC, is a PhD candidate in counseling psychology at the University of British Columbia in Vancouver, British Columbia. She has won the Young Investigator Award in Human Sexuality and is the author of *Mothers, Daughters, and Body Image: Learning to Love Ourselves as We Are.* You can learn more about her work at www.hillarylmcbride.com

Janelle L. Kwee, PsyD, RPsych, is program director and associate professor of counseling psychology at Trinity Western University in Langley, British Columbia and a registered psychologist in private practice at Altus Psychological Services. For more about Dr. Kwee, see www.altuspsychology.com/about/dr-janelle-kwee/

Embodiment and Eating Disorders

Theory, Research, Prevention, and Treatment

Edited by
**Hillary L. McBride and
Janelle L. Kwee**

Routledge
Taylor & Francis Group

NEW YORK AND LONDON

First published 2019
by Routledge
711 Third Avenue, New York, NY 10017

and by Routledge
2 Park Square, Milton Park, Abingdon, Oxon, OX14 4RN

Routledge is an imprint of the Taylor & Francis Group, an informa business

Library of Congress Cataloging-in-Publication Data

Names: McBride, Hillary L., editor. | Kwee, Janelle L., editor.
Title: Embodiment and eating disorders: theory, research, prevention, and treatment / edited by Hillary L. McBride and Janelle L. Kwee.
Description: New York, NY: Routledge, 2018. | Includes bibliographical references and index. Identifiers: LCCN 2018005950 (print) | LCCN 2018017680 (ebook) | ISBN 9781315159645 (eBook) | ISBN 9781138065536 (hbk) | ISBN 9781138065550 (pbk) | ISBN 9781315159645 (ebk) Subjects: LCSH: Eating disorders. | Eating disorders—Prevention. | Eating disorders—Treatment. Classification: LCC RC552.E18 (ebook) | LCC RC552.E18 E47 2018 (print) | DDC 616.85/26—dc23 LC record available at https://lccn.loc.gov/2018005950

ISBN: 978-1-138-06553-6 (hbk)
ISBN: 978-1-138-06555-0 (pbk)
ISBN: 978-1-315-15964-5 (ebk)

Typeset in Bembo
by codeMantra

Contents

Contributors

Christina Bally MA Student in Counselling Psychology, Trinity Western University, Langley, BC, Canada

Chelsea Beyer Doctoral Student in Counselling Psychology, University of British Columbia, Vancouver, BC, Canada

Jazmyn Brown Student Researcher, Nova Southeastern University, Fort Lauderdale, FL, USA

Giovanni Castellini Researcher, Department of Neuroscience, Psychology, Drug Research and Child Health, University of Florence, Florence, Italy

Elizabeth Chan Counsellor, Langley, BC, Canada

Laura Hurd Clarke Professor of Kinesiology, University of British Columbia, Vancouver, BC, Canada

Catherine Cook-Cottone Associate Professor of Counseling, School, and Educational Psychology, University at Buffalo, State University of New York, Buffalo, NY, USA

Natasha Files Family Therapist, Vancouver, BC, Canada

Jenna Fletcher Psychotherapist, Ottawa, ON, Canada

Ian Frampton Senior Lecturer, Center for Clinical Neuropsychology Research, University of Exeter, Exeter, UK

M. Elizabeth Lewis Hall Professor of Psychology, Rosemead School of Psychology, Biola University, La Mirada, CA, USA

Heather L. Jacobson Psychologist, Edmonds, WA, USA

Susan Kleinman Dance/Movement Therapist, The Renfrew Center of Florida, Coconut Creek, FL, USA

Janelle L. Kwee Associate Professor of Counselling Psychology, Trinity Western University, Langley, BC, Canada

Adele Lafrance Associate Professor of Psychology, Laurentian University, Ottawa, ON, Canada

Mihaela Launeanu Assistant Professor of Counselling Psychology, Trinity Western University, Langley, BC, Canada

Anja Loizaga-Velder Director of Research and Psychotherapy, Nierika Institute for Intercultural Medicine, Mexico

Milena Mancini Doctoral Student, Department of Psychological, Health and Territorial Sciences, G.d'Annunzio University Chieti-Pescara, Chieti, Italy

Hillary L. McBride PhD Candidate in Counselling Psychology, University of British Columbia, Vancouver, BC, Canada

Jessica Moncrieff-Boyd Clinical Psychologist at the Adolescent Eating Disorder Service, Priory Hospital Roehampton, London, UK

Andrea Shaw Nevins Professor of History and Political Science, Nova Southeastern University, Fort Lauderdale, FL, USA

Kenneth Nunn Senior Lecturer in the School of Psychiatry, University of New South Wales, Australia

Rhea L. Owens Assistant Professor of Counseling Psychology and Community Services, University of North Dakota, Grand Forks, ND, USA

Peggy Pace Psychotherapist and Developer of Lifespan Integration, LLC, Snoqualmie, WA, USA

Renae Y. Regehr Executive Director, Free to Be Talks, Vancouver, BC, Canada

Marika Renelli MA Student in Psychology, Laurentian University, Ottawa, ON, Canada

Adrienne Ressler Vice President, Professional Development, The Renfrew Center Foundation, For Lauderdale, FL, USA

Valdo Ricca Associate Professor of Psychiatry, University of Florence, Florence, Italy

Kelsey Siemens Counsellor, Langley, BC, Canada

Giovanni Stanghellini Professor of Dynamic Psychology, University Chieti-Pescara, Chieti, Italy

Kenneth Tupper Adjunct Professor in the School of Population and Public Health, University of British Columbia, Vancouver, BC, Canada

Barbara Weber Associate Professor of Human Development, Learning and Culture, University of British Columbia, Vancouver, BC, Canada

Meris Williams Psychologist, Vancouver, BC, Canada

Cindy Wuflestad Director of Certification for Lifespan Integration, Woodinville, WA, USA

Introduction

Of all psychiatric diagnoses, eating disorders have the highest mortality rate (Arcelus, Mitchell, Wales, & Nielsen, 2011; Jáuregui-Garrido & Jáuregui-Lobera, 2012). Current trends in eating disorder prevalence are also disturbing: globally, the number of women struggling with eating disorders is rising, new eating disorders have been added to the most recent version of the DSM, and disordered eating has been emerging in even younger populations and increasing among males (Holland, Hall, Yeates, & Goldacre, 2016; Pike & Dunne, 2015). Yet the suffering within the body extends beyond the individual who meets diagnostic criteria for an eating disorder, with an even more overwhelming number of women dissatisfied with their bodies and demonstrating subclinical levels of disordered eating. The scope of this problem demands innovative approaches to understanding the existing problem and how to solve it.

There is a long philosophical tradition conceptualizing the mind and body as distinct and separate parts. Central to this idea is that the self has been within or synonymous to the mind. This dualism has prevailed in the treatment of eating disorders with its distinct focus on correcting cognition and/or behavior. Where there have been distorted thoughts or negative perceptions, individuals have been encouraged to change their thoughts, correct their perceptions, and comply with the externally imposed rules of how to recover.

The construct of embodiment offers the perspective of the self as an integrated whole. Instead of the self being distinct from the body, the body is the self, and therefore struggle with the body is also an existential struggle with the pain of being a self. The body is also political, and women's bodies reflect the narrative and receive the pain of their oppression within their social and historical context. Although obvious when stated, the body has a role in eating disorders. We have envisioned this book to begin a conversation with a specific focus on the philosophical concept of embodiment as it is related to a holistic vision for eating disorder prevention and treatment. For this reason, this book is positioned within the existential and phenomenological framework.

Eating disorders do not develop and thrive in isolation: they must be understood as situated within a particular sociocultural context and can be understood from a variety of standpoints. In this way, the book is also conceptualized from a feminist perspective as it is decidedly critical of the sociopolitical influences which shape the social construction of the body, and women's bodies in particular. Together, the integration of feminism and existentialism provides a conceptualization of the embodied self in eating disorder prevention and treatment as representing resistance to sociocultural objectification of women's bodies. These perspectives provide language for exploring eating disorders which honor the aspects that are deeply personal and also contextualized within the larger social story.

Numerous books have been written on eating disorders and their treatment, which we acknowledge have been helpful for the advancement of understanding of how eating disorders develop and what to do to help end the suffering of so many people. Often, the literature addressing eating disorders is found within the disciplines of psychology and medicine. Embodiment and eating disorders are situated at the crossroads of a variety of disciplines, and together they represent an integration of psychology, philosophy, medicine, politics, literature, culture, and neuroscience. In this edited volume, we have brought together interdisciplinary and international dialogue about eating disorders with an embodiment focus. Mirroring the integration central to the notion of embodiment, we desired to bring an integration of perspectives into one collaborative volume. We sought out voices representing a wide variety of disciplines to represent the most current empirical research, practical examples, and strategies for prevention and treatment. With contributions from multiple experts, we have designed this book for a variety of readers interested in eating disorders and embodiment, and the book will be particularly useful for readers who intend to interact academically with theory and research and those who will benefit from having new skills and practical examples of eating disorder prevention and treatment.

In much of our research and writing together, we have found Bronfenbrenner's (1979) ecological systems model to provide a helpful framework for exploring women's experiences in and through their bodies. Within this model, human development is conceptualized as occurring within various contextual systems. The individual is at the center of the model but is considered to be nested within the microsystem (family unit, school, peers, religious community, and health services), the exosystem (industry, social services, mass media, local politics, and neighbors), and the macrosystem (the attitudes and ideologies of the culture). These systems interact to shape what is at the center of the model, the developing self.

Within Bronfenbrenner's ecological systems model, we can make sense of the intersection of eating disorders and embodiment. At the center is the lived experience of the body and of disordered eating. The individual does not develop disordered eating (or healing) alone, but within a microsystem. At the level of the individual, there are chapters in this volume addressing neuroscience, emotion, the feelings of being a body, and the use of medicines. We address the microsystem when talking about how family and schools can be powerful sources of influence for the development of embodiment. The microsystem is also addressed through the chapters focusing on therapies for eating disorders, as the relationship with the therapist is at the microsystem level. The larger ecosystem is addressed in the chapters discussing media, the fashion industry, and change in the conceptualization of eating disorder treatments. Lastly, the feminist perspective throughout this book names the way that patriarchal ideologies and the oppression of women, as the broadest circle, permeate all levels of the systems nested within it.

Ultimately, this book was compiled with the intention of creating change. Through having more voices and perspectives represented in the conversation about eating disorders, it is our hope that this will contribute to even more advancement in the understanding of eating disorder prevention and treatment, and ultimately to less human suffering in this form. We hope that the contributions in this volume will inspire a vision and strategy to pursue a world where we all have more freedom to be ourselves in our bodies and to explore new ways of thinking, doing, and relating.

References

Arcelus, J., Mitchell, A. J., Wales, J., & Nielsen, S. (2011). Mortality rates in patients with anorexia nervosa and other eating disorders: A meta-analysis of 36 studies. *Archives of General Psychiatry, 68*(7), 724–731. doi:10.1001/archgenpsychiatry.2011.74

Bronfenbrenner, U. (1979). *The ecology of human development: Experiments by nature and design,* Cambridge, MA: Harvard University Press.

Holland, J., Hall, N., Yeates, D. G., & Goldacre, M. (2016). Trends in hospital admission rates for anorexia nervosa in oxford (1968–2011) and England (1990–2011): Database studies. *Journal of the Royal Society of Medicine, 109*(2), 59–66. doi:10.1177/0141076815617651

Jáuregui-Garrido, B., & Jáuregui-Lobera, I. (2012). Sudden death in eating disorders. *Vascular Health and Risk Management, 8,* 91–98. doi:10.2147/VHRM.S28652

Pike, K. M., & Dunne, P. E. (2015). The rise of eating disorders in Asia: a review. *Journal of eating disorders, 3*(1), 33–47.

Part I

Theoretical and Philosophical Perspectives of Embodiment and Eating Disorders

What is embodiment, and what is its role in the prevention and treatment of eating disorders? This section includes chapters that explore this question from a theoretical perspective, weaving together existential, phenomenological, and feminist perspectives on eating disorders. This includes a chapter addressing how body image and embodiment are different, an exploration of eating disorders as a feminist issue, and the re-centering of the body in eating disorder work, the development of embodiment, the history of embodiment in the discipline of philosophy, and how we may begin to better understand embodiment through research and measurement of experiences and constructs which are difficult to explore through traditional academic approaches.

1 Embodiment and Body Image

Relating and Exploring Constructs

Hillary L. McBride

Our bodies, and our relationships with them, are rife with paradox: known and unknown, constant and changing, often visible to others in ways invisible to ourselves. The skin on my face is made up of different cells than when I was first born, but looking at a photo of my face in childhood, people would recognize the face they see in the photo as my face: different, yet paradoxically the same. My body has always been me and been my own. Yet moving through the world and time, depending on the stage of life, the context, the need, the choice, our bodies can feel less 'our own' and more an object to be seen and judged, touched, used, had. These paradoxes reveal the tensions wrapped up in our human bodies, hinting at the richness and complexity of our existence, the body itself, our relationships to our own bodies and the bodies of others, and our intellectual understanding of 'body'.

With something as apparently concrete as the body, it is intriguing that there is such little consensus among academics about how we understand and describe our relationship to our bodies, as it parallels the domains of human experience: somatic, affective, cognitive, relational/spiritual. Although there are constructs such as *body image* and *embodiment* which have even been used empirically and philosophically to better understand the body-self relationship, there has been no conclusive resolution to the decades-long theoretical debate about what those words mean and how they are related to each other or not (Garner & Garfinkel, 1981; Smolak, 2006).

The divergent approaches to conceptualizing our relationships to and experiences of our bodies give us opportunity for rich dialogue and nuanced understandings. How these theories fit together, and do so within a particular sociopolitical context – where bodies are sites of power and oppression – requires further exploration. In this chapter, we explore the relationship between body image and embodiment as constructs that can inform research, treatment, and prevention of eating disorders.

Body Image

Body image was defined in the early 20th century by Schilder as "the picture of our own body which we form in our mind, that is to say, the way which the body appears to ourselves" (1950, p. 11). Currently, certain definitions of body image appear more regularly than others in the academic literature, even though there is no consistently agreed-upon theoretical definition. Most often, these definitions describe body image as the cognitive appraisal, perception, or evaluation of one's own appearance and body shape, and the related or resulting affect (Smolak, 2006). These cognitive and affective dimensions of body image include appearance evaluation and orientation, esteem of one's body, and the accuracy of size perception (Avalos, Tylka, & Wood Barcalow, 2005; Thompson, Heinberg, Altabe, & Tantleff-Dunn, 1999). Theories of body image differ as to what is included in the umbrella term of body image and what is not. For example, Cash's definition of body image is the "multifaceted psychological experience of embodiment, especially but not exclusively one's physical appearance" (Cash, 2004, p. 1); he further expanded the definition of body image to "one's body-related self-perceptions and self-attitudes, including thoughts, beliefs, feelings, and behaviors" (p. 1). Unlike other theorists, Cash includes a dimension of embodiment in his definition of body image. The addition of a person's body- or appearance-related *behavior* is not included in all definitions of body image and has been identified as the cognitive behavioral theory of body image (Cash, 2002). The behavioral component is sometimes referred to as *appearance or body investment*, implying a body/appearance behavior influenced by cognition and affect (Cash, 2002).

Although body image appears to reside within the person and is attributed to one's own subjective thoughts and feelings, there is research to indicate that a person's cognition and affect about his or her own appearance is influenced by the sociopolitical context (Hardit & Hannum, 2012). Certain appearances are more valuable, and others are less valuable, with some appearances even being oppressed and marginalized (Fisher, 2000; Piran & Cormier, 2005; Young, 2005). Based on what messages are communicated about desirable bodies, a person's cognitive appraisal of his or her own body and the resulting affect can be greatly impacted. We learn how to evaluate our appearance, and against what to evaluate it, based on what is around us and what is considered ideal or desirable. The tripartite model (Hardit & Hannum, 2012) has been helpful in identifying which sources of information are significant in communicating information about desirable bodies: these sources are media, peers, and parents/family. Each of these sources works together reciprocally to perpetuate social discourses about ideal bodies and what kind of appearance is valuable in each society.

Body image has been a central focus of eating disorder research and treatment, and there is evidence that the two may be reciprocally related (Cash & Brown, 1987; Cash & Deagle, 1997). It has been identified that negative body image is not simply the opposite of positive body image. The terms negative body image and positive body image suggest the overall perspective a person has when reflecting on the mental image of his or her body: a positive reflection is one that feels enjoyable and approving, while a negative reflection may be characterized by dissatisfaction, disapproval, or shame (Striegel-Moore & Cachelin, 1999). However, these terms imply, incorrectly, that body image is a single construct with either a positive or a negative dimension. This creates a false binary of polar opposites in which the same ideas exist on either side of the construct, but one is felt positively, while the other is felt negatively. Similar to depression versus happiness, happiness is not simply the absence of depression, and depression is not simply the absence of happiness: positive body image cannot be simplified as the absence of negative body image.

Although positive body image and negative body image both refer to a cognitive evaluation of one's appearance, these terms are actually describing different events, experiences, and qualities in people (Avalos et al., 2005; Smolak, 2006; Tylka, 2011). Despite how difficult it is for a consensus to be reached on what body image is, scholars such as Tylka (2011) and Williams and colleagues (2004) have begun to attempt to identify what healthy body image is and what characterizes the people who possess it. Healthy body image is thought to include a general satisfaction with one's body, less distress in relation to appearance (than those with negative or unhealthy body image), higher levels of optimism and self-esteem, radical self-acceptance, and positive beliefs about their body as it contributes to their functioning and lives overall. Tylka (2011) has identified that healthy body image includes

> favorable opinions of the body regardless of actual appearance; acceptance of the body despite weight, body shape and imperfections; respect for the body by attending to its needs and engaging in healthy behaviours; and protection of the body by rejecting unrealistic media images.
>
> (p. 57)

Although much more simple to understand as a positive or negative binary, this popular conceptualization of body image has created a limited understanding of the complexity of how we relate to our bodies, as well as the multiplicity of cognitive and affective responses people may have when thinking about their appearance. Body image and body appreciation, or body satisfaction, appear to be related terms, in that they all reflect some affective and cognitive response or relationship to one's body. However, their relationship is complicated and difficult to explain. It has since been articulated that women can simultaneously feel pride and joy when reflecting on certain parts of their bodies, while feeling shame and judgment toward themselves when thinking about other aspects of their appearance (Ogle & Damhorst, 2005). For example, researchers exploring women's thoughts and feelings about their bodies at midlife have found that women may feel negatively about one aspect of their appearance, such as increased weight, but feel positively about another aspect of their appearance, such as few wrinkles (Hurd Clarke & Korotchenko, 2011). While these can coexist, it is important to note that a woman's body image, although positive, may reinforce internalization of sociocultural ideals and may not necessarily be a sign of acceptance of one's self. For example, valuing few wrinkles is a result of existing in a culture that believes wrinkles are bad. Further, research addressing midlife women also identifies the complexity of understanding body image as a construct: women may not like their appearance and body size or shape, but may reluctantly accept it. Thus, poor body image and appearance acceptance may coexist.

The Limitations of Body Image as a Construct

Although as a construct body image can be helpful to begin to understand how we cognitively perceive our outward appearance, the term is limited in its ability to capture the complexity of an individual's relationship with his or her body. Moreover, these limitations may be harmful for our understanding of a fully integrated and experiential self.

Read again Schilder's original definition of body image: "*the picture* of our own body which we form in our *mind*, that is to say, the way which the *body appears* to ourselves" (1950, p. 11). The language he uses has a specific focus: notice words like *picture* and *appearance* to capture how we think about what we look like, and the mental construction of an outward reality visible fully to others, but never fully to ourselves. While more current definitions of body image, as described earlier, have expanded to include the cognitive and affective responses, and even for some scholars the behavior resulting from that mental construction of our appearance, the term remains the same: body *image* – where *image* represents the visual, the visible, something seen. Smolak (2006) also highlights that body image includes an evaluative component, in which a person is reflexively judging his or her own appearance or mental image of his or her own body. Evaluation, however, exists in a sociocultural context that is particularly articulate about what is desirable and what is considered good in terms of appearance and image (Piran & Cormier, 2005). This evaluation occurs as a mental measuring up of one's own appearance, or mental image of the body, according to how well it meets expectations, shaped by explicit and implicit narratives of attractiveness, desirability, and social value (Smolak, 2006).

What is missing in these current definitions of body image is the remainder of what it means to be human: the invisible knowing, the experience, the subjective and internal reality. To be *in*-bodied. Body image as a construct can never ever fully capture the complexity of a person's relationship with his or her body, because relationship – especially with one's self – is not limited to appearance alone, to the visible, to what is seen by others. For example, my relationship with myself, with my body, might be one of turmoil and conflict: even though I may like my appearance, and others around me might also find my appearance to be desirable and attractive, an experience of illness makes it difficult for me to move through the world in a way that feels safe. Unfortunately, in a culture that values the image of women's bodies over other and all aspects of the self, for women, it is rare to have the experience of being a self that is not limited to appearance.

In their article *(De)Constructing Body Image*, Gleeson and Frith (2006) critique the manner in which body image as a construct is assumed to be real (and therefore measurable), static, and located within the individual. They state, "assuming that body image 'exists' means that we forget to ask important questions about how this construct comes into being, and how it is deployed and given meaning" (2006, p. 86). Both feminist theory and phenomenology highlight the necessity of critiquing the use of language and constructs as they shape our lived experiences. Thus, in the conceptualization of women's bodies, social oppression, and eating disorders, *body image* as a construct is inadequate for understanding or promoting the fullness of women's experiences of life and self. In our efforts as researchers, theorists, clinicians, educators, and members of society concerned with the prevention and treatment of eating disorders, we must strive for more than positive body image – which reflects only an outside view of the body. Rather, and in addition, we need to consider the experiential aspects of the body: the lived experience of the body from the inside.

Embodiment

Unlike body image, as described earlier, embodiment is the experience of the body as engaged in the world; it is a person's experience of living as a body (Piran & Teall, 2012). The work of philosophers, particularly in the field of phenomenology, made significant contributions to the development of the construct, as noted in the work of Sartre, Merleau-Ponty, Levinas, and Henry (see Weber, this volume). Later utilized in the field of critical sociology, embodiment has come to represent not only the solitary, individual, and inner experience of the body but also the way that the experience of the lived body is shaped by social discourse, relationships, and the *other* (Allan, 2005; Piran & Teall, 2012).

Phenomenologist Max van Manen makes an important epistemological case for the importance of embodiment when considering human experience. His work, *Phenomenology of Practice*, indicates that our body is a source of knowing. Through our body, we can know the world, what it is to feel, to be a self, which ultimately contributes to and is the source of our aliveness. Not limited to cognitive kinds of knowing, he states that knowing "resides in our actions, situations, relations, and, of course our bodies" (van Manen, 2014, p. 270). It is through our embodied being, our corporeality, that we can relate to others (know others) and experience the world (know the world). He describes this corporeal knowing as the feelings that live within our bodies that allow us to sense others and things, to communicate with others nonverbally while receiving their nonverbal communication. It is through the knowing and experience within our bodies that we feel the soothing and empathic touch of a loved one, smell and taste a favorite meal, and sense ourselves aroused during an erotic or sexual encounter. It is through our full awareness and experience of our bodies that we *know* (in a noncognitive manner) how to pour hot water from a kettle without burning ourselves, while also carrying on a conversation with someone nearby.

We can become consciously aware of what we are knowing through our body (i.e. being able to report to another that one has 'learned' through 'experience' not to touch a hot log in a fire, as was 'learned' initially through the experience of pain). However, often the knowings of and through the body are not identified, or made conscious, as is described by Sartre through the phrase *"le passé sous silence"* – or what is being passed over or passed by in silence (van Manen, 2014, p. 327). Often, we are unaware of ourselves as a body, not stopping to notice what our body is doing or not doing, rather focusing on our motivation and intent. For example, we focus on getting to the grocery store while mentally making a list of what to buy, without noticing the experience of walking or the sensation in the body. However, it is through our body that we exist in this world. Through our embodied experience, we can most readily know life and all of its pleasure, pain, and feelings. Interestingly, it becomes most difficult to ignore or forget the body when there are sensations of pain or discomfort, especially in the case of illness (van Manen, 2014, p. 329).

For those of us who are able-bodied, it may have been possible for a time for us to remain unconscious of our embodiment or repress it altogether, leading to a dissociated self within the body; it is the sensations of pain or dis-ease which most often require a person to notice their body in a way that they may not have before (van Manen, 2014). As stated by van Manen, "as long as we are healthy, we may not have reason to take notice of our corporeal being" (p. 330). He then indicates that while the body can be passed over or silenced, it is still "the center of our existence" (p. 330); thus, the mandate of health-care professionals in particular is to support the patient to learn to give voice back to the body, teaching the patient to listen, feel, notice, and thus to live wholly. As can be the case for individuals with physical disabilities, difficulties performing activities that others do not have to think about is a reminder of the body. In these instances, the focus of the body is not (necessarily) the appearance of the body, rather the embodied experience of feeling limited as a body, as a self in the world.

Differences between Embodiment and Body Image

As indicated earlier, body image and embodiment are constructs which both refer to the body, but in different capacities. Body image represents the cognitive attention on the appearance or image of the body, while embodiment refers to the lived body. Dionne (2002) identifies that embodiment is different from body image in several ways. These include the breadth of the construct (including a wide range of emotions, attunement to the body, and functionality), the focus on inner experience, and the social construction of the embodied experience (Piran & Teall, 2012). However, body image is limited to the "evaluation of oneself from the outside and therefore reflects the internalization of the external gaze towards one's body" (Piran & Teall, p. 175). While it is helpful to have a construct that captures one's evaluation of appearance, body image as a construct does not capture the complexity of the human experience, with a focus limited to appearance alone while neglecting the lived body (Dionne, 2002). One possible example of the difference between body image and embodiment is to compare it to the difference between looking at food and actually tasting and digesting it. While the appearance of food may be important to some, one could argue that the primary purpose of food is for it to be eaten, to be experienced, and thus to receive the pleasure and nourishment from it. While helpful to describe a particular dish from its appearance alone, how it appears will never fully capture the various dimensions (smell, texture, taste, body response) to eating it. Imagine, for a moment, that explaining to someone how a dish of spaghetti looks will help them know and experience the eating and tasting of it.

The Sociopolitical Disembodiment and Objectification of Women

Women's fixation on appearance does not develop in isolation, but it emerges in a patriarchal context in which the social value of women is portrayed as being limited to how closely her appearance resembles that of the sociocultural ideal and if her body can be used as a tool for reproduction or the sexual arousal of men (Piran & Cormier, 2005). The tripartite model (Hardit & Hannum, 2012) explains that the primary pathways for the dissemination of sociocultural messages are parents, media, and peers. From a young age, girls and women are prized and valued for their appearance or the sexual or reproductive capacity of their bodies over the other dimensions of human experience often valued in men (Piran & Cormier, 2005). This devaluating of women is particularly clear when observing the portrayal of the female body in media, in which women's bodies are made into objects, cut down to desirable pieces used to sell products (Fredrickson & Roberts, 1997). Through the lens of social learning theory, it is evident how girls and women learn from their social environment (including media, parents, and peers) to leave the fullness of their embodied selves, at times learning about the safety of leaving a body which is constantly evaluated, objectified, and disembodied (Hardit & Hannum, 2012; Piran & Teall, 2012). Girls and women are socialized to abandon their experience of the lived body for the cognitive and evaluative focus on appearance and the attainment of the appearance ideal, and having done so are often socially rewarded as being more desirable (Fredrickson & Roberts, 1997). Disembodiment is obvious during puberty as girls' bodies change, and the preoccupation with the appearance of the changing body becomes a central focus (Smolak, 2006). It is then, if not earlier, that girls begin to objectify themselves, viewing their own bodies from the outside, as if seen through the hypothetical gaze of the other (Smolak, 2006).

In a chapter about women's relationships with their bodies, written from a feminist perspective, it would be remiss to not mention the high prevalence of sexual assault and violence against women and how that impacts women's lived experiences, as these experiences are situated within the body. A woman may evaluate her appearance as pleasing, or not. Yet, based on the fact that she is a woman, she may have the experience of shame about her body or felt the sense of fear within her body because of the likelihood of violation to her body simply because she is born female (Fisher 2000; Piran & Teall, 2012; Young, 2005). A felt sense of fear and unsafety because of the high prevalence of sexual assault (not including the constant sexual objectification of women's bodies) make it difficult for women to stay in their bodies. Women who have experienced sexual assault or violence may also unconsciously and spontaneously dissociate; learning through trauma leaves the experience within the body as a way of surviving (Ogden, Minton, & Pain, 2006). In fact, sexual abuse and assault are significant predictors of eating disorders; distress within the body becomes too much to tolerate; existing 'cerebrally' outside the body becomes a way to survive; and unlike trauma, the body can be controlled (Schwartz & Cohn, 1996; Schwartz & Galperin, 1996). Women with eating disorders are obvious examples of leaving the experience of the body, often referring in clinical settings to their phenomenological experience of self as existing exclusively within their cognitions. Their thoughts, it seems, are the safest places to be. They have the sense of living within their mind, and as they live within their mind, they are carried around in the world by a meat puppet – the body.

The threat of sexual violence must be considered when examining women's relationships with their bodies and the sociopolitical context within which that relationship exists. It is a reminder that, as a construct, body image is helpful for considering how individuals think about and evaluate their appearance, but it does not capture the intricacy of sense and the fullness of the experience of living as and in a body.

Embodiment and Body Image in Eating Disorder Work

The pervasive sexualization, objectification, and devaluation of girls and women and the persistent threat of sexual violence facilitate the fragmentation of women's experience within themselves, forging a divide between their disembodied self and their body (Fisher, 2000; Young, 2005). While it is common for women who have eating disorders to have erroneous perceptions or negative evaluations of their body size and shape, these alone are not the exclusive cause of eating disorders (Katzman & Lee, 1997; Piran & Teall, 2012). Eating disorders may be best understood as "not in any way related to body image but, instead, related to a lived experience of restricted agency" (Piran & Teall, 2012, p. 176). While it is worth exploring body image as a construct, the disembodiment and felt experience of restricted agency related to eating disorders necessitate an approach to eating disorder work (both prevention and treatment) that focuses on the development of the self as an embodied agent. The focus on restructuring of cognitive distortion about the body and food in eating disorder treatment may only serve to further facilitate disembodiment and compliance, reinforcing the compliance imposed on women in the sociocultural and political spheres (Katzman & Lee, 1997; Piran & Teall, 2012). Instead of compliance with the patriarchal construction of femininity, Bordo (1993) describes embodiment as a meaningful resistance and response to complex sociocultural narratives. Eating disorder treatment needs to be an invitation into more agency, whole-person participation in life, and the restoration of the experience of a self which is fully inhabited within the body, especially as it exists within social structures oppressive to women.

Conclusion

Scholars who research and theorize about body image do not completely agree on a singular definition of what body image is, or even that it is (Gleeson & Frith, 2006). Yet, it is still of value to reflect on how people, particularly women, conceptualize, perceive, and evaluate their outward appearance or the image of their body. The final lines of Yeats' poem, *Among Schoolchildren,* capture the inextricable connection between self and body: "O body swayed to music, O brightening glance/How can we know the dancer from the dance (1989, p. 325)?" The construct of body image is limited in its capacity to reflect the intricacy of lived experience as it is situated within the body. This demands a move toward the language of embodiment – the experiential and lived body – in research, prevention, and treatment of eating disorders as a resistance to the construction of women's bodies focused on appearance.

References

Allan, H. T. (2005). Gender and embodiment in nursing: The role of the female chaperone in the infertility clinic. *Nursing Inquiry, 12,* 175–183.

Avalos, L., Tylka, T. L., & Wood-Barcalow, N. (2005). The Body Appreciation Scale: Development and psychometric evaluation. *Body Image: An International Journal of Research, 2,* 285–297. doi:10.1016/j.bodyim.2005.06.002

Bordo, S. (1993). *Unbearable weight: Feminism, western culture, and the body.* Berkeley, CA: University of California Press.

Cash, T. F. (2002). Cognitive behavioral perspectives on body image. In T. F. Cash & T. Pruzinsky (Eds.), *Body image: A handbook of theory, research, and clinical practice* (pp. 38–46). New York, NY: Guilford Press.

Cash, T. F. (2004). Body image: Past, present, and future. *Body Image: An International Journal of Research, 1*(1), 1–5. doi:10.1016/S1740-1445(03)00011-1

Cash, T. F., & Brown, T. A. (1987). Body image in anorexia nervosa and bulimia nervosa: A review of the literature. *Behavior Modification, 11*, 487–521. doi:10.1177/01454455870114005

Cash, T. F., & Deagle, E. A., III. (1997). The nature and extent of body image disturbance in anorexia nervosa and bulimia nervosa: A meta-analysis. *International Journal of Eating Disorders, 22*, 107–125.

Dionne, M. (2002). *The variability of body image: The influence of body-composition information and emotional reactivity on young women's body dissatisfaction* Ph.D. dissertation, psychology department, York University, Toronto.

Fisher, L. (2000). Phenomenology and feminism: Perspectives on their relation. In L. Fisher & L. Embree (Eds.), *Feminist Phenomenology* (pp. 17–38). Netherlands: Springer.

Fredrickson, B. L., & Roberts, T. A. (1997). Objectification theory: Toward understanding women's lived experiences of mental health risks. *Psychology of Women Quarterly, 21*, 173–206. doi:10.1111/j.1471–6402.1997.tb00108.x

Garner, D. M., & Garfinkel, P. E. (1981). Body image in anorexia nervosa: Measurement, theory, and clinical implications. *International Journal of Psychiatry in Medicine, 11*, 263–284.

Gleeson, K., & Frith, H. (2006). (De)Constructing body image. *Journal of Health Psychology, 11*(1), 79–90. doi:10.1177/1359105306058851

Hardit, S. K., & Hannum, J. W. (2012). Attachment, the tripartite influence model, and the development of body dissatisfaction. *Body Image: An International Journal of Research, 9*, 469–475. doi:10.1016/j.bodyim.2012.06.003

Hurd Clarke, L., & Korotchenko, A. (2011). Aging and the body: A review. *Canadian Journal on Aging/La Revue Canadienne Du Vieillissement, 30*(3), 495–510. doi:10.1017/S0714980811000274

Katzman, M. A., & Lee, S. (1997). Beyond body image: The integration of feminist and transcultural theories in the understanding of self starvation. *International Journal of Eating Disorders, 22*, 385–394.

Ogden, P., Minton, K., & Pain, C. (2006). *Trauma and the body: A sensorimotor approach to psychotherapy.* New York, NY: W. W. Norton & Co.

Ogle, J. P., & Damhorst, M. L. (2005). Critical reflections on the body and related sociocultural discourses at the midlife transition: An interpretive study of women's experiences. *Journal of Adult Development, 12*(1), 1–18. doi:10.1007/s10804-005-1277-2

Piran, N., & Cormier, H. C. (2005). The social construction of women and disordered eating patterns. *Journal of Counseling Psychology, 52*, 549–558.

Piran, N., & Teall, T. (2012). The developmental theory of embodiment. In G. L. McVey, M. P. Levine, N. Piran, & H. B. Ferguson (Eds.), *Preventing eating-related and weight-related disorders: Collaborative research, advocacy, and policy change* (pp. 171–199). Waterloo, ON: Wilfrid Laurier University Press.

Schilder, P. (1950). *The image and appearance of the human body.* New York, NY: International Universities Press.

Schwartz, M., & Cohn, L. (1996). Introduction: Eating disorders and sexual trauma. In M. Schwartz & L. Cohn (Eds.), *Sexual abuse and eating disorders*. New York, NY: Brunner-Routledge.

Schwartz, M., & Galperin, L. D. (1996). Reenactment and trauma. In M. Schwartz & L. Cohn (Eds.), *Sexual abuse and eating disorders*. New York, NY: Brunner-Routledge.

Smolak, L. (2006). Body image. In J. Worell & C. Goodheart (Eds.), *Handbook of girls' and women's psychological health* (pp. 69–76). New York, NY: Oxford University Press.

Striegel-Moore, R. H., & Cachelin, F. M. (1999). Body image concerns and disordered eating in adolescent girls: Risk and protective factors. In N. G. Johnson, & M. C. Roberts (Eds.), *Beyond appearance: A new look at adolescent girls* (pp. 85–108). Washington, DC: American Psychological Association.

Thompson, J. K., Heinberg, L., Altabe, M., & Tantleff-Dunn, S. (1999). *Exacting beauty: Theory, assessment, and treatment of body image disturbance*. Washington, DC: American Psychological Association.

Tylka, T. L. (2011). Positive psychology perspectives on body image. In T. F. Cash & L. Smolak (Eds.), *Body Image: A handbook of science, practice, and prevention* (2nd ed., pp. 56–65). New York, NY: Guilford Press.

van Manen, M. (2014). *Phenomenology of practice: Meaning giving methods in phenomenological research and writing*. New York, NY: Routledge.

Williams, E. F., Cash, T. F., & Santos, M. T. (2004). Positive and negative body image: Precursors, correlates, and consequences. Paper presented at the 38th annual Association for the Advancement of Behavior Therapy.

Yeats, W. B. (1989). Among schoolchildren. In A. N. Jeffreys (Ed.), *Yeats's Poems: Edited and Annotated by A. Norman Jeffares with an Appendix by Warwick Gould*. London: Macmillan Press.

Young, I. M. (2005). *On female body experience: "Throwing like a girl" and other essays*. New York, NY: Oxford University Press.

2   Understanding Disordered Eating and (Dis)embodiment through a Feminist Lens

Hillary L. McBride and Janelle L. Kwee

Susan Bordo interprets "the psychopathologies that develop within a culture, far from being anomalies or aberrations, as characteristic expressions of that culture, as the crystallization... of much that is wrong with it" (1988, p. 89). A fitting example of this observation, eating disorders are a gendered and culturally situated phenomenon: girls and women receive approximately 90%–95% of all eating disorder diagnoses (Levine & Piran, 2004; Wilson, Becker, & Heffernan, 2003), and the likelihood of developing an eating disorder increases with time spent in Westernized cultures (Franko, 2007). The following words from Brownmiller capture cultural-level factors that perpetuate disordered eating:

> Appearance, not accomplishment, is the feminine demonstration of desirability and worth. In striving to approach a feminine ideal, by corsetry in the old days or by a cottage-cheese-and-celery diet that begins tomorrow, one arms oneself... Because she is forced to concentrate on the minutiae of her bodily parts, a woman is never free of self-consciousness. She is never quite satisfied, and never secure, for desperate, unending absorption in the drive for a perfect appearance – call it feminine vanity – is the ultimate restriction of freedom of the mind.
>
> (1984, pp. 50–51)

Because of the gendered nature of eating disorders and their development within patriarchal and Western societies, we begin this book with a feminist evaluation of disordered eating and the context within which they most readily develop.

For girls, eating disorders most often emerge during puberty when significant physical and social changes occur (Wertheim & Paxton, 2011). Research has shown that later in adolescence during college or university, women are again at high risk for developing an eating disorder due to increased social pressures for thinness and exposure to disordered eating behaviors (Jung & Forbes, 2007; Neighbors & Sobal, 2007; Smith-Jackson, Reel, & Thackeray, 2011). Research has also identified that as women age, they are not exempt from appearance pressures, but they may again become at increased risk for eating disorders (Kally & Cumella, 2008; Maine

& Kelly, 2016). During the postpartum period, and during menopause, when their bodies move further from the ideals of youthfulness, thinness, and sexiness, women may increase measures of appearance management in an effort to maintain the bodies they used to have (Maine & Kelly, 2016; McKinley & Lyon, 2008). It is during these developmental transitions as women that women can feel increased shame about their bodies and consequently themselves (Bedford & Johnson, 2006). The appearance comparison that occurs between and within women during these developmental stages reinforces the internalization of the thin ideal, leading to destructive eating behaviors (Shroff & Thompson, 2006). Women may compare their current appearance to the sociocultural ideal or to how their own body used to look, which was likely closer to the ideal. Disordered eating is so implicated in the female experience for women, regardless of life phase, that Piran (2010) identified that being born a female itself is a risk factor for the development of eating disorders.

For those unfamiliar with the sociopolitical factors contributing to the development of eating disorders, they may at first interpret a woman with an eating disorder as being vain, judging her preoccupation with her appearance as a form of moral failure. Considered through a feminist lens, this is not the case; the person with the eating disorder is, in fact, being a compliant woman, being who the culture has always asked her to be, controlling her body in the way she has always been urged to by her context (Piran & Cormier, 2005; Piran & Teall, 2012). It is imperative, then, to understand eating disorders as a disorder of society, rather than of the individual. In fact, the women and girls who are the most "ill" with eating disorders may be the most compliant to the appearance-based sociocultural rules of femininity.

In this chapter, we provide a feminist evaluation of the context in which eating disorders develop and of the dominant treatment models for eating disorder intervention. We then explore the importance of embodiment to understanding and treating eating disorders, emphasizing the relevance of "taking up space" physically and socially as a form of resistance to patriarchal oppression.

The Patriarchal Context of Disembodiment and Eating Disorders

In this section, we explore the impact of sociocultural narratives of femininity, the reality of normative body dissatisfaction, and its relationship to self-esteem and eating disorders, and conclude by describing eating disorders as a cultural rather than individual sickness.

Narratives of Femininity

The narratives of femininity socially constructed in patriarchal cultures that foster the objectification of girls and women are damaging (Basow,

Foran, & Bookwala, 2007; Lamb & Brown, 2006) and have been linked to internalized objectification (self-objectification), body shame, low self-esteem, lack of internal awareness, and disordered eating (Calogero, Davis, & Thompson, 2005; Fredrickson, Roberts, Noll, Quinn, & Twenge, 1998; Moradi, Dirks, & Matteson, 2005; Piran & Cormier, 2005; Tylka & Hill, 2004). The standards for women's physical appearance are particularly destructive as they are unrealistic and largely unattainable (Cusumano & Thompson, 1997; Signorielli, McLeod, & Healy, 1994; Silverstein, Perdue, Peterson, & Kelly, 1986): in the past 40 years, the body weight of fashion models has decreased, while the weight of the average woman in Westernized nations has increased (Byrd-Bredbenner, Murray, & Schlussel, 2005; Garner, Garfinkel, Schwartz, & Thompson, 1980; Spitzer, Henderson, & Zivian, 1999; Sypeck, Gray, & Ahrens, 2004; Sypeck et al., 2006; Wiseman, Gray, Mosimarm, & Ahrens, 1992). When young women insist they would rather get run over by a truck than be "fat", it becomes evident that being thin has become one of the most important parts of feminine life itself (Martin, 2007).

Normative Negative Body Image

In the context of these unattainable yet seemingly required standards for women's bodies, negative body image has become increasingly prevalent (Arbour & Martin Ginis, 2008; Frederick, Peplau, & Lever, 2006) with studies reporting that the large majority of women feel dissatisfied with their body appearance and weight (Frederick et al., 2006). Over 70% of adolescent girls experience body dissatisfaction (Kenardy, Brown, & Vogt, 2001) with numbers as high as 80% in women in college and university settings (Spitzer et al., 1999). Body dissatisfaction has become so widespread that it is now understood to be normative (Cash, 2002; Cash & Henry, 1995; Rodin, Silberstein, & Striegel-Moore, 1985); girls aged 6 already demonstrate a strong anti-fat bias, body dissatisfaction, and weight concerns (Davison, Markey, & Birch, 2000; Flannery-Schroeder & Chrisler, 1997; Smolak, 2011; Smolak & Levine, 2001), and girls as young as 3 display an anti-fat bias against others (Latner & Stunkard, 2003; Meers, Koball, Wagner Oehlhof, Laurene, & Musher-Eizenman, 2011). Girls and women hating "fat", and despising their bodies, their own selves, is not always normative; this phenomenon is specifically located in Westernized, patriarchal, and capitalist cultures which devalue women, in comparison to men. In these contexts, value for women is located in their bodies: they are sexual objects and wombs for reproduction.

Negative Body Image and Self-Esteem

Appearance esteem and body satisfaction are major contributors to overall levels of individuals' self-esteem and how individuals feel about themselves as a whole (Tiggemann, 2005). When girls and women believe how they look is a significant contributor to their worth, but feel their appearance does not meet cultural expectations for attractiveness and beauty, body dissatisfaction is inevitable. Body dissatisfaction is not benign; it is directly related to decreased self-esteem (Cash & Pruzinsky, 2002; Richetin, Xaiz, Maravita, & Perugini, 2012; Stice & Bearman, 2001), perfectionism (Mushquash & Sherry, 2013), body dysmorphic disorder (Cash & Pruzinsky, 2002; Neziroglu, Khemlani-Patel, & Veale, 2008; Phillips, Pinto, & Jain, 2004), extreme measures of weight control (Cash & Pruzinsky, 2002; Marshall, Lengyel, & Utioh, 2012; Polivy & Herman, 1993), and eating disorders (Cash & Pruzinsky, 2002; Juarascio, Perone, & Timko, 2011; Levine & Piran, 2004; Neumark-Sztainer, Paxton, Hannan, Haines, & Story, 2006).

Negative Body Image and Eating Disorders

Hilde Bruch (1962) was an early contributor to the relationship between pathological body dissatisfaction and anorexia nervosa and described it as "the absence of concern about emaciation, even when advanced, and the vigor and stubbornness with which the often gruesome appearance is defended as normal and right" (p. 189). Since then, body dissatisfaction has been found to predict frequent dieting (Ackard, Croll, & Kearney-Cooke, 2002; Neumark-Sztainer et al., 2006), bulimic and anorexic eating behaviors (Cooley & Toray, 2001; Neumark-Sztainer et al., 2006), and weight gain (van den Berg & Neumark-Sztainer, 2007). Listed as one of the three diagnostic criteria for anorexia nervosa, the writers of the Diagnostic and Statistical Manual of Mental Disorders (DSM-5; American Psychiatric Association, 2013) describe body dissatisfaction as "an intense fear of gaining weight or of becoming fat" (p. 338), which is "not alleviated by weight loss" (p. 340). Similarly, when describing the diagnostic features of bulimia nervosa, the writers indicate that "individuals with bulimia nervosa place an excessive emphasis on body shape or weight in their self-evaluation" (p. 346) and, like individuals struggling with anorexia nervosa, exhibit fear of gaining weight, desire to lose weight, and heightened dissatisfaction with their bodies.

Conclusion: Eating Disorders as a Sociocultural Sickness

Although it is our tendency in an individualistic medical model to pathologize "sick" people, the prevalence of disordered eating must be understood as a reflection of the sociocultural context where women's worth is measured by their appearance and where appearance standards are often unattainable. The structures of power and privilege that shape Western gender constructs have resulted in the objectification and sexualization of women's bodies; this has communicated to women that their worth lies in appearance (Flaake, 2005; McKinley, 1999; Smolak & Murnen, 2011). This pressure on appearance, and the accompanying anti-fat bias, is so oppressive and widespread that some women use disordered eating as a means of protecting themselves from the potential societal threats associated with unattractiveness (Goss & Gilbert, 2002).

The Tripartite Model: Factors in the Development of Disordered Eating

How do women and girls internalize the values and ideals of their context, where their worth is measured by appearance? For girls and women in particular, the seriousness of this problem has resulted in recent research exploring factors related to body image development in girls and women (Avalos, Tylka, & Wood-Barcalow, 2005; Cash, 2004). The sociocultural model, also called the Tripartite model (Hardit & Hannum, 2012), is used to explain the process by which individuals internalize societal ideals of beauty: an individual's internalized desire for thinness results from sociocultural reinforcement of cultural pressure, leading to disordered eating behaviors and negative affect which contribute, in turn, to the development of eating disorders (Stice, 1994).

These pathways of reinforcement have been identified as media, peers, and parents. The link between media and unhealthy body image has been proven repeatedly (Cusumano & Thompson, 1997; Lamb & Brown, 2006; Quigg & Want, 2011; Smolak & Murnen, 2011), as has the bullying, teasing, and social reinforcement occurring between peers (Ferguson, Munoz, Contreras, & Velasquez, 2011; Menzel et al., 2010). Research exploring parents' contribution to children's body image has demonstrated the overwhelmingly significant relationship between parents' eating and dieting behaviors, body image, comments to their children, and the unhealthy body image in their child (Abraczinskas, Fiask, & Barnes, 2012; Back, 2011; Byely, Archibald, Graber, & Brooks-Gunn, 2000; Canals, Sancho, & Arija, 2009; Coulthard, Blissett, & Harris, 2004; Galioto, Karazsia, & Crowther, 2012). Together media, parents, and peers highlight the pathways through which oppressive messages about women's bodies and value are relayed.

Objectification and (Dis)embodiment

In this section, we discuss the importance of integral unity of the mind-body-self in relation to bodies as sites of both oppression and freedom, and the threat of objectification and mind-body dualism in maintaining embodied wholeness. We then describe eating disorders as an expression of social compliance and in connection with sexual violence and trauma.

The Personal is Political: Bodies as Sites of Oppression and Freedom

Reflecting the popular feminist phrase "the personal is political", feminist theory offers a critique of the broader cultural context which influences all people, especially oppressed people, on a personal level (McKinley, 2011; Piran, 2010). The body is the site of rights, agency, and freedom. Without a body, one does not exist. The person is expressed and made visible through the body itself. And, a person reflects one's social power and privilege, or lack thereof, through his or her body (Piran & Teall, 2012; Young, 2005). This is particularly true of women's bodies, which, like women's voices, have been a dominant site of the rule of silencing patriarchal gender scripts (Brown & Gilligan, 1993; Trost, 2007), which convey that a woman's worth lies in her appearance (Flaake, 2005; McKinley, 1999; Smolak & Murnen, 2011). How can the rights, agency, and freedom of women be protected in a society which conveys that women's worth is tied directly to appearance domains? How can women ever truly succeed, when the rules of a woman's success are connected directly to attractiveness and attractiveness is connected to thinness (Piran & Cormier, 2005; Smolak, 2006)?

Mind–Body Dualism and Objectification

The emphasis on women's worth and success as being linked to her body reinforces as dualistic split between women's mind and the body, where her thoughts, feelings, experiences, and agency are considered secondary to her appearance as a sexual object. This diminishes the full humanness of women and perpetuates women's oppression. As women seek to attain more social power, they may begin to self-objectify, internalizing the notion that it is their body and their appearance to others that matter most. In doing so, women participate in their own oppression, limiting their own experience and expression of their full selves. While this may be problematic existentially, politically, and health-wise, it is also socially reinforced; women who control their bodies and become smaller and quieter, while still remaining sexual objects, are often praised as being most desirable. Most explicitly, women who begin diets or demonstrate eating disorder behavior and lose noticeable amounts of weight are often praised, told by others "wow you look great". What this further reinforces is that women's bodies are distinct from the fullness of their selves (in particular, thoughts, emotions, agency, creative energy, spirituality, etc.) and that their bodies exist for the other, particularly for men.

Eating Disorders as an Expression of Social Compliance

Women's bodies have been objectified and sexualized by the structures of power and privilege that shape gender constructs. Eating disorders stem out of relentless struggles to attain perfection in a society with appearance-based ideals. In fact, disordered eating can be a form of protection from societal threats associated with weight gain (Goss & Gilbert, 2002). Women with eating disorders ought to be seen in the context of their compliance with appearance-based norms and ideals. Social narratives of femininity foster silencing and disappearing of women, where she is worth more for being less.

Sexual Violence, Trauma, and Eating Disorders

The way that media perpetuates narratives of femininity is the most obvious target when considering the sociocultural influences for eating disorders. However, sexual trauma is another example of how the patriarchal oppression of women can cultivate eating disorders in girls and women (Smolak, 2006; Thompson et al., 2003). Cultures that excuse perpetrators of sexual violence (largely men) by holding the victims responsible normalize the use of violent pornography, hypersexualize the female body for economic profit, and cultivate a landscape in which sexual violence and trauma particularly for girls and women are rampant. These cultures create a cycle of oppression for women, where women are more likely to be victims of sexual trauma, but are often blamed for their experiences or disbelieved. Because the body is the site of agency, and selfhood in this world, when the body is violated, it can send the message to women that their agency does not matter here, they do not matter.

More specifically, sexual trauma impairs a person's sense of body ownership and emotional regulation, resulting in intense emotional distress that feels difficult to manage (Herman, 1992). Not surprisingly, eating disorders are linked to sexual trauma for several reasons (Silverman, Raj, Mucci, & Hathaway, 2001; Thompson et al., 2003). Eating disorders may be a woman's natural attempt to self-regulate, utilizing food and specific eating behaviors to manage emotions which otherwise feel difficult to tolerate (Kearney-Cooke & Striegel-Moore, 1997). Further, eating disorders may be a way that trauma is reenacted, as the individual continues to punish or hurt themselves, or acting out what the abuse made them feel (Schwartz & Cohn, 1996; Schwartz & Galperin, 1996). Eating disorders may also be an avenue for gaining a sense of agency within the oppressive patriarchal culture. Although ultimately harmful, and a product of the disrupted agency caused by the trauma, it may be a woman's way of feeling she can have control over her body in a way which she was unable to during the trauma. Following sexual assault, some women may consciously disrupt their eating behaviors as a method of preventing future abuse, hoping to become so large or small as to become unappealing, unsexual (Schwartz & Cohn, 1996). Ultimately, the eating disorders may reinforce what the trauma impressed upon her – life is too painful and it may be easier to disappear; perhaps, then, there will be no more hurt.

Although women and men are both impacted, women are most often the survivors of sexual trauma, and thus it becomes an inextricable factor in the experience of femaleness: to know oneself is at risk for trauma simply for having a vulva. Experiences of sexual trauma, even in the stories of others, are widespread and terrifying enough to create a fear among women about their powerlessness. As argued by Sheffield (1995), the pervasive fear among women of rape alone is a demonstration of women's inequality and oppression, and restricts agency and freedom. Even sexual harassment perpetuates fear of the possibility of further sexual trauma. As such, this can be termed "sexual terrorism" "because sexual harassment and rape can happen to any woman at any time quite independently of her behavior" (Smolak, 2006, p. 74). Not surprisingly, girls who fear sexual harassment have poorer body image (Murnen & Smolak, 2000). How others treat our body appears linked to how we treat our body.

Patriarchal Dynamics in Current Eating Disorder Treatments

Themes of submission and compliance in mainstream eating disorder treatment parallel, paradoxically, the themes underlying the development of eating disorders. In this section, we challenge the status quo, which we argue perpetuates others' power over women's bodies, and call for a shifting focus to thriving and embodiment in research, policy, and practice.

The Familiar Themes of Submission and Compliance

The traditional medical models of eating disorders focus on the pathology within the individual. Current treatment models for eating disorders, particularly Anorexia Nervosa, focus on weight restoration. In inpatient settings, women must meet certain weight-based criteria before qualifying to be discharged. Unfortunately, treatment models focused on re-feeding the person with an eating disorder perpetuate dynamics of oppression and compliance where women are seen as the problem and are forced into submission by medical professionals. Similar to how the development of disordered eating represents a form of social compliance, treatment focused on meeting external criteria for recovery prioritizes treatment compliance over empowerment, freedom, and agency within one's body. Although not in broader culture, and this time "for their good", women are asked to perform in a way that is most pleasing to those who have power over them.

It is paradoxical that women whose very disorder stems from being victimized by a culture that values their silence, submission, and thinness, are given treatment in a model that perpetuates others' power over the women's bodies. While this model of eating disorder treatment may facilitate re-feeding and weight gain, it fails to connect women and girls to their bodies, to their voices, and to give them permission to take up space in society. The control over women in eating disorder treatment may serve to reinforce one of the causes of eating disorders in the first place: the restriction of agency (Piran & Teall, 2012). Where the body is the very site in which a person can experience rights, agency, and freedom (or lack thereof), treatment that separates the body from the person's agency inherently disempowers and silences the person.

Thriving and Embodiment: Opportunities for Research, Policy, and Practice

Collaborative, holistic, and multidisciplinary efforts are needed to treat and prevent body dissatisfaction and eating disorders among females in Westernized patriarchal cultures. Efforts have been made to devise and evaluate methods of treatment for the most serious cases of disordered eating, and to further understand the construct of negative body image, and how it takes root (Cash, 2004). However, a great need remains for research, policy, and clinical practice to focus on the understanding and promotion not just of positive body image (Avalos et al., 2005; Steck, Abrams, & Phelps, 2004) but also of the embodied experience of the self. Facilitating an embodied experience of the self would be a therapeutic intervention, providing an opportunity to feel the self in the body, to restore a sense of safety, goodness, and pleasure in a body.

Shifting from a Disease Model

The existing literature has concentrated "on repairing damage within a disease model of human functioning. This almost exclusive attention to pathology neglects the fulfilled individual and the thriving community" (Seligman & Csikszentmihalyi, 2000, p. 5). As Seligman and Csikszentmihalyi (2000) have suggested, the clinical and research preoccupation with pathological functioning, or "victimology" is insufficient for understanding prevention of pathology or healthy functioning. This gap in academic and clinical practice renders a professional community unable to prevent pathology or to understand and guide individuals toward human strengths and optimal functioning.

The focus of the current literature further implies through omission of the non-pathology-focused content that the pathology is normal (Seligman & Csikszentmihalyi, 2000). This frame is particularly true within the literature addressing eating disorders, body image, and embodiment or disembodiment. Considerably less is known about how women develop a healthy relationship with their body and how to foster the development of an embodied connected sense of self and healthy body image in children and adults so as to protect them while they exist within a social context that is preoccupied with achieving thinness (Piran, 2001). When addressing the problem of body dissatisfaction and its significant effects on the lives of girls and women, it is not enough to consider tertiary treatment (though this is also critical) as sufficient for the resolution of such widespread and dangerous discontent (McKinley, 2011).

Taking Up Space

The feminist perspective has illuminated the gendered power dynamic behind the preference for thin; it is merely an illusion that deprives women of resources, energy, time, and sense of self, to achieve nothing more than oppression and mental health issues in return (Pienaar & Bekker, 2007; Piran & Cormier, 2005). New narratives of what it means to be a woman, and what makes women valuable, must be forged. In the meantime, new pathways for healing and protection for girls and women in this culture must be identified and promoted to prevent suffering and oppression in the majority of women (Rortveit, Astrom, & Severinsson, 2009). Recommendations for effective prevention programs will impact both the individual, and the social environments that influence children most, home and school, to create lasting systemic changes (Greenberg, Domitrovich, & Bumbarger, 2001).

Embodiment as Resistance

From a feminist perspective, we explore in this section how embodiment represents a form of resistance to the objectification and silencing of women. Embodiment has both personal and political dimensions, and is connected to a person's literal and symbolic "voice" in the world.

Embodiment as Personal and Political

As bodies are the very sites of rights, agency, and freedom for the person, our bodies are the battlefields where we fight for liberation. In reclaiming and fully inhabiting one's body as her own, resisting the internalization of the culturally ubiquitous objectification of the female body, a woman speaks with her life against oppression. In healing through embodiment, women reintegrate with what is theirs, fully inhabiting the space they are entitled to take up through their body, as it is. Piran and Teall (2012) state that women with eating disorders are not vain; rather, they are complying with the sociocultural narrative of femininity, which has encouraged them to disappear. They are, in fact, doing what they have always been instructed to do. Instead of being "full of themselves", an expression that implies self-absorption and narcissism, as is often implied for women who are preoccupied with their body and weight, women with eating disorders are self-eviscerating, reducing the self and the full expression and experience of their self in the world. For women to intentionally inhabit their bodies, in a sociopolitical context that grooms them to dissociate from their bodies, is an act of political resistance. It is a form of social noncompliance. Through this, they are saying "you are asking me to shrink, to be silent, to be invisible, but I refuse".

Voice and Embodiment

Voice often represents a metaphor of the embodied self, which exists in relationship with others. Voice, like body itself, is an expression and dimension of the self through which the person interacts with the outside world and is enabled to be oneself. Through voice and body, the person finds her ability to interact with the world and to be herself. Without the body, there is no voice, no capacity to express the self. Thus, voice refers to the literal audible voice of a person, utilized to convey thought, experience, pain, connection, imagery, and terror. Voice also represents the person's expressed self in the world, the capacity for agency and power, and the capacity to advocate for one's self. Consequently, as the fragmentation of the relationship between a woman and her body occurs, it is reflected in both the literal and symbolic dimensions of voice. Voice, like body, is silenced in eating disorders. In her book, *Shrill*, Lindy West (2016) writes about how her shame about her body (and other's shame about her body) translated to other expressions of the self of which she could have more control:

> You fold yourself up like origami, you make yourself smaller in others ways, you take up less space with your personality, since you can't with your body.... I got good at being small early on – socially, if not physically. In public, until I was eight, I would speak only to my mother, and even then, only in whispers, pressing my face into her leg.
>
> (pp. 12–13)

Conclusion: Feminism, Embodiment, and Disordered Eating

A feminist analysis of the messages women receive about themselves and their bodies makes it clear that the concept of embodiment is a necessary lens for understanding and treating eating disorders. The overwhelming problem of women being dissatisfied with their bodies and experiencing life-threatening eating disorders does not exist in isolation to each individual; eating disorders must be understood as situated within a sociocultural context that is oppressive and silencing to women and which teaches them to manage their bodies for the pleasure and consumption of others. From a feminist perspective, it is essential to understand embodiment beyond its experiential relevance to the individual person (though this is immensely important), but as a form of resistance to patriarchal oppression.

In one's body – not in spite of it – one claims her own rights, agency, and freedom to be a person. Prevention and treatment for eating disorders must acknowledge the ubiquitous social disease of patriarchal oppression in which the commodification of women's bodies exists largely for men's pleasure. "Risk factors" for disordered eating are not merely individual vulnerabilities but societal values. Prevention and treatment must avoid individualistic and dualistic tendencies that have largely prevailed in treating eating disorders as personal diseases of faulty cognition or behavior (or most broadly conceptualized as a symptom of a family system), in which the body must be dominated for recovery. Eating disorders are disorders of a patriarchal society in which women are objectified. Promoting integration of the mind-body unity of the self is essential not only to guide the courageous journey of personal healing but also as an act of political resistance.

References

Abraczinskas, M., Fisak, B., & Barnes, R. (2012). The relation between parental influence, body image, and eating behaviors in a nonclinical female sample. *Body Image: An International Journal of Research, 9,* 93–100. doi:10.1016/j.bodyim.2011.10.005

Ackard, D. M., Croll, J. K., & Kearney-Cooke, A. (2002). Dieting frequency among college females: Association with disordered eating, body image, and related psychological problems. *Journal of Psychosomatic Research, 52,* 129–136.

American Psychiatric Association. (2013). *Diagnostic and statistical manual of mental disorders* (5th ed.). Arlington, VA: American Psychiatric Publishing.

Arbour, K. P., & Martin Ginis, K. A. (2008). Improving body image one step at a time: Greater pedometer step counts produce greater body image improvements. *Body Image: An International Journal of Research, 5,* 331–336. doi:10.1016/j.bodyim.2008.05.003

Avalos, L., Tylka, T. L., & Wood-Barcalow, N. (2005). The body appreciation scale: Development and psychometric evaluation. *Body Image: An International Journal of Research, 2,* 285–297. doi:10.1016/j.bodyim.2005.06.002

Back, E. A. (2011). Effects of parental relations and upbringing in trouble adolescent eating behaviors. *Eating Disorders, 19,* 403–424. doi:10.1080/10640266.2011.609091

Basow, S. A., Foran, K. A., & Bookwala, J. (2007). Body objectification, social pressure, and disordered eating behavior in college women: The role of sorority membership. *Psychology of Women Quarterly, 31*(4), 394–400. doi:10.1111/j.1471-6402.2007.00388.x

Bedford, J. L., & Johnson, C. S. (2006). Societal influences on body image dissatisfaction in younger and older women. *Journal of Women & Aging, 18*(1), 41–55.

Bordo, S. (1988). Anorexia nervosa: Psychopathology as crystallization of culture. In I. Diamond & L. Quinby (Eds.), *Feminism and foucault: Reflections on resistance.* Boston, MA: Northeastern University Press.

Brown, L. M., & Gilligan, C. (1993). Meeting at the crossroads: Women's psychology and girls' development. *Feminism & Psychology, 3*(1), 11–35.

Brownmiller, S. (1984). *Femininity.* New York, NY: Ballantine Books.

Bruch, H. (1962). Perceptual and conceptual disturbances in anorexia nervosa. *Psychosomatic Medicine, 24,* 187–194.

Byely, L., Archibald, A., Graber, J., & Brooks-Gunn, J. (2000). A prospective study of familial and social influences on girls' body image and dieting. *The International Journal of Eating Disorders, 28*(2), 155–164.

Byrd-Bredbenner, C., Murray, J., & Schlussel, Y. R. (2005). Temporal changes in anthropometric measurements of idealized females and young women in general. *Women and Health, 41,* 13–30.

Calogero, R. M., Davis, W. N., & Thompson, J. K. (2005). The role of self-objectification in the experience of women with eating disorders. *Sex Roles, 52,* 43–50.

Canals, J., Sancho, C., & Arija, M. V. (2009). Influence of parents' eating attitudes on eating disorders in school adolescents. *European Child Adolescent Psychiatry, 18,* 353–359. doi:10.1007/s00787-009-0737-9

Cash, T. F. (2002). Cognitive behavioral perspectives on body image. In T. F. Cash & T. Pruzinsky (Eds.), *Body image: A handbook of theory, research, and clinical practice* (pp. 38–46). New York, NY: Guilford Press.

Cash, T. F. (2004). Body image: Past, present, and future. *Body Image: An International Journal of Research, 1*(1), 1–5. doi:10.1016/S1740–1445(03)00011-1

Cash, T. F., & Henry, P. E. (1995). Women's body images: The results of a national survey in the U.S.A. *Sex Roles, 33,* 19–28.

Cash, T. F., & Pruzinsky, T. (Eds.). (2002). *Body image: A handbook of theory, research, and clinical practice.* New York, NY: Guilford Press.

Cooley, E., & Toray, T. (2001). Body image and personality predictors of eating disorder symptoms during the college years. *International Journal of Eating Disorders, 30,* 28–36.

Coulthard, H., Blissett, J., & Harris, G. (2004). The relationship between parental eating problems and children's feeding behavior: A selective review of the literature. *Eating Behaviors, 5,* 103–115. doi:10.1016/j.eatbeh.2003.07.003

Cusumano, D. L., & Thompson, J. K. (1997). Body image and body shape ideals in magazines: Exposure, awareness and internalization. *Sex Roles, 37,* 701–721.

Davison, K., Markey, C., & Birch, L. (2000). Etiology of body dissatisfaction and weight concerns among 5-year-old girls. *Appetite, 35,* 143–151.

Ferguson, C. J., Munoz, M. E., Contreras, S., & Velasquez, K. (2011). Mirror, mirror on the wall: Peer competition, television influences, and body image dissatisfaction. *Journal of Social and Clinical Psychology, 30*(5), 458–483. doi:10.1521/jscp.2011.30.5.458

Flaake, K. (2005). Girls, adolescents and the impact of bodily changes: Family dynamics and social definitions of the female body. *European Journal of Women's Studies, 12*(2), 201–212. doi:10.1177/1350506805051241

Flannery-Schroeder, E., & Chrisler, J. (1997). Body esteem, eating attitudes, and gender-role orientation in three age groups of children. *Current Psychology: Developmental, Learning, Personality, Social, 15,* 235–248.

Franko, D. L. (2007). Race, ethnicity, and eating disorders: Considerations for DSM-V. *International Journal of Eating Disorders, 40*(Suppl.), S31–S34. doi:10.1002/eat.20455

Frederick, D. A., Peplau, L. A., & Lever, J. (2006). The swimsuit issue: Correlates of body image in a sample of 52,677 heterosexual adults. *Body Image: An International Journal of Research, 4,* 413–419.

Fredrickson, B. L., Roberts, T. A., Noll, S. M., Quinn, D. M., & Twenge, J. M. (1998). That swimsuit becomes you: Sex differences in self-objectification, restrained eating, and math performance. *Journal of Personality and Social Psychology, 75,* 269–284.

Galioto, R., Karazsia, B. T., & Crowther, J. H. (2012). Familial and peer modeling and verbal commentary: Associations with muscularity-oriented body dissatisfaction and body change behaviors. *Body Image: An International Journal of Research, 9,* 293–297. doi:10.1016/j.bodyim.2011.12.004

Garner, D. M., Garfinkel, P. E., Schwartz, D., & Thompson, M. (1980). Cultural expectations of thinness in women. *Psychological Reports, 47,* 483–491.

Goss, K., & Gilbert, P. (2002). Eating disorders, shame and pride: A cognitive-behavioural functional analysis. In P. Gilbert & J. Miles (Eds.), *Body shame: Conceptualisation, research and treatment* (pp. 219–255). New York, NY: Brunner-Routledge.

Greenberg, M. T., Domitrovich, C., & Bumbarger, B. (2001). The prevention of mental disorders in school-aged children: Current state of the field. *Prevention & Treatment, 4,* 1–59.

Hardit, S. K., & Hannum, J. W. (2012). Attachment, the tripartite influence model, and the development of body dissatisfaction. *Body Image: An International Journal of Research, 9,* 469–475. doi:10.1016/j.bodyim.2012.06.003

Herman, J. (1992). *Trauma and recovery: The aftermath of violence.* New York, NY: Basic Books.

Juarascio, A. S., Perone, J., & Timko, C. A. (2011). Moderators of the relationship between body image dissatisfaction and disordered eating. *Eating Disorders, 19,* 346–354. doi:10.1080/10640266.2011.584811

Jung, J., & Forbes, G. B. (2007). Body dissatisfaction and disordered eating among college women in China, South Korea, and the United States: Contrasting predictions from sociocultural and feminist theories. *Psychology of Women Quarterly, 31,* 381–393. doi:10.1111/j.1471–6402.2007.00387.x

Kally, Z., & Cumella, E. (2008). 100 midlife women with eating disorder: A phenomenological analysis of etiology. *The Journal of General Psychology, 135*(4), 359–377.

Kearney-Cooke, A., & Striegel-Moore, R. (1997). The etiology and treatment of body image disturbance. In D. M. Garner & P. E. Garfinkel (Eds.), *Handbook of treatment for eating disorders* (2nd ed.) (pp. 295–306). New York, NY: Guilford.

Kenardy, J., Brown, W., & Vogt, E. (2001). Dieting and health in young Australian women. *European Eating Disorders Review, 9,* 242–254.

Lamb, S., & Brown, L. M. (2006). *Packaging girlhood: Rescuing our daughters from marketers' schemes.* New York, NY: St. Martin's Press.

Latner, J. D., & Stunkard, A. J. (2003). Getting worse: The stigmatization of obese children. *Obesity Research, 11,* 452–456. doi:10.1016/j.bodyim.2008.03.003

Levine, M. P., & Piran, N. (2004). The role of body image in the prevention of eating disorders. *Body Image: An International Journal of Research, 1,* 57–70. doi:10.1016/S1740-1445(03)00006-8

Maine, M., & Kelly, J. (2016). *Pursuing perfection: Eating disorders, body myths, and women at midlife and beyond.* New York, NY: Routledge.

Marshall, C., Lengyel, C., & Utioh, A. (2012). Body dissatisfaction among middle-aged and older women. *Canadian Journal of Dietetic Practice and Research, 37*(2), 241–247. doi:10.3148/73.2.2012.e241

Martin, C. E. (2007). *Perfect girls, starving daughters: How the quest for perfection is harming young women*. New York, NY: Free Press.

McKinley, N. M. (1999). Women and objectified body consciousness: Mothers' and daughters' body experience in cultural, developmental, and familial context. *Developmental Psychology, 35*(3), 760–769.

McKinley, N. M. (2011). Feminist perspectives on body image. In T. Cash & L. Smolak (Eds.), *Body image: A handbook of science, practice, and prevention* (2nd ed.) (pp. 48–55). New York, NY: The Guilford Press.

McKinley, N. M., & Lyon, L. (2008). Menopausal attitudes, objectified body consciousness, aging anxiety, and body esteem: European American women's body experiences in midlife. *Body Image, 5*, 375–380.

Meers, M. R., Koball, A. M., Wagner Oehlhof, M., Laurene, K. R., & Musher-Eizenman, D. R. (2011). Assessing anti-fat bias in preschoolers: A comparison of a computer generated line-drawn figure array and photographic figure array. *Body Image: An International Journal of Research, 8*, 293–296. doi:10.1016/j.bodyim.2011.04.006

Menzel, J. E., Schaefer, L. M., Burke, N. L., Mayhew, L. L., Brannick, M. T., & Thompson, J. K. (2010). Appearance-related teasing, body dissatisfaction, and disordered eating: A meta-analysis. *Body Image: An International Journal of Research, 7*, 261–270. doi:10.1016/j.bodyim.2010.05.004

Moradi, B., Dirks, D., & Matteson, A. V. (2005). Roles of sexual objectification experiences and internalization of standards of beauty in eating disorder symptomatology: A test and extension of objectification theory. *Journal of Counseling Psychology, 52*, 420–428.

Murnen, S. K., & Smolak, L. (2000). The experience of sexual harassment among grade-school students: Early socialization of female subordination? *Sex Roles, 43*, 1–17.

Mushquash, A. R., & Sherry, S. B. (2013). Testing the perfectionism model of binge eating in mother-daughter dyads: A mixed longitudinal and daily diary study. *Eating Behaviors, 14*, 171–179. doi:10.1016/j.eatbeh.2013.02.002

Neighbors, L. A., & Sobal, J. (2007). Prevalence and magnitude of body weight and shape dissatisfaction among university students. *Eating Behaviors, 8*, 429–439.

Neumark-Sztainer, D., Paxton, S. J., Hannan, P. J., Haines, J., & Story, M. (2006). Does body satisfaction matter? Five-year longitudinal associations between body satisfaction and health behaviors in adolescent females and males. *Journal of Adolescent Health, 39*, 244–251.

Neziroglu, F., Khemlani-Patel, S., & Veale, D. (2008). Social learning theory and cognitive behavioral models of body dysmorphic disorder. *Body Image: An International Journal of Research, 5*, 28–38. doi:10.1016/j.bodyim.2008.01.002

Phillips, K. A., Pinto, A., & Jain, S. (2004). Self-esteem in body dysmorphic disorder. *Body Image: An International Journal of Research, 1*, 385–390. doi:10.1016/j.bodyim.2004.07.001

Pienaar, K., & Bekker, I. (2007). The body as a site of struggle: Oppositional discourses of the disciplined female body. *Southern African Linguistics and Applied Language Studies, 25*(4), 539–555.

Piran, N. (2001). The body logic program: Discussion and reflections. *Cognitive and Behavioral Practice, 8*(3), 259–264. doi:10.1016/S1077–7229(01)80062–6

Piran, N. (2010). A feminist perspective on risk factor research and on the prevention of eating disorders. *Eating Disorders, 18*, 183–198. doi:10.1080/10640261003719435

Piran, N., & Cormier, H. C. (2005). The social construction of women and disordered eating patterns. *Journal of Counseling Psychology, 52,* 549–558.

Piran, N., & Teall, T. (2012). The developmental theory of embodiment. In G. L. McVey, M. P. Levine, N. Piran, & H. B. Ferguson (Eds.), *Preventing eating-related and weight-related disorders: Collaborative research, advocacy, and policy change,* (pp. 169–198). Waterloo, ON: Wilfred Laurier University Press.

Polivy, J., & Herman, C. P. (1993). Etiology of binge eating: Psychological mechanisms. In C. G. Fairburn & G. T. Wilson (Eds.), *Binge eating: Nature, assessment and treatment* (pp. 50–76). New York, NY: The Guilford Press.

Quigg, S. L., Want, S. C. (2011). Highlighting media modifications: Can a television commercial mitigate the effects of music videos on female appearance satisfaction? *Body Image: An International Journal of Research, 8,* 135–142. doi:10.1016/j.bodyim.2010.11.008

Richetin, J., Xaiz, A., Maravita, A., & Perugini, M. (2012). Self-body recognition depends on implicit and explicit self-esteem. *Body Image: An International Journal of Research, 9,* 253–260. doi:10.1016/j.bodyim.2011.11.002

Rodin, J., Silberstein, L. R., & Striegel-Moore, R. H. (1985). Women and weight: A normative discontent. In T. B. Sonderegger (Ed.), *Nebraska symposium on motivation: Vol. 32. Psychology and gender* (pp. 267–307). Lincoln, NE: University of Nebraska Press.

Rortveit, K., Astrom, S., & Severinsson, E. (2009). The feeling of being trapped in and ashamed of one's own body: A qualitative study of women who suffer from eating difficulties. *International Journal of Mental Health Nursing, 18,* 91–99. doi:10.1111/j.14470349.2008.00588.x

Schwartz, M., & Cohn, L. (1996). Introduction: Eating disorders and sexual trauma. In M. Schwartz & L. Cohn (Eds.), *Sexual abuse and eating disorders.* (pp. ix–xi). New York, NY: Brunner-Routledge.

Schwartz, M., & Galperin, L. D. (1996). Reenactment and trauma. In M. Schwartz & L. Cohn (Eds.), *Sexual abuse and eating disorders.* (pp. 210–215). New York, NY: Brunner-Routledge.

Seligman, M., & Csikszentmihalyi, M. (2000). Positive psychology. An introduction. *The American Psychologist, 55*(1), 5–14. doi:10.1037//0003–066X.55.1.5

Sheffield, C. (1995). Sexual terrorism. In J. Freeman (Ed.), *Women: A Feminist Perspective.* Mountain View, CA: Mayfield.

Shroff, H., & Thompson, J. K. (2006). Peer influences, body-image, dissatisfaction, eating dysfunction and self-esteem in adolescent girls. *Journal of Health Psychology, 11*(4), 533–551. doi:10.1177/1359105306065015

Signorielli, N., McLeod, D., & Healy, E. (1994). Gender stereo types in MTV commercials: The beat goes on. *Journal of Broadcasting and Electronic Media, 38,* 91–101.

Silverstein, B., Perdue, L., Peterson, B., & Kelly, E. (1986). The role of the mass media in promoting a thin standard of bodily attractiveness for women. *Sex roles, 14*(9), 519–532.

Silverman, J., Raj, A., Mucci, L., & Hathaway, J. (2001). Dating violence against adolescent girls and associated substance use, unhealthy weight control, sexual risk behavior, pregnancy, and suicidality. *Journal of the American Medical Association, 286,* 572–579.

Smith-Jackson, T., Reel, J. J., & Thackeray, R. (2011). Coping with "bad body image days": Strategies from first-year young adult college women. *Body Image: An International Journal of Research, 8,* 335–342. doi:10.1016/j.bodyim.2011.05.002

Smolak, L. (2006). Body image. In J. Worell & C. D. Goodheart (Eds.), *Handbook of girls and women's psychological health: Gender and well-being across the lifespan* (pp. 69–76). New York, NY: Oxford University Press.

Smolak, L. (2011). Body image development in children. In T. Cash & L. Smolak (Eds.), *Body image: A handbook of science, practice, and prevention* (2nd ed.; pp. 67–75). New York, NY: The Guilford Press.

Smolak, L., & Levine, M. P. (2001). Body image in children. In J. Thompson & L. Smolak (Eds.), *Body image, eating disorders, and obesity in youth: Assessment, prevention, and treatment* (pp. 41–66). Washington, DC: American Psychological Association. doi:10.1037/10404–002

Smolak, L., & Munstertieger, B. (2002). The relationship of gender and voice to depression and eating disorders. *Psychology of Women Quarterly, 26*(3), 234–241. doi:10.1111/1471–6402.t01-1-00006

Smolak, L., & Murnen, S. K. (2011). The sexualization of girls and women as a primary antecedent of self-objectification. In R. M. Calogero, S. Tantleff-Dunn, & J. Thompson (Eds.), *Self-objectification in women: Causes, consequences, and counteractions* (pp. 53–75). American Psychological Association. doi:10.1037/12304-003

Spitzer, B. L., Henderson, K. A., & Zivian, M. T. (1999). Gender differences in population versus media body size: A comparison over four decades. *Sex Roles, 40*, 545–565.

Steck, E. L., Abrams, L. M., & Phelps, L. (2004). Positive psychology in the prevention of eating disorders. *Psychology in the Schools, 41*(1), 111–117. doi:10.1002/pits.10143

Stice, E. (1994). Review of the evidence for a sociocultural model of bulimia nervosa and an exploration of the mechanisms of action. *Clinical Psychology Review, 14*(7), 633–661.

Stice, E., & Bearman, S. K. (2001). Body image and eating disturbances prospectively predict increases in depressive symptoms in adolescent girls: A growth curve analysis. *Developmental Psychology, 37*, 597–607.

Sypeck, M. F., Gray, J. J., & Ahrens, A. H. (2004). No longer just a pretty face: Fashion magazines' descriptions of ideal female beauty from 1959–1999. *International Journal of Eating Disorders, 36*, 342–347.

Sypeck, M. F., Gray, J. J., Etu, S. F., Ahrens, A. H., Mosimann, J. E., & Wiseman, C. V. (2006). Cultural representations of thinness in women, redux: Playboy magazine's depiction of beauty from 1979 to 1999. *Body Image: An International Journal of Research, 3*, 229–235.

Thompson, K., Crosby, R., Wonderlich, S., Mitchell, J., Redlin, J., Demuth, G., ... Haseltine, B. (2003). Psychopathology and sexual trauma in childhood and adulthood. *Journal of Traumatic Stress, 16*, 335–338.

Tiggemann, M. (2005). Body dissatisfaction and adolescent self-esteem: Prospective findings. *Body Image, 2*(2), 129–135.

Trost, A. (2007). The Healthy Image Partnership (HIP) parents program: The role of parental involvement in eating disorder prevention. *Dissertation Abstracts International Section A, 68*, 1–165. University of Texas, Austin, Texas.

Tylka, T. L., & Hill, M. S. (2004). Objectification theory as it relates to disordered eating among college women. *Sex Roles, 51*, 719–730.

van den Berg, P., & Neumark-Sztainer, D. (2007). Fat 'n happy 5 years later: Is it bad for overweight girls to like their bodies? *Journal of Adolescent Health, 41*, 415–417.

Wertheim, E. H., & Paxton, S. J. (2011). Body image development in adolescent girls. In T. Cash & L. Smolak (Eds.), *Body image: A handbook of science, practice, and prevention* (2nd ed.; pp. 76–84). New York, NY: The Guilford Press.

West, L. (2016). *Shrill.* New York, NY: Hachette Books.

Wilson, G. T., Becker, C. B., & Heffernan, K. (2003). Eating disorders. In E. J. Mash & R. A. Barkley (Eds.), *Child Psychopathology* (2nd ed.). New York, NY: Guilford Press.

Wiseman, C. V., Gray, J. J., Mosimarm, J. E., & Ahrens, A. H. (1992). Cultural expectations of thinness in women: An update. *International Journal of Eating Disorders, 11,* 85–89.

Wolf, N. (1991). *The beauty myth: How images of female beauty are used against women.* New York, NY: William Morrow.

Young, I. M. (2005). *On female body experience: "Throwing like a girl" and other essays.* Oxford University Press.

3 Embodiment

A Non-Dualistic and Existential Perspective on Understanding and Treating Disordered Eating

Mihaela Launeanu and Janelle L. Kwee

Introduction

Broadly, embodiment refers to the engagement of the body with the world, wherein the mind and body are inextricably linked and reciprocally influence one another (Allan, 2005; Piran & Teall, 2012). Although intuitively it makes sense that the experience of embodiment is critical in understanding eating disorders, given the pervasive body-related struggles that persons suffering from these disorders describe (Stanghellini, Castellini, Brogna, Faravelli, & Ricca, 2012), the importance of embodiment in the onset of, maintenance of and recovery from eating disorders has only recently become the focus of some research studies (Underwood, 2013).

In line with the more recent focus on exploring the role of embodiment in eating disorders, this chapter proposes an integrative, non-dualistic, existential perspective to understanding embodiment with respect to conceptualizing and treating disordered eating. The chapter begins with a brief review of the philosophical and theoretical underpinnings of contemporary conceptualization of embodiment. Then, Existential Analysis (EA) (Längle, 2013) is discussed as a holistic framework of understanding embodiment in people diagnosed with eating disorders. A clinical case provides a practical illustration about how the EA conceptualizing framework informs the treatment approach for individuals diagnosed with eating disorders. A discussion about implications and future directions concludes this chapter.

Embodiment: Philosophical and Theoretical Underpinnings

Philosophical Heritage

The concept of embodiment is grounded in the existential philosophy of Heidegger (1962), Merleau-Ponty (1945/2012), Sartre (1943), and Foucault (1978). Although this chapter does not aim to provide a comprehensive review of the philosophical underpinnings of embodiment, it is worth noting the main influences that shape our understandings of this concept as relevant to eating disorders.

Embedded and Embodied

By conceiving Being as essentially 'Being in the world' or Dasein, Heidegger (1962) has not only explicitly rejected the Cartesian notion of subject-object/self-body split but also defined human existence as fundamentally embedded and embodied. For Heidegger, there is a reciprocal relationship of the body constituting the self as something in the world and the self constituting the body as an agent.

Merleau-Ponty (1945/2012) further elaborated Heidegger's departure from Cartesian self-body dualism and fully developed the phenomenological understanding of embodiment. Essentially, for Merleau-Ponty, human beings are embodied beings, and the experience and knowing of the world is intrinsically embodied. Thus, we can perceive and interact with the world only to the extent that our bodies enable or constrain us, and our body is our means of being in the world.

Lived Corporeality

Sartre (1943) contributed to the philosophical understanding of embodiment by introducing the distinction between the lived body or lived corporeality (Leib) and the physical body (Koerper). This distinction is also referred to as body-subject versus body-object. The lived body/body-subject refers to one's own direct experience of the body from within. This direct experience of the body in a first-person perspective is also called interoceptive awareness or cenesthetic perspective (Stanghellini et al., 2012). On the other hand, the physical body/body-object refers to the body thematically observed or scrutinized from outside and from a third-person perspective. For Sartre, both the implicit acquaintance with our own body from the first-person perspective and experiencing it as a physical, objective body are key dimensions of corporeality.

Political Body

Foucault (1978) expanded the discussions about embodied existence by affirming the body and corporeality as the nuclear axis of human identity and by critically acknowledging the role of sociopolitical aspects in defining corporeality (i.e., the politics of the body) as the potentially oppressive social counterpart of the inner experience of the body. Objectification theory (Fredrickson & Roberts, 1997) furthers some of Foucault's insights on the sociopolitical influences on the body by discussing the internalization of the external gaze of the other and the oppressive message of 'body for the other' that Westernized culture promotes.

Conclusion

These philosophical ponderings are still shaping our understanding of embodiment in connection with eating disorders. Both Heidegger (1962) and

Merleau-Ponty (1945/2012) affirm embodiment as an existential given, and from this perspective, the struggles with the body for people suffering from eating disorders can be understood as existential struggles to exist as a body in the world. Sartre's distinction between body-object (Koerper) and lived body (Leib) is crucial for understanding the split between the lived experience and objectification of the body that is profoundly relevant for people suffering from eating disorders; it is typical that these people tend to perceive their body as an object scrutinized from an outside perspective rather than a lived, subjective body (Stanghellini et al., 2012). Further, Foucault's (1978) and Fredrickson and Robert's (1997) reflections on the oppressive external gaze and the politics of the body bring the struggles with body and eating into the sociopolitical arena and see the torments of the body in eating disorders as a form of political resistance, not just as an individual disease.

Theoretical Perspectives

Embodiment is now conceptualized through several theoretical lenses: as embodied cognition (Winkielman, Niedenthal, Wielgosz, Eelen, & Kavanagh, 2015), as unity of physiology and consciousness (Maturana, 2002; Varela, 1996), and as developmental and sociocultural phenomenon (Piran & Teall, 2012. Each of these perspectives has its merits and limitations, and shapes our understanding of embodied experience in eating disorders.

Embodied Cognition

This theoretical perspective on embodiment recognizes that all information processing is shaped by the body, primarily by the brain. From such a perspective, processing of information about sights, sounds, and other sensory stimuli, as well as other kinds of information such as abstract social, emotional, or moral concepts is influenced, informed, connected to, and reliant on perceptual, proprioceptive, and somatosensory resources of the body (Niedenthal, 2007; Niedenthal, Barsalou, Weinkielman, Krauth-Gruber, & Ric, 2005; Winkielman, Niedenthal, & Oberman, 2008). This view has been influenced by the remarkable progress in neuroscience and, thus, at times, tends to minimize the role of subjective aspects of embodiment. It nonetheless acknowledges the centrality of body-based knowledge and its disruptions in the course of eating disorders.

Neurophenomenology

Varela (1996) coined the term 'neurophenomenology' to encourage the synergy between neuroscience and the phenomenology of consciousness and subjective experience as a way of understanding embodied experience. Specifically, a neurophenomenological view of embodiment suggests that phenomenological experience and its neurocognitive correlates are intimately connected to each other through reciprocal constraints (Varela, 1996). Thus, matters of embodied lived experience are situated at the intersection of fleshy physiology and subjective phenomena transcending biological processes. This view has important implications for conceptualizing embodiment in eating disorders not only as a cognitive, brain-related experience but also as a profoundly personal yet shared experience of the body.

Sociocultural Frameworks

Moving beyond an exclusively individualistic and static focus in understanding embodiment, Piran and Teall (2012) elaborated a Developmental Theory of Embodiment (DTE) that emphasizes the role of developmental transitions and sociocultural factors in shaping the embodied experience (Piran & Teall, 2012). This framework recognizes and reflects the complex, interactive relationship between the embodied self and culture in which the self is situated. This approach has significant implications for understanding the developmental and sociocultural influences that shape the embodied lived experience in persons with eating disorders.

Existential Analysis: A Holistic Framework for Understanding Embodiment

Within this philosophical and theoretical context, EA elaborates a theoretical framework that promotes a holistic understanding and treatment of eating disorders. In this section, we will discuss the definition of EA, offer an overview of the dialogical and structural models of EA, and then describe the EA view of the body as these pertain to the experience of embodiment in individuals suffering from eating disorders.

Existential Analysis: Main Tenets

EA is a phenomenological and person-oriented psychotherapy. The International Society of Existential Analysis and Logotherapy was founded in 1983 in Vienna and represents the fruit of the collaboration between Viktor Frankl and Alfried Längle. The central aim of EA is to help a person discover a way of living in which he or she is able to give "inner consent" for one's actions. In other words, this aim is to guide a person toward mental and emotional freedom, and the ability to make authentic and responsible decisions (Kwee & Längle, 2013; Längle, 2012). To be authentic means it corresponds to the *person*. Thus, the Existential-Analytic view supports a holistic view of the embodied person with personal agency and freedom. The existential task of *being a person* is the aim of the phenomenological therapeutic process.

Dialogical Model

In the existential-analytical framework, human lives are dynamic possibilities, each one representing a *chance for something* ("Das Leben ist nie etwas, es ist nur die Gelegenheit zu einem Etwas;" Hebbel, 2013). The human being is fundamentally enabled for dialogue (Längle, 2003). Human beings are in inner dialogue with themselves and outer dialogue with life. Längle (2003) describes three constituent elements for dialogue to be possible: (a) dialogue has an addressee, (b) the addressee understands what is said, and (c) dialogue requires a response. When the person is addressed by any situation in their life, they subjectively experience being touched or impressed upon in some way. Through understanding, the person is able to take a personal inner position, and the person's subjective capacity to express oneself enables him or her to give a response.

Giving inner consent is part of a dialogical existence, representing an answer, offered as part of this active exchange with oneself and with the world. To give inner consent is a personal capacity containing the philosophical concept of freedom. One experiences oneself as free in giving inner consent. Consider the example of an eating disorder patient, Leah, who has been diagnosed with Anorexia Nervosa. Aware of its dangers, she knows she *should* increase calorie consumption and work toward better health. She has received medical and nutritional advice and is aware of the multiple, severe, and immediate physical risks facing her. While Leah has cognitively agreed that she needs to follow medical advice in what she eats, she often doesn't feel a sense of inner personal consent or freedom in eating. Leah describes feeling like she is losing control or giving up control to others when she takes a bite.

While getting help for her eating disorder has become a clear goal for Leah, the process of experientially feeling "yes" (or giving inner consent) to eating is cultivated in dialogue with herself and with her situation. She learns to ask herself, *How do I feel about eating this particular bite of food, in this moment? Do I give my own personal consent to swallowing this piece of food? Is there something that I feel hungry for? What tastes good to me?* The more she does this, the more she gives her own self the opportunity to feel consent and agreement to nourishing her body. Leah begins to notice sometimes feeling a "yes" to some food, and in choosing to give her "yes" by eating, she expresses her own agency and freedom. Leah would also begin to ask herself if she gives consent not to eat something at a given time: *Is it OK for me to not eat this bite even though I am starving?* She may not always feel inner consent not to eat, but often still refuse food, consistent with the pattern she has long followed. However, by engaging this space of dialogue and contemplation, Leah as a person enters the situation of eating and enters her own body, giving herself increasing opportunities to respond with embodied agency and authentic action. If Leah lets herself be asked and still fails to give consent to starvation even while continuing to restrict out of her long-established habit, she will become increasingly frustrated in refusing food.

Through cultivating freedom in giving inner consent to her actions, Leah can discover a personally responsible way of dealing with her own life and with the world. To be *personally responsible* in the framework of EA means that one can stand behind what one does, with authenticity. In Leah's case, she is invited, through dialogue, to give an answer to each real situation, considering the givens in her existence. To deal with herself requires that she be in dialogue with herself, taking a personal position toward her own feelings, wishes, hopes, and anxieties that come up around the themes of food, eating, body, relationships, etc. To deal with the outer realities, Leah must also maintain active dialogue with the constraints outside of her, which may include aspects of weight restoration treatment protocols.

Structural Model

Elaborating from the anthropology of Viktor Frankl who developed Logotherapy and identified meaning-seeking as the deepest human motivation (Frankl, 1988), the framework of EA is built on three other existential motivations that exist in parallel to the search for meaning (Längle, 2005). These include the motivations to *be*, to experience *value*, and to be *oneself*. Corresponding to each of the Fundamental Motivations (FM) is a primary existential question (Längle, 1999, 2012):

- I am here. Can I be? Do I have the necessary space, protection, and support?
- I am alive. Do I like to live? Do I feel my emotions and experience the value of my life?
- I am me. May I be myself? Am I free to be me?
- Finally, the primary question of meaning-focused logotherapy: What am I here for? What do I live for? What gives my life meaning?

Within the theoretical framework of EA, these four existential FMs provide the structure for existence. One experiences fulfillment in being able to affirm the existential questions corresponding to each of the four FMs: "yes" to the world (FM1), "yes" to life (FM2), "yes" to one's self/person (FM3), and "yes" to meaning (FM4). Inner consent represents an active "yes" to each of these existential questions of the four FMs.

Existential Analysis View of the Body

Anthropological Background

Grounded in Frankl's (1969) tridimensional anthropological model of the human being, EA acknowledges the body as a fundamental given of the human being and existence. Together with the psychological and the noetic (spiritual) anthropological dimensions, the body represents a constitutive dimension of the human being. Although each dimension is distinguishable from the others, all three are integrated in the lived experience of the body; thus, embodiment represents a holistic experience that reflects the physical, psychological, and spiritual integrity of the human being. Moreover, there is an ongoing, mutual dialogue among these three anthropological dimensions, and, as a result, sometimes tension or conflict may develop leading to imbalances in the holistic sense of the embodied experience (e.g., when the body is sick, psychologically we may feel down or fatigued, whereas our spiritual undertakings may remain strong as our main source of support in times of crisis).

This anthropological model has implications for understanding the embodied experience in eating disorders where the body is rejected or dismissed as a fundamental aspect of one's existence, and concomitantly the psychological life (e.g., emotionality, thinking) becomes constricted while the person may be preoccupied with spiritual strivings toward perfection and a nonmaterial existence. In this process, the person's will may zealously pursue a dangerous ideal of thinness and a disembodied existence at the expense of one's somatic and psychological integrity.

Being and Having a Body

The theoretical framework of EA further elaborates the paradox of 'I am a body' and 'I have a body'. On the one hand, 'I am a body' means that constitutively I exist as an embodied being (Heidegger, 1962; Merleau-Ponty, 1945/2012) and that my body provides the primordial, prelinguistic basis of who I am; on the other hand, 'I have a body' distances me from my body, as my body becomes the object of my relating, possessing, and acting.

The human being resides at the center of this existential paradox, which plays a critical role in understanding the lived experience of embodiment in people with eating disorders where the body itself is called into question and heavily scrutinized. This external gaze further deepens the rift between being and having a body and, eventually, turns the body into an object to be controlled and altered from the outside. Most people diagnosed with eating disorders have difficulties experiencing 'I am a body' and overcompensate for this in distancing from their bodies through an excessive focus on 'I have a body' where the body becomes the object of merciless exercising, starvation, and other projects meant to render it invisible (Skårderud, 2007). Essentially, in the course of an eating disorder, the body becomes a saliently oppressive object (the body-object or Koerper; Sartre, 1943) profoundly estranged from the identity of the person, and this estrangement fractures or even breaks the anthropological somato-psycho-spiritual unity/integrity of the human being.

Embodiment and the Fundamental Existential Motivations

Body as the Physical Structure of Human Existence (FM1)

The existential theme and question of the first FM (FM1) is 'can I be?' More specifically, 'can I exist as a human being in this physical world with my own physicality?' or 'can I exist as a body in the world?' In order to answer 'yes' to these questions, one has to experience ground, support, space, and protection in one's embodied existence.

For people suffering from eating disorders, these questions represent a crucible of anguish, resistance, and perplexity and may be experienced as terrifying. Indeed, some of these people prefer not to have a physical body or at least choose to minimize it close to disappearance (Beyer, 2016; Beyer & Launeanu, in press). Being contained by the hard, physical structure of the body is experienced as imprisonment in heavy, dense materiality with all the limitations that a physically constrained existence brings: pain, hunger, longings, and imperfections. Thus, it may be preferable to reduce one's physicality to a minimum, or to the bare bones.

Body as Existential Ground

Our bodies provide a firm, solid, stable ground to our existence. We live intuitively trusting that our body is holding and carrying us in this world. A deep, implicit trust in our body capacity to hold us through the multitudes of our existence gives us the confidence that all is good in our body and we can rely on it. This trust is so fundamental that rarely do we pause to wonder about it. We are enjoying our life as embodied beings without questioning. In a way we take our embodied existence for granted, and, under regular circumstances, our body is largely a 'forgotten body' (Merleau-Ponty, 1945/2012; Sartre, 1943).

In contrast, people diagnosed with eating disorders develop a salient and even hyper-salient awareness of the body. Rather than being a 'forgotten body' implicitly trusted and relied upon, the body with its external characteristics (i.e., shape, weight, length) becomes the center of preoccupations and, essentially, an undesirable obstacle to be controlled and diminished. The implicit interoceptive awareness and unquestionable trust transform into the obsessive, exteroceptive, scrutinizing gaze of the body-object. This leads to a profound mistrust and suspicion in one's somatic capacities as one of the hallmark symptoms of eating disorders (Beyer, 2016).

Body as Space

Our body creates space both outwardly and inwardly. Outwardly, since we are born in the physical world, we take up space with our bodies. By occupying space, we become visible and set physical boundaries between our own and what is different from us. As our body grows during our development, the space we take grows as well and we install more comfortably in the physical reality of the world. Inwardly, our body is spacious and allows us to experience the space inside. For instance, our lungs are filled with air, and if we take a deep breath, we can create more physical space within our body. This leads to an expansive experience of spaciousness inside and outside our body.

During the course of an eating disorder, this sense of spaciousness tends to be significantly restricted. The body is constrained and minimized close to invisibility. Instead of taking up space and feel expansive in their body, individuals diagnosed with eating disorders avoid their bodies, work incessantly to reduce the physicality of the body via weight loss, and submit their body to excessive physical demands to avoid experiencing the sense of space and visibility that come through the body. An intriguing research finding pointing to the loss of inner spaciousness during anorexia is women's self-reported inability to take a deep breath or to be aware of their breath even late in the recovery process (Launeanu & Beyer, in press). It seems that restoring the inner spaciousness of the body as a good space of dwelling is a slow process fraught with many obstacles.

Body as Protection

By design, our body is meant to offer us protection. Our skin acts as a live, flexible membrane that allows us to optimally relate with the world without being damaged or wounded, and without being poisoned by foreign influences or substances. Our skull keeps our brain safely enclosed, and our thorax protects our heart. Our backbone shields our spinal cord. Our body is fundamentally designed to provide protection and safety.

For people suffering from eating disorders, the body is a source of pain and discomfort (Beyer 2016; Beyer & Launeanu, in press). Rather than protecting, it unsafely exposes personal vulnerabilities in a way experienced as deceitful. Rather than concealing and protecting, the body is too revealing. Rather than providing a safe haven, it makes one too visible and too exposed. Fundamentally, for persons with eating disorders, body is the most unsafe place (Beyer, 2016), and the only pale possibility of safety comes at the expense of beating the body into submission via overexercising, starvation, and/or purging.

Lived Body (FM2)

Our body is not just a firm, protective physical structure that supports our existence but is also filled with life and is experienced as alive, akin to Sartre's (1943) lived body (Leib) or body-subject. The aliveness of the body-subject is experienced as vibrant emotionality in addition to sensuality and interoceptive experiences.

The existential theme of the second FM (FM2) is 'do I like to be?' Body-wise, this means 'do I like my body?' and 'do I like my embodied existence?' In other words, do I experience my existence in my body as fundamentally good, and do I experience pleasure and goodness in and through my body? In order to answer 'yes' to these questions, one has to experience one's body sensuality, emotionality, and relationality.

People diagnosed with eating disorders experience a profound dislike toward their bodies and their body-based experiences (Beyer, 2016). In order to cope with this deep aversion, most of them dissociate from their bodies, which further leads to a pervasive sense of emotional numbness and an experience of inner deadness where emotionality is very limited or distorted. These experiences then percolate their relationships with others and with life itself.

Sensual Body

Physically, we experience the goodness and beauty of life in and through our bodies. As sensual beings, we enjoy food, art, nature, the pleasures of the senses, and take comfort in all these. For persons suffering from eating disorders, sensuality as the body-based capacity to enjoy life and experience life as good is severely restricted. For instance, the food meant to nurture and offer pleasure becomes poison and brings upon indescribable pain. Sexual desire and eroticism vanish as nothing from the rich sensuousness of the world reaches the starved, emaciated bodies.

Emotional Body

Embodied experience is imbued with emotionality. The sensorial pleasures or comfort and the physical pain are accompanied by affective overtones and categorical emotions. Our emotions grow clearer and more powerful when they resonate and are expressed through our bodies.

This ineffable connection between body and emotionality explains why people diagnosed with eating disorders suffer from severe and pervasive emotional deficits such as alexithymia (Fox, 2009; Kyriacou, Easter, & Tchanturia, 2009; Racine & Wildes, 2013). The more severe the eating disorder, the deeper the emotional numbness and incapacity to experience and identify emotions. Disconnection from the body leads to significant losses with respect to emotionality.

Relational Body

Through our bodies, we relate to ourselves, to each other, and to the world. We turn our faces toward each other, we look each other in the eyes, we greet or comfort each other with hugs, we show tenderness in our touch, and we love each other through our body embraces. We are embodied relational beings, and our bodies are meant to communicate, relate, touch, and love. Moreover, we also relate to our own body. We like and appreciate our body as good and beautiful, and we enjoy its sensuality. We experience our body inwardly as a rich source of life and beauty.

The burden of an eating disorder not only disconnects the person from his or her own body, but in so doing, it also severs the relational capacity which is constitutive for the body. Thus, individuals suffering from eating disorders struggle not only with dissociation and numbness within their body but also with feeling alienated and disconnected from others (Beadle, Paradiso, Salerno, & McCormick, 2013; Rommel, Nandrino, Antoine, & Dodin, 2013).

'I Am My Body' (FM3)

The third FM highlights that embodiment is not just another lived experience but rather a core experience of who I am as a person. Simply put it, I am not just a body, I am *my* body. The questions asked here are: 'may I be my body?' or 'am I allowed to be myself in my body?' Does my body show or express authentically who I am in my essence? To answer 'yes' to these questions, one needs to experience attention toward one's body, justice, and appreciation for one's body.

Embodied Person

Our body not only carries us through life and ensures the basic structure of our existence but also reveals who we are as persons. As embodied beings, the uniqueness of our person shines through the materiality of our body, not in an objective, voyeuristic way but in the inimitable manner in which we carry and express ourselves. We do not only possess and alter our body. We essentially are our body, and our body makes our essence visible in the material world.

This is a point of great suffering for people with eating disorders because of the profound disdain for their bodies, which leads to a painful estrangement from their bodies as the material receptacle of their person, and ultimately, from themselves. This way eating disorders severely impact one's sense of identity and the capacity for authentic living. It also makes the person more opaque to being known by the others, which deepens the experience of isolation and alienation (Rommel et al., 2013).

Becoming My Body (FM4)

The existential theme of fourth FM is to experience meaning of existence. For what is my body? For whom is it good? Where is my body needed? What is most important for my body? What should I do with my body? When one can see the value of being a body and feel "yes" toward this value, direction is given for what one should be and do. In this, one affirms being needed in a particular way in his or her embodied existence. In one's body, there is opportunity for freedom and movement, creativity, and belonging to a larger context.

Freedom and Movement

For people suffering with eating disorders, the body can be experienced as a burden, a liability, or an obstacle, and as something that needs to be controlled and reduced. An embodied journey of recovery aims to reclaim the body as a site of agency and freedom, something that offers movement and presence to be in and interact with this physical world. The body, rather than inhibiting the possibilities of the person, is actually the vehicle for giving voice to one's full existence. In one's body, one can affirm freedom and purposeful action.

Creative Body/Giving Birth

Birthing and the capacity to give life represents the ultimate creative potential for the woman's body. Dance and movement, gardening, and sculpturing or other art all represent creative purposes for the embodied self. In the lived experience of eating disorders, the creative body is silenced and controlled. The themes of the fourth FM remind us that the body is generative and full of creative capacity.

Body in the Larger Context

Considering the larger context, what one does with one's embodied existence is larger than oneself. In and through one's body, one chooses to engage cultural and family traditions and spiritual practices. In this larger context, one experiences meaning by choosing the most valuable possibility in a given situation. Given all the possible things one can do and that one may like to do, and that are authentic, the most valuable possibility becomes what one should do. The greater context of embeddedness in family, culture, and spirituality can provide a sense of belonging and rootedness for choosing meaningful action.

Embodiment and EA Personal Activities and Capacities

In EA, a personal activity is a fundamental stance and engagement with the existential theme of each of the four FMs, whereas a personal capacity or faculty represents the capability to accomplish these personal activities in order to realize the existential theme of each FM. For FM1, the personal activities are endurance and acceptance, and the personal capacities are awareness and perception. For FM2 the personal activity is turning towards, and the personal capacities are valuing and feeling. For FM3, the personal activity is encounter, and the personal capacities are taking a stance and moral decision-making. For FM4, the personal activity is creativity and acting in accordance with a broader vision, and the personal capacities are work and action, devotion, and spirituality.

Disturbances in the embodied lived experience encountered in people suffering from eating disorders are reflected in distorted personal activities and capacities. For instance, acceptance as FM1 activity is profoundly impacted, and the awareness and perception of the body are distorted (e.g., seeing oneself as fat when one is emaciated). Instead of turning toward one's body, people suffering from eating disorders turn away from and reject their bodies while suffering massive emotional losses and deficits in the process. Hence, their feelings and capacity to value life and one's body are numbed. Given the significant disconnect from the body, the personal encounter with one's self via one's body is virtually inexistent, and the possibility to develop authentic attitudes toward one's self is almost completely distorted.

Conclusion

EA understands embodiment as a holistic, integrated experience of the body, mind, and spirit. In this view, the body represents the primary physical structure of our existence, the sensual, earthy connection to life, ourselves and others, the receptacle of our person, and the vehicle for our acting in the world, and becoming. People suffering from eating disorders struggle with major disturbances at all these levels of embodied lived experience: physical, emotional, relational, personal, and spiritual. Existentially understood, their suffering is not mainly about food and eating habits but rather about being and becoming one's body in the world, a profound suffering of the totality of the embodied human existence. In this context, food and eating symbolically represent the existential struggle of how to exist as a living body in the world.

Clinical Illustration of EA Treatment Principles

Suffering from an eating disorder needs a holistic understanding and treatment, not a partial one exclusively focused on eating behaviors and attitudes surrounding food. Recovering the integrity of lived embodied experience (Beyer, 2016) requires working along the four FMs and restoring the body as a safe space of hold and support (FM1); as sensual, emotional, and relational body (FM2); as embodied identity and moral compass (FM3); and as free, creative body (FM4).

This section addresses the main EA treatment principles using an illustration from a clinical case provided by the first author of this chapter. After a brief description of the case, a case conceptualization and treatment plan along the four FMs will be discussed.

Case Description

Jane is a woman who was referred to psychotherapy by her physician after her weight dropped dangerously and her blood tests showed significant nutritional deficits. She believes that she is eating too much and desires to further restrict her eating because she feels that her body cannot process food. She is also exercising a lot to keep her weight down. She dreams about becoming invisible, not having a body, and reducing her body to a "bag of bones". She describes how her weight loss and vigorous exercise help to stop her menstruation and how she hates being a woman. She never had any intimate relationships and is terrified about the possibility of falling in love or getting pregnant. She is 38, does not have a permanent job, lives with her parents, and says that her focus on "shaping the body to perfection" gives her a purpose and a sense of accomplishment.

Case Conceptualization

In the next paragraphs, we apply the EA conceptualization framework to Jane's clinical situation. Jane experiences struggles in all of the four FMs, and the following conceptualization reflects the holistic, existential nature of her suffering.

FM1: 'A Bag of Bones'

With respect to FM1, Jane finds her embodied existence oppressive and restrictive, and she dreams to become invisible or to reduce her existence to a 'bag of bones'. It is apparent that she cannot be in her own body, and, after further exploration, she confesses that she feels utterly unsafe in her body because she experiences her body as unpredictable (e.g., Jane recounted some overwhelming incidents around the time she was menstruating). In this context, Jane's desire to shrink her body symbolically means to reduce her existence to its bare essence (the bag of bones) and a clear refusal of living an embodied existence. Although Jane is not actively suicidal, she is entertaining fantasies about leaving her body behind to become lighter and to be able to fly.

FM2: 'The Beast'

From the FM2 perspective, Jane's relationship with her body is tenuous at best, and during our therapy sessions, she disclosed several times that she finds her body 'ugly and disgusting'. In addition, Jane experiences her body like a 'beast' full of rage and other unspeakable emotions that can only be tamed with heavy exercise and fasting. Thus, Jane's emotional life mirrors the unsafety experienced in her physical body, and it is felt as unpredictable and chaotic as her body menstruating. Hence, in extremis, Jane implements severe measures to ensure a safe disconnection from threatening emotions. In so doing, she is also cutting off opportunities for meaningful connections with others in favor of the familiarity of living with her parents.

FM3: 'The Invisible Me'

Perhaps the most striking difficulty during therapy sessions is when Jane is invited to speak about herself, about what she likes and what she would like to do. Her terror when faced with these questions reveals her underdeveloped sense of who she is. Her eyes avert therapist's attention, and her body shrinks even more in the chair. Her tiny body seems too small for her person. Jane softly murmurs that she prefers to be unnoticeable and that she likes to hide in her room for long periods of time. In these moments, Jane resembles a very young child scared to be and fearful of what might come. Thus, her fear of interpersonal intimacy and encounter is not surprising.

FM4: 'Shaping My Body to Perfection'

Paradoxically, Jane has a very strong will and a lot of purpose in spite of her frail body and overwhelming fears. Her voice becomes stronger when she describes in detail and with conviction how much she exercises, the type of exercises, and how much weight she lost as a result. For the first time, she looks as if she accomplished something important. She looks proud and speaks vivaciously about her purpose: 'to shape her body to perfection'. When asked what that meant she quickly and compellingly indicates that it would be a very thin body, 'transparently thin' that would ensure that she will never experience the horror of menstruating or the danger of pregnancy. Besides this purpose, Jane is very confused about what to do with her life and has no hobbies or other enjoyable activities besides exercising.

EA Treatment Principles

A later chapter is devoted to exploring practical strategies for cultivating embodiment. A summary of EA treatment principles that follows the four FMs includes (a) restoring body space and safety; (b) cultivating body sensuality; (c) practicing embodied sense of self; and (d) expressing movement, creativity, and spirituality.

Working with Jane begins with restoring her body space and safety by cultivating awareness of the body from within and experiencing her body's strength and support. Strategies including practicing relaxation, stretching, and yoga postures are all part of restoring safety in her body. Jane would be supported in taking up physical space through her body and visualizing her body as her home in which she is safe and supported.

To cultivate body sensuality, Jane's therapeutic work would also include working with earth elements, such as gardening, observing and being in nature, sculpture, and sand tray work. She would reconnect to emotionality through her body. How does she experience sadness, joy, grief, pleasure, fear, and hope? To what and to whom does she feel a sense of connection? Jane would work with her body to give her access to being in life and to being connected to self, nature, and others. Jane would also explore her relational body. With whom is she close? Whose company does she enjoy and with whom does she want to spend time?

Jane's embodied sense of self is explored as she comes to grapple with not just having a body, or being a body, but actually being her own body. Through this body, Jane's personhood is visible. Moving from the 'invisible me', Jane's therapeutic work would support her authentic and embodied self-expression. In taking up physical space in the world (corresponding to FM1), Jane also reveals herself to the world (corresponding to FM3), resulting in a felt sense that she can be herself through being in her body and that she can be known.

Finally, Jane's therapeutic work would be focused on the direction of her existence. Where is she yearning? Where is she creative? Where does she experience spirituality? Jane's will is ultimately affirmed purposefully through her body. For what is her body? Given the capacities of the body, what is the most valuable thing she can do with her body? Jane would be encouraged to pursue hobbies, interests, spirituality, and creative arts.

Conclusion: EA as a Framework for Understanding and Treating Eating Disorders

Consistent with the focus of this book on exploring the role of embodiment in eating disorders, the authors propose that EA provides a holistic framework for conceptualizing and treating eating disorders. An EA framework provides an integrative, non–dualistic, and existential perspective for understanding and promoting embodiment. Embodiment is understood in EA as a holistic, integrated experience of the body, mind, and spirit. In this view, the body is the physical structure of our existence, the connection to life, the expression of personhood, and the vehicle for action in the world. Eating disorders impact the body on each of these levels, resulting in disturbances that are physical, emotional, relational, personal, and spiritual. Treatment of eating disorders with an EA framework avoids the objectification of the body as something to be controlled and instead promotes agency in and through the existential unity of the body-self. In this approach to understanding and treating eating disorders, EA provides an alternative lens and an alternative approach to clinical interventions, which preserves and promotes the integral unity of the whole person.

References

Allan, H. T. (2005). Gender and embodiment in nursing: The role of the female chaperone in the infertility clinic. *Nursing Inquiry, 12*, 175–183.

Beadle, J. N., Paradiso, S., Salerno, A., & McCormick, L. M. (2013). Alexithymia, emotional empathy, and self-regulation in anorexia nervosa. *Annals of Clinical Psychiatry, 25*(2), 107–120.

Beyer, C. (2016). Seeking the body electric: The role of embodied affective experience in the process of recovery from anorexia nervosa (unpublished Master's thesis). Trinity Western University, BC.

Beyer, C., & Launeanu, M. (in press). Poems of the past, present and future: Becoming a more embodied self in recovering from anorexia nervosa. In H. L. McBride & J. K. Kwee (Eds.), *Healthy embodiment and eating disorders: Theory, research, prevention and treatment.* New York, NY: Routledge.

Foucault, M. (1978). *The history of sexuality.* New York, NY: Penguin Books.

Fox, J. R. E. (2009). A qualitative exploration of the perception of emotions in anorexia nervosa: A basic emotion and developmental perspective. *Journal of Clinical Psychology and Psychotherapy, 16*, 276–302.

Frankl, V. E. (1988). *The will to meaning.* New York, NY: Penguin Books.

Frankl, V. E. (1969). *The will to meaning: Foundations and applications of logotherapy.* New York, NY: The World Publishing Company.

Fredrickson, B. L., & Roberts, T. A. (1997). Objectification theory: Toward understanding women's lived experiences and mental health risks. *Psychology of Women Quarterly, 21*, 273–306.

Hebbel, F. (2013). *Tagebücher.* Stuttgart: Reclam, Eintrag No. 1854.

Heidegger, M. (1962). *Being and time.* Oxford, UK: Blackwell Publishers Ltd.

Kwee, J., & Längle, A. (2013). Phenomenology in psychotherapeutic praxis: An introduction to personal existential analysis. *Experiencing EPIS, A Journal of the Existential and Psychoanalytic Institute and Society, 2*, 139–163.

Kyriacou, O., Easter, A., & Tchanturia, K. (2009). Comparing views of patients, parents and clinicians on emotions in anorexia: A qualitative study. *Journal of Health Psychology, 14*, 843–854.

Längle, A. (1999). Was bewegt den Menschen? Die existentielle Motivation der Person. *Existenzanalyse, 16*(3), 18–29.

Längle, A. (2003). The method of "personal existential analysis." *European Psychotherapy, 4*(1), 37–53.

Längle, A. (2005). The search for meaning in life and the existential fundamental motivations. *Existential Analysis, 16*(1), 2–14.

Längle, A. (2012). The Viennese school of existential analysis. The search for meaning and affirmation of life. In L. Barnett & G. Madison (Eds.), *Existential therapy: Legacy, vibrancy, and dialogue* (2012, pp. 159–170). New York, NY: Routledge.

Längle, A. (2013). 4th fundamental motivation: The fundamental conditions for MEANING in life. Unpublished manuscript, Gesellschaft für Logotherapie und Existenzanalyse, Vienna, Austria.

Maturana, H. (2002). *Biology of cognition and epistemology.* Temuco: Universidad de la Frontera.

Merleau-Ponty, M. (2012). *Phenomenology of perception.* (D. L. Landes, Trans.). New York, NY: Routledge. (Original work published 1945.)

Niedenthal, P. M. (2007). Embodying emotion. *Science, 316,* 1002–1005. doi:10.1126/science.1136930

Niedenthal, P. M., Barsalou, L., Weinkielman, P., Krauth-Gruber, S., & Ric, F. (2005). Embodiment in attitudes, social perception, and emotion. *Personality and Social Psychology Review, 9,* 184–211.

Piran, N., & Teall, T. (2012). The developmental theory of embodiment. In G. McVey, M. P. Levine, N. Piran, & H. B. Ferguson (Eds.), *Preventing eating-related and weight-related disorders: Collaborative research, advocacy, and policy change* (pp. 169–198). Waterloo, ON: Wilfred Laurier University Press.

Racine, S. E., & Wildes, J. E. (2013). Emotion dysregulation and symptoms of anorexia nervosa: The unique roles of lack of emotional awareness and impulse control difficulties when upset. *International Journal of Eating Disorders, 46*(7), 713–720. doi:10.1002/eat.22145

Rommel, D., Nandrino, J., Antoine, P., & Dodin, V. (2013). Emotional differentiation and parental bonding in inpatients suffering from eating disorders. *British Journal of Clinical Psychology, 52,* 215–229.

Sartre, J. P. (1943). *Being and nothingness.* New York, NY: Washington Square Press.

Skårderud, F. (2007). Eating one's words, part I: 'Concretised metaphors' and reflective function in anorexia nervosa – An interview study. *European Eating Disorders Review, 15*(3), 163–174. doi:10.1002/erv.777

Stanghellini, G., Castellini, G., Brogna, P., Faravelli, C., & Ricca, V. (2012). Identity and eating disorders (IDEA): A questionnaire evaluating identity and embodiment in eating disorder patients. *Psychopathology, 45,* 147–158. doi:10.1159/000330258

Underwood, M. (2013). Body as choice or body as compulsion: An experiential perspective on body-self relations and the boundary between normal and pathological. *Health Sociology Review, 22,* 377–388.

Varela, F. J. (1996). Neurophenomenology: A methodological remedy for the hard problem. *Journal of Consciousness Studies, 4,* 330–349.

Winkielman, P., Niedenthal, P., & Oberman, L. (2008). The embodied emotional mind. In G. R. Semin & E. R. Smith (Eds.), *Embodied grounding: Social, cognitive, affective, and neuroscientific approaches* (pp. 263–288). New York, NY: Cambridge University Press. doi:10.1017/CBO9780511805837.012

Winkielman, P., Niedenthal, P., Wielgosz, J., Eelen, J., & Kavanagh, L. C. (2015). Embodiment of cognition and emotion. In M. Mikulincer, P. R. Shaver, E. Borgida, J. A. Bargh, M. Mikulincer, P. R. Shaver, … J. A. Bargh (Eds.), *APA handbook of personality and social psychology, volume 1: Attitudes and social cognition* (pp. 151–175). Washington, DC: American Psychological Association.

4 From Having a Body to Being Embodied

Phenomenological Theories on Embodiment

Barbara Weber

The body has been a topic of philosophical deliberations for humans as long as they ponder about themselves. It is, after all, due to embodiment that an irreversible rift occurs, rending the fundamental condition of human existence. Because of its spatiotemporal relationality, the body functions as the backbone of grammar – of the grammar of speech and of the grammar of space: I and Not-I, Here and There. However, in the natural, social or political sciences, the body is often understood in a Cartesian mode, i.e. a *physically extended object* (Lat. *res extensa*) that exists disconnected from the "thinking mind" (Lat. *res cogitans*). This dualistic and reductionist view of the body has led to a constrained understanding of the body as "lived" as well as its impact on our physical and emotional well-being.

In this chapter, I will start by tracing back this reductionist vocabulary to its origin and outline its main criticism. I will then show why and how phenomenology tries to overcome the Descartes, i.e. by understanding "embodiment" as lived and intersubjective (*intercorporité*). In order to demonstrate the relevance of this paradigm shift within the context of eating disorders, I will concentrate on two thinkers, namely Jean-Paul Sartre and his "three dimensions of the body" in relationship with "the gaze" as well as Maurice Merleau-Ponty and his notion of the "I can." I will show how the disconnection from the "body-for-myself" as well as the pathological attempt to control "how our body looks for Others" may lead to severe distortions in a person's body image. My intention is to explain that such doubts about one's own body are not just faulty perceptions of a subjective mind, but rather touch upon the primordial grounding of our existence. This chapter is written in a phenomenological style, inviting the reader to participate in simple thought experiments by providing everyday examples and using poetic languages. The goal is to push through a reductionist language of embodiment and sensitize for the complexity of our lived experience.

From the Body as "Extended Object" to the Body as "Lived": A Short (His)Story of Embodiment

A dualistic interpretation of the body-mind problem alone is not new, but rather can be found throughout the history of ideas and in almost all cultures.[1] Nonetheless, the famous Canadian-American phenomenologist James Mensch summarizes in a recent presentation on embodiment: "And we are still recovering from the sharp separation between the mind and the body that the Cartesian language has created".[2]

Thus, let us begin with René Descartes: In his pivotal work *Meditations on First Philosophy* (1641/1996), Descartes intensifies the abyss between minds and bodies by identifying them as two absolutely distinct substances with very different attributes: Bodies (*res extensa*) are characterized by spatiotemporal physical properties, while minds (*res cogitans*) are characterized by properties of thinking (including seeing, feeling, etc.). By associating body and mind with two different substances, he was able to cut any lingering connection between the two. He turned the body into a mere object that can be studied, taken apart and controlled, while the mind "watches," analyzes, thinks and understands. This classification sees the mind as the aspect that has access to "the truth," while the body (i.e. perceptions, etc.) can be misleading. In fact, we can doubt the existence of the body in itself, while the mind cannot be doubted (Descartes, 1996, p. 55).

And it was this intention and hubris, which Descartes ascribed to the mind, that centuries later the phenomenologist Edmund Husserl criticized sharply. In fact, he sees the Cartesian separation of *res extensa* and *res cogitans* as a *huge disaster* [German: "große[s] Unheil"] (Husserl, 1956, Hua (Husserliana) VII, p. 73). In opposition to Descartes, Husserl does not see the body as a physical substance, but rather as a lived "here" from which all "there's" are "there". The body is point zero or groundless ground within which all our perceptions and sensations are located. Yet, the subjective "living" of such sensations is fundamentally different from the objective localizations of those from an outsider perspective. He writes, "Although my body is nothing else then a thing among things, it is different as a lived body" (Hua XVI, p. 162). Or in other words, we cannot be replaced or substituted in our embodied perceiving, existing and experiencing: Just as no one can die for us,[3] no one can ever eat or drink for us. Husserl tries to get to the exceptional positioning of one's own body, which is very different from how one relates to all other bodies. It is not through "thinking," but rather is "lived through" and towards the world. Only through being embodied, I am alive and experience the world (Hua XXXIX, p. 615). The lived body therefore *only* exists in "the first person singular" (Aloa & Depraz, 2012, p. 11). In Husserl's phenomenology of embodiment, then, the lived body as the center of experience plays a key role in how we encounter other embodied agents in a shared space of a coherent and ever-explorable world. The Husserl expert Elisabeth Behnke writes, "[We are a] coherent system of movement possibilities allowing us to experience every moment of our situated, practical-perceptual life as pointing to 'more' than our current perspective affords" (Benkhe, 2016, p. 5). Husserl tries to engage with the complex experiences of the lived body (in time). And he therefore does not so much criticize the dualistic language that Descartes uses, but rather the reductionism that comes with his two-substance thinking (Aloa & Depraz, 2012, p. 8f). This Cartesian reductionist language and mode of thinking has not only penetrated the natural, social and political sciences, but moreover silently taken over our everyday language and become part of how we interpret, feel and think about our daily life. Consequently, when Husserl tries to disclose and *undo* these underlying structures of language, he needs to write in a seemingly unusual, eccentric way.[4]

After Husserl and the Beginnings of a "Phenomenology of Embodiment"

This distinction between Descartes' notion of the body as object and Husserl's notion of the "body as lived" was then picked up and further developed by a variety of thinkers. It formed what can be called the "phenomenology of embodiment" (*Leibphaenomenologie*).[5] In the following, I will briefly outline some prominent ideas of this school of thought by referring to Hermann Schmitz, Maurice Merleau-Ponty, Jan Patocka, Michel Henry, Helmut Plessner, Jean-Paul Sartre, Emmanuel Levinas, and Bernhard Waldenfels,[6] as they each disclose a different aspect of the "lived body."[7] I will then focus on Merleau-Ponty and Sartre in more depth.

One of the first philosophers who picked up Husserl's criticism of Descartes' reductionist vocabulary was the German phenomenologist Hermann Schmitz. He made it the task of his life to develop a complex theory of embodiment, for which he tried to meticulously explore all of the various aspects of the body as lived. He uses a phenomenological approach pushing through unreflected, essentialist, everyday language and replaces it with a rich, poetic and systematic repertoire of words that aims to capture (or point towards) the complexity of each phenomenon more adequately. Schmitz himself calls his project a "sky survey" of embodiment (Schmitz, 1990, p. 115). Eventually, the body becomes a "hinge" for many other central philosophical topics like emotions, consciousness and personhood as well as cultural fields, such as art, law, morality, religion and politics (Andermann, 2012, p. 140ff). Schmitz's project was picked up by a number of social scientists and psychologists who use his rich vocabulary to engage with and explore the convolutions of bodily experiences, including the emotions (Seewald, 1992), the space (Fuchs, 2000) and identity (Haneberg, 1995) as well as the pathologies of those.

The German philosopher and sociologist Helmut Plessner is one of the primary advocates for what can be called "philosophical anthropology". He became famous for his reinforcement of Husserl's dualism by distinguishing between "Leib-Sein" (*being a living body*) and "Koerper-haben" (*having an objectifiable body*). Plessner (1928) claims that because we are temporal beings, we always already escape ourselves. At the same time, we are a *lived space* in space, and consequently we can look back and try to *understand* or *see* ourselves. However, what we see, as we look back, i.e. the objective body, is no longer identical with the person who is looking. Thus, the very nature of being human can be grounded in the eccentric positioning. For Plessner, this eccentric positioning of the human is necessary for the open dispositioning of the humans towards the world. Or in other words, because we are not completely in possession of our own embodied self, we remain open to the world and other perspectives. And while Plessner sees this as a potential of the human nature, it can also be experienced as *decentering* or even threatening.[8] Plessner's theoretical deliberations are helpful when one tries to understand embodiment in relationship to identity, the world of "things" [Orig.: *Dingwelt*] and the social world [Orig.: *Mitwelt*] as well as how those elements are interwoven (Plessner, 1928; Weber, 2013).

While both Schmitz and Plessner mainly refer to Husserl for their deliberations, the Czech philosopher Jan Patocka is largely a Heidegger scholar. And although the importance of the body can be intuited in Heidegger's work, the body is only present in its very absence. Here, Patočka (1968; Patočka, Neller, Němec, & Srubar, 1991) picks up Heidegger's blind spot and shows how the body plays a central role when we explore human affections (e.g. fear, boredom) as well as our situatedness within the world. Moreover, in his lectures on embodiment from 1968, Patocka points out that the human, as embodied, is made of the same very *fabric* that the world is made of: We are in the world through world. This embodied existence of world in world is a harmonic intertwining (Novotny, 2012, p. 81). Patocka's intention is to overcome the traditional oppositions of body and mind, incarnation and freedom: By focusing on the primordiality and irreducibility of the first movement of life (Novotny, 2012, p. 83), the body becomes the anchor of Heidegger's "being in the world" and discloses the world in its different appearances. Instead of focusing on the body as object, the lived body becomes like a musical instrument through which different melodies ("ways of being in the world") can be heard or experienced.

In France, embodiment was the focus of four main philosophers, namely Jean-Paul Sartre, Maurice Merleau-Ponty, Emmanuel Levinas and Michel Henry.[9]

The French phenomenologist Emmanuel Levinas emphasizes on the ethical aspects of embodiment, when he turns all of his attention towards the Other. It is no longer the embodied self and his/her relationship to the world that is being explored, but rather how the Other appears to us. To do this, Lévinas (1961) shows how our experience of the lived body changes when we are being looked at. The gaze of the Other petrifies us within our embodied self – we cannot escape, we are vulnerable.

Moreover, the way we are seen by the other (her perceptions, feelings) elude our grasp, and this elusion becomes the pointer towards the radical Otherness of the Other.

> One wants to flee one's own nakedness, hide from the other, but also from oneself. Shame arises when we cannot hide what we want to hide. [...] Shame is exactly this impossibility [...] to hide that we are chained to ourselves, that we are unforgivingly exposed to the Other.
> (Lévinas, 1961, p. 41)

This inexorability of existence is a burden for Levinas, because we are completely thrown back to our existence that we cannot escape; we are trapped in our limited possibilities and reality. Yet, Levinas' account does not stop here. Instead, what brought us into this existential situation, i.e. the gaze of the Other, is also the door to redemption: The fact that I cannot know the Other becomes the epiphany that pulls me away from my own existence and reorients me and all my thinking, feeling and actions towards the other.

The French existentialist Jean-Paul Sartre enters into this topic of embodiment from a similar viewpoint, i.e. the gaze of the Other. From here, he extracts three ontological dimensions of the body: (a) the body for myself as lived, (b) the other's body as an object and (c) my own body disclosed as object to another subject (Sartre, 1943/1992). I will show how the attempt to *control* this third dimension might lead to an unhealthy attitude towards one's own body.

Sartre's colleague Maurice Merleau-Ponty (1945/2012) gives a far more optimistic outlook on the intertwining of the Self and the Other. For him, the gaze of the other is only *objectifying* in situations of power imbalance, i.e. where we want to suppress the subjectivity of the other. Most of the times though, our perspectives and experiences coincide, intersect and inspire one another. In fact, because I'm not completely transparent to myself, my gaze is open towards the encounter with the Other. Thus, Merleau-Ponty interprets this as a healthy and welcomed addition to my own limitations – we coexist in one world.

Michel Henry's theory of a *transcendental embodiment* has been received less frequently, although his central question leads right into the heart of a philosophy of embodiment. In his work *"Philosophie et phénoménologie du corps"* from 1965, he asks, "In what way is the body given to us? In what way do we experience the body as *our* body? How do we know that our consciousness is embodied? He says that we cannot just 'have a body', because then the body would not be an essential part of our consciousness" (p. 22). This is where Henry develops the notion of a *transcendental embodiment* and explores this idea in the context of other central philosophical questions like thinking, acting, as well as the problem of the "Other".

The problem of the Other within the context of embodiment is also a core topic for the German contemporary phenomenologist Bernhard Waldenfels. For him, the body is the fundamental phenomenon that constitutes all other experiences like time, language and the social world. Similar to Plessner, Waldenfels distinguishes between the *Leib* (*lived body*) in its *entity of the self* from the *body as pure matter* (Waldenfels, 2000, p. 9). Within the *gearing of life*, the body resembles a pendulum: It is always both active-living and objective body, subject and object, outside and inside, etc. Yet, instead of reenforcing Husserl's dualism, he tries to explore the ambiguous intertwining of the body with the world (Waldenfels, 1994, p. 465). He shows how the body invades the realm of ideas and nature, necessity and freedom, nature and culture, and thus escapes our attempt to *capture it as something* (1994, p. 465). Here, the Other becomes very important, because my body always already belongs to the Other: as seeing and touching I am by definition also visible and touchable for the Other. Within this context, Waldenfels develops his notion of the "re-sponsivity of the body" (Sternagel, 2012, p. 122).

Since the 1990s, phenomenology of embodiment has grown and influenced many other disciplines like pedagogy, psychology (e.g. Gallagher & Depraz, 2004; Thompson, 2007; Thompson & Varela, 2001), neurology (e.g. Damasio, 1999) and even robotics. And while this chapter cannot trace every one of those developments further, I suggest that exploring the specific vocabularies and viewpoints of existing theories helps to understand the existential qualities of our body perceptions and discloses the complexity that lies behind the lived experience of eating disorders. To show this, I will focus on the notion of the *gaze of the Other* and how the situation of being seen is problematized differently in Sartre and Merleau-Ponty. I theorize that becoming aware of the complexity of our existential state of being visible will help to understand our urge to control our appearance. At the same time, we will see that controlling is not a solution, but rather disturbs deeply the experience of our body *as lived* as well as our ability to actualize our identity as embodied.

Jean-Paul Sartre: On Embodiment, the Gaze and the Other

If we start with the first revelation of the Other as a look, we must recognize that we experience our inapprehensible being-for-others in the form of a possession. I am possessed by the Other; the Other's look fashions my body in its nakedness, causes it to be born, sculptures it, produces it as it is, sees it as I shall never see it. The Other holds a secret - the secret of what I am.

(Sartre, 1943/1992, p. 475)

From Husserl's Dualism to the Three Dimensions of Embodiment

This rather dramatic description is paradigmatic for the existentialist writing style of the French philosopher Jean-Paul Sartre. Born in Paris, Sartre was not only one of the most influential philosophers of his time, but also a play writer, novelist, political activist, biographer and literary critic. He was one of the key figures in existentialism, phenomenology and Marxism, and his work has been highly influential to sociology, critical theory, postcolonial theory and literary studies.

Yet, we might ask how does Sartre arrive at such a pessimistic evaluation of our relationship with the Other? And what role does the body play here? To understand this, we must follow his development of three ontological dimensions of embodiment. These dimensions, however, are not *essences*; they do not exist by or in themselves, but rather describe aspects of our existence. Learning about them might sensitize us for the various nuances of how we experience embodiment.

Sartre (1943/1992) starts out with Husserl's notion of the lived body, which he calls *the body as being-for-itself*. For him, this forms the foundation of human experience, because it is the immediate and pre-reflective experience of the world through the body. Imagine yourself walking through the landscape: You hear birds singing, see the trees, or feel the wind; the body does not appear consciously in that moment, but rather forms the zero point of your coordination system, while the world unfolds in front of you. "Thus by the mere fact that there is a world, this world cannot exist without a univocal orientation in relation to me" (1943/1992, p. 406). In other words, the very fact that my body is seeing and perceiving means that it perceives from a place within the world as world. We disclose the world with our eyes, our fingers. But in the exploration of my surroundings, my body is not standing in the way, but rather a lived instrument that discloses the world ahead of me. And it is my facticity to be "inner-worldly" as I transcend myself towards the world (Sartre, 1943/1992, p. 406). The body-as-being-for-itself remains unproblematized; it exists only lateral, just like we do not think about the fork as we are eating, or we forget about our shoes as we are walking.

And by highlighting this *pre-reflective being-for-itself* of the body, Sartre criticizes that Descartes bypasses this primordial dimension of the body. Instead, Descartes immediately jumps to what Sartre calls the Second Dimension of Embodiment, i.e. the ontological stage of the *body-for-Others*. This second dimension resembles the attempt to capture the existence of the body as an observer and from outside: It becomes a distanced and objectified thing among things. This second dimension can never be experienced from within, i.e. I can never be "objectified body" for myself, because I am always the zero point of all my experiences and perceptions. Consequently, only the Other's body can be objectified in this way.

However, the objectification of the Other's body has to be understood as a process in time. And so I can constitute and capture the Other's body as an object only shortly. The moment the Other looks back at me, I realize that I am myself visible; I am myself flesh and object for the Other. A very simple example might help to illustrate this: When we walk through the busy streets of a city, our eyes might linger on a person who appears interesting to us. We watch them from behind and feel safe in our observation of the objectified Other. Yet, then, the person suddenly turns around and looks right into our eyes; the person sees us watching, and now we become the object to the person's gaze. We feel caught and become ashamed. We are transcended in our transcendence and fall back into the facticity of the moment.

Here is where Sartre's third ontological dimension comes into play: Not only do I exist for myself as a lived body and I can see the Other's body as a thing among things, but "I exist for myself as a body known by the Other" (1943, p. 460). Through the gaze of the Other, I no longer transcend my body towards the world, but rather am thrown back to how I am in this world, i.e. as this object that I am for the Other. Thus, the very thing that makes me share one world with the other, I can never see myself.

We might ask, "Why is this so? Can we not look into the mirror or have a photo/video of ourselves before us?" However, neither the mirror image nor the photo/video is us in the way we would naturally interact with the world or the Other. Furthermore, we need to understand how our perception functions: Perceptions are never a passive recording device, like a camera that is recording a scene from a specific viewpoint. Rather, our perception always works by foregrounding and back-grounding specific aspects of any given scene or object. When the Other looks at my body, she will always focus on some aspect of my appearance (e.g. my hair), while something else fades into the background (e.g. my chin). Moods, emotions and affections often influence what we foreground. For example, when we are in love with a person, we more likely will focus on aspects that we find appealing, like a soft line around the nose or a wise melancholy below the eyes; while when we are arguing with that same person, we might disclose the Other's narrowness of the eyes or a harsh line as their mouth. The Other shapes our appearance with his gaze like a sculptor. And while we can feel the sculpting gaze on our body, we cannot exactly know how the other sees us. Furthermore, the angle from where we are seen also influences how we are actualized as embodied, i.e. from the side, the back, the front, from far away or close up. Every viewpoint makes a difference. The popularity of selfies is an indicator of how important it is for people to find just the right angle. Yet, even a "selfie" does not tell us how we appear to Others. It is popular, because we can control many aspects of our appearance in a selfie (make up, right angle, still photo, Photoshop adjustments, etc.), yet it still does not show us *how* we look when we engage with the world and interact with the Other, nor how the Other actualizes our appearance – it will remain a secret, i.e. the secret of who I am for the Other. The Sartre expert Maier writes,

> As soon as the other sees me, I feel at the same time, that his gaze hits me, it looks at me in a way where I am as I am and where I cannot change how I am. I'm ashamed, because I am helplessly extradited to the Others gaze. I have an outside and the Other possesses this outside with his gaze; yet this is also part of who I am and I'm responsible for it.
>
> (Maier, 1964, p. 3)

My Body as Visible: Phenomenology of the Gaze

> Everywhere are eyes and behind every pair of eyes lives a conscious-ness that sees me, that takes possession of me, that digests me. And this means that I am being classified, packaged and labeled; yet a label that I cannot even see and that now lives within the heart of the Other.
>
> (Sartre, 1943/1992, p. 371)

Sartre eloquently reveals the most vulnerable point of our existence: The fact that we live in a shared world requires that we are embodied, yet it is this embodiment and openness towards the world that prevents us from seeing ourselves in the way that Others see us. Or in other words, our ve-hicle towards the world, as body-for-myself, is out of our control when it is seen by the Other. Based on Sartre's three ontological dimensions of the body, we will now explore in more depth in what ways our pre-reflective bodily experience of the world, as body-for-myself, is being interrupted by the gaze of the other. In order to do this, we will again use some thought experiments.

Imagine again that we sit in a park on a bench. We look at the trees in the wind, the birds flying in the sky and the meadow unfolding in front of our gaze. We transcend our body towards the world; we own this scene as we embrace the horizon. Then, a reading man comes walking through the park. I first try to arrange him just as a thing among things, yet as he comes closer, I fail to fully reduce him to an object:

> If I were to think of him as being only a puppet, I should apply to him the categories which I ordinarily use to group temporal-spatial things. [...Yet] instead of a grouping toward me of the objects, there is now an orientation, which flees from me.
>
> (Sartre, 1943/1992, p. 342)

With the appearance of the Other, the things I see gain a backside – the side that is visible for the Other, but not for myself.[10] The wind in the trees, the birds and the meadow are now seen and heard by someone else, but the way those things are being perceived eludes my grasp. Here, I become aware of the problem of other minds – the Otherness of the Other penetrates by consciousness. The trees, birds, flowers are no longer just part of my own engagement with the world, but rather estranged by another consciousness.

> [the meadow], this green turns toward the Other a face which escapes me. I apprehend the relation of the green to the Other as an objective relation, but I cannot apprehend the green as it appears to the Other. Thus, suddenly a person has appeared which has stolen the world from me. Everything is in place: everything still exists for me; but everything is traversed by an invisible flight and fixed in the direction of a new magnet. The appearance of the Other in the world corresponds therefore to a fixed sliding of the whole universe, to a decentralization of the world which undermines the centralization which I am simultaneously effecting. [...] it appears that the world has a kind of drain hole in the middle of its being and that it is perpetually flowing off through this hole.
>
> (Sartre, 1943/1992, p. 343)

With the presence of the Other, the things show me their no face, they escape my own interpretation, because now there is someone else who sees the world in a way that will always be strange and unknown to myself.

Yet, this is only the first chapter of this event: The man's gaze is still fixed on the book, and I just experience his Otherness in an oscillation between seeing him as an object and the things fleeing my horizon or being oriented towards the other. The moment, though, the man lifts his face and looks at me, everything changes: I am now object to his consciousness. No longer is my body vehicle towards the world, no longer am I diving into the sensuality of the scenery. Instead, I am reduced to the here and now: the present inertia of my material body. I am as I appear to the Other, reduced to the small piece of space that my body indwells. His gaze robs my future, because he sees me just in this one way, from only this viewpoint, then his gaze wanders back into his book. From now on, I live in his heart, as this one image that I do not know and over which I have no control. "In order for me to be what I am, it suffices merely that the Other look at me" (Sartre, 1943/1992, p. 473).

Through the gaze of the Other, we also experience our vulnerability and mortality: I am visible and as this *thing* that can be seen by the Other, I can be touched, held, pushed. The Other can hurt me, not only physically but also emotionally through his perception: He reduces my existence to the facticity of my presence and I am left behind, without future. With his gaze he robs my possibility to transcend the presence, transcend this objectified body. In reality and for myself, I may change, of course, or become someone completely different. Yet, the Other might decide to stop looking at me and I lose my chance to become someone else for him. The image is gone, my future is lost and a part of me is imprisoned within the other's heart. In the end, the encounter with the Other always remains a struggle: "The essence is not the *Mitsein* [being with Others], but rather the conflict" (Sartre, 1943/1992, p. 483).

In summary, the gaze of the Other first robs me my exclusive perspective of the world; then when he looks at me, he sees my blind spots, i.e. the very space in the world that I can never see, because I am this space. And although my encounter with the Other happens in time, his gaze reduces me to my presence: He sees me and walks away with a still image, which I neither know nor can change anymore.

In our next sequence about Merleau-Ponty, we will try to develop a more positive outlook. Instead of focusing on our body as it is for the Other, we will try to (a) focus on the body-for-the-self as a vehicle towards the world and (b) try to turn around Sartre's claim by seeing the encounter with the Other as *Mitsein*, rather than just conflict.

Maurice Merleau-Ponty: With Descartes against Descartes' Reductionism

Merleau-Ponty was born in 1908 in Rochefort-sur-Mer in France and studied alongside Sartre, Simone de Beauvoir, and Simone Weil. He taught at the University of Lyon, then lectured on child psychology and education at the Sorbonne after the war and was awarded the Chair of Philosophy at the Collège de France from 1952 until his death in 1961. Yet, besides his teaching, Merleau-Ponty was also one of the political editors for *Les Temps modernes* together with Sartre, who were colleagues and friends, but later had a falling out regarding their intellectual relationship with communism.

In the following sequence, we will first show why Merleau-Ponty sees human beings as fundamentally intersubjective and not in conflict (as Sartre stated). And while also Merleau-Ponty is aware of the permanent possibility of conflict, for him this is not the primordial way of relating with the Other. We will then follow his transformation of Descartes' Cogito into his famous notion of the "I can." On that basis, we will revisit the gaze of the Other and see how the intertwining of embodiment, Other and world (which is called *flesh* in his later work) leads to a healthier interpretation of the encounter with the Other.

Primordial Intersubjectivity and the "I Can"

"Consciousness is being at the thing through the medium of the body" (Merleau-Ponty, 1945, p. 168f). This simple sentence already entails Merleau-Ponty's later concept of *chair* (flesh), which elaborates on the intertwining of senses, meaning and world: We are visible beings who see, we are feeling beings who can be felt by others and we are embodied beings who understand the world through the medium of the body. Or as Merleau-Ponty says himself in his last and unfinished work *The Visible and the Invisible*,

> One can say that we perceive the things themselves, that we are the world that thinks itself / or that the world is at the heart of our flesh. [...T]here is a ramification of my body and a ramification of the world and a correspondence between its inside and my outside, between my inside and its outside.
>
> (Merleau-Ponty, 1968, p. 136)

A newborn is not yet aware of her body. Her arms and legs do not yet belong to herself, i.e. she does not indwell her body. However, by feeling her own body with her hands, by biting into her finger and feeling the pain, then biting into a toy and not feeling any pain, the child learns to distinguish her own body from the world, while exploring the world through her body. We feel this *double-sensation* all the time, e.g. when we touch a piece of fabric, our finger not only feels the softness of the blanket, but at the same time feels the fabric felt from within ourselves. To become aware as an individual indwelling the world, we need to become aware of the difference between touching an external object with our finger and touching ourselves. In the latter case, we not only feel the finger touching but simultaneously also feel ourselves being palpated. The Merleau-Ponty expert James Mensch writes,

> Each hand through the other thus becomes aware of itself as a sensing object. Each is grasped as an object that, qua sensing, is also a subject. The ability of flesh to be taken as both subject and object gives it the special character of its self-awareness.
>
> (Mensch, 2009, p. 221)

The body is a vehicle towards the world: It continuously engages with and brings out aspects and nuances of the world that are being actualized through our meaning-making perception. In return, my actualization of the world shapes who I am. The material world and the self are not two separated substances (like in Descartes), but rather two sides of the same coin.

Yet, the body is not only the necessary condition for the development of individuality but also the precondition for primordial intersubjectivity. And in fact, for Merleau-Ponty, the bodily intersubjectivity (called inter-corporealite)[11] is prior to the concept of individuality. In his book *La Phenomenologie de la Perception*, he describes the infant as having no concept of "you" or "me", because its bodily scheme has not yet developed. The baby inhabits a world, which she believes is accessible for everybody. She does not think of Others as "private subjectivities" nor does she believe that we are all "limited to one perspective on the world" (Merleau-Ponty, 1945/2012, p. 407). "Only for adults is the perception of others and the intersubjective world a problem" (Merleau-Ponty, 1945/2012, p. 407f); for children, the co-existence with others is primary and only later do they recognize themselves as separate.[12] This is why Merleau-Ponty argues that there is an immediate connection between bodies: A child will always intentionally imitate our movements. Although she has neither seen herself in the mirror nor is her body the same as mine, if we open our mouth when we raise a spoon to feed her, she intentionally opens her own mouth. "She perceives in her body her intentions, my body with my intentions and thus my intentions within her body" (Merleau-Ponty, 1945/2012, p. 404f). This immediate imitation is also how children learn to use tools and thus to dwell in the world of cultural objects. Otherwise, the things around us would be like "aeroliths from an alien planet" (Merleau-Ponty, 1945/2012, p. 406). And it is because our bodies are similar, that we learn to relate to the things around us, and ultimately find them as extensions of our own body. There is no other way to learn how to eat with a fork, scribble with a crayon, or tie one's shoes except by watching another person doing these actions and then feeling the corresponding movements within one's own body. With these examples and by using a psychological lens, Merleau-Ponty tries to explain that for the child, the Other does not appear as a separate entity; the Other's body is not a wall, but rather a door that leads into a shared world. And this is why for Merleau-Ponty, the problem of solipsism is a problem that can only be posed retrospect, i.e. after we have already grown up in a shared world:

> I can escape from society into nature, or from the real world into an imaginary [... yet we can] only call such perceptions into question in the name of a truer one that would correct it: if I am able to deny each thing, that is always by affirming that there is something in general. [...] I can construct a solipsistic philosophy, but by doing so I presuppose a community of speaking men, and I address myself to this community. [...] Solitude and communication must not be two terms of an alternative, but rather two moments of a single phenomenon.
> (Merleau-Ponty, 1945/2012, p. 376)

This continuous intertwining of the Self and Other also occurs in the process of language acquisition. Here, Merleau-Ponty elaborates on Immanuel Kant's account on concepts and perceptions. We enact our *senses* (perceptions) by putting the objects to the uses that disclose their specific *sense* (meaning). Concepts arise from the sense-making of our senses. Merleau-Ponty concludes,

> Consciousness is originarily not an 'I think that,' [in the sense of Descartes' *cogito*] but rather an 'I can'. [...] Vision and movement are specific ways of relating to objects and, if a single function is expressed

throughout all of these experiences, then it is the movement of existence, which does not suppress the radical diversity of contents, for it does not unite them by placing them all under the domination of an 'I think,' but rather by orienting them towards the inter-sensory unity of a 'world'.

(Merleau-Ponty, 1945/2012, p. 139)

Merleau-Ponty's notion of the "I can" is the enactment and actualization of meaning through the medium of the body. Thus, it can entail anything from "I can ride a bike" to "I can pick a flower" to "I can climb up this hill." This is why the "I can" lies at the heart of any concept formation because we do not know or learn or discover concepts abstractly, but rather discover them through our bodily engagement with the world and with others. "Language takes on a sense for the child when it *creates a situation* for him" (Merleau-Ponty, 1945/2012, p. 423). For example, we learn the concept of a flower while going for a stroll and smelling it with our family. Within the same context, we might also learn that some plants belong to the category of flower, but that there are also other plants called mushrooms and trees and so forth. Each concept functions like a joint that we put into our perceived world around us in order to distinguish one thing from the other: e.g. we learn to perceive the leaf as different from the branch, the branch as different from the tree, the tree as different from the giraffe eating the leaf, etc. Yet, those concepts are only filled with meaning to the degree as they are tied to our bodily projects: e.g. we can use a leaf for a play boat and let it float on the river or we use a branch to make fire or pick flowers to make a bouquet that fills our living room with the smell of Spring. Only through these bodily enactments of the projects that are tied to those concepts (in the form of *I cans*), they become meaningful and create a grid that we put onto the perceived world around us. Different from Descartes, where the mind is separated from the body, for Merleau-Ponty, it is the body that discloses meaning and vice versa, the way we disclose meaning shapes our being and becoming (i.e. our identity).

Now, for all our language acquisition, from learning to pick the right fruit to eat or a flower to make a bouquet, to learning how to ride a bike or drive a car, we do not learn those concepts in isolation, by ourselves, but rather as part of a pattern of our bodily engagement with other people (our social environment). And we are able to engage with the Other and create meaning, because we share a similar (not identical) body, whose structure of perception is open to the world. This openness comes with the impossibility to gain a complete vision of ourselves (how we appear to the Other). And this is why, for Merleau-Ponty, we experience the world as shared and ourselves as fundamentally intersubjective. This entails that the Other is not a threat to my absolute perspective (i.e. that we own our outlook and interpretation of the world, like in Sartre), but rather that this Other becomes a welcome colleague, who can augment my limited perspective on the world and disclose ever new ways of engaging with the world. And because my identity is so closely related to my "I can," i.e. my bodily engagement with the world, the Other helps me to increase my meaning making and engagement with the world.[13]

Of course, this intersubjective world can be forsaken and, to a certain degree, it necessarily will be left behind, as we grow older or withdraw from the Other. But we need to become aware of our interdependence and our connection with others if we want to live in an intersubjective world rather than in isolation: "In fact, if there is to be one intersubjective world (also for adults), then the child's worldview must be acknowledged as having been correct all along, despite the opinions of adults or Piaget" (Merleau-Ponty, 1945/2012, p. 408).

In the following, we will show how Merleau-Ponty's deliberations change the way we interpret our encounter with the Other. We will see that for him, "the Other as object remains only a devious modality of the Other" (Merleau-Ponty, 1945/2012, p. 511f), i.e. when the gaze that reduces the Other to an object supplants communication (Merleau-Ponty, 1945/2012, p. 414f). By contrast, when we acknowledge our primordial intertwining with the Other, then our gazes embrace each other: Each one complements the Other's perspective. More specifically, I will explicate the yearning for the invisible as a crucial experience of being embodied and argue that the gaze of the Other not only makes us aware of the invisibility of our own body but also of the invisibility of the world. Merleau-Ponty's account of the visible and the invisible can almost be seen as an antipode to Sartre's deliberations about the gaze.

The Yearning for the Invisible: Gaze and Flesh

Already in Merleau-Ponty's earlier work, the body constitutes a third dimension between subject and object. Yet by withdrawing the body from the objective world, it also loses its purity and transparency for itself. And here again, Merleau-Ponty tries to work against Descartes' separation of consciousness and the body by saying:

> It will never be made clear how signification and intentionality could inhabit molecular structures or cellular masses, here Cartesianism is correct. But then again, there is no question of such an absurd undertaking. We must recognize that the body – as a chemical structure of a collations of tissues – is formed through a process of impoverishment beginning from a primordial phenomenon of the body-for-us, of the body of human experience, of the perceived body, which objective thought encompasses but whose completed analysis it has no need to postulating. With regard to consciousness, we must no longer conceive of it as a constituting consciousness and as a pure being-of-itself,

but rather a perceptual consciousness, as the subject of a behavior, as being in the world of existence, for only in this way will another person appear in control of his phenomenal body and receive a sort of 'place'.

(Merleau-Ponty, 1945/2012, p. 367)

This leads Merleau-Ponty to the distinction between the corps *objectif* [objective body] and the *corps propre* [body-for-ourselves]. And as the body withdraws from the objective world, it becomes a third genre that can be located somewhere between being a subject and an object. In his unfinished late work *Visible and the Invisible*, Merleau-Ponty calls this *third genre* flesh (orig.: *la chair*): It expands to become the entire world, is neither matter, mind nor substance, but is instead an element (Merleau-Ponty, 1968, p. 139). Body and world relate to each other like the inside and outside of a glove. The boundary between them can no longer be unambiguously drawn because body is world that has become conscious and begun to communicate with itself from within itself. "We will therefore have to realize that there is an ideality that is not alien to the flesh that gives it its eyes, its depth, its dimensions" (Merleau-Ponty, 1968, p. 152). This reciprocal grasping around ourselves and being grasped means that my body is not merely one object of perception among others, but is also the zero point of my coordinate system, the starting point of all dimensions into the world. "To say that the body is a seer is, curiously enough, not to say anything else than: it is visible" (Merleau-Ponty, 1968, p. 273). Thus, similarly to Sartre, Merleau-Ponty concludes that seeing and being able to see are interconnected, or in other words that seeing requires that there be an invisible side of my own body, like the blind spot in the eye that is necessary if we are to see at all.

> The touching itself, seeing itself of the body is itself to be understood in terms of what we said of the seeing and the visible, the touching and the touchable. [...] [T]o escape oneself, to be ignorant of oneself, the self in question is by divergence (d'écart), is Unverborgenheit of the Verborgen [sic!] as such, which consequently does not cease to be hidden or latent.
>
> (Merleau-Ponty, 1968, p. 249)

Therefore, being visible means living in a common world that has an invisible backside.

Here, Merleau-Ponty expands on his metaphor of optics, but now states that not unlike the way the mutually complementary viewpoints of my own two eyes create the perception of depth, so too a third dimension is added due to the slightly shifted perspective of the other onto the world. Messages repeatedly intersect in the anonymous field of our shared world. Messages received by the other come to me and vice versa: When another person sees something that I cannot see, I can see his response to the sight and thus empathically feel what he has seen. The same can happen to him when he sees me respond. A double chiasm is created by the relationships between the I and the Other (which refers to the invisibility of our own body), as well as by the relationships between I, Other and the shared world (which refers to the invisibility of the world). Through this reciprocal meshing of viewpoints, what I see (although it isn't identical with what the other sees) remains open to the other's gaze. Together with the being of the other, it forms "a sole vertical existence" (Merleau-Ponty, 1968, p. 216) to a mutual world. "Chiasm, instead of the For the Other: that means that there is not only a me-other rivalry, but a co-functioning. We function as one unique body" (Merleau-Ponty, 1968, p. 215). This notion is very different from Sartre's idea. For Sartre, the gaze of the other is a threat, whereas for Merleau-Ponty, the strangeness of the other's gaze reveals the backside of the world for each other and enables us to live in a common world in which we mirror for each other what we cannot see at firsthand.

And so, instead of seeing the Other as a threat, Merleau-Ponty interprets the Other as the complementing side to my own being in the world:

> Here there is a being-shared-by-two, and the other person is no longer for me a simple behavior in my transcendental field, nor for that matter am I a simple behavior in his. We are, for each other, collaborators in perfect reciprocity: our perspectives slip into each other, we coexist through a single world.
>
> (Merleau-Ponty, 1945/2012, p. 370)

My own body (for Others), though, remains invisible for myself. Yet, here too, the Other is not my enemy: Through his loving gaze, he gives back to me what I cannot see. I *feel* myself through the Other's eyes, when he looks at me; he gives me the space to transcend myself into the future.

Body, Gaze and Chiasm: The Ballet of Encounter

Our journey into the phenomenology of embodiment led us through a number of ideas, including the body-for-myself (Sartre, 1943) or the *corps propre* (Merleau-Ponty, 1945/2012), the body-for-Others (Sartre, 1943/1992) or *corps objectif* (Merleau-Ponty, 1945/2012), the body-as-seen-by-the-Other (Sartre, 1943/1992), the Other as the complementary perspective to my own bodily existence (Merleau-Ponty, 1945/2012) as well as the replacement of the Cogito by the *I can* (Merleau-Ponty, 1945/2012). We explored the preconditions of embodiment and encounter and saw that the pre-reflective, dialogical intertwining with the Other is a fragile equilibrium: On the one hand, the invisibility of our own body is a precondition for our openness towards the Other and the world. On the other hand, because this aspect of our body is invisible to ourselves, we are tempted to focus on it. Yet, this automatically destroys our relationship to or connection with the other as well as the ability to actualize ourselves through our body in the world (i.e. the I-can). Vice versa, the Other's objectifying gaze can likewise interrupt our communal engagement with the world or with each Other. Eventually, it can destroy our ability to feel our body for ourselves (i.e. what Sartre called the First Ontological Dimension).

Eating disorders are often related to body image disorders, and various instruments for measurements have been developed (e.g. Stanghellini et al., 2012, Tury, Gulec, & Kohls, 2010). For example, in a recent empirical study on embodiment, identity and eating disorder by Stanghellini et al. (2012), the group developed and validated a new self-reported questionnaire called IDEA (Identity and Eating disorders). They used Sartre's vocabulary on embodiment to develop a questionnaire that explores the *lived corporeality* in connection with personal identity. It is a cross-sectional study and, for sure, a longitudinal study would be needed to see if the results are specific to eating disorder patience or state-related features. However, in their comparison of 147 eating disorder patients with 187 healthy people, they found that those with eating disorders felt in a very specific way about their embodiment: e.g. they felt themselves only through the gaze of the other and were defining themselves only through the evaluation of the other. Furthermore, they were feeling themselves only through objective measures, felt extraneous from their own body or even needed to feel themselves through starvation. In this last section, we will use Sartre's and Merleau-Ponty's ideas in order to understand better what circumstances might influence the development of such unhealthy body images.

Let us begin with a concrete situation: Imagine you get ready to go out for dinner with your partner. You both put on your nicest clothes in anticipation of an inspiring evening. Each of you dresses for the Other. Now, we suddenly feel how our partner looks at us from the side or even from behind. His warm gaze lingers on our neckline. We don't need to see our partner's gaze in order to feel it; rather, like the white cane of a blind person, his gaze is probing our back. Now, as we walk over to the wardrobe, our gait begins to swing in a particular way. We become aware how our body is for the other. Of course, we do not *see* our body for the Other, like we see the lamp over there or our clothes in the wardrobe. Rather, we feel our body through the Other's gaze; we experience it like a latent or a lateral knowledge. And this is only possible because feeling our lived body from within as *urpräsentierbar* (primordial present-ability) also includes the possibility to feel how it appears for other people. My partner's face, his expression and the softness of his eyes show me how he sees me; his gaze becomes my mirror; yet at the same time, my own gaze does not come to an end here; rather, his facial expressions, the love that shines back from his sudden smile makes me see him as this person who I love.

In this situation, and different from Sartre's account, the body is not just an object, not a naked thing; rather, we each are actualized in our subjectivity and Otherness.[14] Merleau-Ponty calls this the *chiasm of encounter*:

> The coupling of the bodies, that is, the adjustment of their intentions to one sole *Erfüllung* [fulfillment], to one sole wall they run into from two sides, is latent in the considerations of one sole sensible world, open to participation by all, which is given to each.
>
> (Merleau-Ponty, 1968, p. 233)

Unfortunately, seeing and being seen does not remain in the private sphere or between lovers only. Instead, it is played over and over again by the throngs of people all over the world, on boulevards, in Cafés, in parks and nowadays also in the virtual space. Interestingly enough, especially the anonymity of the metropolis[15] has made seeing and being seen the primary form of exchange. People derive a certain undeniable pleasure from allowing their invisibility to blossom in the crossfire of gazes – because it is the gaze of Others that make this invisible side laterally accessible for them. "[H]enceforth, through others' eyes we are to ourselves fully visible; that lacuna where our eyes, our back lies, is filled, filled still by the visible, of which we are not the titulars" (Merleau-Ponty, 1968, p. 143).

The shadow side of this exchange is that people mostly remain objects to us. The language of self-staging compensates for this paucity of direct communication. The message is the medium, and the medium is the body for others. Of course, the world of fashion exploits precisely this uncertainty and insecurity; it discovered this undeniable aspect of the human condition as a unique selling point and reminds us of this blind spot in our existence. Therefore, there is a great temptation to try to "overcome" our invisibility by controlling this side as much as possible – e.g. through fashion, jewelry, tattoos, piercing, etc.[16] Another mechanism to control our body-as-it-appears-for-others is through measurements (Stanghellini et al., 2012): e.g. if we have the perfect shape, BMI, the perfect weight, etc., then we again can control our appearance and make sure that we are perfect for the gaze of the Other. Yet, the compulsion to control our invisible side of the body[17] can easily get out of balance. We may even loose our connection to how our body feels for ourselves. This First Ontological Dimension then is being replaced by Sartre's third dimension: i.e. how our body appears through the gaze of the Other or through the evaluation of the Other (Stanghellini et al., 2012). It is important though to understand that this is not the loving gaze of a friend, like in our thought example before, but rather it is the objectifying gaze of the observer. Merleau-Ponty also calls this "the observing gaze of an insect at a distance" (1945/2012, p. 410, translated by B. Weber) that eradicates the possibility for communication. In that case, one's body can feel "extraneous" (Stanghellini et al.,

2012). Starvation or injuring of the body can be interpreted as attempts to regain some kind of connection with our estranged body.

Seeing is seizing – the Other's gaze can kill me in an instance, chain me up in my objectivity, construe an unchanging image that will exist apart from me, without my knowledge even. However, this is not the only modality of encounter. It may also happen that the Other looks with love, with hope or just with an open, inviting gaze that creates the space for me to occur. Then, I'm not reduced to my past, but rather encouraged and invited into the future of coexistence. And weather to do the former or the latter is the responsibility and decision of the Other. Yet, what remains for us to decide is whether or not we allow ourselves to let go of control, to expose our body in its vulnerability, to send it out into the world and to trust the Other's gaze. And like a tree, whose roots reach deep down into the earth, so that it can grow up tall, we too need to indwell our body as it feels to us, so that we can be courageous and reach out into existence.

> Those, you almost envied them, the forsaken, that you
> found as loving as those who were satisfied. Begin,
> always as new, the unattainable praising:
> think: the hero prolongs himself, even his falling
> was only a pretext for being, his latest rebirth.
> But lovers are taken back by exhausted Nature
> into herself, as if there were not the power
> to make them again. Have you remembered
> Gastara Stampa sufficiently yet, that any girl,
> whose lover has gone, might feel from that
> intenser example of love: "Could I only become like her?"
> Should not these ancient sufferings be finally
> fruitful for us? Isn't it time that, loving,
> we freed ourselves from the beloved, and, trembling, endured
> as the arrow endures the bow, so as to be, in its flight,
> something more than itself? For staying is nowhere.
>
> (Rainer Maria Rilke, The First Elegy)

Notes

1 I.e. in the form of the "Body-Mind Problem" reincarnation theories or discussions around idealism, realism and materialism, etc.
2 "A Theory of Human Rights," presented as the keynote speech opening the Society for Continental Philosophy conference in St John's Newfoundland, October 2011. An shorter version was presented at the International Association of Philosophy and Literature in Regina, June 2010.
3 See Martin Heidegger's account on death in 'Sein und Zeit' (1976).
4 Husserl's way of writing has often been described as 'cryptic'.
5 Especially German and French phenomenologists like Max Scheler, Helmut Plessner, Maurice Merleau-Ponty, Jean-Paul Sartre, Michel Henry, Bernhard

Waldenfels or Hermann Schmitz separated the body as lived (German: Leib) from the body as object for others (German: Koerper).

6 The German anthology edited by Alloa, Bedorf, Grueny, and Klass (2012) gives an excellent overview of theories about embodiment within continental philosophy.

7 I am focusing on German and French philosophers, because it seems that those are less known within the English-speaking academic world. However, there are, of course, a number of English-speaking scholars who picked up the notion of embodiment from the phenomenological tradition, e.g. James Mensch (2009), Shaun Gallager (2005), David Abram (1996) to only name a few.

8 The philosophical anthropologist Max Scheler is working on similar topics on embodiment around that time. However, I only focus on Plessner here, because he focuses on embodiment more explicitly.

9 In the meantime, more contemporary philosophers have picked up this topic and developed it further; yet, here I focus on the line of thinkers who directly followed Husserl's and Heidegger's thinking.

10 See Husserl's notion of 'apprehension' (Hua X).

11 The German Merleau-Ponty scholar Bernhard Waldenfels writes: "*Intercorporiaet* [in Merleau-Ponty] means that I discover the Others within myself even before I consciously let the Other in or withdraw from the social world." (Waldenfels, 1999, S. 52; translated by B. Weber.)

12 See here the extensive writings of the child psychologist Juergen Seewald on 'Leib und Symbol [embodiment and symbol]' (1992).

13 For example, it is the Other who shows me that I can use this paper not only to write on, but also to make a fire or to build an airplane (see Mensch, 2009, p. 191); this enriches my 'I can', i.e. the way I can engage with the world. And by enriching my "I can", it also increases my freedom (i.e. possible ways to engage with the world from which I can choose from); it means that the more possibilities I have, the freer I am.

14 Very similarly, the Other can sensitize us to the invisibility or 'back side' of the world.

15 Nowadays, we observe something similar within the 'virtual space' (e.g. Facebook, Instagram, etc.), however, under slightly different conditions; unfortunately, this chapter does not allow to go deeper into this matter.

16 As stated before, this is the cradle of 'selfies': i.e. the place, where we can have perfect control from our outfit, make up, the exact right angle, etc. and frozen into the stillness of the one perfect image.

17 Whence the advice by the Valley Girls from L. A., "It doesn't matter how you feel, as long as you look good."

References

Abram, D. (1996). *The spell of the sensuous*. New York, NY: Random House.

Aloa, E., & Depraz, N. (2012). Edmund Husserl – Ein merkwuerdig unvollkommen konsitutiertes Ding. In E. Alloa, T. Bedorf, C. Grüny, & T. Nikolaus Klass (Eds.), *Leiblichkeit. Geschichte und Aktualitaet eines Konzepts* (pp. 7–22). Tübingen, Germany: Mohr Siebeck.

Andermann, K. (2012). Hermann Schmitz – Leiblichkeit als kommunikatives Selbst- und Weltverhaeltnis. In E. Alloa, T. Bedorf, C. Grüny, & T. Nikolaus Klass (Eds.), *Leiblichkeit. Geschichte und Aktualitaet eines Konzepts* (pp. 130–145). Tübingen, Germany: Mohr Siebeck.

Benkhe, E. (2016). *Edmund Husserl phenomenology of embodiment*. Retrieved from www.iep.utm.edu/husspemb/

Buytendijk, F. J. J. (1948). *Über den Schmerz*. Bern, Switzerland: Verlag Hans Huber Bern.

Damasio, A. (1999). *The feeling of what happens. Body and emotion in the making of Consciousness*. New York, NY: Mariner Publisher.

Descartes. (1641/1996). *Meditations on first philosophy* (J. Cottingham, Trans.). Cambridge, MA: Cambridge University Press.

Fuchs, T. (2000). *Leib, Raum, Person. Entwurf einer phänomenologischen. Anthropologie*. Stuttgart, Germany: Klett-Cotta Verlag.

Gallagher, S. (2005). *How the body shapes the mind*. New York, NY: Oxford University Press.

Gallagher, S. & Depraz, N. (2004). Embodiment and awareness. Perspectives from phenomenology and cognitive science. Special Issue of *Theoria et Historia Scientiarum*, 7.1.

Gallagher, S., Depraz, N., & Hanna, R. (2003). Embodiment and awareness. Perspectives from phenomenology and cognitive science. (Series Ed.) *Theoria et Historia Scientiarum* (Vol. 7, no. 1), Toruń, Poland: Nicolas-Copernicus University Press.

Haneberg, B. (1995). *Leib und Identität. Die Bedeutung der Leiblichkeit für die Bildung der sozialen Identität*. Würzburg, Germany: Ergon Verlag.

Heidegger, M. (1927). *Sein und Zeit*. Tübingen, Germany: Max Niwmeyer Verlag Tübingen.

Henry, M. (2011). *Philosophie et phénoménologie du corps. Essai sur l'ontologie biranienne*. Paris, France: Puf. (Original work published 1965).

Husserl, E. (1950ff). *Husserliana (=Hua) as well as Materialien (=HuM)*, Den Haag (later: Dordrecht): Martinus Nijhoff Publisher.

Husserl, E. (1950ff). *VII: Die Philosophie. Erster Teil: Kritische Ideengeschichte*. In Rudolf Boehm (Ed.), 1956.

Husserl, E. (1950ff). *X: Zur Phänomenologie des inneren Zeitbewusstseins*. In Rudolf Boehm (Ed.), 1969.

Husserl, E. (1950ff). *XVI: Ding und Raum. Vorlesungen 1907*. In Ulrich Claesges (Ed.), 1973.

Husserl, E. (1950ff). *XXIX*: Die Krisis der europäischen Wissenschaften und die transzendentale Phänomenologie. Ergänzungsband. In R. N. Smid (Ed.), *Texte aus dem Nachlass 1934–1937*, 1992.

Lévinas, E. (1961). *Totalité et Infini. Essai sur l'Extériorité*. The Hague, Netherlands: Martinus Nijhoff.

Maier, W. (1964). *Das Problem der Leiblichkeit bei Jean-Paul Sartre und Maurice Merleau-Ponty*. Tübingen, Germany: Max Niemeyer Verlag.

Marcel, G. (1985). *Leibliche Begegnung*. In H. Petzold (Ed.), *Leiblichkeit*, Paderborn.

Mensch, J. (2009). *Embodiments: From the body to the body politic*. Evanston, IL: Northwestern University Press.

Mensch, J. (2011). Empathy and rationality. In B. Weber, E. Marsal, A. T. Dobashi (Eds.), *The politics of empathy. New interdisciplinary perspectives on an ancient phenomenon*. Münster, Germany: Lit Verlag.

Merleau-Ponty, M. (1968). *The visible and the invisible*. Evanston, IL: Northwestern University Press.

Merleau-Ponty, M. (2012). *Phenomenology of perception* (D. A. Landes, Trans.). London, UK: Routledge Publisher. (Original work published in 1945).

Novotny, K. (2012). Leiblichkeit: Geschichte und aktualitaet eines konzepts [Embodiment: History and actuality of a concept]. In E. Alloa, T. Bedorf, C. Grüny, & T. Nikolaus Klass (Eds.), (pp. 81–89). Tübingen, Germany: Mohr Siebeck Publisher.

Patočka, J. (1968). Die Kritik des pschologischen Objektivismus und das Problem der phänomenomenolschen Psychologie bei Sartre und Merleau-Ponty. *Archiv des XIV. Internationalen Kongress für Philosophie, 2,* 656–688.

Patočka, J. (1995). *Papiers phénoménologiques.* (E. Abrams, Trans.). Grenoble, France: Jérôme Millon. (The French is a translation of Patočka's manuscript notes for the 1968–1969 lectures held at Charles University, Prague, published in Czech and translated into English on the basis of an unauthorized compilation of his students' notes.)

Patočka, J., Nellen, K., Němec, J., & Srubar, I. (1991). *Die bewegung der menschlichen existenz: Phänomenologische schriften II [The movement of the human existence: Phenomenological papers II].* Stuttgart, Germany: Klett-Cotta Publisher.

Plessner, H. (1928). *Die Stufen des Organischen und der Mensch. Einleitung in die philosophische Anthropologie.* Berlin, Germany: Leipzig.

Sartre, J.-P. (1992). *Being and nothingness.* (P. Smith, Trans.) (New York, NY: Washington Square Press. (Original work published 1943).

Schmitz, H. (1990). *Die person.* Bonn, Germany: Bouvier.

Seewald, J. (1992). *Leib und Symbol. Ein sinnverstehender Zugang zur kindlichen Entwicklung.* München, Germany: Fink.

Stanghellini, G., Castellini, G., Brogna, P., Faravelli, C., & Ricca, V. (2012). Identity and eating disorders (IDEA): A questionnaire evaluating identity and embodiment in eating disorder patients. *Psychopathology, 45*(3), 147–158. doi:10.1159/000330258

Sternagel, J. (2012). Bernhard Waldenfels – Responsitivitaet des Leibes. In E. Alloa, T. Bedorf, C. Grüny, & T. Nikolaus Klass (Eds.), *Leiblichkeit. Geschichte und Aktualitaet eines Konzepts.* Tuebingen, Germany: Mohr Siebeck.

Thompson, E. (2007). *Mind in life: Biology, phenomenology and the sciences of mind.* Cambridge, MA: Cambridge University Press.

Thompson, E., & Varela, F. (2001). Radical embodiment: Neural dynamics and consciousness. *Trends in Cognitive Sciences, 5* (10), 418–425.

Tury, F., Gulec, H., & Kohls, E. (2010). Assessment methods for eating disorders and body image disorders. *Journal of Psychosomatic Research, 69*(6), 601–611.

Waldenfels, B. (1994). *Antwortregister.* Frankfurt am Main, Germany: Suhrkamp Verlag.

Waldenfels, B. (1999). *Sinnesschwellen. Studien zur Phänomenologie des Fremden.* Frankfurt am Main Germany: Suhrkamp Verlag.

Waldenfels, B. (2000). Die Responsivität des Leibes. In B. Waldenfels (Ed.) *Idiome des Denkens. Deutsch-Französische Gedankengänge II* (pp. 76–89). Frankfurt am Main: Suhrkamp Verlag.

Weber, B. (2013). *Vernunft, Mitgefühl und Körperlichkeit. Eine phänomenologische Rekonstruktion des politischen Raumes.* Freiburg, Germany: München.

5 The Developmental Theory of Embodiment

Implications for Treatment and Prevention of Eating Disorders

Heather L. Jacobson and M. Elizabeth Lewis Hall

Introduction

The Developmental Theory of Embodiment (DTE) is a feminist theory that takes as its starting point the observation that gender is a risk factor in the development of eating disorders (Piran, 2010). This theory proposes that women are exposed to a variety of social experiences which shape individuals' embodiment through three pathways: experiences in the physical domain, experiences in the mental domain including exposure to dominant social labels and expectations, and experiences related to social power (Piran & Teall, 2012). Both protective and risk factors are organized along these three pathways of one's social context: physical freedom (versus physical corseting), mental freedom (versus mental corseting), and social power (versus social disempowerment).

The DTE was developed by Niva Piran of the University of Toronto. Her expertise in eating disorders and their prevention led her to develop the DTE based on a mixed-methodology research program in two main phases (Piran, 2001; Piran & Cormier, 2005; Piran & Thompson, 2008). The first phase involved exploration and validation of a three-way risk factor pathway along the domains of physical, mental, and social power. Over a 15-year period, students in over 300 focus groups from a residential ballet school were surveyed regarding factors in the school environment that negatively impacted their experiences of their bodies. Researchers utilized multiple quantitative measures and structural equation modeling to analyze results. They found that three significant risk factor pathways emerged: (1) physical corseting, or violation of one's sense of body ownership; (2) mental corseting, or internalization of constraining social labels; and (3) social disempowerment through exposure to prejudicial treatment.

The second phase of research in the formation of the DTE addressed limitations from Phase 1 and extended the findings to include the protective factors of physical freedom, mental freedom, and social power, in addition to the risk factors noted earlier. Using both qualitative and quantitative methods, researchers surveyed young women and interviewed them about their lives, results of which validated the key concepts of the DTE. Physical freedom, mental freedom, and social power were found to be significant, protective social factors that help shape one's experience of embodiment.

Two key concepts in the DTE are the definition of embodiment and the definition of the protective or risk factors associated with the development of embodiment. Piran and Teall (2012) describe one's "experience of embodiment" as potentially either positive/connected or disrupted. They define positive or connected embodiment in this way:

> Positive/connected embodiment is a complex construct that includes: feeling "at one" with the body, embodied power and agency, body functionality/ competence, a "subjective" experience of living in the body with limited external consciousness, the freedom to act/take space/move especially in private and public spheres, the freedom to challenge external standards, body-anchored joy/passion/comfort/other positive feelings, body care and protection, clarity of needs/rights/desires/internal states, connection to others regarding needs/desires/rights, the freedom to express individuality through the body, connection with the physical environment, and the openness to use the body as a source of knowledge in interacting with the world.
>
> (p. 185)

In other words, positive embodiment involves a sense of connectedness to and freedom in one's body. Importantly, connected embodiment not only includes subjective feelings of "oneness" with the body but also engaging in behaviors and choices that work to protect, care for, and utilize one's body in myriad ways.

Conversely, disrupted or negative embodiment involves a sense of disconnection from one's body. It may include viewing the body as "a site of disempowerment/vulnerability/constrained space" or "as a site of low functionality/competence" (Piran & Teall, 2012, p. 186). Disrupted embodiment also involves harsh self-evaluation of one's body based on external standards regarding appearance and may include behaviors or practices that are dictated by external standards rather than by one's own bodily needs or desires (Piran & Teall, 2012). Self-harming behaviors and neglect of care for one's body both fit into this category. A person who experiences disrupted embodiment may have difficulty identifying his or her needs, desires, or internal states and may feel disconnected from others due to an inability to express these needs. Likewise, he or she may feel disconnected from the physical world and may not use his or her body as a source of information and freedom in interacting with the world (Piran & Teall, 2012, p. 186).

The three social factors that shape connected or disrupted embodiment in girls and women include the protective and risk factors of physical freedom (versus physical corseting), mental freedom (versus mental corseting), and social power (versus social disempowerment), each of which will be discussed in more detail in the following pages. Piran and Teall (2012) emphasize the fact that each of these factors is mediated through various social contexts such as one's family, peer group, and community. These protective and risk factors are also shaped by social location including gender, race, socioeconomic class, sexual orientation, and age.

Piran (2016) has further identified five dimensions among girls and women that elaborate on a construct of "Experience of embodiment": "connection and comfort with one's body, embodied agency, connection and expression of desires, attunement to self-care, and engagement in meaningful pursuits not focused on an objectified gaze upon one's appearance" (p. 54). These dimensions overlap with the three protective social factors initially identified by Piran and Teall (2012). Assessing and conceptualizing embodiment through these five lenses in addition to exploring girls' or women's experiences of physical freedom, mental freedom, and social power provides a richer understanding of how individuals may shift in their experience of embodiment as they age.

When individuals present with disordered eating behaviors, assessment should include a broad evaluation of their experiences of embodiment in addition to the social factors that influence their embodiment. For example, clients should be asked about bodily self-harm and behaviors relating to self-care. Assessment should include questions focusing on individuals' abilities to be aware of and attuned to their bodies, particularly their bodily appetites, changes, and desires. Additionally, inviting girls and women to engage in a chronological account of their "body journey" with related experiences, thoughts, and feelings may be a valuable opportunity for both clinicians and participants to identify when shifts occurred in a client's experience of embodiment (Piran, 2016). Incorporating exploration of these age-related shifts into the assessment process helps the clinician to gain a more particular picture for the disruptive or facilitative social factors that have contributed to an individual's embodied experience.

Several aspects of social factors that have been studied in relation to embodiment include gender, sexuality, eating, dementia, religion, and alcohol use (Jacobson, Hall, Anderson, & Willingham, 2016; Kontos & Martin, 2013; Kristensen, Askegaard, & Jeppesen, 2013; Lyons, Emslie, & Hunt, 2014; Yamamiya, Cash, & Thompson, 2006). Each of these studies has extended Piran and Teall's (2012) theory by highlighting the ways in which social contexts influence how people experience their bodies. For example, body dissatisfaction has been linked to more negative sexual experiences for college-aged women (Yamamiya, Cash, & Thompson, 2006). Religious beliefs about the body have been shown to influence whether or not people feel more or less connected to their bodies and bodily sensations (Jacobson, Hall, Anderson, & Willingham, 2016). Kristensen, Askegaard, and Jeppesen (2013) found that people increasingly turn to their own experiences and bodily sensations for information regarding health risks or benefits of eating behaviors, rather than the internet or other information sources. Similarly, for middle-aged men and women, one's own embodied experience has been found to be more important in regulating alcohol use than health promotion advice (Lyons, Emslie, & Hunt, 2014). Though focused on differing social aspects, each of these studies emphasizes the relationship between one's social context and one's experience of embodiment. As noted earlier, social contexts mediate the protective factors of physical power, mental freedom, and social power, each of which we now consider in more detail. Given the research support for each of these factors in women's experiences of embodiment, each of these social aspects might be a focus of inquiry in facilitating the telling of the "body journey."

Physical Freedom

One of the three protective social factors discussed by Piran and Teall (2012) is that of physical freedom or power, the opposite of which is physical corseting, or having one's body ownership violated. Physical freedom includes

> experiences that enhance a girl's and a woman's sense of her body as a physical site of: (1) safety, care, and respectful ownership; (2) freedom of, and competence in, movement; and (3) comfort with physical desires, appetites, and age-related changes.
>
> (p. 187)

One example of physical freedom is young women being fully immersed in a physical game or activities. Likewise, physical freedom involves feeling free to wear comfortable, non-sexualizing, or non-objectifying clothes. Physical power can also include girls being fully included in family chores without gender stereotypes or limitations placed on them for being female. It involves girls/women feeling safe to explore the natural world, whether through taking walks or jogging, or camping, hiking, and other outdoor activities. Additionally, physical freedom includes paying attention to and being comfortable with one's bodily desires, appetites, and changes: for example, development of sexual interest and desire through puberty, experiences of pregnancy and childbearing, and menopause and other age-related changes.

In the development of the DTE, Piran and Teall (2012) assessed individuals' experiences of the opposite of physical freedom, physical corseting, through measures of childhood sexual or physical abuse, adult sexual coercion, and adult exposure to unwanted sexual attention. They define physical corseting as situations in which a girl or woman experiences her body "as a physical site: (1) which is unsafe, neglected, and/or a target of violations to body ownership; (2) with limited freedom of movement and low functionality; and (3) which restricts physical desires, appetites, and disrupts comfort with age-related changes" (Piran & Teall, 2012, p. 187). Examples of physical corseting include any experiences in which a girl or woman feels that her body ownership has been violated, ranging from more extreme instances such as sexual harassment or abuse, to any unwanted sexual experiences. Sexual abuse, as one extreme example of physical corseting, has been linked to dissociation, somatization, and eating disorders (Young, 1992), all disorders that involve a disconnected experience of embodiment.

Physical corseting also includes advertising and marketing of sexualized, exposing clothing to girls that may restrict their ability to move freely or feel comfortable in their bodies. Research has found that young women experience decreased opportunities for being involved in physical activities as they move toward early adolescence, a more subtle example of physical corseting (Piran, 2015; Piran & Teall, 2012; Robbins et al., 2016). Piran and Teall (2012) also found that girls in their study reported a decreased sense of physical body safety as they aged, indicating a subjective lack of physical freedom or power.

Critical to growing up in an environment supportive of physical power is a context of equality, respect, and support. Girls need to know that they have a right to bodily safety and that their ownership of their bodies is important. Additionally, they need models of self-care to look to as they age and change, not only their parents but also teachers, mentors, and other respected adults. This means it is essential that on an institutional and even national level, policies are in place to protect against body-based harassment or abuse for both young girls and women of all ages (Piran & Teall, 2012).

In preventing and treating eating disorders, Piran (2015) suggests that there are four protective areas within the domain of physical freedom that programs aimed at the prevention and treatment of eating disorders could incorporate to promote positive body image. These four areas are (a) pleasurable engagement in physical activities and the associated freedom from forced compliance with harsh appearance standards, (b) safety, (c) attuned self-care, and (d) pleasurable connection to desires. Specific examples of encouraging physical freedom for girls include opportunities to engage fully and joyfully in non-objectifying physical activities such as sports, yoga, playing outside, physical expression through dance, and gardening. Girls may also be encouraged to connect positively with nature through hiking or wilderness trips. Piran, Carter, Thompson, and Pajouhandeh (2002) suggest that adults who are significant in the lives of children, in addition to their educational institutions, should encourage and model engagement in these activities. Safety in one's physical environment, without fear of violation, is also an important component of being able to engage fully and joyfully in physical activities.

Multiple opportunities for such active, physical engagement for girls and women exist; for example, one such organization seeks to foster positive self-esteem through building a sense of physical security and safety in activities, fostering connection and community among participants, and providing fun and varied opportunities to engage in activities such as rock climbing classes, canoeing trips, leadership development, and adventure camps (www.womenswilderness.org).

Yoga has also been shown to both reduce risk factors and increase protective factors for eating disorders (Neumark-Sztainer, 2014), and people who practice yoga report higher body satisfaction and positive embodiment than those who do not participate in regular yoga (Mahlo & Tiggemann, 2016). Eating disorder treatment might include assignment of engagement in such activities, with a focus on connecting with one's body and processing feelings and experiences that result from being active. Reflection on being engaged in activities could be encouraged through journaling or group discussion (Piran, 2015).

Additionally, treatment of eating disorders should include an emphasis on cultivating an awareness of and attentiveness to one's bodily sensations, appetites, and desires – the area of attuned self-care identified by Piran (2015). As girls age and their bodies change during puberty, they need encouragement and guidance from adults in feeling comfortable with their physical desires and appetites (Piran & Teall, 2012). It is important that adults model respect for their own bodies and self-care in response to what their bodies may be telling them. For example, adults can model recognizing when they are hungry and responding by eating appropriately, or accepting that they feel tired and resting when needed. Significant adults in a girl's life, particularly their mothers, can provide guidance regarding important body-related transitions such as menarche, purchasing a bra, or engaging in body alteration practices such as wearing makeup and shaving one's legs (Piran, 2015). Piran and Teall (2012) also suggest that girls should be encouraged to wear comfortable, non-objectifying, or sexualizing clothing and uniforms as a way of encouraging their sense of physical freedom and body ownership. Parents, particularly mothers, can encourage and model to their daughters the freedom to wear comfortable clothing appropriate to the activity.

A popular blog and website, www.pigtailpals.com, offers resources for adults on how to foster positive body image in their children, as well as providing resources for children themselves. The website suggests that parents engage with their children in activities and comment on their own bodies as a way of healthy role-modeling, for example, stating things like, "My strong legs carried me all the way up that hill!" or "I love my arms because they can throw a Frisbee!" Hearing positive body talk from influential adults about their own bodies provides a healthy example for young people, especially girls navigating the challenge of changing bodies during puberty.

Girls also need opportunities for open, nonjudgmental conversation regarding sexual desire and self-care in the expression of that desire.

It is important that girls feel they have a sense of ownership over their bodies and that a healthy, positive body image is encouraged, as research has demonstrated links between body image and sexual experiences (Yamamiya, Cash, & Thompson, 2006). Yamamiya, Cash, and Thompson (2006) found that young women who were more physically self-conscious reported higher ambivalence about whether or not to engage in sexual activity and felt less emotionally engaged during sex than women with less physical self-consciousness. The researchers suggested that helping women to increase their body image may thus improve sexual functioning, a finding that supports the idea that young women need positive and open role models regarding their sexual desires and experiences.

Physical freedom as a protective factor is essential to the development of healthy embodiment. If a young girl experiences a loss of physical freedom, or physical corseting, her embodiment becomes disrupted, cut off from the most fundamental experience of being a self in a body. If a girl is allowed to experience physical freedom in a variety of areas, she may be more likely to feel connected to and aware of her body. Physical freedom alone is not sufficient, however; a sense of mental freedom and power is also important in developing healthy embodiment.

Mental Freedom

The second protective factor in the development of embodiment is that of mental freedom, or "the freedom to explore and determine one's own sense of identity" (Piran & Teall, 2012, p. 188). Mental freedom involves three protective sub-factors:

> (a) freedom of voice, assertive action, and passionate engagement in activities that are unrelated to appearance; (b) freedom from and a critical stance toward stereotypes of gendered appearance standards; as well as (c) freedom from and a critical stance toward constraining stereotypes of gendered behavior.
>
> (Piran, 2015, p. 152)

Mental freedom, then, involves a critical attitude and approach toward stereotyped social molds, with a sense of freedom to reject socially labeled groups such as "tomboy"/"girlie girl," "butch"/"girlie," "slut"/ "prude," and "nice"/"bitch" and instead decide one's own identity without relying on categories or stereotypes. It also involves rejection of pressure to view one's body as an object, especially an object of sexual gratification. Previous research has demonstrated that girls who grow up in an environment where they are protected from the experience of being an object to be gazed at, as well as given the freedom to assert their voice and act in the world, have more positive body image than those who do not (Piran, 2015).

The opposite of mental freedom is internalization of constraining social labels and a sense of powerlessness to reject social molds or labels.
In developing the DTE, Piran and Teall (2012) utilized measures that
assessed self-silencing of needs and voice, the suppression of the outward expression of anger, and the internalization of an objectified gaze
toward one's own body. Fredrickson and Roberts (1997), in their seminal work on Objectification Theory, posited that women experience
objectifying gazes through social and interpersonal encounters and visual
media which often sexualizes the female body. As women internalize
this objectification, they increasingly view their own bodies as objects as
well. This self-objectification results in detrimental effects on women's
health and well-being including increased shame, anxiety, and decreased
awareness of internal body states. Fredrickson and Roberts suggested that
women are most targeted for objectification during their years of potential childbearing age as their bodies change and develop. Young women
begin to learn that not only does their new, developing body belong to
them, it is also now "public domain" in the sense that it may be looked
at, evaluated, and commented upon by others (Fredrickson & Roberts,
1997, p. 193). In the process of this change, a young girl comes to realize
that she may be seen and evaluated by others as solely a body, rather than
all of herself including her body, mind, and whole being. Other research
has indicated that internalization of specific discourses about femininity,
one form of self-objectification, is related to disordered eating patterns
(Morrison & Sheahan, 2009; Piran & Cormier, 2005). Specifically, Morrison and Sheahan (2009) found relationships between disordered eating
and gender-related discourses of self-objectification, self-silencing, and
anger suppression.

Consistent with these findings about internalized objectification, Piran
and Teall (2012) found that the young women they surveyed reported
intense pressure to fit into "molds of femininity" (e.g., categories like
"tomboy"/"girlie girl" and "slut"/"prude"), which increased post-puberty
(p. 192). Molds of femininity artificially dictate and label what girls are
or are not, what they like or do not like, and what they participate in or
choose to hold back from. For example, one young woman in their study
described some of her friends as "total girlie girls--they don't play sports at
all" (Piran & Teall, 2012, p. 189).

There are multiple ways of helping young women challenge the pressure to conform to societal labeling and instead to embrace the mental
freedom of defining their own identity (Piran, 2015; Piran & Teall,
2012). It is important that girls have opportunities in their families, in
school, with trusted adults/mentors, and with friends, to become aware
of and critical toward social scripts and labels (Piran, 2015; Piran et al.,
2002, 2007). Attention should be drawn to how these social labels or
molds disrupt their embodied experience and interfere with their developing sense of self. Other research suggests that developing critical

awareness is most effective when interventions are aimed at creating alternative and liberating peer norms (Becker, Ciao, & Smith, 2008; Piran, 2001). Piran and Teall (2012) also suggest that schools cultivate environments that enhance students' critical perspectives on cultural norms and prejudices and normalize the process of challenging social scripts and labels.

The internet, particularly social media websites, is one way in which adolescents build social connections and shape their future behaviors (Wu, Outley, Matarrita-Cascante, & Murphrey, 2015). Wu, Outley, Matarrita-Cascante, and Murphrey (2015) suggest that when used with a particular purpose and design, internet technology is a positive opportunity for adolescents to develop their self-identification and social skills. Online resources may provide another avenue for reaching young women in an attempt to encourage their rejection of social molds and encourage their sense of mental freedom. Amy Poehler, a well-known comedian and activist for women's rights, has created the website https://amyssmartgirls.com, a website dedicated to "helping young people cultivate their authentic selves." Her website features strong, successful women in all areas of life including female musicians, a blind Olympic swimmer, female politicians, and a female marine scientist. It also includes a "take action" section that focuses on current events and provides ways for girls to get involved. Another popular website, www.amightygirl.com, features clothing categories for girls such as "animals/nature," "feminist/girl power," "literary themed," "science/technology," "sports/hobbies," and "princess alternatives." Both of these websites have Facebook pages, and their creators are active on social media, engaging with the young women they hope to reach in positive ways. These are just two examples of ways in which technology can be used positively for young women to encourage critical evaluation and start conversations about confining, artificial social categories for women.

In addition to feeling a sense of physical freedom and safety, mental freedom is also important in the development of healthy embodiment. As young girls feel free to reject social, artificially constructed molds or labels, they are empowered to define their own identity in a more congruent and genuine way. Though social pressure and objectification are real and intense, girls may be encouraged to turn away from falsely dichotomous categories and instead embrace all parts of themselves authentically.

Social Power

The third protective factor in the development of healthy embodiment is that of social power, which relates to experiences in girls' lives that reflect equity, social power, and a connection to their desired communities (Piran & Teall, 2012). It also involves either freedom from being cast in the role of a marginalized "other" or having the opportunity to stand up to inequitable treatment. Sub-factors identified in the protective factor of social power include

> (a) freedom from exposure to prejudicial treatment and discrimination related to the individual's social location (gender, race/ethnicity/ religion, weight, social class, sexual orientation, health); (b) a social environment that provides experiences of social power and equity that are unrelated to one's appearance characteristics; (c) empowering relational connections that provide acceptance, validation, and role-modeling; as well as (d) a positive connection to one's embodied social location.
>
> (Piran, 2015, p. 153)

Additional protective factors involve having a relational forum for critical discussions about social prejudices and for developing effective resistance strategies to these prejudices, as well as a sense of connection to a desired community.

Piran and Teall (2012) state, "Embodying privilege is associated with positive embodiment, which includes all of the aspects of social location in terms of gender, social class, ethno-cultural group membership, and other factors" (pp. 190–191). For example, looking a certain way or having access to privileges such as shopping at particular stores factors into a girl feeling "popular" and therefore significantly influences a girl's sense of social power. Piran and Teall found that a stratification of social power exists based on a girl's social location; for example, blonde, blue-eyed white girls from a higher socioeconomic status (SES) embodying privilege were considered the most "popular" in their interviews.

The opposite of social power is social disempowerment, which may come through exposure to prejudicial treatment or internalization of objectification resulting in a perceived need to maintain one's social standing through one's appearance. In Piran and Teall's (2012) study, girls from a more privileged social background feared losing social power if their appearance changed, whereas girls from more underprivileged communities considered altering their appearance in an attempt to acquire social status and power. In both cases, social disempowerment was experienced through how a girl perceived her looks in relation to others. Piran and Teall assessed social disempowerment using measures of gender harassment and weight harassment and found that consistent with previous research, both gender harassment and weight harassment were significantly related to disordered eating patterns (Piran & Thompson, 2008). Additionally, social disempowerment through problems such as isolation, peer pressure, and social exclusion has been shown to be a contributing factor in disordered eating behavior (Patel, Tchanturia, & Harrison, 2016; Salafia, Jones, Haugen, & Schaefer, 2015). Social sensitivity, particularly mistrust of others or fear of being perceived negatively by others, has also been linked to eating disorders (Patel, Tchanturia, & Harrison, 2016). These results suggest that increasing a young woman's sense of social power, particularly through increasing her sense of social connectedness and equity, may be one factor in mitigating the development of disordered eating behaviors.

In discussing how to facilitate social power for girls/women, Piran and Teall (2012) especially emphasize the role of educational environments. They urge that school environments be closely monitored, not only on a policy level, such as standard procedure in cases of harassment, but also on the level of school norms (e.g., who typically gets teased, who gets voted to be school representatives). Schools could implement a zero-tolerance policy for weight-based harassment or any other discrimination based on gender, race, and other diversity factors. Piran and Teall also suggest that the school should ideally be a community that counters, rather than fosters, dominant social structures regarding gender, ethnicity, health, and SES. For example, school curriculum could include an emphasis on the contributions of women and other diverse groups (Piran, 2015). Schools could work to make sure resources are allocated equally to both genders (e.g., girls' sports). On a broader level, development of critical awareness is needed to identify and challenge social norms and processes in which girls' bodies are used as a way to express social privilege or disempowerment (Piran, 2001, 2002; Piran et al., 2007). This requires parents, teachers, and administrators to share a vision for empowering young women and creating safe spaces for open discussions surrounding these issues.

One example of this is an after-school eating disorder prevention program, REbeL, recently piloted in several high schools (Breithaupt, Eickman, Byrne, & Fischer, 2016). Goals of the REbeL program include empowering students to criticize the "thin ideal" and societal pressure to look a certain way, while also encouraging active involvement as student leaders and agents of change in their schools. Social engagement and connection is fostered by focusing on individual's strengths as well as how those strengths interact with those of their peers. With an emphasis on empowerment, students are given opportunities for involvement in community outreach, mentoring others at elementary schools, and creating social media posts. Students are also encouraged to advocate for themselves and others at a state and national level by challenging societal norms regarding weight and appearance in advertising. Programs such as REbeL provide an example for how schools can work to help facilitate social power in students, particularly young women, as they increasingly connect to their communities and are empowered to stand up to inequitable treatment.

Summary

The DTE (Piran & Teall, 2012) provides a helpful theoretical framework from which to evaluate the development and treatment of eating disorders. Approaches to the treatment of eating disorders are sometimes hampered by an exclusive focus on ameliorating the destructive and potentially lethal symptoms of these disorders. While crucial, the amelioration of symptoms must be supplemented by the development of a healthy relationship with the body. This can be challenging in the absence of a solid theory of healthy embodiment. This deficit is addressed by the DTE. In addition to defining positive (connected) and negative (disrupted) embodiment, its three key concepts of physical freedom, mental freedom, and social power illustrate how social factors influence experiences of embodiment in multiple ways. These concepts expand the clinician's arsenal by suggesting important areas for intervention that have not previously been emphasized.

Approaches to the treatment of eating disorders have also been limited by a focus on what Rose (1985) has called "causes of cases." This kind of causation involves the examination of factors which explain the eating disorder in a specific individual at a specific time, such as weight concerns, internalization of thinness, or perfectionism. However, this approach neglects what Rose has called "causes of incidence," which are the kinds of causes that put specific populations at risk. The two are complementary, akin to examining carefully the trees in a forest, but also broadening one's scope enough to identify the forests in the landscape. The DTE is also unique in providing this kind of broad scope which identifies social and gender-based causes of incidence (Piran, 2010). This also allows for a multilevel understanding of causality and a correspondingly broader base from which to develop interventions. By following this framework and breaking down the factors that influence embodiment into these three categories, clinicians may be better equipped to identify and target the socially mediated challenges that affect their clients presenting with disordered eating behaviors.

References

Becker, C. B., Ciao, A. C., & Smith, L. M. (2008). Moving from efficacy to effectiveness in eating disorders prevention: The sorority body image program. *Cognitive and Behavioral Practice, 15*, 18–27.

Breithaupt, L., Eickman, L., Byrne, C. E., & Fischer, S. (2016). REbeL peer education: A model of a voluntary, after-school program for eating disorder prevention. *Eating Behaviors*. Advance online publication. doi:10.1016/j.eatbeh.2016.10.010

Fredrickson, B. L., & Roberts, T. (1997). Objectification theory: Towards understanding women's lived experiences and mental health risks. *Psychology of Women Quarterly, 21*, 173–206. doi:10.1111/j.1471–6402.1997.tb00108.x

Jacobson, H. L., Hall, M. E. L., Anderson, T. L., & Willingham, M. M. (2016). Religious beliefs and experiences of the body: An extension of the developmental theory of embodiment. *Mental Health, Religion, & Culture, 19*(1), 52–67. doi: 10.1080/13674676.2015.1115473

Kontos, P., & Martin, W. (2013). Embodiment and dementia: Exploring critical narratives of selfhood, surveillance, and dementia care. *Dementia: The International Journal of Social Research and Practice, 12*(3), 288–302. doi:10.1177/1471301213479787

Kristensen, D., Askegaard, S., & Jeppesen, L. (2013). "If it makes you feel good it must be right": Embodiment strategies for healthy eating and risk management. *Journal of Consumer Behaviour, 12*(4), 243–252. doi:10.1002/cb.1427

Lyons, A. C., Emslie, C., & Hunt, K. (2014). Staying "in the zone" but not passing the "point of no return": Embodiment, gender and drinking in mid-life. *Sociology of Health & Illness, 36*(2), 264–277. doi:10). 1111/1467–9566.12103

Mahlo, L., & Tiggemann, M. (2016). Yoga and positive body image: A test of the embodiment model. *Body Image, 18*, 135–142. doi:10.1016/j.bodyim.2016.06.008

Morrison, T. G., & Sheahan, E. E. (2009). Gender-related discourses as mediators in the association between internalization of the thin-body ideal and indicants of body dissatisfaction and disordered eating. *Psychology of Women Quarterly, 33*, 374–383. doi:10.1111/j.1471–6402.2009.01515.x

Neumark-Sztainer, D. (2014). Yoga and eating disorders: Is there a place for yoga in the treatment and prevention of eating disorders and disordered eating behaviors? *Advanced Eating Disorders, 2*(2), 136–145. doi:10.1080/21662630.2013.862369

Patel, K., Tchanturia, K., & Harrison, A. (2016). An exploration of social functioning in young people with eating disorders: A qualitative study. *PLos One, 11*(7). doi:10/1371/journal.pone.0159910

Piran, N. (2001). Re-inhabiting the body from the inside out: Girls transform their school environment. In D. L. Tolman & M. Brydon-Miller (Eds.), *From subjects to subjectivities: A handbook of interpretive and participatory methods* (pp. 218–238). New York, NY: New York University Press.

Piran, N. (2002). Prevention of eating disorders. In C. G. Fairburn & K. D. Brownell (Eds.), *Eating disorders and obesity: A comprehensive handbook* (pp. 367–376) New York, NY: Guilford Press.

Piran, N. (2010). A feminist perspective on risk factor research and on the prevention of eating disorders. *Eating Disorders, 18*, 183–198. doi: 10.1080/10640261003719435

Piran, N. (2015). New possibilities in the prevention of eating disorders: The introduction of positive body image measures. *Body Image, 14*, 146–157. doi:10.1016/j.bodyim.2015.03.008

Piran, N. (2016). Embodied possibilities and disruptions: The emergence of the experience of embodiment construct from qualitative studies with girls and women. *Body Image, 18*, 43–60. doi:10.1016/j.bodyim.2016.04.007

Piran, N., Buttu, D., Damianakis, M., Legge, R., Nagasawa, S., & Mizevich, J. (2007). Understanding intensified disruptions in girls' self and body experiences during adolescence (Annual Convention, Canadian Psychological Association, Ottawa, ON, June).

Piran, N., Carter, W., Thompson, S., & Pajouhandeh, P. (2002). Powerful girls: A contradiction in terms? Young women speak about the experience of growing up in a girl's body. In S. Abbey (Ed.), *Ways of knowing in and through the body: Diverse perspectives on embodiment* (pp. 206–210). Welland, ON: Soleil Publishing.

Piran, N., & Cormier, H. (2005). The social construction of women and disordered eating patterns. *Journal of Counseling Psychology, 52*(4), 549–558.

Piran, N., & Teall, T. (2012). The developmental theory of embodiment. In G. L. McVey, M. P. Levine, N. Piran, & H. B. Ferguson (Eds.), *Preventing eating-related and weight-related disorders: Collaborative research, advocacy, and policy change* (pp. 171–199). Waterloo, ON: Wilfrid Laurier University Press.

Piran, N., & Thompson, S. (2008). A study of the adverse social experiences model to the development of eating disorders. *International Journal of Health Promotion and Education, 46*(2), 65–71.

Robbins, L. B., Ling, J., Toruner, E. K., Bourne, K. A., & Pfeiffer, K. A. (2016). Examining reach, dose, and fidelity of the "Girls on the Move" after-school physical activity club: A process evaluation. *BMC Public Health, 16*, 1–16. doi:10.1186/s12889-016-3329-x

Rose, G. (1985). Sick individuals and sick populations. *International Journal of Epidemiology, 14*, 32–38.

Salafia, E. H. B., Jones, M. E., Haugen, E. C., & Schaefer, M. K. (2015). Perceptions of the causes of eating disorders: A comparison of individuals with and without eating disorders. *Journal of Eating Disorders, 3*(1). doi: 10.1186/s40337-015-0069-8

Wu, Y.-J., Outley, C., Matarrita-Cascante, D., & Murphrey, T. P. (2015). A systematic review of recent research on adolescent social connectedness and mental health with internet technology use. *Adolescent Research Review, 1*(2), 153–162. doi:10.1007/s40894-015-0013-9

Yamamiya, Y., Cash, T. F., & Thompson, J. (2006). Sexual experiences among college women: The differential effects of general versus contextual body images on sexuality. *Sex Roles, 55*(5–6), 421–427. doi:10.1007/s11199-006-9096-x

Young, L. (1992). Sexual abuse and the problem of embodiment. *Child Abuse and Neglect, 16*(1), 89–100. doi: 10.1016/0145–2134(92)90010-O

6   Conceptualizing and Measuring Embodiment

Lessons from a Response Processes Inquiry with Women Recovering from Anorexia Nervosa

Mihaela Launeanu, Chelsea Beyer, and Christina Bally

This chapter proposes an innovative perspective to understanding and measuring embodiment based on examining how women recovering from anorexia nervosa (AN) respond to questions and scenarios assessing body connection and emotional awareness, two essential facets of embodied lived experience. To begin, this chapter opens by briefly reviewing the contemporary frameworks of conceptualizing embodiment and the current practices in the assessment and measurement of embodied experience in individuals living with eating disorders. Then, a holistic, phenomenologically grounded theoretical-methodological framework for conceptualizing and measuring embodiment is proposed. This framework is illustrated by the presentation of key findings of an empirical investigation on response processes underlying answering questions and scenarios assessing body connection and affective experience. The results of this response processes inquiry suggest that women articulate their experience of embodiment via several interlocking processes: (a) interoceptively, by tuning into their body sensations; (b) affectively, by attending to the bodily experienced emotional cues; (c) kinesthetically, by moving and engaging expressively with their body; (d) cognitively, by constructing/imagining scenarios or accessing episodic and declarative memories; and (e) relationally, by attuning to and empathizing with others' emotional states through their body. These processes are mapped onto women's recovery journey in order to establish potential benchmarks for monitoring the recovery process in a manner that honours women's lived experience of their bodies. A discussion of the theoretical and clinical implications of the proposed framework for understanding and measuring embodiment will conclude this chapter.

This chapter contributes to conceptualizing and measuring embodiment by (a) complementing the quantitative data on embodiment measurement with subjective, personally rich accounts of how embodiment is experienced and articulated by women recovering from AN; (b) proposing a response processes model of self-reporting on embodied lived experience; (c) laying the foundation for developing person-centred measures of embodied affective experience; and (d) promoting a more holistic conceptualization of embodied experience that includes sensorial, affective, kinesthetic, and relational aspects in addition to the cognitive and body image-related ones.

Embodiment: Frameworks of Understanding

Existential Foundations

The concept of embodiment has deep roots in the continental philosophy (Heidegger, 1962; Merleau-Ponty, 1945/2012) and has recently become an intensely discussed topic in social sciences. Reviewing the philosophical underpinnings of this construct or the current intellectual debates surrounding embodiment is beyond the scope of this chapter, but it is explored further by Barbara Weber in Chapter 4. Therefore, for the purpose of this chapter, we adopt a broader definition of embodiment as engagement of the body with the world, wherein the mind and body are inextricably linked and reciprocally influence one another (Allan, 2005; Piran & Teall, 2012).

Experientially, embodiment is lived through the subjective body-based experience, and this embodied experience encompasses components of lived human experience that involve the body, such as the sensorial, kinesthetic, emotional, and relational experiences. Moreover, being embodied means being a self in a body in the world (Heidegger, 1962) or a body-self (Beyer, 2016), to interact with one's surroundings and with others through sensory and kinesthetic processes, and to experience affective responses during this interaction. Lived embodied experience is a coherent, integrated, body-based experience of one's self, and it is imbued with affective nuances and atmospheres.

Contemporary Perspectives

Partially shaped by this philosophical heritage, contemporary conceptualizations of embodiment are often a place of tension between the neurocognitive focus of the embodied cognition paradigm (Winkielman et al., 2015) and the more integrative, neurophenomenological models proposed by Varela (1996) and Maturana (2002). More recently, Piran and Teall (2012) addressed the developmental and sociological dimensions of embodiment, and Sáenz-Herrero and Díez-Alegría (2015) explored the cultural and gender influences that shape the understanding of embodiment.

Embodied Cognition

The proponents of the embodied cognition approach recognize the crucial role that the body plays in knowing about the world and propose that information processing is directly shaped by the body (Winkielman et al., 2015). According to this view, the body's interactions with its surrounding world, as well as the recollection of previous experiences or information, whether sensory or affective, are at least partially reproduced, re-enacted, or re-experienced through the body (Barsalou, 1999; Clark, 1999; Wilson, 2002). Such re-enactment is referred to as "embodied simulation" and is seen as crucial to reasoning, using emotional concepts, and interpreting language (Winkielman et al., 2015).

This neurocognitive view of embodiment has made considerable strides in examining the brain and body states implicated in embodied experience. In particular, the studies on embodied affective simulation mediated by abstract mental states may inform the understanding of some deficits in emotional awareness and processing encountered in people suffering from eating disorders. Notwithstanding these contributions, the embodied cognition framework has been largely fueled by the enormous progress in neuroimaging and experimental cognitive psychology and, thus, tends to minimize the subjective aspects of the embodied experience.

The Neurophenomenology of Embodiment

An attempt to offer a more integrated framework to understand embodiment was proposed by Varela (1996) who coined the term "neurophenomenology" to encourage the synergy between neuroscience and the phenomenology of consciousness as a way of understanding embodied experience. Varela argued that consciousness extends beyond introspection of internal physiological awareness and perception, and incorporates reflexive capacities enabling a fluid dialogue between objective and subjective realities. Matters of embodied lived experience are, thus, situated at the intersection of fleshy physiology and subjective phenomena transcending biological processes.

Varela's (1996) attempt to bridge the findings from neuroscience and phenomenology represents a remarkable contribution with important implications for conceptualizing embodiment in eating disorders not only as a cognitive, brain-related experience but also as a profound experience of the entire body. In spite of its promise, Varela's invitation to integrate these domains awaits more empirical studies and theoretical elaboration.

Sociocultural Frameworks

Moving beyond an exclusively individualistic focus in understanding embodiment, Piran and Teall (2012) elaborated the Developmental Theory of Embodiment (DTE) that emphasizes the role of developmental transitions and sociocultural factors in shaping the embodied experience. This framework serves as a bridge between sociology and psychology, between the body, as approached by the critical social theory, and embodied experience of individual development (Piran & Teall, 2012). Such a perspective on embodiment recognizes and reflects the complex, interactive relationship between the embodied self and culture in which the self is situated. This approach has significant implications for understanding the developmental and sociocultural influences that shape the embodied lived experience in persons with eating disorders.

Summary and Challenges

There seems to be an ongoing tension within contemporary theoretical perspectives on embodiment between the objective focus of the neuro-cognitive science and the subjective focus of exploring phenomenologically the lived experience of embodiment. An attempt to bridge the two frameworks was made by Varela's (1996) neurophenomenology model, but the need to integrate neuroscientific findings with subjective experiences persists. More recently, the sociocultural dimensions of embodiment were more carefully examined (Piran and Teall, 2012; Sáenz-Herrero & Díez-Alegría, 2015). Notwithstanding these important developments, there is no integrated model of conceptualizing embodiment, and the phenomenological aspects of the embodied lived experience tend to be somewhat underrepresented at the expense of investigating the neurological correlates of embodiment.

Measuring Embodiment

A solid measurement model requires well-elaborated theoretical frameworks in order to accurately capture the core dimensions or the experience of a characteristic or phenomenon. Hence, it comes as little surprise that the relatively underdeveloped conceptualization of embodiment has a significant impact on the current measurement models in the area of embodiment and assessment practices in this field.

Disembodied and Objectifying Practices

In spite of the growing research evidence indicating that the lived experience of one's body is intimately related to the onset of, maintenance of, and recovery from AN (Beyer, 2016; Beyer & Launeanu, in press; Jenkins & Ogden, 2012; Piran & Teall, 2012; Stanghellini, Castellini, Brogna, Faravelli, & Ricca, 2012), the measurement models in the field of eating disorders are largely disembodied and dominated by traditional quantitative tests geared towards inventorying cognitions and behaviours surrounding food and eating. For instance, the "golden standard" in eating disorders assessment, the Eating Disorders Questionnaire (EDQ-E;

Fairburn & Beglin, 1994), consists almost exclusively of behavioural items focused on eating behaviours.

These measurement models and assessment practices can easily collude with the socioculturally driven body objectification and preoccupation with external symptomatic behaviours and, thus, may become oppressive. The exclusive focus on evaluating the external characteristics of the body such as shape and weight, and on counting the frequency of eating behaviours promotes the body-mind disconnect right at the heart of assessment and perpetuates the split that has generated the problem in the first place. During most of these assessments, participants move from seeing themselves as a number on a scale or on the measuring tape to becoming a number on a test while their holistic experience of themselves and their lived body is dismissed.

Moreover, the few tests which purposefully intend to assess various facets of embodiment (e.g., body awareness and dissociation, emotional awareness) target these experiences in the general population only and are not geared towards assessing individuals suffering from eating disorders. Hence, validity studies for these measures used with individuals suffering from eating disorders are largely missing, and this situation renders these tests largely unhelpful in assessing embodied experiences in these individuals.

Rays of Hope

In this context, it is salutary that two recent measures have been developed with the aim of specifically assessing embodiment in relationship with eating disorders: the Identity and Eating Disorders Questionnaire (IDEA; Stanghellini et al., 2012) and the Embodiment Scales for Women (ESW; Piran & Teall, 2012; Teall, 2006, 2015). The latter has not yet been published; thus, the following review is based on the general brief description of this measure provided by its authors.

Identity and Eating Disorders Questionnaire

The IDEA (Stanghellini et al., 2012) is a measure that targets the abnormal attitudes towards one's own corporeality and the difficulties in the definition of one's own identity. Founded on Sartre's (1943) distinction between the lived body (Leib) or body-subject and the physical body (Koerper) or body-object, IDEA was grounded in the hypothesis that "persons with eating disorders experience their own body first and foremost as an object being looked at by another, rather than coenesthetically or from a first-person perspective" (Stanghellini et al., 2012, p. 148). Research findings using IDEA seem to confirm that people suffering from eating disorders experience their body first and foremost as an object being looked at by another and define their selves primarily in terms of the way one is looked at by others and through one's ability to control one's shape and weight. Stanghellini and Castellini discuss IDEA and this work further in Chapter 8.

Although IDEA offers valuable information about attitudes towards the body and how one defines one's identity through the body, it provides little insight into the actual experience of lived corporeality. This may be partly because of the authors' attempt to integrate a more phenomenological stance around lived corporeality with the mainstream cognitive-behavioural framework of conceptualizing eating disorders.

The Embodiment Scales for Women

This measure (Piran & Teall, 2012; Teall, 2006, 2015) stems directly from Piran's research on the DTE (Piran & Teall, 2012; Piran et al., 2002; Piran et al., 2007). Among its six scales, the ESW includes the Experience of Embodiment Scale (Teall, 2006, 2015). Although currently unpublished, the Experience of Embodiment Scale is described as consisting of six factors: positive connection with body, body disrupted adjustment, agency and expression, experience and expression of sexual desire, self-care and attunement versus body harm and neglect, and self-objectification (Teall, 2006, 2015).

Given that the scale is unpublished, it is impossible to directly evaluate how the items address each of these dimensions or the psychometric properties of the scale. However, based on the descriptions offered by the authors, it is valuable to see that body connection, agency and expression as well as self-care and resisting self-objectification are considered important domains of defining and assessing embodiment.

Limitations and Challenges

Notwithstanding these recent developments in measuring embodiment, significant limitations and challenges remain. Whereas the mainstream assessment practices have largely overlooked the role of embodied experience in eating disorders, the few measures that target body connection and emotional awareness as part of embodied experience have not been validated with people diagnosed with eating disorders, which makes these tests unusable for this population. Although newer developments in the field have focused specifically on embodied experience as related to eating disorders, IDEA (Stanghellini et al., 2012) has focused on attitudes towards body and external perception of one's body rather than on the lived experience of embodiment, and, for the time being, it is impossible to evaluate ESW (Teall, 2006, 2015) because these scales are not yet published.

Thus, several challenges remain with respect to measuring embodiment: (a) limited, partial conceptualization of embodied experience in the existing measurement models (e.g., the emotional experience tends to be overlooked and kinesthetic aspects virtually absent); (b) measurement models follow traditional quantitative practices of assigning numbers to external characteristics without paying attention to process and subjective experiences; and (c) marked disconnect between the theoretical conceptualization of embodied experience and measurement models.

Alternative Theoretical-Methodological Perspective

In response to these limitations, we propose an alternative theoretical-methodological perspective for conceptualizing and measuring embodiment, and will subsequently illustrate some of its aspects by drawing on the findings of an empirical investigation with women recovering from AN. The contributions and implications of this proposed framework will also be addressed.

Embodied Lived Experience as Sensorial-Affective-Kinesthetic Unity

Experientially, embodiment is lived as embodied experience encompassing sensual, affective-relational, and kinesthetic ways of experiencing one's body, others and the world. Whereas there has been a surge of research studies in the area of embodied cognition focused on the body-based information processing (Winkielman et al., 2015), the investigation and theoretical elaboration of the other facets of this construct (e.g., affective, kinesthetic) is less represented. Hence, drawing on relevant research literature, we conceptualize embodiment as lived experience consisting of a dynamic interplay among sensorial-somatic, affective, and kinesthetic relational experiences. The focus of this conceptualization is on elaborating the facets of the lived experience of corporeality following the philosophical tradition of Merleau-Ponty (1945/2012) and Sartre (1943).

Embodied Experience as Affective Experience

The experience of the lived body is spontaneously accompanied by emotional tone and affective experiences. It is very rarely that our sensorial embodied experience is devoid of any emotional states or influences. In this sense, it is important to distinguish between interoceptive awareness and embodied experience, as embodied experience involves interoception, yet is not comprised of interoception alone. Thus, embodied experience extends beyond interoceptive awareness, by incorporating reflexive engagement of the self with the lived body and the world (Varela, 1996), and it is through recognizing and engaging with body sensations and states that affective experience is uncovered, which may then facilitate identification of differentiated emotions.

Affective Experience as Embodied Kinesthetic Experience

Reciprocally, emotionality is lived in and through the body. Echoing the centrality of the body in affective experience, Mazis (1993) focused on the word emotion itself, which implies movement and furthermore embodiment as it requires a vehicle (i.e., the body), through which existence in space is made possible. As Spackman and Miller (2008) observed, "The embodiment of the emoter is, then, essential to the emotion itself; it is not a secondary aspect of the subject's appraisal of his environment" (p. 369).

The body also serves as a symbolic tool or "concretized metaphor" used to physically represent non-physical phenomenon such as emotional experience (Skårderud, 2007, p. 164). Particularly salient in eating disorder cases, the body and body-related behaviour (e.g., eating, purging) have been identified as representing emotional, social, or moral phenomenon such as purification, vulnerability, and the desire for control, further illustrating emotional experience as embodied (Skårderud, 2007).

Embodied Experience as Relational Experience

Theories of embodiment suggest that awareness and identification of others' emotions go beyond recognition or cognitive "knowing." Just as subjective affective experience involves activation of physiological processes, perceiving and identifying the others' emotions involve a degree of vicarious experiencing of the others' emotional states facilitated through embodied experience (Winkielman et al., 2008). Moreover, the ability to perceive and identify emotional experience in others involves experiencing of emotion in the bodily-self (Winkielman et al., 2015).

In particular, certain differentiated emotions such as embarrassment, guilt, shame, and pride require the existence and awareness of, as well as differentiation from, the other. The ability to experience and recognize such emotions requires self-awareness, recognition and referencing of external standards, and awareness of the mental states and perspectives of the other, all of which involve the bodily-self in relation to the bodily-other (Lagattuta & Thompson, 2007; Tangney & Fischer, 1995).

Summary

Embodied lived experience represents a unity of sensorial-physiological, affective, relational, and kinesthetic aspects. Emotional experience is embodied and arises from physiological responses to the environment, which are then interpreted and integrated via the central nervous system (Barrett & Bliss-Moreau, 2009; Damasio, 1994; Damasio, Everitt,

& Bishop, 1996; Spackman & Miller, 2008). Thus, the body serves as a vehicle through which emotions are experienced, affective information becomes nuanced, and emotions are physically represented (Mazis, 1993; Skårderud, 2007; Winkielman et al., 2015). Reciprocally, embodied experience lends itself to affective experience. Engaging with embodied experience facilitates the uncovering of affective experience and identification of differentiated emotions, in addition to facilitating connection with the emotional experience of the other in relationships and dialogue (Winkielman et al., 2015). Thus, it is important that in conceptualizing and measuring embodiment, both the interoceptive-sensorial, affective and kinesthetic aspects of embodied lived experience are included.

Beyond the Measuring Tape: An Alternative Measurement Model

Traditional measurement models like those currently employed in research and clinical practice are primarily if not exclusively focused on measuring variables and aggregates of variables at the expense of personal subjective experience and individual differences. These measurement models are exclusively nomothetic and falsely assume ergodicity (Molenaar, 2012) at the expense of idiographic understandings. In the area of eating disorders, these measurement models directly contribute to disembodied assessment practices and mirror the obsession with scrutinizing the numbers on the scale or measuring tape reported by individuals diagnosed with eating disorders. Although the phenomenological tradition has provided rich descriptive characterizations of embodiment and has used these as starting point for theories of the self, it has not offered the operational working definitions and measures needed for rigorous empirical research (Longo, Schüür, Kammers, Tsakiris, & Haggard, 2008).

A Phenomenologically Grounded Measurement Model

In response to these challenges and in line with the original philosophical conceptualization of embodiment as lived corporeality, we propose and elaborate a measurement model rooted in the phenomenology of embodied experience understood as somatic–affective–kinesthetic experience. To accomplish this goal, the preliminary steps are (a) to uncover the core processes of this experience as articulated by participants during a systematic, rigorous interview focused on understanding how the interviewees articulate their answers to questions or scenarios targeting embodiment, and (b) to elaborate a model of understanding the process of responding to such questions and scenarios. This chapter addresses these preliminary steps of developing such a measurement model.

Response Processes

The term coined for the inquiry into the underlying processes of responding to items, questions, or scenarios is "response processes" (Launeanu & Hubley, 2017). Response processes inquiry may serve different roles (Launeanu, 2016), but for the purpose of developing a measurement model of embodiment, these response processes represent both theoretical building blocks and psychometric variables that can be further mathematically formalized, if and as needed.

Response processes were traditionally defined as "the theoretical mechanisms that underlie item responses" (Embretson, 1983, p. 179). Borsboom, Mellenbergh, and Van Heerden (2004) and Zumbo (2009) suggested that response processes represent the explanatory mechanisms of test score variation, and one of the main purposes for identifying response patterns and processes is to be able to integrate this knowledge in a coherent, explanatory model of test score variation. Moreover, response processes may help uncover the experiential, phenomenological structure of a phenomenon or characteristic in order to provide a deeper understanding of that phenomenon (Launeanu, 2016), and this is the main objective of the current study.

Measuring Embodiment

In this view, to measure embodiment means essentially to uncover the phenomenological structure of the embodied experience as articulated by participants in a way that would further allow for fine-grained distinctions regarding changes in the thresholds of that experience so that a meaningful subjective assessment of this experience takes place. In contrast with "numerics" (Kline, 1990) where numbers are arbitrarily assigned to various characteristics, measuring embodiment would then mean to detect the processes that are intrinsic and constitutive of the embodied experience, to investigate the systematic structure that emerges in the patterns of responses, and to integrate these processes in a model.

Empirical Illustration

In this section of the chapter, we illustrate the preliminary steps of developing a holistic, phenomenologically grounded model for measuring embodiment by using the data collected during an empirical investigation of women's embodied affective experience throughout the process of recovering from AN (Beyer, 2016). The main objectives of this empirical investigation were (a) to identify the core processes that constitute the structure of the embodied experience in women recovering from AN, (b) to build a process-based model of responding to questions and scenarios targeting embodied experience, and (c) to explore mapping these processes on the recovery journey. A future objective not addressed in this chapter is to develop a protocol of measuring embodied experience that includes the phenomenological processes identified in these preliminary steps.

Brief Description of the Study

Participants and Procedure

Six women previously diagnosed with AN, aged 21–28, participated in the study. All participants self-identified as being recovered and reported cessation of energy intake restriction and restoration of body weight. Each woman participated in a one-on-one response processes interview where she completed a measure of body connection (Scale of Body Connection [SBC]; Price & Thompson, 2007) and emotional awareness (Levels of Emotional Awareness Scale [LEAS]; Lane, Quinlan, Schwartz, Walker, & Zeitlin, 1990), respectively, while articulating aloud her process of responding to questions or scenarios (Launeanu & Hubley, 2017). Following the completion of each measure, women were then asked a series of questions regarding the clarity and applicability of items to their own lived experience. All interviews were video recorded, transcribed, and analyzed for emergent themes and response processes.

Measures

The SBC and LEAS are both self-report measures. The SBC was designed to assess body awareness and body dissociation (Price & Thompson, 2007). Items are responded to using a Likert scale, denoting the degree or frequency of applicability of an item for the respondent. The LEAS was designed to assess emotional awareness (Lane et al., 1990). To do so, a variety of scenarios are presented, and the respondent is asked to identify what they might feel in addition to how another person in the described scenario might feel.

Embodiment Deconstructed

Interviewing women recovering from AN as participants for this study was purposeful. Struggling with an eating disorder profoundly disjoints the existential mind-body unity (Beyer, 2016; Piran & Teall, 2012; Stanghellini et al., 2012). The primordial unity of embodied lived experience is fragmented or dissolved during the course of the disorder and, hopefully, restored during the recovery process (Beyer, 2016; Jenkins & Ogden, 2012). Paradoxically, this process of disrupting and restoring of embodied lived experience offers rich insights into the lived meaning of embodiment as a dynamic, subjective experience that brings together interoceptive and affective experiences as well as an intimate connection with the body and the visceral knowing of the bodily-self. Inviting women recovering from AN to reflect on and articulate how they experience their bodies provides the opportunity to uncover the processes involved in the delicate yet strenuous process of unraveling and reconstructing of embodied experience, and these processes represent the foundation for a phenomenological understanding and measuring of embodiment.

Findings: Articulating Body Connection

Four categories of response processes were observed while women in recovery from AN responded to questions targeting their experience of body connection: (a) interoceptive processes or tuning into the sensorial experience of the body; (b) affective processes or attending to emotional body cues; (c) cognitive processes such as remembering, rationalizing, or building scenarios; and (d) behavioural processes mainly related to emotional regulation of embodied experience. A more detailed presentation of these results is displayed in Figure 6.1.

These response processes mobilized during answering questions targeting body connection were nuanced and varied in relation to where women found themselves in the process of recovery from AN. For example, earlier in recovery, women had difficulties accessing interoceptive or affective information directly and relied mainly on cognitive processes while a significant degree of body disconnection or numbness was noticed. This picture changed considerably as women moved through recovery, with women accessing interoceptive and affective information while increasing connection with the body was noticed. Figure 6.2 exemplifies

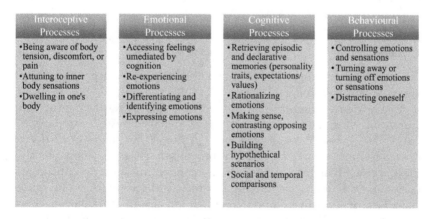

Interoceptive Processes	Emotional Processes	Cognitive Processes	Behavioural Processes
•Being aware of body tension, discomfort, or pain •Attuning to inner body sensations •Dwelling in one's body	•Accessing feelings umediated by cognition •Re-experiencing emotions •Differentiating and identifying emotions •Expressing emotions	•Retrieving episodic and declarative memories (personality traits, expectations/values) •Rationalizing emotions •Making sense, contrasting opposing emotions •Building hypothethical scenarios •Social and temporal comparisons	•Controlling emotions and sensations •Turning away or turning off emotions or sensations •Distracting oneself

Figure 6.1 Processes Involved in Self-Reporting on Body Connection.

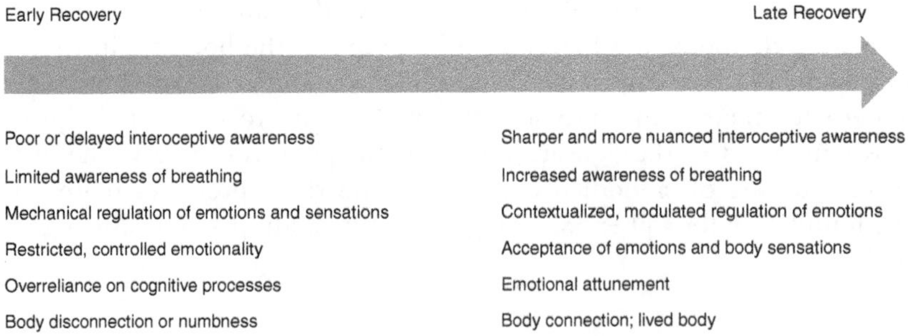

Early Recovery   Late Recovery

Poor or delayed interoceptive awareness	Sharper and more nuanced interoceptive awareness
Limited awareness of breathing	Increased awareness of breathing
Mechanical regulation of emotions and sensations	Contextualized, modulated regulation of emotions
Restricted, controlled emotionality	Acceptance of emotions and body sensations
Overreliance on cognitive processes	Emotional attunement
Body disconnection or numbness	Body connection; lived body

Figure 6.2 Mapping Body Connection Processes on AN Recovery Continuum.

this observed progression in greater detail. These observations suggest that an accurate measurement and assessment of embodied experience should differentiate among various response processes that are connected with different points in recovery, rather than assessing recovery as a definitive, one-time event or outcome.

Findings: Articulating Embodied Affective Experience

Response Processes

Similar to the response processes underlying answering questions on body connection, women recovering from AN articulated their affective embodied experience differently at various points in recovery. To that end, they made use of interoceptive, kinesthetic, affective, and cognitive processes to articulate their embodied affective experience. Table 6.1 presents these results in detail following the recovery continuum.

Response Processes Model of Self-Reporting on Embodied Affective Experience

Figure 6.3 presents the model of responding to scenarios targeting embodied emotional awareness.

As depicted in Figure 6.3, there were shifts in response processes employed when answering items as women progressed through recovery from AN. Women who were in the earlier stages of recovery tended to show limited capacity for imagining scenarios. Subsequently, these women had difficulty personally connecting with described scenarios and relied on generalizing as a means of responding. The result was a lack of identified emotion (e.g., "I don't know if I'd be conscious of the feeling"). Women who were further along in recovery tended to

Table 6.1 Response Processes Affective Awareness

Early Recovery	Mid Recovery	Late Recovery
Difficulty or inability to access feelings	Constructive processes Scenario building Imagined or hypothetical feelings	Kinesthetic processes Engaging in body movements to amplify core affective experiences, or to facilitate the identification of emotions Body postural engagement such as tensing one's body
Censoring and holding back feelings	Cognitive processes Rationalizing feelings Overriding feelings by general beliefs Counterfactual thinking; meta-thinking	Somatic re-experiencing
Tentativeness and uncertainty in identifying feelings	Declarative memory Broad, enduring personality attributions to infer or justify a feeling/ emotional experience	Episodic memory Personal body-based memories and experiences
Polarized, black and white feelings	Kinesthetic processes Limited body movement and activation during accessing or identifying feelings	Accessing and holding opposite emotions
Emotional disconnection, depersonalization	Inferring feelings from behaviours and socially sanctioned expectations Interpersonal processes Need for interviewer's validation	Accessing clearly identified emotion Contextualizing emotions Effective emotional self-regulation

make assumptions about the described scenario, enlisting social norms and motivations, declarative memory, and inferences about possible behaviour. This resulted in a number of plausible options and outcomes, with tentatively identified and undifferentiated emotions (e.g., "I would probably feel anxious"). Women who were later in recovery tended to enact and engage with described scenarios. They often utilized episodic memory and experienced, or re-experienced emotions through their bodies. This was evidenced by notable shifts in posture, facial expression, and physical movement. The result of such emotional re-experiencing and somatic activation was identification of differentiated, integrated, and contextualized emotion (e.g., "I'd feel, not quite angry, but irritated").

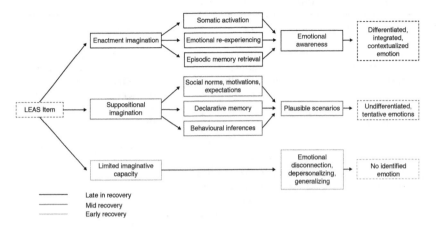

Figure 6.3 Response Processes Model LEAS.

Summary of Findings

The journey of restoring the embodied experience during recovery from AN is mirrored by changes in how women access and articulate their embodied affective experience. In early recovery, women either re-sponded to questions about their bodies and affective experience using abstract cognitive processes disconnected from direct somatic experiencing or had significant difficulties answering these questions (e.g., long pauses, silences, no response). These processes illustrate the tenuous experience of embodiment and the reliance on memories or intellectual hypotheses instead of directly accessing the interoceptive or affective body states. As women advance in their recovery process, they tended to rely more and more on body cues, and engaged kinesthetically with their body to help access emotions. Moreover, their emotional identification became more precise, nuanced, and contextualized later in recovery.

Conclusion

These results indicate that women recovering from AN self-evaluate and articulate their embodied experience using several response processes: interoceptive, affective, kinesthetic, and cognitive. These processes suggest an emerging phenomenological structure of articulating embodiment along somatic-affective processes. Furthermore, these findings suggest several shifts along these processes that could be considered thresholds in how embodied lived experience is articulated: (a) for interoception, the threshold between disconnection and somatic activation; (b) for emotional processes, the threshold between emotional disconnection and emotional re-experiencing; (c) for kinesthetic processes, the threshold between numb-ness to activating and moving the body; and (d) for cognitive processes, the threshold between declarative memory and cognitive inferences to episodic memory and enactment imaginative-constructive processes. These thresholds need to be elaborated in further studies in order to specify a measurement protocol.

Theoretical and Clinical Implications

The results of this response processes inquiry hold important implications for how embodiment is conceptualized and subsequently measured in both research and clinical spheres. Given the inextricable connection between emotional experience and the body (Mazis, 1993; Skårderud, 2007; Winkielman et al., 2015), it is foundational that affective-kinesthetic experience is acknowledged and included not only in the assessment of embodiment, but as a key indicator in women's recovery from AN. At a basal level, this requires broadening of the construct of embodiment to include the affective, interoceptive, and kinesthetic components of embodied lived experience.

Moreover, due to the symbolic, affective, and dynamic nature of embodied experience, measurement models and applied assessment should allow for qualitative reports including metaphorical or allegorical components to complement quantitative measurement scales. It is also valuable to note that for women recovering from AN, a traditional measurement scale may evoke anxiety, disorientation, uncertainty, or resistance after an extensive focus on measuring one's body and weight while suffering from AN. Similarly, a traditional measurement scale may also limit acknowledgement of affective, interoceptive, and kinesthetic capacities, promoting continued bifurcation of the body-self and disrupted embodied experience associated with AN. Thus, acknowledging and inviting affective, interoceptive, and kinesthetic ways of responding to assessment tools contribute to the rigour of assessment while also encouraging engaged embodied experience in the respondent. It is also recommended that future measurement tools incorporate an awareness of changes in response processes used across recovery while allowing for distinction between cognitive and interoceptive, kinesthetic, affective, and relational ways of responding to assessment items so as to provide a more nuanced picture of the AN recovery progress.

Appendix A

Response Process Follow-Up Questions

1 To what extent did you understand the questions?

    i Were there any specific questions that you did not understand?

    ii If so, which one(s) and why?

2 To what extent did you feel the questions fit or were applicable to your own experiences?

    iii Were there any specific questions that you felt very strongly applied to your own experiences?

    iv If so, which one(s) and why?

3 To what extent did you feel the questions did not fit or were not applicable to your own experiences?

    v Were there any specific questions that you felt did not apply to your own experiences?

    vi If so, which one(s) and why?

References

Allan, H. T. (2005). Gender and embodiment in nursing: The role of the female chaperone in the infertility clinic. *Nursing Inquiry, 12*, 175–183.

Barsalou, L. W. (1999). Perceptual symbol systems. *Behavioral and Brain Sciences, 22*, 577–660.

Barrett, L. F., & Bliss-Moreau, E. (2009). Affect as a psychological primitive. *Advances in Experimental Social Psychology, 41*, 167–218. doi:10.1371/journal.pone.0064959

Beyer, C. (2016). Seeking the body electric: The role of embodied affective experience in the process of recovery from anorexia nervosa (unpublished Master's thesis). Trinity Western University, BC.

Beyer, C., & Launeanu, M. (in press). Poems of the past, present and future: Becoming a more embodied self in recovering from anorexia nervosa. In H. L. McBride & J. K. Kwee (Eds.), *Healthy embodiment and eating disorders: Theory, research, prevention and treatment*. New York, NY: Routledge.

Borsboom, D., Mellenbergh, G. J., & Van Heerden, J. (2004). The concept of validity. *Psychological Review, 11*, 1061–1071.

Clark, A. (1999). An embodied cognitive science? *Trends in Cognitive Sciences, 3*, 345–351. doi:10.1016/S1364–6613(99)01361–3

Damasio, A. R. (1994). Decartes' error: Emotion, reason, and the human brain. New York, NY: G. P. Putman's Sons.

Damasio, A. R., Everitt, B. J., & Bishop, D. (1996). The somatic marker hypothesis and the possible functions of the prefrontal cortex. *Philosophical Transactions: Biological Sciences, 351*(1346), 1413–1420.

Embretson, S. (1983). Construct validity: Construct representations versus nomothetic span. *Psychological Bulletin, 93*, 179–197.

Fairburn, C. G., & Beglin, S. J. (1994). Assessment of eating disorders: Interview or self-report questionnaire? *International Journal of Eating Disorders, 16*, 363–370.

Heidegger, M. (1962). *Being and time.* Oxford, UK: Blackwell Publishers Ltd.

Jenkins, J., & Ogden, J. (2012). Becoming 'whole' again: A qualitative study of women's views of recovering from anorexia nervosa. *European Eating Disorders Review, 20*, 23–31. doi:10.1002/erv.1085

Kline, M. (1990). *Mathematical thought from ancient to modern times* (Vol. 2). New York, NY: Oxford University Press.

Lagattuta, K. H., & Thompson, R. A. (2007). The development of self-conscious emotions: Cognitive processes and social influences. In J. L. Tracy, R. W. Robins, J. P. Tangney (Eds.), *The self-conscious emotions: Theory and research* (pp. 91–113). New York, NY: Guildford Press.

Lane, R. D., Quinlan, D. M., Schwartz, G. E., Walker, P. A., & Zeitlin, S. (1990). The levels of emotional awareness scale: A cognitive-developmental measure of emotion. *Journal of Personality Assessment, 55*(1–2), 124–134. doi:10.1207/s15327752jpa5501&2_12

Launeanu, M. (2016). Response processes as a source of validity evidence in self-report measures: Theoretical and methodological implications (unpublished Doctoral dissertation). The University of British Columbia, BC.

Launeanu, M., & Hubley, A. (2017). A model building approach to examining response processes as a source of validity evidence for self-report items and measures. In B. D. Zumbo & A. M. Hubley (Eds.), *Understanding and investigating response processes in validation research* (pp. 115–136). New York, NY: Springer International Publishing.

Longo, R. M., Schüür, F., Kammers, M. P. M., Tsakiris, M., & Haggard, P. (2008). What is embodiment? A psychometric approach. *Cognition, 107*, 978–998. doi:10.1016/j.cognition.2007.12.004

Maturana, H. (2002). *Biology of cognition and epistemology.* Temuco: Universidad de la Frontera.

Mazis, G. (1993). *Emotion and embodiment.* New York, NY: Peter Lang.

Merleau-Ponty, M. (2012). *Phenomenology of perception* (D. L. Landes, Trans.). New York, NY: Routledge. (Original work published 1945).

Molenaar, P. C. M. (2012). A dynamic factor model for the analysis of multivariate time series. *Psychometrica, 50*, 181–202.

Piran, N., & Teall, T. (2012). The developmental theory of embodiment. In G. McVey, M. P. Levine, N. Piran, & H. B. Ferguson (Eds.), *Preventing eating-related and weight-related disorders: Collaborative research, advocacy, and policy change* (pp. 169–198). Waterloo, ON: Wilfred Laurier University Press.

Piran, N., Buttu, D., Damianakis, M., Legge, R., Nagasawa, S., & Mizevich, J. (2007). *Understanding intensified disruptions in girls' self and body experiences during adolescence* (Annual Convention, Canadian Psychological Association, Ottawa, ON, June).

Piran, N., Carter, W., Thompson, S., & Pajouhandeh, P. (2002). Powerful girls: A contradiction in terms? Young women speak about the experience of growing up in a girls' body. In S. Abbey (Ed.), *Ways of knowing in and through the body: Diverse perspectives on embodiment* (pp. 206–210). Welland, ON: Soleil Publishing.

Price, C. J., & Thompson, E. A. (2007). Measuring dimensions of body connection: Body awareness and bodily dissociation. *The Journal of Alternative and Complementary Medicine, 13*(9), 945–953. doi:10.1089/acm.2007.0537

Sáenz-Herrero, M., & Díez-Alegría, C. (2015). Gender and corporality, corporeality, and body image. In M. Sáenz-Herrero (1st ed.), *Psychopathology in women: Incorporating gender perspective into descriptive psychopathology* (pp. 113–142). Switzerland: Springer International Publishing. doi:10.1007/978-3-319–05870-2_6

Sartre, J. P. (1943). *Being and nothingness*. New York, NY: Washington Square Press.

Skårderud, F. (2007). Eating one's words, part I: 'Concretised metaphors' and reflective function in anorexia nervosa – An interview study. *European Eating Disorders Review, 15*(3), 163–174. doi:10.1002/erv.777

Spackman, M. P., & Miller, D. (2008). Embodying emotions: What emotion theorists can learn from simulations of emotions. *Minds & Machines, 18*, 357–372. doi:10.1007/s11023-008-9105–7

Stanghellini, G., Castellini, G., Brogna, P., Faravelli, C., & Ricca, V. (2012). Identity and eating disorders (IDEA): A questionnaire evaluating identity and embodiment in eating disorder patients. *Psychopathology, 45*, 147–158. doi:10.1159/000330258

Tangney, J., & Fischer, K. (1995). *Self-conscious emotions: The psychology of shame, guilt, embarrassment, and pride.* New York, NY: Guildford Press.

Teall, T. (2006). *The construction of the embodiment scale for women* (unpublished Master's thesis). University of Toronto, ON.

Teall, T. L. (2015). A quantitative study of the developmental theory of embodiment: Implications to health and well-being (unpublished Doctoral dissertation). University of Toronto, ON.

Varela, F. J. (1996). Neurophenomenology: A methodological remedy for the hard problem. *Journal of Consciousness Studies, 4*, 330–349.

Wilson, M. (2002). Six views of embodied cognition. *Psychonomic Bulletin and Review, 9*, 625–636. doi:10.3758/BF03196322

Winkielman, P., Niedenthal, P., & Oberman, L. (2008). The embodied emotional mind. In G. R. Semin & E. R. Smith (Eds.), *Embodied grounding: Social, cognitive, affective, and neuroscientific approaches* (pp. 263–288). New York, NY: Cambridge University Press. doi:10.1017/CB09780511805837.012

Winkielman, P., Niedenthal, P., Wielgosz, J., Eelen, J., & Kavanagh, L. C. (2015). Embodiment of cognition and emotion. In M. Mikulincer, P. R. Shaver, E. Borgida, J. A. Bargh, M. Mikulincer, P. R. Shaver, … J. A. Bargh (Eds.), *APA handbook of personality and social psychology, volume 1: Attitudes and social cognition* (pp. 151–175). Washington, DC: American Psychological Association.

Zumbo, B. D. (2009). Validity as contextualized and pragmatic explanation, and its implications for validation practice. In R. W. Lissitz (Ed.), *Thike concept of validity: Revisions, new directions and applications* (pp. 65–82). Charlotte, NC: Information Age Publishing.

7 Moving Toward Embodied Research

Elizabeth Chan

Many of the women I work with use the language of hunger to describe their longings and desires. For most, it is an aching sort of sensation rooted in the very core of their being.

Sometimes I ask them, "Where do you carry your hunger?" – a tongue-in-cheek reference to the fact that, so often, women speak to where they carry their weight.

"What do you mean?" they ask.

"Where do you feel your hunger?" I persist. "Where do you feel it in your body?"

"Everywhere," they say, "I feel it everywhere in my body."

I distinctly remember my encounter with one particular woman whom I met in residential care. During graduate school, I was moonlighting as a residential support worker. This gave me a unique opportunity to know human beings who spend almost all their time searching for an escape, since they are otherwise trapped in states of unbearable fear, rage, despair, and anxiety. At the residential home, they find reprieve – though, at first, only in a physical and practical sense. The painful longing in their hearts gives way to an aching emptiness. Still they seek something that might curb their insatiable yearning for relief or fulfillment.

On a golden afternoon in late January, I met a woman who had entered the home just a few days before I had gotten hired to work there. Her face was drawn with a hungry look as she sat by the alcove, gazing out the window. When I sat down next to her, she turned to me abruptly. There was a strange expression on her face: defiance and fierce pride, and something that looked like concern, all jumbled up together. For a moment, we sat in silence. Even then, her wordlessness did not mask a profound intelligence. I cleared my throat and was about to introduce myself when, suddenly, she spoke: "It's awful to sit here. You almost feel ill."

"Tell me what it's like," I said.

"My ill-ness? What it's like?" She laughed, almost harshly, but then again, mostly to herself. "It's like perpetual emptiness. It's like desperation. It's like emancipation. It's frantic like starvation. It's hunger."

"Tell me about your hunger."

"My hunger is like a hurricane," she said, "and it tears me up from inside. It claws at me, bites at me, threatens to devour me. It leaves nothing but desire and desperation in the wake of its disaster."

I almost asked the question, "And where do you feel it?" but she already appeared to be thinking. Then, with startling clairvoyance, she responded to my unspoken question, "It's in the pit of my stomach. No, deeper still…deeper than my stomach. No. Maybe…" she paused. With a wry grimace of amusement, she finished her sentence, "I guess I feel it everywhere. I feel it everywhere and all the time. But it starts in a deep, deep place inside of me. I don't know what is at the very core of human beings but that's where it starts. It starts in the core of my being."

Human Experience in Research

Human experience, the target of much critical activity in the humanities and social sciences, is, as Chadwick (2017) describes, "messy, in-between, on the edge and ontologically challenging" (p. 70), especially to those tasked to explain and describe it. Incompleteness is the baseline state of research which looks at the churning, inchoate states of mind, body, and psyche. Yet, despite the glaring ineffability of intimate, embodied, and at the same time, daily and unexceptional aspects of human existence, researchers have sought to answer questions not only to do with the "what" of lived experience, but also the "how" and the "why." A keen fascination with human life has, over past decades, donned the starched uniform of interrogator − determined to query, prod, demand, and yield findings, which front a level of understanding regarding a whole plethora of complex human phenomena.

Can questions about affect and emotion, feelings and sensations, and sensual bodily drives and psychic energies truly become subjects of fruitful inquiry? Can we unmask the elements which give rise to that clawing, aching, and biting quality characterizing the human experience of longing and desire? On the one hand, we can say, for example, that longing gives way to anxiety, which, in the experience of renowned writer and self-proclaimed behavioral addict Gabor Maté (2008a,b),

> clothes itself in concerns about body image or financial security, doubts regarding loveability or the ability to love, self-disparagement and existential pessimism about life's meaning and purpose − or… [otherwise] manifests itself as grandiosity, the need to be admired, to be seen as special.

> (p. 334)

Yet, the sensation itself, Maté goes on to explain, is, at bottom, "nameless and formless" (p. 334).

Social scientists have recruited thoughts and explanations to serve as indicators and descriptions of the phenomenon; nonetheless, those living with the felt sense of deep and desperate desire in the face of stark hollowness within themselves will find these ideas, identifications, and explanations vague and unconvincing at best. So what is the first step to take in order to allow the truth of lived experience to emerge? Joseph Campbell (2008), in *The Hero with a Thousand Faces*, writes that the first step of one's quest into discovery and greater understanding of the human soul is, in fact, a kind of exile – to stand in diametric opposition to that of social duty and the popular cult. Only then can one realize that "each carries within himself the all; therefore it may be sought and discovered within" (p. 332).

Traditional post-positivist methods of research may at times contribute to the silencing of women and the disconnection of women from their felt sense of self. In this chapter, feminist, transformative, and embodied methods of inquiry are discussed, as they may be helpful in both better understanding women's experiences of their bodies and their experiences of eating disorders and body shame. A discussion is also included on how these methods can contribute both literally and symbolically to women's freedom in their bodies and to giving voice to their experiences.

Background and Challenges

In the modern era, post-structural theories have driven a widespread "turn to the text" (Hook, 2003). Chadwick (2017) propones that the result has been a heavy reliance upon "analyses of language, talk, text and discourse" (p. 55) for developing critical understanding of human phenomena. She states that this poses some concerns, however, "principally regarding that which is potentially 'left out' of discursive analyses" (p. 55). Of course, the predominant methodological approaches and analytic practices in research are indelibly tied to ontological assumptions regarding the nature of subjectivity, human experience, bodily articulations, and language. From the perspective of theorists, researchers, and scientist-practitioners engaging in discursive approaches for their work, questions about the subjective and ontological experience of human beings must give way to more conventional means of scientific investigation with the goal of producing precise and scientific knowledge, which can then be told and represented in speech and proliferated through written and verbal expositions. In the end, the means of talking about what we know is as important as what we know. Yet, the paucity and taciturnity of language when speaking about fleshly, emotional, and intensely embodied experience highlights the difficulties of translation when it comes to the wordless stories embedded in the bare facts of human experience and existence.

Tracing Bodily Expressions of Inner Experience

Perhaps language floods in where primordial connectivity to essential experience is lacking. To fill the void, we become attached to descriptions and explanations which, in the end, cannot compensate us for the loss of ability to give deep and embodied expression to the parts of our experience which feel as if they are beyond name and form. While working at the residential home, I noticed that the women struggled constantly with the conundrums of psychic disruption to identity and to the integrity of embodiment following conversations in which they felt stuck or stilted in attempts to explain their inner experience. It was as if elements of their bodily and emotive experience always escaped capture in the codifying practices of a fully formed, communal language or vocabulary. As they grappled with a whole host of strong feelings including distress, rage, pain, fear, and occasionally, pride, delight, and pleasure, a distinctive lack of words to describe bodily affect seemed to disturb the relationship between the woman speaking and the one listening.

At the time, I was honing my ability to help people go into emotional, mental, and physical blocks as they felt them. As I witnessed struggles in the process of interactions, I sought to establish a subjective, sensory frame of reference for speaking about integral and intrinsic human experience. I asked questions such as "What was that like for you?", "Where did you feel it in your body?", "How did that impact you emotionally?", "What came up for you when he/she/they said that?", "Did you experience any thoughts or feelings at that time?" Again and again, the women appeared perplexed, if not somehow abashed by my line of questioning. In the end, it was not elegant, stripped away, thin slices of life that surfaced for observation and consideration amid our conversations, but shards. I remember a woman had once coyly said to me:

> I'm here – a grown woman, a full-fledged adult – living in a place where other people tell me when to get up and when to go to sleep, whether I can go outside or go to the bathroom, what to eat and how much. If that doesn't tell you how I'm doing and what it feels like to be me, I don't know what will.

Her comment and others like it were the most consistent forms of protest against the ambiguity, the emptiness, and the silence which threatened to "sweep away all traces of the specificity, corporeality, of their own processes of production and self-representation" (Grosz, 1995, p. 2). Despite the desire to express their visceral and emotional experiences, it became clear that standard linguistic and discursive expressions were insufficient. Consequently, the women often felt scared, baffled, enraged, and isolated by their deeply felt and embodied experiences. These private and seemingly incommunicable pieces of their lives at once resisted expression yet demanded interpretation.

Anthony Storr (1997) writes that

> When a person is encouraged to get in touch with and express [her] deepest feelings in the secure knowledge that [she] will not be rejected, criticized, nor expected to be different, some kind of rearrangement or sorting-out process often occurs within the mind which brings with it a sense of peace; a sense that the depths of the well of truth have really been reached.
>
> (p. 22)

For many of these women, such a peace felt distant and unapproachable. The unsettling effects of perpetual dissatisfaction with the small sliver of their experience made visible through their words continuously gnawed at them. Out of passionate curiosity about the life histories, the daily experiences, and the self-perceptions of these women, I continued to believe that what was often taken to be incomprehensible was, in fact, subject to expression, though that expression could not be fixed and was constantly disruptive vis-à-vis language in its conventional aspect. These expressions, I felt, "could outrun any specific attempt to interpret them" (Inahara, 2012, p. 191), and yet could be (re)found and (re)situated through conversation that worked on a more instinctual and primal level than words. Grosz (1995) explains that there are as many versions of subjectivity as there are bodies involved in its construction (see also Barad, 2003; Wilson, 2004). Through this lens, I was able to see that some women found expression in music, dance, poetry, art, tone, gestures, outbursts, and silence. Beyond words, their experiences manifested in all kinds of signifying practices suffused with bodily and semiotic energies. Their experiences were also the source of ideas, identifications, deeds, beliefs, and relational dynamics. I began to listen to the small sermons of their faces, their bodies, their postures, and their tones. I became aware of their movements, their grace, their nervous twitches, their eyes looking over my shoulder, and their eyes looking down for fear of intensity or transparency or inadequacy. I discovered that it was all saying something. For me, this was, as Padfield (2003) writes,

> an attempt to experience loss of what is 'known', not as an absence but as a chance for change and transformation – an acceptance of the states of 'unknowing' and 'impermanence' as part of a continuum we are all part of.
>
> (p. 37)

My experience at the home helped inform my understanding of subjectivity, language, expression, and bodies. This has influenced my practice in both research and therapy. Discursive approaches are important, providing means to both dialogue and clarify on what is felt; yet, at the same time, language is often inadequate when it comes to representing bodily sensations, feelings, and experiences (Brown, Cromby, Harper, Johnson, & Reavy, 2011; Gilles et al., 2004). There is a need for methodological innovation that goes beyond language and looks with interest at exploring various aspects of bodily life and embodied experience. And, indeed, this observation is salient today (Frank, 1995; Harris & Guillemin, 2012; Sandelowski, 2002). Theorists and scholars have heavily expounded on the limits of discursivity in qualitative research (Chadwick, 2017). While this has generated thoughtful discussions pertaining to the nature of experience and outlined flaws in our current research paradigm, there remains a dearth of practical solutions or answers addressing the limits of language in articulating the "fleshy and sensual lived body" (Chadwick, 2017, p. 58). It appears that we lack tangible methodological structures that integrate the paradigmatic insights of a turn to body and to sensory, "fleshy" experience into research practice. As a result, there have been substantive challenges to developing concrete body-centered qualitative methodological strategies. Up to now, efforts to "embody" qualitative methodology have largely mirrored the goals and processes of qualitative research on embodied reflexivity. More specifically, experimental strategies for centering the bodily experiences of research participants have often kept the basic storyline of describing and interrogating talk *about* the body, rather than focusing on talk in and through the body (Frank, 1995). It is not that research thus far has not focused on the body; it is that research has not considered the body as "simultaneously the cause, topic and instrument of whatever new stories are told" (Frank, 1995, p. 2). In other words, the language of the body has often been overlooked amidst our attempts to access the embodied qualities of human life and experiences.

Describing stories as told through the body requires a special level of attention (Frank, 1995), which effectively reframes and redirects our ways of approaching, tracing, and representing bodily experience. Finding different ways of listening to and for the body in qualitative analyses installs new extra-discursive methods into our research practice.

Art and Hunger: Strategies for Dynamic Engagement with Extra-Discursivity

Interestingly, the arts have always provided a means for seeking to illustrate all the invisible things which we know but find exceedingly difficult to articulate – images, metaphors, movement, tone, pixels, all commingled into a creative weaving of elements which we hope will conjure resonance and understanding. Here, we turn to that which is extra-discursive – in other words, that which is beyond the bounds of discourse – to tap into a reality that is more metaphysical than rational/logical.

A poignant example of this in literature is the psychologically driven work of fiction written by Norwegian author Knut Hamsun in 1890. The novel portrays an artist who wanders the streets of Christiana (now Oslo), struggling from the effects of starvation, all the while trying to sell his articles to the local newspaper. The hunger ravages his body and takes hold of his mind. The man begins his dark descent into a kind of madness characterized by paranoia and despair. He becomes increasingly anarchic as he allows himself to be driven by nothing other than whim and ungovernable urge in the face of profound hunger. At every moment, his self-imposed misery exhausts him, overwhelms him. All the while, the progressive mental and physical decay are being recounted in detail, written from the perspective of the protagonist who Hamsun (1890/2008) explains

> was conscious all the time that [he] was following mad whims without being able to do anything about it. [For] despite [his] alienation from [himself]…, and even though [he] was nothing but a battleground of invisible forces, [he] was aware of every detail of what is going on around [him].
>
> (p. 15)

In the midst of emptiness and desperation so dense that it seems to suffocate the very possibility of life, Hamsun's hero continues to strive for lucidity in his writing. Of course, he grows ever weaker in mind and body, hunger affecting his prose in the same way it affects his life. In the end, the protagonist's autobiographical account gives way to the demented moans of a consciousness starving to express itself, to "the whisper of the blood and the pleading of the bone marrow" (Hamsun, 1890/1994, p. 8).

What we can learn from art more generally and *Hunger* more specifically is the means by which to achieve more dynamic engagement with the extra-discursive. The ingenuity of *Hunger* as literary artwork has to do the fact that it is, first of all, an art that is indistinguishable from the life of the artist who makes it. All aspects of lived experience – whether "strange and inexplicable moods and thoughts that invade the mind [or] things that are often too elusive to be seized and held fast" – are therefore deposited into the text even as experiential fragments and incongruities which appear to exceed or rupture the narrative frame. What appears, then, is a dynamic inner life of immediacy and spontaneity, "a tiny drama closely observed, but narrated before us and not enacted" (Cohn, as cited in Slavin, 1994, p. 14). Slavin (1994) writes that

> Hamsun uses a vocabulary of mental states: train of thought, mood, shock, sensations, nerves, feelings, single thoughts. We have direct discourse – "Getting weak" and "harsh" and sensible phrases – without any of the conventional marks of punctuation or other signs to separate these words from there indirect, narrated stance consistently.

There is no hindsight, generalizing, analyzing – nothing breaks the recording of inner happenings, in their succession, without causal links.
The temporal adverbs – suddenly, in this instant, at that moment – put
before us a wide shade of feelings: depression, illumination, anger,
pathos. But there is no reach for a pattern, as Hamsun's narrator presents consciousness as a series of strange and even fantastic moods. A
metaphor that occurs to me is that of a very sensitive seismograph
recording with accuracy movements similar to the 'tiny leaping movements' of his feet. We find no digression, no gnomic statement, no
explication"

(p. 14)

Through his art, Hamsun constructs a world held together not exclusively,
or even primarily, by words themselves, but by the act of storytelling
within poetics expressive of a most profound subjectivity. Throughout the
course of the entire fiction, Hamsun purges any reference to the narrating
self as distant from the experiencing self and draws upon epiphanic moments of the narrator, forged from the chain of free associations, in order
to access and explore inexplicable states of perception. Can the same be
said of research which tries to capture the fleshy, sensual experiences being
articulated in and through participants' narratives? Are our representation
and analysis of bodily modes of telling indistinguishable from the ambiv-
alent, multivocal, and contradictory subjectivity of narrators as they tell
their stories? According to Auster (2003), Hamsun's *Hunger* does not aim
to be "an art of autobiographical excess, but rather an art that is the direct
expression of the effort to express itself. In other word, an art of hunger:
an art of need, of necessity, of desire" (p. 323). Through the depiction of a
starving young man whose sense of reality is giving way to a delusionary
existence on the darker side of Pascalian terror, Hamsun produces art of
such a type that "admits the chaos and does not try to say that the chaos is
really something else….To find a form that accommodates the mess, that
is the task of the artist" (Beckett, 1961).

In some ways, art seeks to be unburdened of social propriety and its
arbitrary imposition of order. It is concerned with the mess that is often shirked by more conventional approaches for expounding on bodily
emotional experiences. It does not reduce the particularity and the ex-
cessiveness of bodily expression and bodily responses to the lived experience to philosophical abstraction. Rather, it embraces the situated
expressiveness of the body and seeks to highlight ways in which people
are transparent to each other (Wittgenstein, 1953/1986). Unfortunately
for research, a decade's worth of grappling with "embodied methodologies" has not yet provided us with means by which to capture much of
the messy and lively qualities of subjective and embodied human experience. Chadwick (2017) believes that the problem arises in the *critical
moment* of turning talk into text. She explains that "it is in the process

of transcription that embodied voices [of participants] are often rendered mute and are lost to analysis/interpretation" (p. 60). In other words, we run across issues of embodying sensual bodily drives and energies of talk and storytelling when we seek to seamlessly convert entire narrative passages into transcript text or written summaries based on constituents of the experience being described. Ultimately, there are questions as to whether meaningful analysis can stem from what is now static and devoid of bodily energies and rhythms which, according to Kristeva (1984), are an essential part of the meaning-making process surrounding embodied experience. Indeed, various strategies presently used in an effort to grapple with and apply practical and analytic ways of embodying qualitative methodology – for example, grounded theory (Charmaz, 2006), thematic analysis (Braun & Clarke, 2006), interpretative phenomenological analysis (Smith, Flowers, & Larkin, 2009), and critical discourse analysis (Van Dijk, 1999) – have "tended to take a denaturalized approach to transcription in which the substantive content [i.e., *what* is said], rather than the form and bodily intricacies of speech acts [i.e., the saying itself], is foregrounded" (Chadwick, 2017, p. 60; see also Oliver, Serovich, & Mason, 2005).

Semiotic Dimensions of Embodied Experience: Preserving Bodily Energies in Research

It is the work of Julia Kristeva (1984) and her theory of the "speaking body" or "subject-in-process" that highlights the lag in research with regard to considering semiotic aspects of the lived experience. Here, what Kristeva describes as the semiotic is akin to "the energies, rhythms, forces and corporeal residues necessary for representation" (Grosz, 1989, p. 43). Such expressions of the semiotic "resist any simple definition" (Inahara, 2012, p. 185) and, as expressions, "cannot be replaced by other terms...to do the same communicative job, as is often the case with conventional dimensions of meaning" (Inahara, 2012, p. 185). Semiotic expression is concerned with distinctive ways of telling and represents "as much of the embodied, performative and breathy qualities of speech as possible" (Chadwick, 2017, p. 61). It depicts the "visceral force of speaking bodies" (Chadwick, 2017, p. 60). So long as we perceive that bodily and semiotic energies are superfluous in our analysis of the multidimensional expressions of living and embodied experience, we will fail to capture the meaning and significance of multiple layers of richness and complexity embedded in ways of talking about difficult to articulate embodied experiences. As long as we fail in attending to the undercurrent of "living energy which converts static words into a sensual matrix of meaning and which constantly threatens to disrupt univocality, coherence and symbolic logic" (Chadwick, 2017, p. 59; see also Boulous-Walker, 1998), we sever the connection between the one who is speaking and what is spoken about and between research subjects and researchers.

How, then, can we listen to the intricacies of the performative "speaking being" telling/talking about her embodied experience in research contexts? Minae Inahara (2012) suggests that attention to the affective aspects captured in embodied modalities, including bodily eruptions in speech (intonation, pitch, rhythm, laughter, etc.), points us toward the multitude of expressive possibilities which can otherwise be overlooked. These possibilities, in fact, help to undermine the boundaries of the un-shareable and to expand the confines of the shareable; through the semiotic, there are means of expressing aspects of an embodied being which are unintelligible in the symbolic. Kristeva's (1984) theory of the speaking body-subject provides a rich framework for considering "*both* the manifest content of stories/talk and its underside which disrupts clear and orderly meaning (see McAfee, 2004) and emerges in storytelling as moments of excess, contradiction, incoherence and ambiguity" (Chadwick, 2017, p. 65). Rather than discounting moments of "narrative excess" (Chadwick, 2017, p. 65), what McKendy (2006) calls "the rough spots" (p. 474) in narratives which do not conform to univocal or tidy analytic interpretations, efforts to conduct embodied analysis must start with acknowledging these moments of excess and ambiguity as theoretically and analytically important.

Approaches and Strategies for Conducting Embodied Research

Chadwick (2017) writes that "embodied methodologies need to be able to make sense of the embodied energies alive in talk and stories and of experiences as lived and felt in the flesh" (p. 59). In other words, these methods must facilitate a focus on aspects of the embodied being that are largely unintelligible in the context of a public and objective system of language and when governed by what is irreducibly normative and fixed. Embodied research should enable the possibility of capturing direct, semiotic, and "extra-verbal" (McAfee, 2004, p. 17) dimensions of subjective bodily experiences. In her own work researching the experience of childbirth for various women, Chadwick (2017) has leveraged poetic representational and methodological devices to highlight the performative aspects of talk/telling. She explains that the form and "rhetorical architecture" (Moore, 2013, p. 62) of more poetic forms of transcribing what is said can, in some ways, seek to "more closely [approximate] the rhythm and emotion of an oral narrative" (O'Dell & Willim, 2013, p. 319). Indeed, the structural and aesthetic elements of poetry can create an opportunity for evoking "the disruptive bodily qualities of storytelling which cannot be contained as transcript codes" (Chadwick, 2017, p. 64). The architectural use of the page; the alignment (or dysalignment) of certain segments of transcript; and the italicizing, underlining, or bolding of certain elements can all provide means of reproducing the lively and pulsating qualities of embodied narratives. In this way, the texture of the text infuses it with sensory qualities. Similar to Hamsun's style of writing, Chadwick (2017) was careful, in her transcription work, to try and respect the "rhythms of speech" (p. 61) and therefore "did not impose artificial grammatical regulations such as full-stops or commas" (p. 61); rather, it was her "chief goal...to try and represent as much of the embodied, performative and breathy qualities of speech as possible" (p. 8). She states, "Respecting participants' embodied tellings by attempting to transcribe as much of the messy and lively qualities of their utterances as possible, was a methodological move which later enabled a focus on 'ways of telling' as analytically important" (p. 61). Chadwick concedes that, evidently, any attempt to transform sounds and utterances of such visceral experience as childbirth into words on a page will always "be limited, flawed and partial re-productions" (p. 64). Nonetheless, the reenvisioning of transcriptions as "open and sensory texts rather than closed, realist and empirical reflections of what was really communicated" (p. 64) is an important stride toward moving embodied methodologies into the realm of qualitative interpretation and analysis. Accessing alternative, even arts-based, approaches to phenomenologically explore, sift through, and represent qualitative data may afford creative opportunities for revealing aspects of lived experience in distinctive ways – moreover, ways that are open to a plurality of readings and to more multilayered analysis.

Embodied Analysis

Embodied analysis starts with a turn to the living body. Rather than deny the body of its materiality, which ultimately leaves the body powerless and inanimate, this process looks to recapture the lost corporeal space and body by expanding methodological practices/approaches toward an emphasis of "body-as-flesh," rather than a disembodied "body-as-text." According to a number of feminist scholars, particularly Grosz (1994), Barad (2003), and Wilson (2004), bodily expressions acquire their salience through naturalistically oriented, sensory approaches to engaging with bodies/corporeality. Becoming "up close" with bodies can prove to be insightful and can help to reveal the ways in which corporeality itself affects or is affected by concrete experience. As researchers interacting with the body, not as a Cartesianized subject, but as the nuclear axis of presence and identity (Foucault, 1966/1973; Heidegger, 1962/2001), we can register the significance of its manifest vocality, sensoriality, spatiality, and mobility for improving upon the purpose in conducting embodied research: to reevoke a sense of corporeality, fleshiness, and embodied performance in the analysis and representation of findings.

In their efforts to access the embodied being, Carol Gilligan and Lyn Mikel Brown proposed a conceptualization of the inner self/psyche, which can be represented and has embodied significance through the metaphor of *voice*. In line with Moore's (1984) beliefs that "internal experiences and their physical expression are unbreakably united" (p. 17), Brown and Gilligan (1992) developed the idea of the voice as a channel of psychic expression embedded in the body, in the experiences and in the realities of relationship, of time, and of place. They explained that voices are grounded in their physicality – their sounds, resonances, vibrations – and that the resounding of our voices is impacted by the physics of relationship and is affected by the relational acoustics surrounding us: whether we feel heard or not heard, how our feelings and thoughts, brought out into the open, are received by others and responded to by ourselves and by other people. Brown and Gilligan (1992) believed that by focusing on, listening to, and tracing the movement of voices in story, it is possible to peel back intertangled layers of the semiotic, anarchic, bodily, and contradictory aspects of the self.

Seeking to delve deeply into the bodily and affective dynamics alive in multiple, complex, and competing voices, Carol Gilligan and her colleagues developed the listening guide, a method that fuses psychoanalytic and relational theory and involves a series of "listenings" through which the researcher "tunes-in" and distinguishes different voices embedded within narratives (Gilligan, Spencer, Weinberg, & Bertsch, 2003). Among qualitative methods, the listening guide distinguishes itself from other existing forms of research in that it provides a set of analytic steps which facilitate listening to stories at multiple levels. This process encourages consideration of not only the content of a narrative, but also the structure, the conglomeration of voices shaping the narrative, the points of view denoted by various voices, the symbolism, patterns of repetition, omissions, etc. By elucidating the complex interplay between body/self configurations in and through a multiplicity of voices, the researcher is challenged to engage with discontinuities, differences, and contradictions that present in stories rather than seeking to assimilate what is nuanced, ambiguous, or indeterminate into "singular interpretations or neatly manicured themes" (Chadwick, 2017, p. 65). Chadwick (2017) argues that "efforts to 'smooth over' ambiguity and discontinuities in qualitative analyses is antithetical to any project to foreground the bodily/fleshy aspects of stories and experience" (p. 70). The "myriad of different types of laughter, repetitions, incoherent utterances and narrative inconsistences and contradictions" (Chadwick, 2017, p. 65) reflects raw, unaffected, and lively elements of human experience and is the very "stuff" of subjectivity (Grosz, 1994). The listening guide pulls together these various elements to support the creation of multiple pathways into relationship with the subject, rather than a single, fixed framework for interpreting human experience. Here, we see the possibility for a more polyphonic dialogue.

Part of the analytic process of the listening guide highlights the fluidity of self-knowledge and fluctuations in expressions of what is personally known, deeply felt, and experienced. The use of "I-poems," in particular, helps in illustrating moments in which an individual's sense of knowing is dense and palpable as well as moments when that sense becomes blurred, troubled, and indeterminate. These poetic devices trace the thick and thin layers of embodied and ontological knowledge. They detect the ebb and flow of subjectivity in the shifting presence of the first person voice carried through individual stories. Focusing on the force and rhythm of pronouns, especially self and/or personal pronouns, is conducive to listening for embodied voices present in narratives. Through the creation of "I-poems," researchers can represent the complex, polylogical aspects of individuals' lived experiences. These poems somehow articulate and give form to the radical indeterminacies and ongoing internal negotiations between what is known, what is felt, what is experienced, and what has been dismissed.

In my research which looks at the impacts of trauma on the embodied sense of self, I discovered that "I-poems" clearly delineate the process of bringing together various, seemingly disparate, aspects of one's self in order to achieve a felt sense of acceptance and wholeness. "I-poems" enabled the representation of specific moments of confusion or struggle along with moments of restitution, resolve, and relief in the midst of the healing journey. For example, consider the following two poems constructed from Kara's (pseudonym) narrative. The first comes from the beginning of the therapeutic process and the second emerges near the end. Here, the first depicts Kara's frustration, her felt sense of helplessness, and her experience of loneliness in the midst of traumatic effects:

I… I, um, I had done a lot of work on my own
I did a lot
I
I
We process
We process everything
I had done so much work
On my own
I…I tried so *hard*
You know
I was doing
But
I
I *wasn't*
Wasn't fixing
I couldn't
I *couldn't*

> Couldn't change
> I had <u>failed</u>
> I was *not* being

The second poem conveys an internal shift toward wholeness and acceptance of the self which Kara experiences having undergone therapy – part of which entailed "[going] to the dark places to receive [her] healing" (Kara, personal communication, April 25, 2016) and part of which was learning to live more freely in the present:

> Even with my warts and my bumps and my imperfections
> I *know*
> I'm <u>wonderful</u>
> I feel <u>good</u>
> I walk in that
> I just long to see
> I *just feel*
> Healing is a wonderful thing

In particular, representing part of Kara's story in poetic form allows the audience to take in diverse elements of her process – both in terms of her therapeutic journey and her attempts to describe that experience. The varied modes of articulation demonstrated by the poem's architectural formulation draw attention to the starts and stops in speech, to where tone underscores the importance of certain words, and to redundancies and repetitions inherent to working out parts of the lived experience. The listening guide offers researchers a way of engaging transcript texts and of foregrounding messy and distinctive ways of telling present in people's narratives regarding embodied experience. By attuning to the micro-details of talk and by capturing the microanalytic interactions of embodied storytelling, we are able to legitimize all the various kinds of subversive and alternative modes of expressing one's bodily and felt sense of experiencing.

Conclusion

I recall an afternoon of sitting in the gathering room at the residential home where I was playing the guitar and singing. I was startled when a resident called out, "Wait! What was that line? Sing it again!"

"Which one?" I asked her.

She furrowed her brow, trying to recall. "Something about a wolf howling."

I obliged and sang the line again: "Like a wolf at midnight howls you'll use your voice in darkest hours to break the silence and the power holding back the others from their glory" (Garrels, 2011).

The resident, now appeased, let out a sigh. "Use your voice to break the silence and the power," she murmured to herself. Then, looking at me, she said, "I want my voice to be real. I want it to mean something. I want to be heard and understood. I want it to break silence and power. I want..." she stopped, thinking, "I guess I just want it to be the sign of my aliveness. I want to be alive and I want to speak life."

The development of embodied methodologies should be centered upon ways of accessing and capturing the living energies flowing in and through the visceral channels of storytelling. Unfortunately, methodological challenges persist due to a continued focus on talk *about* bodily life rather than on talk which stems out of embodied living. Qualitative researchers are attempting to move past discursive strategies for articulating bodies and embodied experience. The bulk of these efforts have incorporated elements of embodied reflexivity, embodied data collection methods, and embodied writing and representation of findings. While important, these strategies appear to have had limited success in producing concrete methodological and analytical tools with which to conduct research about embodied experience. In this chapter, I drew on literary, clinical, and feminist influences in proposing ways to reframe the goals of embodied methodologies. Taking the example of Knut Hamsun's novel *Hunger*, I suggested that phenomenological engagement with the extra-discursive could open up spaces for grappling with ways of telling that fall outside of what might strictly be considered the "narrative frame." In other words, I highlight a naturalistic approach in which all utterances, sounds, and idiosyncrasies are considered within the enactment of sensory mood and bodily dimensions in talk/telling. This directly corresponds to Julia Kristeva's (1984) work regarding semiotic and symbolic modes for the production of meaning and subjectivity. Indeed, Kristeva's theory of the "speaking body" or "subject-in-process" highlights the bodily and fleshy rhythms, the desires and sensual residues that imbue static words with a living energy which both threatens rational, univocal discourse and stimulates meaning-making at the affective, bodily level.

Looking to tap into bodily and semiotic energies, I turned to the methodological strategies developed by Carol Gilligan and colleagues in and through the listening guide. This work is based on the concept and metaphor of *voice* which, in feminist scholarship, is often taken to represent the embodied sense of self. According to Brown and Gilligan (1992), maintaining voice has embodied significance (see also Bourdieu, 1990; Bourdieu & Wacquant, 1992; Merleau-Ponty, 1945/2012). We use our voices as expressed modes of underscoring the realities of our lived experience. Interestingly, our speaking carries with it the polyphony of voice, the complexities of the lived experience, as well as the "ever-changing or moving-through-time quality of the sense of self and the experience of relationship" (Brown & Gilligan, 1992, p. 23).

The listening guide tries to capture the multiple dimensions living and being in psycho-corporeal existence. Through several "listenings," the researcher attunes to the embodied, performative, and breathy qualities of speech in its articulation of lived experience. The use of poetic devices from the listening guide can then be used to map the alternative, subterranean story lines evident in the characterizing ways in which individuals tell their stories.

While the recapturing of voices in qualitative research represents an effort to move embodied methodologies into the realm of qualitative data analysis, this certainly does not represent a definitive solution to the challenges of embodying qualitative methodologies. Rather, it is my hope that suggestions of this ilk can contribute to ongoing conversations and debates about creative and innovative means by which to further develop and envision embodied modes of qualitative analysis.

References

Auster, P. (2003). *Collected prose*. New York, NY: Picador.

Barad, K. (2003). Posthumanist performativity: Toward an understanding of how matter comes to matter. *Signs, 28*, 801–831.

Beckett, S. (1961). *Beckett by the Madeleine/Interviewer: Tom F. Driver*. The Columbia University Forum (Vol. 4), New York, NY: Columbia University.

Boulous-Walker, M. (1998). *Philosophy and the maternal body: Reading silence*. London, UK: Routledge.

Bourdieu, P. (1990). *The logic of practice* (R. Nice, Trans.). Stanford, CA: Stanford University Press.

Bourdieu, P. & Wacquant, L. J. D. (1992). *An invitation to reflexive sociology*. Chicago, IL: University of Chicago Press.

Braun, V. & Clarke, V. (2006). Using thematic analysis in psychology. *Qualitative Research in Psychology, 3*(2), 77–101.

Brown, L. M. & Gilligan, C. (1992). The harmonics of relationship. In L. M. Brown & C. Gilligan, *Meeting at the crossroads: Women's psychology and girls' development* (pp. 18–41). Cambridge, MA: Harvard University Press.

Brown, S., Cromby, J., Harper, D., Johnson, K., & Reavy, P. (2011). Researching 'experience': Embodiment, methodology, process. *Theory and Psychology, 21*(4), 493–515.

Campbell, J. (2008). *The hero with a thousand faces* (3rd ed.). Novato, CA: New World Library.

Chadwick, R. (2017). Embodied methodologies: Challenges, reflections and strategies. *Qualitative Research, 17*(1), 54–74.

Charmaz, K. (2006). *Constructing grounded theory: A practical guide through qualitative analysis*. London, UK: SAGE.

Foucault, M. (1973). *The order of things: An archaeology of the human sciences* (A. Sheridan, Trans.). New York, NY: Vintage (Original work published 1966).

Frank, A. (1995). *The wounded storyteller: Body, illness and ethics*. Chicago, IL: The University of Chicago Press.

Garrels, J. (2011). White owl [Recorded by J. Garrels]. On *Love & war & the sea in between* [CD]. Portland, OR: Small Voice Records.

Gilles, V., Harden, A., Johnson, K., Reavy, P., Strange, V., & Willig, C. (2004). Women's collective constructions of embodied practices through memory work: Cartesian dualism in memories of sweat and pain. *British Journal of Social Psychology, 43*(1), 99–112.

Gilligan, C., Spencer, R., Weinberg, K., & Bertsch, T. (2003). On the listening guide: A voice-centred relational method. In P. M. Camie, J. E. Rhodes, & L. Yardley (Eds.), *Qualitative research in psychology: Expanding perspectives in methodology and design* (pp. 157–172). Washington, DC: American Psychological Association.

Grosz, E. (1989). *Sexual subversions: Three French feminists.* Sydney, AU: Allen and Unwin.

Grosz, E. (1994). *Volatile bodies.* Bloomington, IN: University of Indiana Press.

Grosz, E. (1995). *Space, time, and perversion: Essays on the politics of bodies.* New York, NY: Routledge.

Hamsun, K. (1994). *From the unconscious life of the mind* (M. Skramstad De Forest, Trans.). Louisville, KY: White Fields Press (Original work published 1890).

Hamsun, K. (2008). *Hunger* (R. Bly, Trans.). New York, NY: Farrar, Straus and Giroux (Original work published 1890).

Harris, A. & Guillemin, M. (2012). Qualitative interviewing: A portal into the otherwise explored. *Qualitative Health Research, 22*(5), 689–699.

Heidegger, M. (2001). *Being and time* (J. Macquarrie & E. Robinson, Trans.). London, UK: SCM Press (Original work published 1962).

Hook, D. (2003). Language and the flesh: Psychoanalysis and the limits of discourse. *Pretexts, 21*(1): 43–64.

Inahara, M. (2012). The voice of pain: The semiotic and embodied subjectivity. In S. Gonzalez-Arnal, G. Jagger, & K. Lennon (Eds.), *Embodied selves* (pp. 180–195). Houndsmill (Basingstoke): Palgrave Macmillan.

Kristeva, J. (1984). *Revolution in poetic language.* New York, NY: Columbia University Press.

Maté, G. (2000a). *Scattered minds: A new look at the origins and healing of attention deficit disorder.* Toronto, ON: Vintage Canada.

Maté, G. (2008b). *In the realm of hungry ghosts: Close encounters with addiction.* Berkeley, CA: North Atlantic Books.

McAfee, N. (2004). *Julia Kristeva.* New York, NY: Routledge

McKendy, J. (2006). 'I'm very careful about that': Narrative and agency of men in prison. *Discourse & Society, 17*(4), 473–502.

Merleau-Ponty, M. (2012). *Phenomenology of perception* (D. L. Landes, Trans.). New York, NY: Routledge. (Original work published 1945)

Moore, R. (2013). Reinventing ethnopoetics. *Journal of Folklore Research, 50*(1–3): 13–39.

Moore, S. (1984). *The Stanislavski system: The professional training of an actor* (2nd ed.). New York, NY: Penguin.

O'Dell, T., & Willim, R. (2013). Transcription and the senses. *The Senses and Society, 8*(3): 314–334.

Oliver, D., Serovich, J., & Mason, T. (2005). Constraints and opportunities with interview transcription: Towards reflection in qualitative research. *Social Forces, 84*(2), 1273–1289.

Padfield, D. (2003). *Perfections of pain.* Stockport: Dewi Lewis Publishing.

Sandelowski, M. (2002). Reembodying qualitative inquiry. *Qualitative Health Research, 12*(1), 104–115.

Slavin, J. A. (1994). *The wound, the world, and the word: Narrating consciousness and continuity of Hamsun's authorship.* Louisville, KY: White Fields Press.

Smith, J., Flower, P., & Larkin, M. (2009). *Interpretative phenomenological analysis: Theory, method and research.* London, UK: SAGE.

Storr, A. (1997). *Solitude.* London, UK: HarperCollins.

Van Dijk, T. (1999). Critical discourse analysis and conversation analysis. *Discourse & Society, 10*(4), 459–460.

Wilson, E. (2004). Gut feminism. *Differences: A Journal of Feminist Cultural Studies, 15*(3), 66–94.

Wittgenstein, L. (1986). *Philosophical investigations* (G. Anscombe, Trans.). Oxford, UK: Blackwell Publishers (Original work published 1953).

8 Eating Disorders as Disorders of Embodiment and Identity

Theoretical and Empirical Perspectives

Giovanni Stanghellini, Milena Mancini,
Giovanni Castellini, and Valdo Ricca

Eating disorders (EDs) are severe psychopathological syndromes that likely result from, and are sustained by, sociocultural, psychological, and biological factors (Jacobi, Hayward, de Zwaan, Kraemer, & Agras, 2004; Klump, Bulik, Kaye, Treasure, & Tyson, 2009). According to the last edition of the Diagnostic and Statistical Manual (American Psychiatric Association, 2013) they encompass three main diagnoses: anorexia nervosa, bulimia nervosa, and binge eating disorder.

Longitudinal studies indicate that most patients migrate among diagnoses over time (Fairburn & Harrison, 2003; Milos, Spindler, Schnyder, & Fairburn, 2005) without a substantial change in basic psychopathological features (Castellini et al., 2011; Eddy et al., 2008; Fairburn & Cooper, 2007; Tozzi et al., 2005, see Figure 8.1), suggesting the existence of a common psychopathological core. Indeed, these disorders consist in abnormalities that are shown on two different domains, one behavioral (e.g. dietary restraint, compensatory purging, etc.) and the other experiential (e.g. pathological concerns about body shape and weight).

In the DSM-5 (American Psychiatric Association, 2013), EDs "are characterized by severe disturbances in eating behaviour", but, as a matter of fact, the abnormal eating behavior can be considered the epiphenomenon of different specific cognitive and emotional disturbances (Dalle Grave, 2011; Fairburn, Cooper, & Shafran, 2003; Williamson, White, York-Crowe, & Stewart, 2004), including an overestimation of the shape and weight concerns and of the personal identity (Carter, Blackmore, Sutandar-Pinnock, & Woodside, 2004; Loeb et al., 2007; Ricca et al., 2010). Persons affected by EDs have a tendency to overvalue their body shape and weight (Fairburn & Harrison, 2003) and "tend to define themselves on the basis of their shape and weight and their ability to control them" (Fairburn & Harrison, 2003, p. 407), whereas most people evaluate themselves on the basis of the way they perceive their performance in other domains, e.g. work, relationship, etc.

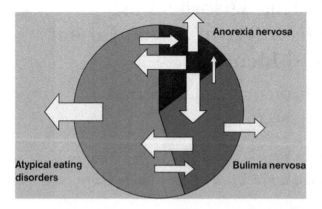

Figure 8.1 Migration of Diagnoses in ED Spectrum (Fairburn, Cooper, & Shafran, 2003).

The present chapter aims to overcome the simplistic behavioral assessment suggested by the DSM and to provide a comprehensive description of the main psychopathological dimensions in the persons affected by EDs – especially focusing on the subjective perception of their own body and their personal identity. The basic idea is that ED patients can be better understood as suffering from a specific disorder of lived corporeality contributing to an anomalous constitution of one's identity. We believe that a comprehensive understanding of these dimensions can improve diagnosis and clinical approach to patients (see Figure 8.2).

Lived Body

Patients with EDs overvalue their body shape and weight. The concept of "lived body" may help to better understand these anomalies. The concept "lived body" is taken from phenomenology and addresses the body experienced from within. Since the beginning of the 20th century, phenomenology has developed a distinction between lived body (*Leib*) and physical body (*Koerper*), or between body-subject and body-object (Husserl, 1912–1915). The lived body is the coenesthetic apprehension of one's own body, the primitive experience of oneself, the basic form of self-awareness, or direct, unmediated experience of one's own body, and not a representation of it mediated by reflection (as the case with "body image") (Merleau-Ponty, 1996; Stanghellini et al., 2014). In other words, this is my own direct experience of my body in the first-person perspective, myself as a spatiotemporal embodied agent in the world (Dillon, 1997; Husserl, 1912–1915; Merleau-Ponty, 1996; Stanghellini, 2009; Stanghellini & Rosfort, 2013; Stanghellini et al., 2014). The physical body or body object is the body thematically investigated from without,

Figure 8.2 Abnormal Eating Behavior as Epiphenomenon of Abnormal Body Experience and Identity Constitution.

as for example by the natural sciences such as anatomy and physiology, in the third-person perspective (Husserl, 1912–1915; Merleau-Ponty, 1996; Stanghellini, Castellini, Brogna, Faravelli, & Ricca, 2012). The physical body refers to the body that can be manipulated, e.g. by surgery. The lived body turns into a physical, objective body whenever we become aware of it in a disturbing way. Whenever one's movement is somehow impeded or disrupted, then the lived body is thrown back on itself, materialized or "corporealized". It becomes an object for oneself.

The unmediated and pre-reflexive experience of my body is the implicit background of my day-to-day experiences against which I develop a coherent sense of self as a unified, bounded entity, naturally immersed in a social world of meaningful others. The lived body is the center of three main dimensions of experience (Stanghellini, 2009):

1   *The experience of myself, and especially of the most primitive form of self-awareness.* I experience myself as the perspectival origin of my experiences (i.e. perceptions or emotions), actions, and thoughts. This primordial access to myself, or primitive form of egocentricity, must be distinguished from any explicit and thematic form of I-awareness, since it is tacit and implicit, although experientially present. This

primitive self-awareness is not a conceptual or linguistic representation of oneself, but a primordial contact with oneself or self-affection in which who feels and who is felt are just one thing. Last but not least, it must be also distinguished from a kind of object-awareness, since it is does not arise from an objectifying or observational perception of oneself. Henry (1973) uses the term "ipseity" to express this basic or minimal form of self-awareness. Thus, ipseity is the implicit, pre-reflexive, immediate, nonconceptual, non-objectifying, and non-observational sense of existing as a subject of awareness. It is prior to, and a condition of, all other experience. Two basic and closely related aspects of minimal self-awareness are self-ownership and self-agency. Self-ownership is the pre-reflexive sense that I am the one who is undergoing an experience. Self-agency is the pre-reflexive sense that I am the one who is initiating an action. The immediate awareness of the subjectivity of my experience or action involves that these are in some sense owned and generated by myself. These are the basic components of the experienced differentiation between self and nonself, myself and the object I perceive, and my representation of that object and the object itself. This basic form of self-experience is rooted in one's bodily experience and its situatedness among worldly objects and other people. Ipseity is indiscernible from "inhabiting" one's own world, i.e. being engaged and feeling attuned to one's own environment. It is the lived body that provides this engagement and attunement. Being conscious is dwelling in (*être-à*) the world through one's own lived body (Merleau-Ponty, 1996).

2   *Object-experience and meaning-bestowing.* The power of organizing experience is grounded in motility and perception. A modification in one's lived body implies a modification in the perception of the external world. To Husserl (1912–1915), the shape of material things, just as they stand in front of me in an intuitive way, depends on my configuration, on the configuration of myself as an experiencing embodied subject. By means of the integrity of kinesthesia – the sense of the position and movement of voluntary muscles – my own body is the constant reference of my orientation in the perceptive field. The perceived object gives itself through the integration of a series of prospective appearances. The lived body is not only the perspectival origin of my perceptions and the locus of their integration, it is the means by which I own the world, insomuch as it structures and organizes the chances of participating in the field of experience. The lived body perceives worldly objects as parts of a situation in which it is engaged, of a project to which it is committed, so that its actions are responses to situations rather than reactions to stimuli. The body seeks understanding from the things with which it interacts; the lived body is silently at work whatever I do. I understand my environment as I inhabit it, and the meaningful organization of the field of experience

is possible because the active and receptive potentials of my own body are constantly projected into it (Sheets-Johnstone, 1999). Knowledge is enacted (Varela, Thompson, & Rosch, 1991) or action-specific, and perception is always tangled up with specific possibilities of action (Clark, 1997). Perception is constantly geared up to tracing possibilities for action; these possibilities for action are what we called "meaning", since the meaning of an object is how we put it at use. The basic kind of knowledge I have of objects I encounter in the world is not a kind of mere theoretical cognition, but rather a kind of concern which manipulates things and "puts them to use" (Heidegger, 1962). Objects appear to my embodied self as something *in-order-to*, as *equipment*, "ready to hand", for manipulating reality and so for cutting, sewing, writing, etc. I literally grasp the meaning of one thing, since this meaning is exactly the specific "manipulability" (*Handlichkeit*) of one thing.

3   *The experience of other people, i.e. intersubjectivity.* The lived body is also at the center of intersubjectivity, setting the stage for the immediate, pre-reflexive perceptual linkage between my own and the other's body (*intercorporeality*) through which I recognize another being as an alter ego and make sense of his actions. From the angle of intercorporeality, intersubjectivity is a communion of flesh and not a relationship between separate persons. Intercorporeality means the transfer of the corporeal schema, the primary bond of perception by which I recognize others as being similar to myself. This phenomenon is the phenomenal basis of syncretic sociability, i.e. of pathic identification with the other – in a word, of intersubjectivity (Dillon, 1997). Intercorporeality is never fully evident, but it is the bearing support of all interaction connected with behavior, already active and present ahead of any explicit communication. The perceptive bond between myself and another person is based on my possibility to identify with the other person's body by means of a primary perceptive tie. Developmental psychologists support the hypothesis that proprioception is involved in understanding other persons through body-to-body attunement (Stern, 2000).

Lived Body-for-Others

In addition to the two dimensions of corporeality (body-subject and body-object) discussed before, Sartre (1943/1992) emphasized that one can apprehend one's own body also from another vantage point, i.e. as one's own body when it is looked at by another person. When I become aware that I am, or better my own body is, looked at by another person, I realize that my body can be an object for that person. Sartre calls this the "lived body-for-others". With the appearance of the Other's look, writes Sartre, I experience the revelation of my being-as-object. The upshot of this is a feeling of having my being outside, the feeling of being an object (Stanghellini, 2017). Thus, one's identity becomes reified by the Other's gaze and reduced to the external appearance of one's own body. When this way of apprehending one's body crystallizes, and so becomes the only way to experience one's own body, one cannot have an experience of one's own body from within, but only through the gaze of the Other. The body, so to say, takes the shape that the Others' gaze imposes upon it. This, on the one hand, makes one feel shame or disgust for one's own body, but on the other hand, helps one recover a sense of "unity" and "condensation" – as it is the case with people suffering from EDs (Stanghellini & Mancini, in press; Stanghellini et al., 2012).

Persons affected by, or vulnerable to, EDs often report their difficulties in perceiving their emotions and that they do not "feel" themselves (Goodsitt, 1997; Malson, 1999; Piran, 2001; Sands, 1991). They have difficulties in feeling their own body in the first-person perspective and to have a stable and continuous sense of themselves as embodied agents.

This entails a fleeting feeling of selfhood and an evanescent sense of identity. Indeed, feeling oneself is a basic requirement for achieving an identity and a stable sense of one's self (Stanghellini et al., 2012). The experience of not feeling one's own body and emotions involves the whole sense of identity. Indeed, we construe our personal identity on the basis of our feelings, that is, of what we like or dislike. For these persons, since they can hardly feel themselves and their feelings are discontinuous over time, identity is no longer a real psychic structure that persists beyond the flow of time and circumstances. They also feel extraneous from their own bodies and attempt to regain a sense of bodily self through starvation (Stanghellini, 2017). In other words, the basic phenomenon seems to be that these people experience own body first and foremost as an object being looked at by another, rather than coenesthetically or from a first-person perspective. Since they cannot have an experience of their body from within, they need to apprehend their body from without through the gaze of the Other. What they seem lack is the coenesthetic apprehension of their own body as the more primitive and basic form of self-awareness. As a consequence of that, the way one feels looked at by other persons is the only possibility to feel oneself and define one's identity.

Identity

In persons with EDs, the disturbance of the experience of one's own body is interconnected with the process of shaping one's personal identity. The body shapes identity in the course of social situations. Sensations of attraction/repulsion, desirability/disgust, as well as all emotions as embodied phenomena (Stanghellini & Rosfort, 2013) are the basis to establish what I like and who I am.

Research in this area has provided two main constructs pertaining to disorders of identity as maintaining factors in EDs: severe clinical perfectionism and core low self-esteem (Murphy, Straebler, Cooper, & Fairburn, 2010). Clinical perfectionism is a system for self-evaluation in which self-worth is judged largely on the basis of striving to achieve demanding goals and success at meeting them (Shafran, Cooper, & Fairburn, 2002). The patient's perfectionist standards apply to her attempts to control eating, shape, and weight, as well as other aspects of her life (e.g. performance at work or sport).

The psychodynamic perspective underscores impairments in overall identity development and the failure to establish multiple and diverse domains of self-definition. In particular, Bruch (1979) suggested that the dissatisfaction and preoccupation with body image that characterizes persons with EDs reflect a maladaptive "search for selfhood and a self-respecting identity" (Bruch, 1979, p. 255). The basis for the development of the sense of a core subjective self is represented for Stern (2000) by the interaction between mother and infant in sharing affective states and experiences.

We assume that identity impairments are related to the alienation from one's own body and the difficulties to experience one's own emotions as stable and reliable ways to establish a representation of oneself. Feeling extraneous from oneself is the core phenomenon in people with EDs, from which several typical although secondary features derive, namely the need to feel oneself only through the gaze of the others, through objective measures, and through self-starvation (see Figure 8.3).

The coenesthetic apprehension of one's own body is the more primitive and basic form of self-awareness or core Self. Indeed, feeling oneself is a basic requirement to achieve a stable sense of one's Self and the basic condition of possibility for developing a narrative apprehension of oneself or autobiographical Self. Patients with EDs often report their difficulties in feeling themselves, especially their own body, and in perceiving their emotions. Therefore, there is the need to resort to one's own body weight as a viable source of definition of the Self. According to Nordbø, Espeset, Gulliksen, Skårderud, and Holte (2006), persons with anorexia nervosa may explain their behavior as a tool for achieving a new identity since changing one's body is a tool to become another (Skårderud, 2007a,b). They want to change, and changing one's body serves as a concrete and symbolic tool for such ambition. Thus, shaping oneself is a "concretized metaphor", establishing equivalence between a psychic reality (identity) and a physical one (one's body shape). The shaping of one's own body becomes a substitute for the construction of one's own identity: body building is the replacement for identity *Bildung* (Stanghellini, 2005). For persons affected by EDs identity is a task, not a taken for granted datum (Stanghellini, 2017; Stanghellini & Mancini, in press). They have the necessity to perpetually construct themselves. This construction is based on the way they feel seen and judged by other persons. In this perspective, they

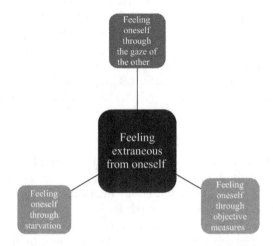

Figure 8.3 A Tentative Pathogenetic Model.

seem to share with the late-modern mind an aesthetic or pornographic conceptualization of the Self based on seeing and been seen and on the approval of Others. Another feature ED patients share with late modernity is the obsession with measures and numbers. These persons are constantly engaged in a sort of conceptual and mathematical process for establishing their own identity (Stanghellini & Mancini, in press).

The Idea Questionnaire

This model is supported by the data we collected by a self-reported questionnaire called IDEA (IDentity and EAting disorders) (see Table 8.1). It allows to identify different phenotypes that express a gradient of vulnerability to EDs along a continuum, rising from high-risk nonclinical subjects toward the clinical population of ED patients. In fact, IDEA is a tool able to identify a vulnerability in persons with abnormal eating patterns over threshold (Stanghellini et al., 2012). The IDEA questionnaire is available in English and Italian and is being adapted and translated into several languages, including Chinese and Spanish.

The basic questions and the clinical characteristics upon which IDEA is built are reported in Table 8.2. The questionnaire was developed focusing on the following phenomenal areas, derived from unstructured interviews of patients in a clinical setting: (1) feeling oneself through the gaze of the other, (2) defining oneself through the evaluation of the other, (3) feeling oneself through objective measures, (4) feeling extraneous from one's own body, (5) feeling oneself through starvation, (6) defining one's identity through one's own body, and (7) feeling oneself through physical activity and fatigue. Theoretically, the questionnaire assumed that most

Table 8.1 The Idea Questionnaire

	Not at all (0)	Just a little (1)	Enough (2)	Much (3)	Very much (4)
1 For me it's very important to see myself through the eyes of the others.	0	1	2	3	4
2 Eating according to my own rules is the only way to feel myself.	0	1	2	3	
3 If I could not eat the way I want, I would not be myself anymore.	0	1	2	3	4
4 Sometimes, the emotions I feel are extraneous to me and scare me.	0	1	2	3	4
5 If my measures remain the same over time, I feel that I am myself, if not I feel I am getting lost.	0	1	2	3	4
6 I see myself fuzzy/hazy, as if I had no boundaries.	0	1	2	3	4
7 Sometimes I focalize myself through the gaze of the others.	0	1	2	3	4
8 Seeing myself from their point of view makes me feel very anxious.	0	1	2	3	4
9 In all this confusion, knowing that my weight is under control reassures me a little bit.	0	1	2	3	4
10 Only if I have my weight under control does being looked at by the others make me feel alright.	0	1	2	3	4
11 The way I feel depends on the way I feel looked at by the others.	0	1	2	3	4
12 The flesh is unimportant; it doesn't let me feel my bones.	0	1	2	3	4
13 I am dependent on the evaluation of the others.	0	1	2	3	4
14 I see myself out of focus, I don't feel myself.	0	1	2	3	4
15 Knowing what the others think of me calms me down.	0	1	2	3	4
16 Even if I think that the way the others evaluate me is wrong, I can't do without it.	0	1	2	3	4
17 If I follow your dietary prescriptions, I cannot recognize myself when I look at myself in the mirror; this does not happen if I do things in my own way.	0	1	2	3	4

(Continued)

	Not at all (0)	*Just a little (1)*	*Enough (2)*	*Much (3)*	*Very much (4)*
18 I can't stand not to know what the others think of me.	0	1	2	3	4
19 Changing my own eating habits scares me to death, as does any other change in my life.	0	1	2	3	4
20 The fear of change is an emotion that I can't tolerate.	0	1	2	3	4
21 Having control of my weight means having control of the possible changes that happen in my body.	0	1	2	3	4
22 Having my weight under control makes me feel in control of my emotional states.	0	1	2	3	4
23 When I meet someone I can't stay without knowing what he thinks of me.	0	1	2	3	4

pathological eating behaviors and features are a consequence of the severity of abnormal bodily experiences and identity disorders. To validate the questionnaire, we administered it to a sample of women with EDs. Factor analyses showed the presence of four main dimensions, namely (1) feeling oneself through the gaze of the other and defining oneself through the evaluation of the other, (2) feeling oneself through objective measures, (3) feeling extraneous from one's own body, and (4) feeling oneself through starvation. These subscales showed a different pattern of association with the EDs features. Feeling oneself through the gaze of the other and defining oneself through the evaluation of the other were associated with overvalued thoughts regarding body shape. A measure of alienation from one's own body and emotions, and feeling extraneous from one's own body significantly correlated with concerns about weight and body shape. Finally, feeling oneself through objective measures and feeling oneself through starvation were associated with overvalued thoughts regarding weight and eating concerns and with dietary restriction, respectively. In line with these results and with their theoretical framework, some characteristic abnormal eating patterns, such as starvation and the fixated checking of objective measures, might be interpreted as an alternative coping strategy aimed to feel oneself for those patients who are unable to feel themselves coenesthetically. These results were confirmed for patients reporting anorexia nervosa, bulimia nervosa, and binge eating disorder (Stanghellini et al., 2012). Moreover, it was also applied beyond the boundaries of the DSM diagnostic categories, and abnormal bodily experiences were observed not just for "over-threshold" ED patients. First of all, it was tested in a large population of university students who did not suffer from EDs. In this population, IDEA appeared to be able to identify vulnerability in subjects without full-blown EDs but with abnormal eating patterns. Moreover, the questionnaire provided a numerical threshold to discriminate clinical vs. nonclinical populations. Indeed, in people who develop clinically relevant eating behavior, extraneousness from one's own body is a phenomenon that is significantly more manifest and penetrant than in people who display over-threshold, but non-full-blown abnormal eating patterns. This could represent the first step to demonstrate that IDEA is able to identify candidate experiential intermediate phenotypes that express a gradient of vulnerability from healthy to clinical persons with EDs (Stanghellini et al., 2014). Another study proposes a model of interactions between genetic vulnerability – represented by fat mass and obesity-associated (FTO) gene – and stable psychopathological traits, such as bodily disorders and emotion dysregulation for ED patients. The distribution of a polymorphism of the FTO (rs9939609 T>A) was evaluated in a series of 250 ED patients and in a group of 119 healthy control subjects. Clinical data were collected through a face-to-face interview and several self-reported questionnaires were applied, including the Emotional Eating Scale and the IDEA questionnaire for bodily disorders and self-identity. The A-allele was associated with an increased vulnerability to EDs. The presence of the A-allele was associated with binge eating behavior, higher emotional eating, and higher IDEA scores. Finally, the FTO rs9939609 SNP was found to influence the relationship between these variables, as an association between disorder of corporeality and emotional eating was found only in A-allele carriers. A-allele seems to represent a potential additive risk factor for ED persons with bodily disorders to develop emotional eating and binge eating behavior (Castellini et al., 2017).

Finally, the questionnaire was applied to morbidly obese patients, which is a high-risk population for the development of ED behaviors. Our results confirmed the hypothesis that abnormal bodily experiences are a core feature not just for "over-threshold" ED patients but also for a high-risk population such as morbidly obese patients (Castellini et al., 2015).

The vulnerability to ED behaviors, such as binge eating, appeared to be associated with abnormal bodily experiences in a dimensional pattern. Moreover, abnormal bodily experiences measured by IDEA represent the psychological underpinning of the relationship between binge eating behaviors and impulsivity, which has been frequently associated with such behaviors. A mediation model clarified that not impulsivity in itself, but the presence of impulsivity in persons affected by abnormal bodily experiences, may lead to ED psychopathology and abnormal eating behaviors. We concluded that the disturbance in lived corporeality may represent the core vulnerability trait that is one of the psychological characteristics underlying the association between personality traits such as impulsivity and the development of ED's features.

Table 8.2 Key Questions

Questions	Clinical characteristics
✓Are behaviors psychopathologically specific?	✓Alienation from one's own body and from one's own emotions.
✓Are abnormal eating behaviors typically subtended by abnormal experiences?	✓Disgust for own body.
	✓Shame.
✓Are abnormal eating behaviors just symptoms in different psychopathological domains?	✓Exaggerated concern to take responsibility for the way one appears to the others.
✓Are there many kinds of EDs or just one?	✓Capacity to feel oneself only through the look of the others.
✓Do ED(s) share one (or more) core phenomena?	✓Capacity to feel oneself only through objective measures.
✓Do ED(s) (totally or in part) overlap with other psychopathological syndromes?	✓Capacity to feel oneself only through self-starvation.

Conclusion

There are theoretical as well as clinical reasons to consider abnormal eating behaviors as epiphenomena of a more profound disorder of lived corpo- reality and self-identity. Especially one dimension – the lived body-for- others as described by J.-P. Sartre – seems to represent the core concept to grasp the anomalies of lived corporeality in ED patients. Until recently, a valid and reliable methodology was lacking to develop and empirically support this hypothesis. IDEA represents a new, multidimensional, easy- to-perform instrument for assessing the abnormal experiences and atti- tudes of persons affected by EDs.

The anomalous phenomena explored and measured by IDEA are mainly two: abnormal attitudes toward one's own corporeality, and difficulties in the definition of one's own identity. We suggest that specific abnormalities in lived corporeality, namely experiencing one's own body first and fore- most as an object being looked at by another (rather than coenesthetically and from a first-person perspective), and of personal identity, namely de- fining one's own self largely in terms of the way one feels looked at by the others and through one's ability to control one's shape and weight (rather than through other kinds of performance), are supposedly core features of ED psychopathology. Future longitudinal research should establish if these abnormalities are permanent core vulnerability traits underlying acute symptoms in clinical populations, and the diachronic distribution of each of these features along the pathogenetic steps toward full-blown ED symptoms. Also, large-scale studies should assess the presence of these features in the general population, and especially their correlation with social, ethnic, and cultural features. Last but not least, translational studies should look for their correlation with biological markers in order to ex- plore if they can be candidate endo-phenotypes.

References

American Psychiatric Association. (2013). *Diagnostic and statistical manual of mental disorders: DSM-5* (5th ed.). Arlington, VA: American Psychiatric Association.

Bruch, H. (1979). Developmental deviations in anorexia nervosa. *Israel Annals of Psychiatry & Related Disciplines, 17*, 255–261.

Carter, J. C., Blackmore, E., Sutandar-Pinnock, K., & Woodside, D. B. (2004). Relapse in anorexia nervosa: A survival analysis. *Psychological Medicine, 34*(4), 671–679.

Castellini. G., Franzago, M., Bagnoli, S., Lelli L., Balsamo, M., & Mancini, M. et al. (2017). Fat mass and obesity-associated gene (FTO) is associated to eating disorders susceptibility and moderates the expression of psychopathological traits. *PloS One, 12*(3), doi:10.1371/journal.pone.0173560

Castellini, G., Lo Sauro, C., Mannucci, E., Ravaldi, C., Rotella, C. M., Faravelli, C., & Ricca, V. (2011). Diagnostic crossover and outcome predictors in eating disorders according to DSM-IV and DSM-V proposed criteria: a 6-year follow-up study. *Psychosomatic Medicine, 73*(3), 270–279.

Castellini, G., Stanghellini, G., Godini, L., Lucchese, M., Trisolini, F., & Ricca, V. (2015). Abnormal bodily experiences mediate the relationship between impulsivity and binge eating in overweight subjects seeking for bariatric surgery. *Psychotherapy and Psychosomatics, 84*(2), 124–126.

Clark, A. (1997). *Being there. Putting brain, body, and world together again.* Cambridge, MA: MIT Press.

Dalle Grave, R. (2011). Eating disorders: Progress and challenges. *European Journal of Internal Medicine, 22*(2), 153–160.

Dillon, M. C. (1997). *Merleau-Ponty's ontology.* Evanston, IL: Northwestern University Press.

Eddy, K. T., Dorer, D. J., Franko, D. L., Tahilani, K., Thompson-Brenner, H., & Herzog, D. B. (2008). Diagnostic crossover in anorexia nervosa and bulimia nervosa: Implications for DSM-V. *American Journal of Psychiatry, 165*(2), 245–250.

Fairburn, C. G. & Cooper, Z. (2007). Thinking afresh about the classification of eating disorders. *International Journal of Eating Disorders, 40*(S3). doi:10.1002/eat.20460

Fairburn, C. G. & Harrison, P. J. (2003). Eating Disorders. *The Lancet, 361*(9355), 407–416.

Fairburn C. G., Cooper, Z., & Shafran, R. (2003). Cognitive behavior therapy for eating disorders: a 'transdiagnostic' theory and treatment. *Behaviour Research and Therapy, 41*(5), 509–528.

Goodsitt, A. (1997). *Eating disorders: A self-psychological perspective.* D. Garner, & P. Garfinkel (Ed.). New York, NY: Guilford Press, 205–228.

Heidegger, M. (1962). *Being and time* (J. Macquarrie, Trans.). New York, NY: Harper and Row.

Henry, M. (1973). *The essence of manifestation.* Den Haag, Netherlands: Martinus Nijhoff.

Husserl, E. (1912/1915). *Ideen zu einer reinen Phaenomenologie und phaenomenologische Philosophie. II. Phaenomenologische Untersuchungen zur Konstitution.* Den Haag, Netherlands: Martinus Nijhoff.

Jacobi, C., Hayward, C., de Zwaan, M., Kraemer, H. C., & Agras, W. S. (2004). Coming to terms with risk factors for eating disorders: application of risk terminology and suggestions for a general taxonomy. *Psychological bulletin, 130*(1), 19.

Klump, K. L., Bulik, C. M., Kaye, W. H., Treasure, J., & Tyson, E. (2009). Academy for eating disorders position paper: Eating disorders are serious mental illnesses. *International Journal of Eating Disorders, 42*(2), 97–103.

Loeb, K. L., Walsh, B. T., Lock, J., Le Grange, D., Jones, J., & Marcus, S. U. E., et al. (2007). Open trial of family-based treatment for full and partial anorexia nervosa in adolescence: Evidence of successful dissemination. *Journal of the American Academy of Child & Adolescent Psychiatry, 46*(7), 792–800.

Malson, H. (1999). Women under erasure: Anorexic bodies in postmodern context. *Journal Of Community and Applied Social Psychology,* 9(2), 137–153.

Merleau-Ponty, M. (1996). *Phenomenology of perception* (C. Smith, Trans.) New York, NY: Humanities Press.

Milos, G., Spindler, A., Schnyder, U., & Fairburn, C. G. (2005). Instability of eating disorder diagnoses: prospective study. *The British Journal of Psychiatry, 187*(6), 573–578.

Murphy, R., Straebler, S., Cooper, Z., & Fairburn, C. G. (2010). Cognitive behavioral therapy for eating disorders. *Psychiatric Clinics of North America, 33*(3), 611–627.

Nordbø, R. H., Espeset, E., Gulliksen, K. S., Skårderud, F., & Holte, A. (2006). The meaning of self-starvation: Qualitative study of patients' perception of anorexia nervosa. *International Journal of Eating Disorders, 39*(7), 556–564.

Piran, N. (2001). V. Reinhabiting the body. *Feminism & Psychology,* 11(2), 172–176.

Ricca, V., Castellini, G., Lo Sauro, C., Mannucci, E., Ravaldi, C., Rotella, F., & Faravelli, C. (2010). Cognitive-behavioral therapy for threshold and subthreshold anorexia nervosa: A three-year follow-up study. *Psychotherapy and Psychosomatics, 79*(4), 238–248.

Sands, S. (1991). Bulimia, dissociation, and empathy: A self-psychological view. In Earlier versions of the chapter were presented at the 12th Annual Conference on the Psychology of the Self, San Francisco, CA, Oct 12–15, 1989, and at the Division 39 (Psychoanalysis) American Psychological Association meeting, New York, NY: Apr 5–8, 1990. New York, NY: Guilford Press.

Sartre, J. P. (1992). *Being and nothingness.* New York, NY: Washington Square Press. (Original work published 1943).

Shafran, R., Cooper, Z., & Fairburn, C. G. (2002). Clinical perfectionism: A cognitive–behavioural analysis. *Behaviour Research and Therapy, 40*(7), 773–791.

Sheets-Johnstone, M. (1999). *The primacy of movement.* Amsterdam, Netherlands: John Benjamins.

Skårderud, F. (2007a). Eating one's words, Part I: Concretised metaphors' and reflective function in anorexia nervosa—An Interview Study. *European Eating Disorders Review, 15*(3), 163–174.

Skårderud, F. (2007b). Eating one's words, part II: The embodied mind and reflective function in anorexia nervosa—theory. *European Eating Disorders Review,* 15(4), 243–252.

Stanghellini, G. (2005). For an anthropology of eating disorders. A pornographic vision of the self. *Eating and Weight Disorders-Studies on Anorexia, Bulimia and Obesity,* 10(2), 21–27.

Stanghellini, G. (2009). Embodiment and schizophrenia. *World Psychiatry, 8*(1), 56–59.

Stanghellini, G. (2017). *Lost in dialogue.* Oxford, England: Oxford University Press.

Stanghellini, G., Castellini, G., Brogna, P., Faravelli, C., & Ricca, V. (2012). Identity and eating disorders (IDEA): a questionnaire evaluating identity and embodiment in eating disorder patients. *Psychopathology, 45*(3), 147–158.

Stanghellini, G. & Mancini, M. (in press). *The therapeutic interview. Emotions, values, and the life-world.* Cambridge, MA: Cambridge University Press.

Stanghellini G. & Rosfort R. (2013). *Emotions and personhood. Exploring fragility. Making sense of vulnerability.* Oxford, England: Oxford University Press.

Stanghellini, G., Trisolini, F., Castellini, G., Ambrosini, A., Faravelli, C., & Ricca, V. (2014). Is feeling extraneous from one's own body a core vulnerability feature in eating disorders? *Psychopathology, 48*(1), 18–24.

Stern, D. N. (2000). *The interpersonal world of the infant.* New York, NY: Basic Books.

Tozzi, F., Thornton, L. M., & Klump, et al. (2005). Symptom fluctuation in eating disorders: correlates of diagnostic crossover. *American Journal of Psychiatry, 162*(4), 732–740.

Varela, F., Thompson, E., & Rosch, E. (1991). *The embodied mind.* Cambridge, MA: MIT Press.

Williamson, D. A., White, M. A., York-Crowe, E., & Stewart, T. M. (2004). Cognitive-behavioral theories of eating disorders. *Behavior Modification, 28*(6), 711–738.

Stanghellini et al. (2012). IDEA: a questionnaire evaluating identity and embodiment in ED patients. *Psychopathology, 45*(3), 147–158.	Validation of IDEA questionnaire (population: 147 ED patients and 187 healthy controls). The questionnaire showed good test-retest reliability and internal consistency; IDEA scores were specifically associated with ED psychopathology. Four factors were extracted: "feeling oneself only through the gaze of the other and defining oneself only through the evaluation of the other", "feeling oneself only through objective measures", "feeling extraneous from one's own body", and "feeling oneself through starvation".
Stanghellini et al. (2014). Is feeling extraneous from one's own body a core vulnerability feature in eating disorders? *Psychopathology, 48*(1), 18–24	IDEA identified a vulnerability to EDs in subjects with abnormal eating patterns in the general population (253 university students) and recognized the presence of a significant discomfort related to the body (measured with Body Uneasiness Test). Feeling extraneous from one's own body is the experience that discriminates most between clinical and nonclinical subjects.
Castellini et al. (2015). Abnormal bodily experiences mediate the relationship between impulsivity and binge eating in overweight subjects seeking for bariatric surgery. *Psychotherapy and psychosomatics, 84*(2), 124–126.	Abnormal bodily experiences (measured with IDEA) are a core feature not just for "over-threshold" ED patients (140 patients) but also for a high-risk population such as morbidly obese patients (204 patients). IDEA scores express a gradient of vulnerability to ED psychopathology and behaviors from high-risk subjects (bariatric surgery subjects) up to the clinical groups. Not impulsivity in itself, but the presence of impulsivity in persons affected by abnormal bodily experiences may lead to ED psychopathology and abnormal eating behaviors. The disturbance in the lived corporeality may represent a core vulnerability trait underlying the association between personality traits (impulsivity) and the development of ED features.
Giovanni Castellini et al. (2017). Fat mass and obesity-associated gene (FTO) is associated to ED's susceptibility and moderates the expression of psychopathological traits.	We propose a model of interactions between genetic vulnerability – represented by fat mass and obesity-associated (FTO) gene – and stable psychopathological traits, such as bodily disorders and emotion dysregulation for ED patients (250 ED patients and 119 healthy controls). The *A*-allele was associated with an increased vulnerability to EDs (*AA+AT* genotypes frequency 72.8% in EDs vs. 52.9% in controls). The presence of the *A*-allele was associated with binge eating behavior, higher emotional eating, and higher IDEA scores. Finally, the *FTO* rs9939609 SNP was found to influence the relationship between these variables, as an association between disorder of corporeality and emotional eating was found only in *A*-allele carriers.
	A-allele seems to represent a potential additive risk factor for EDs persons, with bodily disorders to develop emotional eating and binge eating behaviors.

Part II

Embodiment and Eating Disorder Research

Empirical research exploring the body as it relates to the prevention and treatment of eating disorders is a relatively new, and consequently there is ample room for exploration of how these areas intersect. The focus of this section of the book is to make visible recent research which is both academically rigorous and innovative in its findings to forge ahead the existing knowledge in this field. The chapters in this section include research addressing sexuality and spirituality, embodiment and the parent-child relationship, the evaluation of a school-based intervention, age, aging bodies, embodiment in recovering from eating disorders, as well as the neuroscience of eating disorders and embodiment. Together, these chapters contribute to our evidence base related to embodiment and eating disorders.

9 Sexuality, Disordered Eating, and Embodiment

Kelsey Siemens and Janelle L. Kwee

Women's corporeality, size, appearance, and sexuality have been sites of oppression for many women. Not surprisingly, embodied sexuality is often limited for women who struggle with eating disorders; there is a relationship between experiencing the self through the body and experiencing sexual subjectivity. Where women's bodies are experienced as sites of oppression and objects, they are more likely to experience their bodies as sources of shame rather than as sources of pleasure and joy. In this chapter, the relationship between embodied sexuality, disordered eating, and embodiment is discussed, highlighting the possibility for women to experience their bodies as sources of pain as well as of joy and freedom. This chapter begins with objectification theory as a framework for understanding sociocultural factors that impact women's health and embodiment. Specifically, we discuss contributing factors and consequences of sexual objectification. This section is followed by a discussion of sexual embodiment and reclaiming one's body as a source of agency, pleasure, joy, and freedom.

Objectification and Sexualization

Oppression of women's bodies in Western culture is ubiquitous. Objectification theory (Fredrickson & Roberts, 1997) can provide a helpful framework to understand the ways in which sociocultural factors impact women's overall health, physically, sexually, mentally, emotionally, and relationally (Szymanski, Moffitt, & Carr, 2011). Sexualization, objectification, and violence toward women's bodies manifest on both macro- and microlevels. Objectification occurs when a person is treated as an object (a body or an assortment of body parts) that is valued primarily "for its use to (or consumption by) others" (Fredrickson & Roberts, 1997, p. 174). Sexual objectification, or sexualization, then, is when a person is treated as a *sexual* object; this includes, but is not limited to, sexualized media content, being the target of body appraisal or gaze, and unwanted sexual encroachments (Tylka & Kroon Van Diest, 2015). According to

The APA Task Force on the Sexualization of Girls (2007), sexualization occurs when

1   One's value comes solely from their sexual appeal/behavior;
2   One is held to a narrowly defined standard of beauty that is equated with being "sexy";
3   A person is objectified;
4   And/or sexuality is inappropriately imposed on a person.

Here, sexualization is differentiated from healthful, mutually pleasurable, bonding, respectful, and consenting sexual relationships and/or activity. Objectification theorists assert that sexual objectification potentially contributes to the development of eating disorders, sexual dysfunction, and depression, all of which disproportionately impact women (Fredrickson & Roberts, 1997; Szymanski, Moffitt, & Carr, 2011). Sexualization of girls and women occurs in varying forms across the life span. According to Smolak and Murnen (2011), even infants and preschoolers are "in training" to become sexual objects. The internalization of sexualization, or self-objectification, occurs when the "objectifying gaze is turned inward, such that women view themselves through the perspective of an observer and engage in chronic self-surveillance" (Calogero, 2013, p. 312). Self-objectification, therefore, is a process in which one becomes disembodied, shifting from active subject to passive object. Consequently, sexual objectification subordinates, disempowers, and oppresses women; it reinforces harmful, patriarchal gender roles that limit and constrain sexual expression, choice, and pleasure (Smolak & Murnen, 2011).

Sexual Objectification: Contributing Factors

In the following section, we address contributing factors to sexual objectification, including media and pornography, and gender roles and gender-based violence.

   Media and pornography. The APA Task Force on the Sexualization of Girls (2007) cites the media as both reflecting and contributing to the continued sexualization and objectification of girls and women in mainstream culture. Targeting children and adults alike, television programs, music videos, music lyrics, movies, magazines, sports media, video/computer games, and even cartoons and animation all reinforce a narrow and often unattainable standard of beauty. Through these mediums, girls and women's values are implied to be predicated by one's ability to adhere to the "beauty ideal" (APA, 2007). Consistent exposure to sexualized media content appears to have a negative impact on girls and women's self-concept and embodiment. In a review of the empirical research

(1999–2015) on the impact of sexualization in the media, Ward (2016) found that daily exposure to such content is directly related to increased self-objectification, body dissatisfactions, and greater tolerance of sexual violence toward women. Given estimations that, on average, Americans spend over 15 hours consuming both traditional and digital media each day (Short, 2013), the influence of media on cultural ethos cannot be underestimated.

Pornography, another form of media, creates, illuminates, and perpetuates dominant cultural narratives about bodies, power, and sexuality. Widely consumed, on average, boys will access pornographic websites by age 11, and up to 50% of young men report viewing porn on a weekly basis (Dines, 2010; Tylka & Kroon Van Diest, 2015). Pornography is a multibillion-dollar industry, generating more profit in the United States than football, basketball, and baseball combined (Tylka & Kroon Van Diest, 2015).

At best, mainstream pornography depicts a very narrow image of women's bodies; in pornography, thin or curvaceously thin women are the object of male gaze and male pleasure. Worse, Gail Dines (2010), prolific feminist author and critic of the pornography industry, highlights the growing production and consumption of "gonzo porn," a genre that portrays hardcore, debasing, and derogating sexual scenes. Common features of gonzo pornography include gang rape, forceful and painful oral and anal penetration, slapping and choking despite women gagging and crying (DeKeseredy, 2015; Dines, 2010; Tylka & Kroon Van Diest, 2015). Equally troubling, the distribution of child pornography is increasingly prevalent; in 2015, there were 500,000 child pornography websites (increasing by approximately 5000% since 2006) (DeKeseredy, 2015). Exposures to such images are not benign. Pornography becomes a powerful medium through which both boys and girls, men and women, learn and internalize the nature of patriarchy, idealized gendered bodies, and violent sexuality. Sadly, more and more researchers are finding that the violent, racist, and demeaning sexual depictions in pornography are strongly linked with real violence (DeKeseredy, 2015). Pornography, according to Bergen and Bogle (2000), "is a training manual for abuse" (p. 231) of women and children.

Interpersonal contributors: Gender roles and violence. While both reflecting and contributing to real-life experience, media do not provide the only source of sexualization scripts. Direct, everyday relational lived experiences can facilitate the internalization of sexualization of girls and women. From patriarchal gender role socialization to interpersonal sexual violation, girls and women frequently experience harmful, objectifying interactions. Patriarchal gender role socialization, Szymanski, Moffitt, and Carr (2011) posit, encourages men to be aggressive and powerful and to view women as sex objects and sex as a conquest. The same patriarchal gender roles, on the other hand, socialize women to be passive, submissive to men, and to accept responsibility for men's sexual behavior (Szymanski, Moffitt, & Carr, 2011). These traditional gender norms are often held and implicitly or explicitly reinforced across many domains, including in familial and working relationships and within religious, educational, and judicial systems.

Men and women in North America are frequently exposed to limiting gender roles that perpetuate the sexualization of girls and women. Unfortunately, dehumanizing sexual violence toward girls and women is also commonplace. Sexual objectification also occurs when men stare at women, evaluate or comment on their bodies, touch their bodies without permission, or when women are sexual assaulted and/or raped (Smolak & Murnen, 2011). For example, endemic in college campuses across North America is the sexual victimization of women; it is estimated that more than half of college women experience some form of sexual victimization (four times the amount of sexual victimization as men) (Kelley & Gidycz, 2015; Szymanski, Moffitt, & Carr, 2011). Furthermore, researchers have shown that between 45% and 75% of women in the general population report experiencing sexual victimization, while between 17% and 25% of women experience rape in their lifetime (Kelley & Gidycz, 2015). As we will highlight in the following, women's experiences of sexual violence are related to increased body shame, self-objectification, and adverse psychological outcomes including disordered eating (Szymanski, Moffitt, & Carr, 2011).

Psychological Consequences of Sexual Objectification

Through sexual violence, sexualization, and sexual objectification, women's bodies become sites of oppression and pain. Fredrickson and Roberts (1997) posit that experiences of objectification and self-objectification increase appearance anxiety, body shame, and anxiety about personal safety. They also postulate that women who are ashamed of their bodies (or feel like their bodies fall short of the internalized cultural idea) are more likely to suppress their bodies' internal cues, like hunger and sexual arousal, which can further facilitate disordered eating and sexual dysfunction. More recent research has supported these claims, indicating that self-objectification is associated with increased risk for depression (Johnson & Wardle, 2005; Tiggemann & Kuring, 2004), disordered eating (Tylka & Hill, 2004), and sexual dysfunction (Calogero & Thompson, 2009; Steer & Tiggemann, 2008). Interestingly, Tiggemann and Williams (2012) found that sexual functioning, depression, and disordered eating are significantly intercorrelated among women. Researchers also support the notion that both direct interpersonal experiences of sexualization and exposure to sexually objectifying media, including pornography, are related to self-objectification, the internalization of cultural beauty standards, body shame, body dissatisfaction, and eating disorder symptomatology (APA Task Force on the Sexualization of Girls, 2007; Szymanski,

Moffitt, & Carr, 2011; Tylka & Kroon Van Diest, 2015). In the following section, we will further outline the intersection of self-objectification, body shame, eating disorders, and sexual well-being.

Self-objectification, shame, and sexuality. According to Pujols, Meston, and Seal (2010), 43% of women in the United States experience sexual difficulties, including sexual pain, low desire, and difficulties with lubrication and/or orgasm. While there are undoubtedly multiple, complex intrapsychic, physical, relational, and societal factors related and contributing to sexual difficulties, considerable research underscores the negative impact of self-objectification and body shame on sexual functioning and well-being. For example, a heightened awareness about how one's body might appear to a sexual partner and/or appearance anxiety during sexual intimacy has been found to be associated with decreased sexual functioning and with lower sexual well-being (Vencill, Tebbe, & Garos, 2015; Wiederman, 2000). Furthermore, in a review of the literature, Satinsky, Reece, Dennis, Sanders, and Bardzell (2012) found that women with a negative body image report sexual avoidance, decreased pleasure, decreased orgasmic capabilities, and sexual satisfaction. Likewise, poor body image during sexual activity and dissatisfaction with body parts (e.g., genitalia, stomach, thighs) among college-aged women is related to lower sexual assertiveness and sexual esteem (Pujols, Meston, & Seal, 2010; Schick, Calabrese, Rima, & Zucker, 2010). Sexual objectification and sexual self-objectification heighten one's awareness of one's body as seen through the eyes of others while diminishing one's subjective and embodied experiencing of sensations and desires. Given the influence of media, pornography, gender role scripts, and gender-based violence in shaping the so-called "eyes of the Other," represented by narrow and often unattainable beauty standards, women without a strong internal connection to their bodies are likely to experience body shame.

As mentioned above, experiences of sexualization and self-objectification often result in bodily or sexual shame. Shame is described as "an intensely painful [and universal] feeling or experience of believing we are flawed and therefore unworthy of acceptance or belonging" (Brown, 2010, p. 5). According to Kyle (2013), sexual shame is this aforementioned experience as a reaction to one's current or past sexual thoughts, behaviors, or experiences. In this way, like self-objectification, body and sexual shame develops when one has internalized and feels as though they fall short to set of external standards. The experience of shame can have significant consequences for one's physical and relational experiences of sexuality (Woo, Brotto, & Gorzalka, 2011). Hastings (1998) argued that shame underlies most negative sexual symptoms. Kaufman (1989) concurred, stating that shame is said to be the most critical affect to the development of sexual dysfunction. Sexual shame can dull sexual initiative and limit interest-excitement, resulting in decreased arousal and sexual engagement (Lichtenberg, 2001). In addition to sexual arousability, shame can potentially impact sexual pleasure;

body shame seems to increase sexual self-consciousness and decrease sexual satisfaction, pleasure, and lower sexual desire (Moore & Davidson, 1997; Sanchez & Kiefer, 2007; Woo, Brotto, & Gorzalka, 2011). If body shame and self-objectification negatively impacts sexual functioning, it follows then that body appreciation and embodiment likely increase and promote healthful sexuality (Satinsky et al., 2012).

Sexual Embodiment

The abovementioned experiences of body surveillance, self-objectification, and sexual shame seem to connote a disruption in embodiment during sexual intimacy. Embodiment, as expanded on in other chapters, is a key element of identity or a sense of self and is the experiencing of one's body in the world (Tolman, Bowman, & Fahs, 2013). According to Piran and Teall (2012), embodiment is a complex concept that includes feeling "at one" with the body, feeling agency and power in the body, a feeling of freedom to "take up space" in the world, and a connection with and clarity of one's own needs, desires, and rights. Embodiment is not just awareness of the body as an object; rather, it is awareness *as* a body. Sexual embodiment, then, is the felt experience or "in-touchness" with one's desire and connection to a physical state (Tolman, Bowman, & Fahs, 2013). Simply put, sexual embodiment is when, during sexual expressions, one is connected with their whole selves through and within their body. Experiencing or evaluating one's body as an object, or judging one's body during sexual intimacy, is therefore incongruent with the experience of sexual embodiment.

Disordered Eating and Sexual Shame:
The Present Research

The present study (see Siemens, 2015) was initially undertaken with the aim to understand the lived experiences of sexual shame resilience and embodiment among young adult women who had been immersed in Christian faith-based messaging around sexuality in the formative developmental period of adolescence. The research was conducted as a master's thesis with the first author as the primary investigator and the second author as the thesis supervisor. In order to understand the meaning of these women's experiences, a hermeneutic phenomenological method was utilized. Multiple themes emerged revealing certain areas of commonalities between the women's stories. Although not the research focus, experiences of disordered eating were described by 60% of the participants in sharing their journeys of sexual shame. While this is not surprising given the underlying theme of objectification, it yielded rich data about the lived connection between sexual objectification, shame, and eating disorders. Sexual agency and embodiment appear as avenues for reclaiming one's body-self unity as a source of agency and pleasure.

Methods

Participants. Participants included five women between the ages of 25 and 30. Participants were chosen based on evidence of sexual shame resilience. A shame resilient person is someone that experiences and recognizes their experiences of shame and is able to move through them constructively while maintaining authenticity (Brown, 2006). All of the participants were married within the past three years and had been immersed in Christian faith culture. Purposeful sampling was utilized with the aim to select information-rich cases which would best illuminate the lived experience of developing resilience to sexual shame.

Materials and procedures. In the first phase of recruitment, social media advertisements were used. Participants were first asked to review the informed consent on an online survey, which contained information about the study and criteria for participation. Participants were next contacted via a phone interview. Before commencing the interview, each participant was e-mailed a copy of the consent form and asked to review it. Participants were invited to contact the interviewer with questions. Data from the online survey were discarded once participants were identified as either being appropriate or not appropriate for participation.

Semi-structured interviews took place at private and convenient times and locations for the participants, including their own homes if participants preferred. Hard copies of interviewer notes and consent forms were kept in locked filing cabinets in a locked office. Audio files and digital copies of the transcripts were kept in an encrypted, password-protected computer file.

The hermeneutic phenomenological method (van Manen, 1997), which integrates both descriptive and interpretive phenomenology, was utilized. Hermeneutic phenomenology explores human experience and the meanings of the experience with sensitivity to language, which reflects a historical and cultural context. This method is interpretive and highlights a dialogical process between the participant and reflection on their experience. The methodological structure proposed by van Manen (1997) was followed; this involves a dynamic interplay between the following research activities:

1   turning to a phenomenon which seriously interests us and commits us to the world;
2   investigating experience as we live it rather than as we conceptualize it (data collection);
3   reflecting on the essential themes which characterize the phenomenon;
4   describing the phenomenon through the art of writing and rewriting;
5   maintaining a strong, oriented stance toward the question; and
6   balancing the research context by considering parts and whole

(van Manen, 1997, pp. 30–31)

These steps served as a road map for the research process, which sought to answer the primary research question: "What are Christian women's lived experiences of resilience to sexual shame?" The lived experience of the interconnectedness of sexual objectification, shame, and eating disorders was identified explicitly in the experiences of three of the five participants. These three interviews are the sources of the results that follow.

Strengths and limitations. Criteria for methodological rigor applied to this research include openness, balancing integration, concreteness, resonance, and actualization (De Witt & Ploeg, 2006). The concept of openness refers to the researchers' systematic and explicit accounting for the multiple decisions they make throughout the research process, including tracking shifts in interpretations (De Witt & Ploeg, 2006), consistent with step one of van Manen's hermeneutic phenomenological method in which the researcher attunes and orients themselves to a specific phenomenon, and continuously turns back toward this phenomenon. Consistent with the criterion of openness, we are able to track the discovery of eating disorder themes as they connected to the original guiding research question. Further phenomenological research exploring sexual shame and eating disorders is necessary to deepen this area of inquiry.

Balancing integration represents the weaving of philosophical concepts in the study methods and findings, striking a balance between the voices of study participants and the potential explanations. Consistent with this, we have aimed to keep the participants' experiences, our own personal responses as researchers, and the existing literature speaking to shame and objectification, all in dialogue with each other.

Concreteness is the usefulness for practice of study findings (De Witt & Ploeg, 2006). Bringing the results of this research into the present volume on eating disorder theory, prevention, and treatment is one way in which we make the results practical. This study sheds light on the central theme of objectification in both eating disorders and sexual shame. In doing so, it also offers a vision for the importance of cultivating embodied subjectivity as a stance of resistance to sociocultural objectification.

Resonance relates to the experiential effect of reading study findings upon the reader (De Witt & Ploeg, 2006), occurring when the reader is moved by participants' experiences (van Manen, 2006). We have attempted to capture the richness of participants' experiences and invite the reader to be open to being touched by the participants' lived experiences.

Actualization encompasses the future realization of resonance and study findings (De Witt & Ploeg, 2006), meaning the interpretive process does not end at the conclusion of the research, but is sustained in a continual interpretation of the experiences. To this end, we bring the following findings into dialogue with the other chapters in this volume and invite the reader to engage in their own interpretive processes.

Highlights of Results: Connections between Sexual Shame and Eating Disorders

In this section, we will highlight the experiences of the participants who put words to the connection between body shame and disordered eating.

The body as a holding place for shame and a target of control. In various examples, participants described the body as a target and holding place for shame, which they attempted to control and manage without feeling connected and "in touch" with their physicality. For three of the women, shame and the resulting attempts to control their bodies were manifested in disordered eating. Leah explains this articulately:

> I was severely anorexic throughout my teenager years, so I guess that is really, on one level it's an effort to keep my body childish. To eliminate breasts and curves and thighs, and anything... especially being tall, it was like wanting to stay small. And being skinny is kind of your way of doing it. Yah, so it's probably another way of... you know, you bury it down and then you take it out against your body without conscious thought.

Jennifer, too, shared that she has come to realize that the shame and insecurities that she experienced about herself (as a whole person) were displaced onto her body, as if her body was a separate entity: "I detested my body. I hated it. For how it looked and appeared." Jennifer describes how silence about sexuality and changes in puberty connected to hating and controlling her body:

> And I think that's another part of how I felt a lot of shame about my body. Because I think that I was, I developed pretty late, but at the same time I was very much disgusted with my change in my body. And I think my—I didn't know anything because I didn't go to sex ed classes, that my mom knew about. And so, like, the changes that were happening, I felt almost ashamed of having breasts and what that means. I felt like I was just becoming this sexual being and that was bad. And so, I think it developed into a lot of other things of me trying to control my body and hating my body.

In feeling the foreignness of her developing body as an adolescent, Jennifer shares,

> I seriously wanted to be a guy, because I hated how our culture portrays women, and just being objectified. I just wanted to diminish those parts of me because of that. And I think that's another message I took from culture about my sexuality.

Body shame and relational disconnection. Leah further described putting up a barrier between herself and others as she put up a barrier between herself and her body: "disconnecting from my own relationships, and disconnected from my body. And I was anorexic. So in an extreme way disconnected like on a lot of levels from my body."

Leah's own shame resulted in not feeling alienated from others who were comfortable with their own sexuality. For example, she describes being "like enemies" with her first roommate in university who had "a big chest and she would wear these little tank tops, and just 'woooooahhhhh!' cleavage showing alllll the time. And I was so like, 'OH MY GOSH!'" She compares her own body silencing and inhibition to her roommate's comfort, saying,

> I was like black and white, and Audrey Hepburn style. So covered up and anorexic. And she's so VOLUPTUOUS AND VIBRANT colours and cleavage and laughing and life!!...I was seeing someone who was just more comfortable with their body and not ashamed...it was so shocking.

Parallel shame responses in sexuality and eating behaviors. Lily spoke about how, when she was engaging in sexual behaviors that she felt ashamed of, she would push her feelings aside in the moment. In a sense, Lily allowed herself to temporarily enjoy her sexuality, which opened the door to herself in some ways even though it didn't all come together yet. She had momentary "in-touchness" with her body and her libido. However, she also couldn't fully celebrate her experiences because her sexuality was kept compartmentalized. The following morning, she would experience the shame. Lily, therefore, could not fully celebrate her sexuality or her experience, because it had to be separate. Lily believes that as a result of the oppressive environment of the community she grew up in, she developed an eating disorder as an adolescent. She likened her sexuality to her struggle with binge eating when she said:

"Shame, no eating, but then, you eat, eat, eat, and then the next day it was like, 'I'm gonna starve all day and I'm gonna be good.' Right? So I think I did that with physical [sexual] stuff, too." At this point in time, when Lily was engaging in sexual behaviors, it was "all or nothing" in that either there was complete restraint or abandon, both in response to the shame. Lily described eating followed by starving all day to "be good" as similar to her compartmentalized connection with her sexuality. In both eating and sexuality, Lily couldn't experience and fully own the true goodness of being her body. While separation and fragmentation can be protective when we are experiencing intense shame, when we are able to integrate, thereby experiencing our sexuality with our whole self, we come into closer contact with what it means to be human.

Reclaiming sexual embodiment and agency. All of the participants were able to describe journeys of moving through shame and into embodied wholeness. As the focus of the research was on sexuality and resilience to sexual shame, the participants were able to offer insights into how the movement from an objectified stance to a subjective connection in their bodies and sexuality is a pathway toward embodied wholeness and agency.

Acceptance, freedom, and pleasure. Lily came back to contrasting binge eating in shame with learning to enjoy her sexuality slowly and fully:

> I was surprised how much endurance we had for enjoying each stage really slowly. Just enjoying each stage for a long time, of physicality. And not needing to rush to the next one. I think because there wasn't the shame there, which is kind of like. Like I think I compare it to binge eating because I experienced that, which was like, 'quick, quick, quick, quick, quick' you know…

She says, "you can take your time and enjoy this….I hadn't had physicality without shame…I always went from zero to sixty quite quickly when shame was there." The message was clear for Lily that when you own and accept something, you can experience freedom in it and full embodied presence.

Finding intrinsic value in the body. Lily describes her journey through counseling:

> I developed an eating disorder out of some of the control issues I had.…So a lot of that healing came from the healing process through [counselling]. I think just began to love how powerful my body was and healthy it was, and strong. And really good friendships with women who thought they looked great. Or who hadn't thought they looked great, but were trying to journey into that. And I found that the more confident I was, I grew to the place where I felt like I looked awesome. Like I felt like, I knew I wasn't a certain type, but I thought I was really beautiful. And I truly believed it, which was really awesome after where I've been. And I think out of that came then a new confidence sexually too. And that started to effect relationships with guys, and where I was willing to go, because I thought, "yah, I look great. Others should enjoy this."

Lily demonstrates a shift to finding value in her body, even in her appearance, that she could both subjectively enjoy and offer relationally for others to enjoy. This is a significant shift from the "body for others" objectification that pushed Lily toward bingeing and purging.

Reclaiming spiritual embodiment as intended by God. Jennifer put words to a spiritual journey of reclaiming that her body was created to be an integral part of her to enjoy. Referring to God, Jennifer says, "He created me this way for a reason. And I have these desires that He doesn't want me to just ignore or avoid, but this means that I can channel these desires into connecting with." In contrast to her earlier body hatred and rejection of femininity, Jennifer describes coming to own her feminine body with one example feeling "ok with having breasts" and not limiting her sexuality "to fulfill men's pleasure." She described a shift from seeing herself as a spirit with a body, to being "ok in my skin." She says, "I'm ok with what my body feels or wants....I can feel like, 'this is who I am, and this is ok.'" She shared how she experiences her body in her marriage today:

> Now I think I feel more whole, I guess...feeling in my body. This is good, and like I can feel, am allowed to feel pleasure and to have someone enjoy my body in a sense that this is me, this is all of me. This is not my physical part, but you're enjoying *me*. Which is great.

Later she beautifully says, "I'm not ashamed of who I am so I can have someone enjoy me, and I can enjoy them." Contrasting this with her previous experience, she recalls "before 'I was definitely hiding myself,' and now it's like, 'Here I am!' (laughs)."

Summary

In this study on resilience to sexual shame among young women, connections between sexual objectification, shame, and disordered eating were apparent. Consistently, among participants, the body was described as a target and holding place for shame. More than half of the participants shared experiences of disordered eating. They responded by shutting off, controlling, and managing their bodies at the expense of *being in* and *being* their bodies. Body shame was connected to relational disconnection with partners and friends. Moreover, parallel shame responses to sexuality and eating were identified.

Participants in this study also illuminated how their journeys of developing resilience to sexual shame were connected to experiences of increasing embodied wholeness. Their experiences referenced the transformation from hiding to accepting sexuality so that it could be savored slowly and pleasurably, in contrast to food or sex bingeing followed by restriction. They also described finding intrinsic value in the body and owning it as a site of enjoyment for self and others. In addition, the spirituality of embodiment was highlighted, which is particularly significant given that religious messaging around sexuality had also been highlighted as a source of sexual and body shame. Given that the focus of the research was on sexuality, the participants offered insights into how the movement from an objectified stance to a subjective connection with their sexual bodies is a pathway toward embodiment. Sexual agency and embodiment appear as avenues for reclaiming one's body-self unity as a source of agency and pleasure.

Discussion and Conclusion

Women's corporeality, size, appearance, and sexuality are primary sites of oppression for women, and embodied sexuality is limited for women with eating disorders. Similarly, sexual objectification and shame also appear to be risk factors for disordered eating. Objectification theory provides a framework for understanding the sociocultural factors that impact women's health and embodiment. Sexual objectification, shame, and eating disorders are connected to similar contributing factors such as media and pornography, and gender-based violence. Through these pathways, women's bodies become sites of pain, and objectification increases appearance anxiety, body shame, and anxiety about personal safety.

The central theme in reclaiming embodiment is a movement from objectification to "subjectification" of the whole person, experienced from within one's own senses and physicality. Promoting subjective knowing and felt "in-touchness" with one's senses is also a pathway for taking a stance of resistance to sociocultural objectification of women. In the same way that body surveillance, self-objectification, and sexual shame disrupt embodiment, becoming attuned to one's whole self in and through their sexuality facilitates awareness *as* a body. Embodiment, expanded more fully in other chapters, is a key component of identity, focused on experiencing of the body in the world (Tolman, Bowman, & Fahs, 2013), and feeling agency and power in the body, freedom to "take up space" in the world, and a connection with one's own needs, desires, and rights (Piran & Teall, 2012). In treatment, cultivating ways for women to actively take up space within and through their bodies is important for reclaiming the body as a site of agency, freedom, joy, and connection. Being "in the body" to experience closeness to others, to one's own emotions, and to one's own sense of agency and sensuality is both a personal and a political act which stands against oppression and objectification.

References

American Psychological Association. (2007). *APA task force on the sexualization of girls*. Washington, DC: American Psychologist Association.

Bergen, R. K. & Bogle, K. A. (2000). Exploring the connection between pornography and sexual violence. *Violence and Victims, 15*(3), 227.

Brown, B. (2006). Shame resilience theory: A grounded theory study on women and shame. *Families in Society, 87*(1), 43–52.

Brown, B. (2010). *Gifts of imperfection: Let go of who you think you're supposed to be and embrace who you are*. Center City, MN: Hazelden Publishing.

Calogero, R. M. (2013). Objects don't object: Evidence that self-objectification disrupts women's social activism. *Psychological Science, 24*(3), 312–318.

Calogero, R. M. & Thompson, J. K. (2009). Potential implications of the objectification of women's bodies for women's sexual satisfaction. *Body Image, 6*(2), 145–148.

DeKeseredy, W. S. (2015). Critical criminological understandings of adult pornography and woman abuse: New progressive directions in research and theory. *International Journal for Crime, Justice and Social Democracy, 4*(4), 4–21.

De Witt, L. & Ploeg, J. (2006). Critical appraisal of rigour in interpretive phenomenological nursing research. *Journal of Advanced Nursing, 55*(2), 215–229.

Dines, G. (2010). *Pornland: How porn has hijacked our sexuality.* Boston, MA: Beacon Press.

Fredrickson, B. L. & Roberts, T. A. (1997). Objectification theory: Toward understanding women's lived experiences and mental health risks. *Psychology of Women Quarterly, 21*, 173–206. doi:10.1111/j.1471-6402.1997.tb00108.x.

Hastings, A. S. (1998). *Treating sexual shame: A new map for overcoming dysfunction, abuse, and addiction.* Lanham, MD: Jason Aronson, Incorporated.

Johnson, F. & Wardle, J. (2005). Dietary restraint, body dissatisfaction, and psychological distress: a prospective analysis. *Journal of Abnormal Psychology, 114*(1), 119.

Kaufman, G. (1989). *The psychology of shame.* New York, NY: Springer.

Kelley, E. L. & Gidycz, C. A. (2015). Labeling of sexual assault and its relationship with sexual functioning: the mediating role of coping. *Journal of Interpersonal Violence, 30*(2), 348–366.

Kyle, S. E. (2013). *Identification and treatment of sexual shame: development of a measurement tool and group therapy protocol.* (Unpublished doctoral dissertation) American Academy of Clinical Sexologists, San Antonio, TX.

Lichtenberg, J. D. (2001). Motivational systems and model scenes with special references to bodily experience. *Psychoanalytic Inquiry, 21*(3), 430–447.

Moore, N. B. & Davidson Sr., J. K. (1997). Guilt about first intercourse: An antecedent of sexual dissatisfaction among college women. *Journal of Sex & Marital Therapy, 23*(1), 29–46.

Piran, N. & Teall, T. (2012). The developmental theory of embodiment. In G. L. McVey, M. P. Levine, N. Piran, & H. B. Ferguson (Eds.), *Preventing eating-related and weight-related disorders: Collaborative research, advocacy, and policy change* (169–198). Waterloo, ON: Wilfred Laurier University Press.

Pujols, Y., Meston, C. M., & Seal, B. N. (2010). The association between body image, sexual functioning, and sexual satisfaction. *Journal of Sexual Medicine, 7*, 905–916.

Sanchez, D. T. & Kiefer, A. K. (2007). Body concerns in and out of the bedroom: Implications for sexual pleasure and problems. *Archives of Sexual Behavior, 36*(6), 808–820.

Satinsky, S., Reece, M., Dennis, B., Sanders, S., & Bardzell, S. (2012). An assessment of body appreciation and its relationship to sexual function in women. *Body Image, 9*(1), 137–144.

Schick, V. R., Calabrese, S. K., Rima, B. N., & Zucker, A. N. (2010). Genital appearance dissatisfaction: Implications for women's genital image self-consciousness, sexual esteem, sexual satisfaction, and sexual risk. *Psychology of Women Quarterly, 34*(3), 394–404.

Short, J. E. (2013). *How much media: report on American consumers.* Institute for Communications Technology Management, Marshall School of Business.

Siemens, K. (2015). Embodiment of spirituality and sexuality: Women's lived experience of resilience to sexual shame. *Unpublished thesis in Counselling Psychology* (master's thesis). Trinity Western University, Langley, BC, Canada.

Smolak, L. & Murnen, S. K. (2011). The sexualization of girls and women as a primary antecedent of self-objectification. In Calogero, E., Tantleff-Dunn, & Thompson (Eds.), *Self-objectification in women; Causes, consequences, and counteractions* (pp. 53–69). Washington, DC: American Psychological Association.

Steer, A. & Tiggemann, M. (2008). The role of self-objectification in women's sexual functioning. *Journal of Social and Clinical Psychology, 27*(3), 205–225.

Szymanski, D. M., Carr, E. R., & Moffitt, L. B. (2011). Sexual objectification of women: Clinical implications and training considerations. *The Counseling Psychologist, 39*(1), 107–126.

Szymanski, D. M., Moffitt, L. B., & Carr, E. R. (2011). Sexual objectification of women: Advances to theory and research. *The Counseling Psychologist, 39*(1), 6–38.

Tiggemann, M. & Kuring, J. K. (2004). The role of body objectification in disordered eating and depressed mood. *British Journal of Clinical Psychology, 43*(3), 299–311.

Tiggemann, M. & Williams, E. (2012). The role of self-objectification in disordered eating, depressed mood, and sexual functioning among women: A comprehensive test of objectification theory. *Psychology of Women Quarterly, 36*(1), 66–75.

Tolman, D., Bowman, C., & Fahs, B. (2013). Sexuality and embodiment. In D. Tolman, L. Diamond, J. Bauermeister, W. George, J. Pfaus, & M. Ward (Eds.), *Handbook of sexuality and psychology* (pp. 759–804). Washington, DC: American Psychological Association Books.

Tylka, T. L. & Hill, M. S. (2004). Objectification theory as it relates to disordered eating among college women. *Sex Roles, 51*(11), 719–730.

Tylka, T. L. & Kroon Van Diest, A. M. (2015). You looking at her "hot" body may not be "cool" for me: Integrating male partners' pornography use into objectification theory for women. *Psychology of Women Quarterly, 39*(1), 67–84.

van Manen, M. (1997). *Researching lived experience: Human science for an action sensitive pedagogy* (2nd ed.). London, ON: The Althouse Press.

van Manen, M. (2006). Writing qualitatively, or the demands of writing. *Qualitative Health Research, 16*(5), 713–722. doi:10.1177/1049732306286911

Vencill, J. A., Tebbe, E. A., & Garos, S. (2015). It's not the size of the boat or the motion of the ocean: The role of self-objectification, appearance anxiety, and depression in female sexual functioning. *Psychology of Women Quarterly, 39*(4), 471–483.

Wade, J. (2000). Mapping the courses of heavenly bodies: The varieties of transcendent sexual experience. *Journal of Transpersonal Psychology, 32*(2), 103–122.

Ward, L. M. (2016). Media and sexualization: State of empirical research, 1995–2015. *The Journal of Sex Research, 53*(4–5), 560–577.

Wiederman, M. W. (2000). Women's body image self-consciousness during physical intimacy with a partner. *Journal of Sex Research, 37*(1), 60–68.

Woo, J. S., Brotto, L. A., & Gorzalka, B. B. (2011). The role of sex guilt in the relationship between culture and women's sexual desire. *Archives of Sexual Behavior, 40*(2), 385–394.

10 Intergenerational Journeys

Mothers Raising Embodied Daughters[1]

Hillary L. McBride and Janelle L. Kwee

The serious consequences of eating disorders and the often co-occurring body shame have necessitated research exploring what causes and contributes to the development of eating disorders. Research addressing body image has led to the development of the tripartite model or sociocultural model (Hardit & Hannum, 2012). This model explains how parents, media, and peers work together as the dominant sources contributing to the perpetuation and dissemination of ideals of femininity and beauty centered on thinness. Research further exploring the contribution of parents to their children's body image has repeatedly demonstrated the significant relationship between parent's own eating-dieting behaviors and negative body weight/shape comments, and their children's body dissatisfaction and dieting behaviors (Abraczinskas, Fisak, & Barnes, 2012; Back, 2011; Canals, Sancho, & Arija, 2009; Coulthard, Blissett, & Harris, 2004; Eisenberg, Berge, Fulkerson, & Neumark-Sztainer, 2011; Galioto, Karazsia, & Crowther, 2012). Parental modeling and direct and explicit comments are thought to be the two mechanisms through which parents communicate messages about eating, bodies, weight, and appearance to their children.

Mothers, who act in most homes as the primary caregiver for young children, have a significant role in the biopsychosocial development of their children, also sharing with them the socially constructed narrative of femininity, answering the question with their words and actions "what does it mean to be a woman in this world" (Davison, Markey & Birch, 2000; Elfhag & Linne, 2005; Ogden & Steward, 2000). Jean Baker Miller (1976) explained the connection and likeness girls have to their mother as the source of the relational framework within which they operate in the world. Miller states that all women's relationships, including her relationship to herself, are shaped through one's early experience of relationship with one's mother. Not surprisingly, strong links have been found between eating pathology in mothers and their daughters, identifying an opportunity for focused prevention and treatment efforts. While the importance of understanding what predicts and contributes to eating disorders must continue, the focus on identifying mothers as contributing factors has unfortunately vilified the role of the mother, further contributing to "mother-blaming" (Vander Ven & Vander Ven, 2003).

Although less popular in the academic literature, there is evidence that mothers can also act as agents and advocates in the development of well-being, growth, and thriving in their daughters (Boyd, Ashcraft, & Belgrave, 2006; Gross & McCallum, 2000; Hutchinson, Jemmott, Jemmott, Braverman, & Fong, 2003; McBride, Kwee, & Buchanan, 2017; Usher-Seriki, Bynum, & Callands, 2008). Mothers help shape their daughter's worldviews, equip them with the necessary emotional skills with which they navigate the world, and provide them with the information they need, particularly during the emotionally charged period of pubertal development (Flaake, 2005). The strength of the mother-daughter relationship may also serve as a protective factor against adolescent risk-taking behavior, which includes how the adolescent daughter views and treats her own body (Boyd, Ashcraft, & Belgrave, 2006). Flaake (2005) suggests that it is through the mother's own behavior and involvement in her daughter's life that the mother reinforces gender roles or proposes healthier and more authentic alternatives. Flaake proposes that it is through the mother-daughter relationships that there is the possibility to revise traditional gender roles and interrupt the pattern of objectification which reinforces the thin ideal in girls' and women's lives.

Due to the significant roles mothers have as mental health agents (Maor & Cwikel, 2015; McBride, Kwee, & Buchanan, 2017), especially in the development of girls' body image, this study was designed to better understand the development and journey of embodiment in young women, how the relationship with their mothers contributed to a sense of healthy embodiment, and their mother's struggles with or toward a more embodied life.

Method

Participants

The participants in this study were five Caucasian biological mother-daughter dyads. This included ten participants in total, which meets the standards for qualitative research (e.g., for phenomenology, see Langdridge, 2007; for narrative research methods, see Riessman, 2008). The "daughters" in this study were between 19 and 30 years old, and currently had a relationship with their mothers of varying degrees of closeness. Each daughter who participated was selected based on her self-identified positive body image, which was assessed later using Multidimensional Body-Self Relationship questionnaire (MBSRQ; Avalos, Tylka, & d-Barcalow, 2005) and the Body Appreciation Scale (BAS; Cash & Szymanski, 1995). The daughters had never experienced an eating disorder or body dysmorphic disorder. Once the "daughter" participants had been selected for participation, their mothers were invited to participate regardless of their body image (assessment measures were not utilized to screen mother participants). None of the mother participants reported experiencing an eating disorder, but two of the mothers described what appeared to be some symptoms of disordered eating during adolescence. All of the mothers were between the ages of 50 and 67. All of the daughters and mothers self-identified as Caucasian, Christian, and heterosexual; however, this part of inclusion criteria was only disclosed at the time of each participant's interview, after the participants had been recruited and screened.

The Listening Guide

The assumption underlying the design of the study, and the method of analysis chosen for the data, is that the current cultural gender scripts for women are oppressive and silencing (Piran & Cormier, 2005; Wolf, 1991), affecting both what women say and their way of being in the world (Gilligan, 1982). Born out of Gilligan (1982) and Miller's (1976) work on women's identity and moral development, the Listening Guide comes in response to the influence of patriarchy of psychological theories of development, which were most often created using research with boys and men's experiences, but did not sufficiently address or assess women's experiences in the world and how women find value and make decisions. The themes which are heard in the participant's stories are referred to as the voices with which the participants spoke. To read more about the Listening Guide, please refer to the chapter in this book addressing embodied research methods by E. Chan.

The team of researchers who conducted analysis for this study was comprised of the authors and six female graduate research assistants in a graduate counseling psychology program. In order to code the voices heard in the participants' stories, an interpretive feminist relational lens was used through relational dialogue and researchers' consensus of felt sense of participant's narrative, instead of examining the word choice alone. Having numerous members of the research team provided credibility to the study, as the research team was diverse in individual characteristics, yet together interpreted the data from within the same sociocultural context.

Recruitment and Sampling

Online advertisements as well as snowball sampling were utilized to identify potential participants who were then asked to complete the MBSRQ and the BAS through a survey website to determine their level of appropriateness for the study. Ninety-one women completed the online survey, and the first five participants who met inclusion criteria were contacted for a brief phone interview. Purposive and intensity sampling were used to identify participants who might best contribute depth of information to the study. This was also verified during the phone screening once participants were selected based on their responses to the online questionnaire (Mertens, 2010). The criteria for inclusion were as follows: a woman between the ages of 19 and 30, self-identified as possessing healthy body image, and currently in a relationship with their mother. There were no inclusionary requirements for the mother participants or about the quality of relationship between mother and daughter. Participants were invited to choose a pseudonym to represent themselves if they so desired.

Data Collection Procedures

Once the daughter participant was determined to be eligible to participate and had given her consent, her mother was informed through a phone conversation of the study and consented to participate. Following this, each individual member of the dyad began participation in the data collection phase. The researchers conducted semi-structured interviews with each of the ten participants that were approximately one hour in length.

Rigor

Following the completion of the analysis by the research team, participants were invited to review the written analysis and change or remove parts of the analysis they felt were incongruent with their experience and the information they intended to communicate at the time of the interview. During this process, two of the mother participants reported feeling saddened when reading the analysis because it named their painful and often insecure experiences of their bodies. However, they also chose not to change the analysis, as they believe it reflected accurately their stories and experiences.

Results

This study was designed to explore the experiences of young adult women who experience positive embodiment and the influence their mothers had on their experiences of their bodies. The themes or voices used reflect the ways that the participants spoke about their bodies. Their relationships to themselves and others are then discussed, followed by a discussion about how mothers specifically helped their daughters become embodied, in spite of their own body shame and/or disembodied relationships with themselves.

Voices of the Body

When participants spoke about their bodies, and their experience of themselves as a body, they used the following voices: idealized femininity, silencing, functionality, acceptance, embodiment, and resistance. The voices of embodiment and resistance are expanded in their description due to their relevance to the purpose of this book. The voice of idealized femininity was used when participants spoke about what it meant, and the felt pressure, to be a culturally desirable woman: to be good, seen but not heard, desired, and a sexual object for the pleasure of men. All participants used this voice, but all daughters used this voice when identifying and resisting sociocultural expectations. Participants used the voice of silencing when they were attempting to minimize their literal voices and/or their bodies, effectively to take up less space relationally, conversationally, or physically. When using the voice of silencing, the participants often said "she never said..." or "we just didn't talk about that". When using the voice of functionality, women told stories of their focus on the function of their bodies, particularly as an aspect of the self which deserves care, nourishment, and attention. This voice at times represented a mindful care of the self as the body, while other times it was used to represent a divide between self and body, where the body was a machine which needed to work properly. The voice of acceptance was used to address the process of moving toward embodiment, while not yet fully there. When using this voice, women said things like "learning", "journey", and "healing", giving a sense of a woman moving toward a more whole relationship with her body, loving and repairing her sense of self.

Voice of embodiment. In this study, the voice of embodiment was used passionately by participants to capture their unapologetic love for all aspects of themselves, particularly their bodies. This voice stands in opposition to the voice of silencing or idealized femininity, demonstrating their pride and joy in their embodied identities, physicality, and strength. When using this voice, they used words like "beautiful", "love", "freedom", and "unique", and adamantly resisted narrow and oppressive discourse of the female body/self, expressing instead liberation and joy in the diversity of women's physical selves. They also acknowledged the divine qualities of the body, savoring the experience of the body as spiritual in its sensuality and pleasure. Interestingly, for the research team this was the most satisfying voice to identify, creating a contagious effect of embodiment among the women conducting analysis who reflected on feeling more embodied when reading these participant's stories. We cheered and celebrated together, stopping the formal process of analysis to connect personally with the text, feeling the victory within our own bodies as we read.

Voice of resistance. The voice of resistance is the voice used when women are standing in opposition to the voice of idealized femininity, resisting silencing gender roles and the objectification of women's bodies. This voice represents the speaking out against values and media that oppress women and cause them to believe their bodies are bad or undesirable. In addition to speaking out against cultural views of women, the voice is used when women are speaking truth about their value and beauty. When using the voice of resistance, women often used the words like "lies", "messages", and "disgusting" when speaking about the culture, frequently saying things like "I don't want to" and "I don't need to" to demonstrate their opposition. This voice was used also as they spoke of other women, resisting on their behalf. In a notable example of this, one participant states: "I'm a very protective person, I will push someone away or I will give very dirty looks if men are eyeing people up or my friends up... I don't want girls or women to think that they're objects ever." Interestingly, in providing this example this participant demonstrates her literal resistance on behalf of other women, but also her own embodied resistance to the myth of femininity that as a woman she must be silent and submissive; in this, she resists the cultural script for her as a woman.

Voices of Relationship

The three voices heard when women spoke about relationship included comparison, differentiation, and connection. The description of the voice of connection is expanded due to its specific relevance to this book. The voice of comparison was used to describe how they (and their bodies) were different than or similar to other women. The research team concluded that the voice of comparison was used both as an illustrative tool and as a function of idealized femininity, which keeps women competing with each other. It seems that this voice is used to speak of the body as an object which is evaluated in relationship to other body/objects. For example, this was identified in one participant's interview where she said regularly "compared to my sister", "she is a little heavier than me", or "she has gorgeous legs, whereas I...". The voice of differentiation was used by all participants, both mother and daughter participants, to speak about their desire to be their own person, to have an identity, within the context of relationships. In using this voice, the women were saying, "I know who I am in light of you", or "I'd like to find out who I am in light of you".

   Voice of connection. Although all participants used the voice of connection differently, this voice was featured prominently in each of the interviews, supporting Gilligan's work explaining the relational values governing women's lives (Gilligan, 1982). This voice was used to describe their experiences of relationships and feeling safe or secure with someone. The voice of connection was also used as women reflected on their heritage and their intergenerational narrative as women. Some of the markers used for this voice included "protection", "loving", "safe", and "close". One participant states,

> I was always close with my mom, and I felt this sense of closeness and this sense of safety that my mom was there, that she was taking care of my needs and that she loves me... I felt safe and secure in my relationship.

Interestingly, all participants used this voice when speaking about their mothers, even the mother participants themselves. All of the mothers used the voice of connection when speaking about their daughters. Some women used the voice of connection to speak about their relationship to their partner, to God, or to their own sense of self.

Embodiment, and Mothers and Daughters

Mothers have been found to be particularly influential in how their children come to experience their bodies (Cooley, Toray, Wang, & Valdez, 2008; McBride, Kwee, & Buchanan, 2017). For all of the mothers in this study, their own mothers had been silent about physical and sexual development, and body image, either never speaking about these things, or only doing so in a negative way. Some of the mothers commented on how their mothers were from a different generation, where the focus on family life was survival and health. Interestingly, all of the mothers in this study reported struggling with their body image in the past or were still struggling with a negative body image today. We cannot ascertain if there is a causal relationship between their mother's silence and their own struggle to accept their bodies. However, the literature suggests that it is important for girls to be informed about their bodies and to be shown how to accept and appreciate their bodies, and see their own strength (Piran & Teall, 2012). This is particularly important because as girls develop physically, they need modeling about how to care for themselves and embrace their sexuality and desires in healthy ways.

"Standing on my shoulders". In this study, all mothers spoke about their body insecurity growing up. Although some mothers had begun to move toward acceptance, all mothers made body-disparaging comments that their daughters remember them making. All mothers, however, desired to be more vocal with their daughters about body image and sexuality than their mothers were with them. And when a mother had suffered or struggled with a particular issue, it was her focus to ensure her daughter did not struggle in the same way. Even though the mothers struggled with their bodies, and were not necessarily able to name or identify this struggle, they appeared to be aware of it to some degree, as they desired for their daughters to have a healthier body image. The desire these mothers showed to protect their daughters from their own struggles was something we came to understand using the metaphor "standing on my shoulders". The mothers desired for their daughters to stand on their stories like a platform for growth, going further and reaching higher than they were ever able to. In this way, the mothers were giving a gift to their daughters, desiring more for them than they were able to experience; that their daughters would experience more freedom and health.

Safety and connection. The daughters also felt safe in their relationships with their mothers, even though this too was not communicated explicitly in the dyad. Whether they chose to do so or not, they always felt able to go to their mother for anything they needed, physical or emotional. All the daughters knew that they were accepted fully by their mother, regardless of their appearance or if they disagreed with their mother. When the young women spoke about their bodies, they said kind and affirming things, describing their strength, and their choice to appreciate their own beauty, while not allowing their appearance alone to define their identity. Although they experienced embodiment now, almost all daughters used the voice of silencing to describe their body in the past. This occurred during puberty, when the challenge of feeling out of control with physical changes created insecurity within them. In some cases, the voice of silencing and comparison was used to describe their insecurity when their bodies did not change or develop at the same rate as their peers. Puberty is a particularly important time of development where girls encounter the sexualization of their bodies, and learn from societal messages that their new more womanly bodies define their cultural worth as women (Flaake, 2005; Piran & Cormier, 2005). This disruption of embodiment during adolescence is normal and does not prevent a woman from experiencing reembodiment after adolescence (Piran, Carter, Thompson, & Pajouhandeh, 2002). Unlike many young women, who learn to see their bodies through the eyes of the culture (Smolak & Murnen, 2011), the daughters in this study were able to anchor their identity in areas other than their appearance, which allowed them to resist the experiences of body shame.

Spirituality and the focus on nonappearance domains. The daughters in this study saw value in themselves for reasons other than appearance. It was often their mothers that encouraged them to focus on nonappearance aspects, including having an identity rooted in their spiritual life and faith or religious practices. For the daughter participants, spirituality and religious practices were hugely influential in supporting both their self-worth and identity security, and their intellectual assessment of cultural messages. In striking contrast to the way women are objectified, devalued, and oppressed, only being seen as valuable if they meet narrow appearance standards, one participant states that God "encourages me, and will see more for all that I am and say that I am beautiful." Believing that their Creator sees them as lovable, valuable, and perfect just as they are, and that this is ultimately more important than what the culture says about them as women, they were able to resist the dominant narratives of femininity, reminding themselves that in their relationship with their Creator they are always secure, loved unconditional, and affirmed. The women also had other ways of finding value and joy of corporeality that was outside a cultural influence. They learned to connect with themselves and the earth through gardening, their physical power through sports and exercise, and the rawness of their physical strength through birthing babies. It was these experiences that allowed these women to experience the physical dimensions of themselves as positive and enjoyable. Together, their nonappearance-related positive experiences of themselves and their spirituality gave them the opportunity to experience themselves as a whole self, creating depth and richness which transcends the seemingly ubiquitous normative sexualization and objectification of women.

Discussion

This study affirms the significant role of mothers in shaping women's experiences of their bodies. However, the experiences of the participants in this study offer a counter-narrative to "mother-blaming", demonstrating that mothers can play an instrumental and constructive role in their daughters' development of embodiment and in resisting sociocultural messages of body objectification. Essentially, mothers are seen in this study to play an active role in breaking the cycles of disembodiment, body dissatisfaction, and body objectification, all of which are normative in our culture. In their loving relationships with their daughters, the mother participants in this study are an intergenerational resource, which interrupts and resists patriarchal narratives around body image. This finding offers an important clue to the effective preventive role of mothers as advocates in women's development of well-being, growth, and thriving, even as mothers themselves are navigating their own complicated experiences within the same sociocultural context.

The metaphor that emerged out of this study of "standing on the shoulders" is a promising image that mothers can provide possibilities beyond their own experience for their daughters to reach greater embodiment; these mothers provided "shoulders to stand on" by allowing the daughters to anchor their identity in nonappearance domains, through spiritual and religious practices, in speaking openly about their bodies, in connecting their daughters to their physical power and creativity through sports and gardening, and through actively resisting oppressive gender scripts. Most importantly, the mothers provided a safe relational context of genuine love and acceptance. This connected and loving mother–daughter relationship stands out as a powerful protective factor against disordered eating and against body objectification, and gives us a glimpse into how relational safety and acceptance are central to pathways to self-acceptance and embodiment.

The pathways identified before are consistent with Piran and Teall's (2012) developmental theory of embodiment in which individuals experience embodiment through the physical domain, mental domain, and social power. The mothers encouraged their daughters to feel strong through playing sports (physical domain) and to challenge gender roles (mental freedom). Due to the population of the sample (women from upper-middle-class families), the mothers did not speak about the challenges of poverty and how that intersects with oppression for women, indicating a position of privilege (social power). No existing model of development of body image or embodiment acknowledges the potentially significant influence of spirituality. However, in this study, spiritualty was an important component of the participant's identity, allowing them to resist sociocultural messages about their bodies as women.

Implications for Interventions and Further Research

Implications for practice include working with mothers and creating alternate dialogues. A key contribution from the findings in this study is to shift from mother-blaming to empowering mothers to participate in their daughters' development with a focus on strength and resilience. The mother participants in this study made mistakes and had limitations but had in common the ability to provide relational safety to their daughters and to protect them from the same challenges they faced. Efforts at prevention and treatment of eating disorders require alternate dialogues for women to speak about their bodies. While an overwhelming proportion of women are dissatisfied with their bodies, those who are satisfied with their bodies lack opportunity to vocalize this. Spaces for women to speak positively about their bodies include individual and group counseling contexts, as well as in school and community prevention and health promotion efforts.

Further research about intergenerational journeys of embodiment is needed with larger and more diverse samples, to explore nonbiological mother-daughter dyads and to explore in more depth the role of spirituality as a protective factor. Both qualitative and survey-based research can build effectively on this study.

Conclusion

North American women's experiences of their bodies are troubling, and younger and younger girls are identified as feeling dissatisfied with their bodies (Calogero, Tantleff-Dunn, & Thompson, 2011; Kenardy, Brown, & Vogt, 2001; McKenney & Bigler, 2016; Piran & Cormier, 2005; Spitzer, Henderson, & Zivian, 1999). While this problem has triggered a necessary response to focus on disordered eating, research about "what goes right" for women who experience positive embodiment has lacked. The women in this study have wrestled with and resisted dominant discourses about their appearance and have chosen to see themselves differently. Their mothers played a significant role on this journey, teaching them to care for their bodies and instilling confidence in who they were as people. The stories of these participants reflected a deep sense of connectedness with self and others, and a countercultural desire for the world to be a place where women's beauty is appreciated and where their appearance does not define their worth.

Feminist research aims to explore topics in a way that can create meaningful change in our world, and particularly to improve the lives of women and girls (Yoder, 2015). This study has been focused from the beginning on the question of how women can live healthy lives in a world saturated by silencing and oppressive discourses about women. This study offers hope for women to rewrite the collective story of our bodies, challenging the existing cultural discourse to create freedom for ourselves and for the women who will come after us.

Note

1 Authors Note: The original data from this study have also been published in the *Canadian Journal of Counselling and Psychotherapy*; however, a different scope of the study was represented in that journal article than is presented in this chapter. This article has been cited throughout.

References

Abraczinskas, M., Fisak, B., & Barnes, R. (2012). The relation between parental influence, body image, and eating behaviors in a nonclinical female sample. *Body Image: An International Journal of Research, 9*, 93–100. doi:10.1016/j.bodyim.2011.10.005

Avalos, L., Tylka, T. L., & d-Barcalow, N. (2005). The body appreciation scale: Development and psychometric evaluation. *Body Image: An International Journal of Research, 2*, 285–297. doi:10.1016/j.bodyim.2005.06.002

Back, E. A. (2011). Effects of parental relations and upbringing in troubled adolescent eating behaviors. *Eating Disorders, 19*, 403–424. doi:10.1080/10640266.2011.609091

Boyd, K., Ashcraft, A., & Belgrave, F. Z. (2006). The impact of mother-daughter and father- daughter relationships on drug refusal self-efficacy among African American adolescent girls in urban communities. *Journal of Black Psychology, 32*(1), 29–42. doi:10.1177/0095798405280387.

Calogero, R. M., Tantleff-Dunn, S., & Thompson, J. K. (2011). *Self-objectification in women: Causes, consequences, and counteractions* (1st ed.). Washington, DC: American Psychological Association.

Canals, J., Sancho, C. & Arija, M. V. (2009). Influence of parents' eating attitudes on eating disorders in school adolescents. *European Child Adolescent Psychiatry, 18*, 353–359. doi:10.1007/s00787-009-0737-9

Cash, T. F., & Szymanski, M. L. (1995). The development and validation of the Body-Image Ideals Questionnaire. *Journal of Personality Assessment, 64*(3), 466–477.

Cooley, E., Toray, T., Wang, M. C., & Valdez, N. N. (2008). Maternal effects on daughters' eating pathology and body image. *Eating Behaviors, 9*(1), 52–61. doi:10.1016/j.eatbeh.2007.03.001

Coulthard, H., Blissett, J. & Harris, G. (2004). The relationship between parental eating problems and children's feeding behavior: A selective review of the literature. *Eating Behaviors, 5*, 103–115. doi:10.1016/j.eatbeh.2003.07.003

Davison, K., Markey, C., & Birch, L. (2000). Etiology of body dissatisfaction and weight concerns among 5-year-old girls. *Appetite, 35*, 143–151.

Eisenberg, M. E., Berge, J. M., Fulkerson, J. A., & Neumark-Sztainer, D. (2011). Weight comments by family and significant others in young adulthood. *Body Image: An International Journal of Research, 8*, 12–19. doi:10.1016/j.bodyim.2010.11.002

Elfhag, K., & Linne, Y. (2005). Gender differences in associations of eating pathology between mothers and their adolescent offspring. *Obesity Research, 13*(6), 1070–1076.

Flaake, K. (2005). Girls, adolescents and the impact of bodily changes: Family dynamics and social definitions of the female body. *European Journal of Women's Studies, 12*(2), 201–212. doi: 10.1177/1350506805051241

Galioto, R., Karazsia, B. T., & Crowther, J. H. (2012). Familial and peer modeling and verbal commentary: Associations with muscularity-oriented body dissatisfaction and body change behaviors. *Body Image: An International Journal of Research, 9*, 293–297 doi:10.1016/j.bodyim.2011.12.004

Gilligan, C. (1982). *In a different voice: Psychological theory and women's development.* Cambridge, MA: Harvard University Press.

Gross, P. H., & McCallum, R. S. (2000). Operationalization and predictive utility of mother– daughter synchrony. *School Psychology Quarterly, 15*, 279–294.

Hardit, S. K., & Hannum, J. W. (2012). Attachment, the tripartite influence model, and the development of body dissatisfaction. *Body Image: An International Journal of Research, 9*, 469–475. doi.org/10.1016/j.bodyim.2012.06.003

Hutchinson, M. K., Jemmott, J. B., III, Jemmott, L. S., Braverman, P., & Fong, G. T. (2003). The role of mother–daughter sexual risk communication in reducing sexual risk behaviors among urban adolescent females: A prospective study. *Adolescent Health, 33*(2), 98–107.

Kenardy, J., Brown, W., & Vogt, E. (2001). Dieting and health in young Australian women. *European Eating Disorders Review, 9*, 242–254.

Langdridge, D. (2007). *Phenomenological psychology: Theory, research and method.* New York, NY: Pearson Prentice Hall.

Maor, M., & Cwikel, J. (2015). Mothers' strategies to strengthen their daughters' body image. *Feminism & Psychology, 26*(1), 11. doi:10.1177/0959353515592899

McBride, H. L., Kwee, J. L., & Buchanan, M. J. (2017). Women's healthy body image and the mother-daughter dyad. *Canadian Journal of Counselling and Psychotherapy, 51*(2), 97–113.

McKenney, S. J., & Bigler, R. S. (2016). Internalized sexualization and its relation to sexualized appearance, body surveillance, and body shame among early adolescent girls. *The Journal of Early Adolescence, 36*(2), 171–197. doi:10.1177/0272431614556889

Mertens, D. M. (2010). *Research and evaluation in education and psychology: Integrating diversity with quantitative, qualitative, and mixed methods* (3rd ed.). Thousand Oaks, CA: Sage Publications.

Miller, J. B. (1976). *Towards a new psychology of women.* Boston, MA: Beacon Press.

Ogden, J., & Steward, J. (2000). The role of the mother-daughter relationship in explaining weight concern. *The International Journal of Eating Disorders, 28*(1), 78–83.

Piran, N., Carter, W., Thompson, S., & Pajouhandeh, P. (2002). Powerful girls: A contradiction in terms? Young women speak about the experience of growing up in a girl's body. In S. Abbey (Ed.), *Ways of knowing in and through the body: Diverse perspectives on embodiment* (pp. 206–210). Welland, ON: Soleil Publishing.

Piran, N., & Cormier, H. C. (2005). The social construction of women and disordered eating patterns. *Journal of Counseling Psychology, 52*, 549–558.

Piran, N., & Teall, T. (2012). The developmental theory of embodiment. In G. McVey, M. P. Levine, N. Piran, & H. B. Ferguson, *Preventing eating-related and weight-related disorders: Collaborative research, advocacy, and policy change* (pp. 171–199). Waterloo ON: Wilfred Laurier Press.

Riessman, C. K. (2008). *Narrative methods for the human sciences.* Los Angeles, CA: Sage Publications.

Smolak, L., & Murnen, S. K. (2011). The sexualization of girls and women as a primary antecedent of self-objectification. In R. M. Calogero, S. Tantleff-Dunn,

& J. Thompson (Eds.), *Self-objectification in women: Causes, consequences, and counteractions* (pp. 53–75). Washington, DC: American Psychological Association. doi:10.1037/12304-003

Spitzer, B. L., Henderson, K. A., & Zivian, M. T. (1999). Gender differences in population versus media body size: A comparison over four decades. *Sex Roles, 40*, 545–565.

Usher-Seriki, K. K., Bynum, M. S., & Callands, T. A. (2008). Mother–daughter communication about sex and sexual intercourse among middle- to upper-class African American girls. *Journal of Family Issues, 29*, 901–917.

Vander Ven, T., & Vander Ven, M. (2003). Exploring patterns of mother-blaming in anorexia scholarship: A study in the sociology of knowledge. *Human Studies, 26*(1), 97–119.

Wolf, N. (1991). *The beauty myth: How images of female beauty are used against women.* New York, NY: William Morrow.

Yoder, J. (2015). Asking so what? About our scholarship: Why values matter when planning, doing, and dissemination research. CPA Sponsored Invited Speaker Presentation, Canadian Psychology Association annual convention, Ottawa, ON. June 4, 2015.

11 Poems of the Past, Present, and Future

Becoming a More Embodied Self in Recovering from Anorexia Nervosa

Chelsea Beyer and Mihaela Launeanu

Introduction

Anorexia nervosa (AN) is presently defined by the following: (a) restriction of energy intake leading to a significantly low body weight on the basis of age, sex, development, and physical health; (b) intense fear of gaining weight or becoming fat, or continued behavior interfering with weight gain despite significantly low body weight; and (c) disturbances in the way in which one's body weight or shape is experienced, excessive influence of body weight or shape on self-evaluation, or continued failure to recognize the seriousness of current low body weight (American Psychiatric Association, 2013). Paralleling this definition, recovery from AN is described and understood in terms of restoring body shape and weight, and changing the cognitions and behaviors surrounding food and eating. Principally, recovery from AN is equated with the remission and ultimately the absence of the symptoms outlined in the DSM-5 (American Psychiatric Association, 2013). By these criteria, recovery from AN represents an exceptionally challenging outcome, with only 46.9% of cases reaching full recovery (Steinhausen, 2002), whereas 20.8%–35% of the AN cases becoming chronic or relapsing (Carter, Blackmore, Sutandar-Pinnock, & Woodside, 2004; Steinhausen, 2002). Moreover, this symptom-focused perspective of recovery does not elucidate the process of recovery itself but focuses exclusively on the symptomatic end result.

This chapter proposes an alternative way of understanding recovery from AN in terms of women's own experiences of their body, self, and affective experience. After a brief review of research findings regarding recovery from AN, the chapter will introduce the reader to an innovative methodological approach to investigation of the embodied and affective themes that emerged throughout recovery from AN. The findings of this investigation will be discussed with respect to the current literature on AN and recovery from AN, and the clinical and research implications of these findings will be addressed.

Recovery from AN: A Multifaceted Process

Defining Recovery: An Elusive Endeavor

In the research literature on AN, definitions of recovery are typically built upon a variety of behavioral and physical hallmarks such as cessation of energy intake restriction, restoration of body weight, and normalization of menstruation (Steinhausen, 2002). Depending on which feature was selected to signify recovery, reported recovery rates tended to vary. Specifically, when weight restoration was used as the hallmark of recovery, 60% of cases reportedly reached full recovery. When the global rate of recovery, defined as "recovery from all essential AN symptoms," was used to signify recovery, only 46.9% of cases were reported as recovered (Steinhausen, 2002, p. 1285). Recovery rates tended to vary further still: 57% when normalization of menstruation was used as the main recovery indicator, and 47% when normalization of eating behaviors was taken into account (Steinhausen, 2002). In addition to depicting a polysemous picture of recovery from AN, mainstream notions of recovery dominated by focus on behaviors and the object-body lack consideration of other key features associated with AN, such as emotional and embodied experience. Moreover, the mainstream definitions of recovery are focused on attaining a certain outcome without considering the dynamic and often nonlinear process of recovery.

Affective Dimensions of Recovery

In addition to the behavioral changes highlighted by the mainstream criteria of recovery, emotional experience, regulation, and expression represent key dimensions in the process of recovering from AN. Research studies have found that individuals diagnosed with AN often suffer from difficulties recognizing, understanding, expressing, tolerating, and regulating their own emotions (Fox, 2009; Kyriacou, Easter, & Tchanturia, 2009; Racine & Wildes, 2013). With recovery from AN, these emotional deficits diminish to the point where most recovered individuals demonstrate beliefs about emotions, ability to tolerate emotions, and levels of emotion suppression similar to that of healthy control groups (Oldershaw et al., 2011).

In addition, research has indicated that although individuals diagnosed with AN suffered from severe suppression of emotional expression, during recovery from AN these individuals regained their capacity to express emotions and exhibited a greater degree of facial emotional expression (Dapelo, Hart, Hale, Morris, & Tchanturia, 2016). In particular, the expression of positive affect tended to be significantly increased during recovery (Dapelo et al. 2016), which makes the expression of positive emotions an important hallmark of recovery from AN.

Recovering the Embodied Experience

Intimately connected with these emotional processes, the experience of one's body is also severely impacted during AN and throughout recovery. Research studies that investigated the experience of corporeality in eating disorders concluded that "persons with [eating disorders] experience their own body first and foremost as an object being looked at by another, rather than cenesthetically or from a first-person perspective" (Stanghellini, Castellini, Broga, Faravelli, & Ricca, 2012, p. 148). Consistent with experiencing one's body from an external perspective, individuals with AN tend to exhibit heightened sensitivity to visual information about the body together with reduced somatosensory information processing about the body (Eshkevari, Rieger, Longo, Haggard, & Treasure, 2014). This heightened sensitivity to visual information which overrides the proprioceptive information processing has been described as increased "malleability of the bodily self" (Eshkevari et al., 2014, p. 401) and represents a unique characteristic of AN.

During recovery from AN, although this malleability of body-self diminishes, it continues to persist to a greater degree than that seen in healthy individuals (Eshkevari et al., 2014). Consequently, it is likely that recovered individuals will still tend to over-rely on visual cues in processing information about their bodies. Such an overreliance on visual cues suggests that even with AN symptom remission and weight restoration, the embodied experience of individuals with AN may differ significantly from that of individuals without a history of disordered eating.

Considering such features of AN, emphasis on embodied experience compliments the predominant attention given to body image as a way of approaching eating disorder etiology and recovery. As body image consists of a perceptual evaluation emphasizing experience of the body from an external perspective (Piran & Teall, 2012), concentration on body image adds to the focus on external experience of the body seen in cases of AN. Therefore, an embodied approach to AN recovery redresses imbalances in subjective and objective experience of the body.

Intrapersonal Aspects of Recovery

In addition to affective and embodied experience, intrapersonal dynamics have been cited as shifting with recovery from AN. The findings of a meta-synthesis research study investigating recovery from AN indicated that recovered individuals identified reclaiming power and control and acceptance of oneself as central aspects of the recovery process (Duncan, Sebar, & Lee, 2015). Linked to self-acceptance and increased agency, managing and connecting with emotions was identified as another key element during AN recovery (Duncan et al., 2015).

Also speaking to intrapersonal dynamics, Jenkins and Ogden (2012) found that women diagnosed with AN were prone to experience multiple dichotomies or splits between mind and body, behavior and cognitions, and rationality and irrationality. Remarkably, these women described recovery from AN as a time when these parts of their selves were no longer divided: an experience of becoming 'whole' (Jenkins & Ogden, 2012).

Relational and Sociocultural Dimensions of Recovery

Recent literature has posited AN as located at the intersection of body, self, and sociocultural context (Piran & Teall, 2012; Piran & Thompson, 2008). Exploring embodiment as it relates to eating disorder etiology, the Developmental Theory of Embodiment (DTE) suggests that complex social situations may play a decisive role in explaining how or why certain individuals are more prone to develop eating disorders (Piran & Teall, 2012). For example, violations of body ownership, internalization of social labels or stereotypes, and prejudice or disempowerment were identified as contributing to eating disorder development (Piran & Teall, 2012). Within such a framework, just as development of eating disorders is associated with disruptions in embodied experience, perspectives of recovery likewise must take into account the subjective lived experience of the body.

Summary

Existing literature indicates shifts in emotional experience (Dapelo et al., 2016; Oldershaw et al., 2011) as well as in the way the body-self is experienced (Eshkevari et al., 2014) with recovery from AN. Reclamation of power and control, increased self-acceptance, and the experience of becoming 'whole' also represent unique characteristics of recovery from AN (Duncan et al., 2015; Jenkins & Ogden, 2012). Such findings are congruent with locating eating disorders at the intersection of body, self, and sociocultural context, inferring that mainstream notions of recovery from AN lack consideration of subjective embodied affective experience.

Rationale and Purpose of the Study

Although several research studies have highlighted differences in affective and embodied experience in AN and with recovery (Dapelo et al., 2016; Eshkevari et al., 2014; Jenkins & Ogden, 2012; Oldershaw et al., 2011), research has yet to investigate embodied affective experience throughout the recovery process. In an effort to synthesize existing knowledge of embodied affect experience and develop a more holistic picture of recovery from AN, this study sought to explore the embodied and affective experience of women with AN through the process of recovery using sentence stems generating body-centered poetic discourse as a method of inquiry. In light of this study's aim, the research question was as follows: what are women's embodied affective experiences during the process of recovery from AN?

Method

Participants

Six Caucasian women, aged 21–28, diagnosed with AN within five to twelve years prior to this study, and self-identified as 'recovered,' participated in this study. Five of the participants reported past diagnosis of AN, restricting type, and one of the participants reported past diagnosis of comorbid AN and Bulimia Nervosa. Of the six participants, two reported continuing to limit food intake on a regular basis for weight maintenance purposes. However, each woman reported that she no longer restricted food intake to the point of leading to significantly low body weight; therefore, none of the women met DSM-5 diagnostic criteria for AN at the time of the study. Each woman reported a treatment history of a combination of multiple service providers, ranging from private counseling to residential treatment. Cumulative duration of treatment for AN ranged from just over two to twelve years.

Feminist Paradigmatic Foundation

Given the subjective and complex nature of embodied experience, a feminist approach emphasizing reflexivity, relationality, intimacy, and nurturance is consistent with the aims of this research (Devault, 1990; Gilligan, 1982). Research conducted from a feminist paradigm attends to the voices of the socially silenced or marginalized and actively seeks to eliminate the power imbalance between the researcher and participants, viewing each woman as an expert of her own lived experience (Mertens, 2015).

Body-Centered Poetic Discourse as Method of Inquiry

Body-centered poetic discourse was chosen as the method of inquiry for this study (Chadwick, 2016). As an alternative to semi-structured interviews, participants were guided to reflect on their embodied affective experience throughout recovery from AN using metaphorical and symbolic language. Sentence stems were used as an anchoring strategy to elicit body-centered poetic discourse. The use of sentence stems emerged from balancing the aim of inviting metaphorical reflection with the desire to provide a certain level of structure for reflection. This structure was provided as a means of mitigating anxiety and perfectionist tendencies associated with AN (Farstad, McGeown, & von Ranson, 2016). Previous research investigating embodied and emotional experience has utilized poetry (Bracegirdle, 2012), prompts such as cue cards to facilitate embodied reflection (Sutton, 2011), and thematic analysis of metaphorical discourse (Peltola & Saresma, 2014) as means of exploring such subjective complexities. Previous research has indicated that metaphorical language gives way to expression of subjective, experiential phenomena representing a natural medium for rich description of lived experience (Chadwick, 2016; Peltola & Saresma, 2014; Sutton, 2011). Moreover, due to the symbolic nature of the body and food in AN (Skårderud, 2007a; Woodman, 1980), the use of metaphorical language was congruous with the nature of this study.

Data Collection and Analysis

Each woman participating in the study was invited to complete a set of six body-centric sentence stems, displayed on six individual cards (see Appendix 1). Women were guided to complete as many or as few sentence stems in whatever order they chose, initially completing sentence stems based on how they currently experienced their body. They were then asked to complete the same sentence stems, as many or as few in whatever order, based on how they experienced their body at the worst of their eating disorder. Lastly, they were asked to complete the sentence stems, as many or as few in whatever order, based on how they hope to experience their body in the future. This dialogue was then transcribed and arranged as poetic verse, reflecting the expressive nature and phrasing of each women's words. Poems were analyzed by a research team using thematic analysis in accordance with the phases outlined by Braun and Clarke (2012). The research team consisted of four females, three of which were graduate students and one who held a Ph.D., from the Counselling Psychology department at a Canadian university. A team approach was chosen for data analysis procedures in light of feminist values of relationality and reflexivity (Mertens, 2015), fostering dialogue and reflection from multiple perspectives.

Results

From past-, present-, and future-oriented poetic discourse, reflections on three points of the AN recovery process were articulated: at the worst of the eating disorder, in recovery, and toward body-self unity. Out of each reflection point and corresponding themes that emerged, three body-self patterns were identified: the bifurcated body-self, the recovering body-self, and the unified body-self. In addition, eleven embodiment and three affective themes were identified (see Figure 11.1). With recovery from AN, discourse displayed a shift from negative embodied experience, characterized by experiencing the body as bad, disconnected, and restricting to positive embodied experience, characterized by experiencing the body

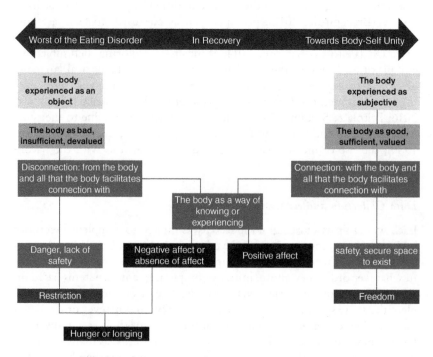

Figure 11.1 Embodied and Affective Themes.

as valuable, connected, and freeing. The shift in affective experience with recovery from AN was intertwined with embodied experience. Negative affect or absence of affect was gradually replaced by positive affect as facets of embodied experience shifted from negative to positive.

Poems of the Past: The Bifurcated Body-Self

At the worst of the eating disorder, women's embodied experience was characterized by a stark division between the object-body and the self. A sense of disenfranchisement prevailed, with the body lacking both value and beauty. Moreover, there was a clear pattern of the object-body being rejected by the self. The body was experienced as foreign and not belonging to the self. The following sections present the main embodiment and affective themes connected with the bifurcated body-self.

The body experienced as a devalued object. The most predominant theme emerging at the worst of the eating disorder was of the body being experienced almost completely as an object-body that did not belong to the self. Moreover, the object-body was perceived as bad, a censured problem never measuring up to expectations or desires. At this point, the body was also experienced as ugly and inferior, symbolizing failure and insufficiency. Women's accounts focused on external aspects of their bodies in a way that became consuming. Attention was placed on the object-body: how it looked externally, what it weighed, and how its shape could be manipulated.

> My body reminds me of clay –
>   clay that could be molded and moved – not hard clay.
>   It could be molded and moved into something that you like,
>   or that other people like, or that you'd feel more
>   comfortable with.
>   And you can control it in that manner.
>   And it's material.
>
>   (Paix)[1]

The body as a way of knowing or experiencing the undesirable. At the worst of the eating disorder, there was a pattern of disconnecting from experiencing one's emotions and inner self, as facilitated by the body. Moreover, the body represented a way of being in the world; of taking up physical space. Women described a persistent desire to take up less space, to disappear.

> My body prevents me from disappearing.
>   I think the purpose of my eating disorder, in some ways,
>   was to try to get as far away from my pain as possible,
>   by trying to disappear.
>   And in some ways, the paradox of the eating disorder is
>   you feel more valuable,
>   the less of you there is.
>
>   (Anna)

Disconnection from the body and all that the body facilitates connection with. Another emerging theme was that of disconnection of the self from body. At the worst of the eating disorder, there was a clear pattern expressed by the women of separation of the object-body and the self. Furthermore, the body was described as being foreign to the self.

> It almost felt like – I don't know because I've never experienced this –
>   but I would imagine it felt similarly to the way that someone feels
>   if they're transgendered.
>   They're in the wrong body.
>   And I felt like I was in the wrong body.
>
>   (Phoenix)

Danger and restriction. The themes of lacking safety and experiencing restriction emerged from the eating disorder discourse. Women's accounts were laden with patterns of antagonism. Battle language pervaded the struggle with the eating disorder and body-self. The body was often described as representing the battle site or the opponent itself. Focus was also on what the body preventing the self from doing. The body was poignantly experienced as a cage.

> My body makes me feel restricted...
> My body feels like a cage...
>> It was something that I was stuck in –
>>> I didn't like it, but I was just stuck in it.

(Paix)

Negative affect or absence of affect. Linked to the body as evoking emotions, the theme of the body being tied to the experience of negative or unwanted emotions, or a lack of emotional experience, emerged at the worst of the eating disorder. Disgust, shame, sadness, anger, anxiety, and numbness were all identified.

> My body makes me feel angry,
>> ashamed,
>> disgusted,
>> and sad because it couldn't be what I wanted.

(Devlin)

Hunger or longing. Lastly, the theme of intense hunger, desire, or longing emerged. Again, the irony of this theme within the context of AN is glaring, with the women's expression of 'hunger,' of insatiable longing for nonphysical needs to be met, juxtaposing with physical rejection of food.

> And what I wanted was what I thought would make me happy;
> or would bring me love – or whatever I wanted.
> And so constantly having that separation between what I was and what
> I wanted
>> made me very sad.

(Devlin)

Poems of the Present: The Recovering Body-Self

The word recovery in this context was chosen to reflect the pattern of the object-body being recovered by the self. Through the present-oriented poetic discourse, it becomes clear that these women were at varying points along the continuum of recovery from AN. Although each account reflects this range in recovery stage, there is an evident shift in how the body is experienced, contrasting with the past eating disorder discourse. Moreover, recovery discourse is characterized by tension between themes of positive and negative embodied and affective experience. There is an overarching pattern of struggling with the body as an object versus the body as subjective, the body as disconnected versus the body as connected, and the body as restricting versus the body as freeing. Affective themes reflect this dynamic, with clear tension between negative and positive affect including the experience of shame versus pride and anxiety versus peace. The following sections present the main embodiment and affective themes connected with the recovering body-self.

The body experienced as a devalued object versus a valuable subjectivity. The body continues to be experienced as an object by the majority of the women, yet the object-body is often perceived as valuable and belonging to the self. The body is experienced as an object-for-self. Remarkably, the body begins to be experienced as a subjective body-for-self in some cases. Extending beyond the self claiming the body as a valuable object, the self begins to identify with the subjective body.

> My body is me.
>> I feel more than ever that there isn't a distinction between
>>> myself and my body,
>>>> in terms of mind-body dualism,
>>>> so I feel very congruent as a self.
>>> I feel just as much that I am my toes,
>>>> as I am in my head,
>>>> walking around in this body...
> My body allows me to be me,
>> because there is no me without a body.
>
> (Anna)

The body as a way of knowing or experiencing the undesirable versus the desirable. Throughout recovery, the body continues to function as a way of knowing emotions, limits, and one's place in the world. In the present-oriented discourse, the body continues to evoke emotion. However, tension characterizing emotional experience is evident as women describe their bodies as evoking mixtures of discomfort and pride. Moreover, the body begins to be embraced as a way of the self existing in the world.

> If I think about my body as representing this journey of being a self
> in this world,
>> that I can see how far I've come, and also
>> it's been a painful experience,
>> to be a self in this body in this world.
>
> (Anna)

Disconnection versus connection from the body and all that the body facilitates connection with. The theme of disconnection persists into recovery, with a pattern of the body being disconnected. The body is still experienced by some women as being disconnected from the self, holding implications for the relationship between the self and the numerous aspects of lived experience that the body facilitates connection with. However, the perception of the body as foreign diminishes greatly with recovery and the theme of connection begins to emerge. In stark contrast with patterns of disconnection between the body, self, and affective experience, a pattern of connection with the body-self and with others surfaces.

> My body allows me to be present with my loved ones.
>
> > (Devlin)

Danger and restriction versus safety and freedom. Language denoting conflict continues into the present-oriented discourse, yet largely lacks the previous pattern of the body being an enemy. Instead, tension pervades the recovery discourse, with women describing a push-pull between past articles (restriction, discomfort, inadequacy) and emerging safety and acceptance. There is tension between what the body-self is and what it is not. Women describe their once restrictive bodies as facilitating freedom, with the body itself feeling free or allowing the self to feel free. This freedom is experienced through movement, power, and sovereignty.

> [My body is] free, too.
>   It feels free in a way that's new and exciting and victorious.
>
> > (Anna)

Negative affect or absence of affect versus positive affect. The theme of negative affect continues into recovery, although it becomes less dominating of the women's lived experiences. Disgust, shame, anxiety, and numbness are notably less present in recovery discourse. In contrast, women begin to express emotions that contradict previously prevailing negative affect including peace, happiness, and pride.

> My body makes me feel happy…
> My body feels at peace.
> My body feels rested…
> My body allows me to express joy.
>
> > (Paix)

Hunger or longing. The dominant theme of insatiable hunger or longing seen at the worst of the eating disorder begins to dissipate with recovery. Pangs of desire for the body-self to be more acceptable or different from how it actually is continue to emerge. However, the present-oriented discourse is characterized by a restlessness, lacking the fervent drive seen at the worst of the eating disorder.

> I'd say my body is trying to accept itself.
> Or my body is trying to get me to accept it.
>
> (Rebekah)

Poems of the Future: The Unified Body-Self

Recovery of the body by the self is sometimes followed by unification of the self with the body. With reflection on future hopes, perceiving the body as an object nearly entirely dissipates, along with ownership language referring to the body. In its place emerges the desire for and experience of body-self unity. The only trace of the body-as-object that remains in the future-oriented discourse is one instance of the self claiming the body, which is stated in conjunction with an expression of body-self unity:

> This is me,
> this is my body.
>
> (Devlin)

The following sections present the main embodiment and affective themes associated with the unified body-self.

The body experienced as a valuable subjectivity. A pattern of the body experienced as valuable and subjective emerges, characterized by a rejection of the body-as-object. Moreover, a pattern of the self identifying with the body surfaces within the future-oriented discourse. There is a resounding sense of unity between the body and self that emerges, with the body being described as integral to who the self is. The body does not become all-consuming, nor does it become eclipsed by the self. Rather, the body and the self become unified; paradoxically two entities as one whole person.

> I want to continue looking at my body as me.
>> My body is me.
>> I've just started to feel that way, and I want to even more so
>>> have that unity,
>>>> knowing that my body is me,
>>>> and it's my mind and my body and my soul.
>>
>> (Paix)

The body as a way of knowing or experiencing the desirable. The quality of valuing flows into the notion of the body as a way of knowing or experiencing. Within the future-oriented discourse, the body continues to evoke emotions, but such emotions are no longer unwanted. Likewise, the body also continues to function as a way of knowing limits, yet this is perceived as a crucial part of caring for oneself or even caring for others.

> My body prevents me from – as an experiential thermometer –
>   it prevents me from hurting myself, or other people,
>   or making mistakes
>   or from getting into danger.
> My body prevents me from doing things I don't want to do,
>   or are unhealthy for me.
>
> (Anna)

Connection with the body and all that the body facilitates connection with. A pattern of connection between the self, body, and others in the external world continues in the future-oriented discourse. In some cases, emerging is a sense not only of connection but of congruency between the self and the body.

> My body feels open
>   and connected...
> My body allows me to connect with myself,
>   and to others.
>
> (Lorelai)

Safety and freedom. Other themes that remain evident in future-oriented discourse are that of safety and freedom. The body continues to be experienced as a safe, secure place promoting a desire to care for the body-self. Additionally, themes of restriction present even into recovery are entirely absent here. Freedom is again experienced through movement, through the body facilitating expression of the self, and through feeling powerful.

> My body allows me to express who I feel like I really am.
>
> (Rebekah)

Positive affect. The final theme emerging from future-oriented discourse is that of positive affect. Emotions including peace, happiness, and gratitude continue to emerge, entirely replacing difficult emotions like anxiety, sadness, and shame that pervaded eating disorder discourse. The body becomes as a source of peace, contentment, and happiness, and prompts gratitude stemming from its ability to endure and be healthy.

> My body makes me feel grateful.
>   I'd like to feel what it's like to be in my body
>   or look at my body

and be grateful that it's still going – after everything I put it
   through.
My body is a gift.
      I'd like to recognize that it's a gift
      and be grateful for it
      and really recognize that it is special and created.

(Devlin)

Discussion

Recovery from AN and restoration of embodied experience.
Poetic discourse gathered through this study conveys restoration of embodied experience as intrinsic to women's journey of recovery from AN.
Recovery here is used to describe the physical and psychological process
of healing from AN, while restoration refers to the embodied experience,
defined as (re)engagement of the body with the world (Piran & Teall,
2012). Depicting this process, at the worst of each woman's battle with
AN, a pattern of body-for-other emerged, with the object-body separated from the self. The body was experienced as devalued and disgusting,
symbolizing insufficiency and struggle. It was an antagonist to the self, an
encasing enemy that was both foreign and tormenting. A sense of disenfranchisement, of the object-body belonging to, and existing for the other
prevailed. Moreover, the self was consumed by insatiable hunger rooted
in a sense of inadequacy. The 'body-that-is-not-mine' accompanied a self
characterized by the desire to diminish or disappear.

As the recovery journey progressed, a pattern of the self recovering
the body emerged. Women's accounts vividly illustrated how, through
recovery from AN, the self gradually claimed ownership of the previously
estranged object-body. Although at this stage, the body remained pre-
dominantly experienced as an object that the self possessed and inhabited,
'body-for-self' language entered the discourse. Additionally, the 'body-
that-is-mine' became associated with strength, power, and agency, while
tension in the relationship between self and body were evident.

Although potentially idyllic, a pattern of the self identifying and finding
unity with the body emerged when women reflected on how they envision their future. Each woman was not only able to identify and conceive
of this picture but also expressed striving for such a possibility. When
observed in contrast with alarming accounts of disgust and disdain for the
one's own body at the worst of the eating disorder, it is astounding that
these women would eventually desire to experience body-self unity. The
'body-that-is-me' becomes a symbol of victory and a subjective site of
lived experience, expansive, and free in the world.

Implications and recommendations. The findings of this study further the understanding of the AN recovery process. Notably, this study's
results parallel previous research findings of increased 'malleability' of the

186 Chelsea Beyer and Mihaela Launeanu

body enduring even when the individual is considered recovered from AN (Eshkevari et al., 2014). Just as women participating in the study may be considered recovered by mainstream diagnostic standards, yet still spoke of vexing relationships with their bodies to varying degrees, previous research suggests that disruptions in embodied experience may remain after external signs of the eating disorder remiss (Eshkevari et al., 2014). The implications of this observation extend to the dilemma of defining recovery, termination of treatment, and perhaps even rates of relapse. If women are deemed recovered based on behavioral and physical symptom remission despite persistent disruptions in embodied affective experience, and treatment is ended, it is reasonable to speculate that the likelihood of relapse would be high.

When questioning what constitutes full recovery from AN, one is also confronted with the hopes of the women who participated in the study and the stark realities of what it means to be a self in a female body in today's world. Illustrating such complexities of recovery, one woman described having a "normal level of discontent with [her] body," when discussing her relationship with her body prior to her eating disorder (Phoenix). A second woman echoed this sentiment when speaking of her current stage of recovery:

> I'll always be a 9.5 out of 10 in recovery, because... the normative discontent for women in their experience of their bodies in North America, and so I think we all need to recover. I think, as women in North America, we all need to recover. I would say that most people, their journey of recovery might be different, and maybe it's not as severe, where they start, but that we need to have a total sociocultural revolution in the way that we view our bodies and ourselves as women. And I think that until I'm in perfect unity with myself, I think I'll always be in recovery.
>
> (Anna)

What these women described mirrors verbatim what has been coined 'a normative discontent,' linking the experience of shame with women's prevailing state of preoccupation with bodily physical appearance (Rodin, Silberstein, & Striegel-Moore, 1984). The elusiveness of full recovery from AN is often attributed to individual factors or the nature of the disorder itself (Carter et al., 2004). Yet such a baseline for female lived experience in Western society, a *normal* discontent with the body-self, presents a barrier to body-self unity. Recovery from AN then shifts from being a matter of the individual to a systemic matter of sociocultural perceptions of and interactions with the female body-self.

The study's findings also contribute to existing literature illustrating recovery from AN as a process of becoming 'whole' (Jenkins & Ogden, 2012). Moreover, poetic discourse links this process of becoming whole with themes of reclaiming power and agency and connecting with emotions, which are previously identified key elements in recovery from AN (Duncan et al., 2015). Such findings illustrate that for women to 'recover' their bodies as belonging to their selves represents great progress, yet unification of the female body-self lies beyond reclamation. Moreover, seeking this unity involves connecting with emotions through engaging with the body and encouraging the female body-self to exist as expansive, powerful, and free.

As a whole, this study's findings support the need for reframing AN and AN recovery as at the intersection of embodied affective experience and sociocultural factors, complimentary to the dominant yet inadequate emphasis on food and the object-body. Focusing research efforts on investigating factors influencing positive embodied affective experience may further elucidate the AN recovery process. Likewise, emphasizing intrapersonal relational dynamics of the self, body, and emotions represents a promising therapeutic alternative to mainstream behavior- and object-body-focused approaches to treatment of AN.

Note

1 All participants chose pseudonyms to be represented by.

References

American Psychiatric Association. (2013). *Diagnostic and statistical manual of mental disorders* (5th ed.). Washington, DC: American Psychiatric Association.

Bracegirdle, C. E. (2012). Discovering embodiment: A poetic method. *Body, Movement and Dance in Psychotherapy: An International Journal for Theory, Research and Practice, 7*, 201–214. doi:10.1080/174332979.2011.645879

Braun, V., & Clarke, V. (2012). Thematic analysis. In H. Cooper. (Eds.), *APA handbook of research methods in psychology: Vol. 2. research designs*. (pp. 57–71). Washington, DC: American Psychological Association.

Carter, J. C., Blackmore, E., Sutandar-Pinnock, K., & Woodside, D. B. (2004). Replase in anorexia nervosa: A survival analysis. *Psychological Medicine, 34*, 671–679. doi:10.1017/S0033291703001168

Chadwick, R. (2016). Embodied methodologies: Challenges, reflections and strategies. *Qualitative Research, 21*, 1–21. doi:10.1177/1468794116656035

Dapelo, M., Hart, S., Hale, C., Morris, R., & Tchanturia, K. (2016). Expression of positive emotions differs in illness and recovery in Anorexia Nervosa. *Psychiatry Research, 246*, 48–51. doi:10.1016/j.psychres.2016.09.014

Devault, M. L. (1990). Talking and listening from women's standpoint: Feminist strategies for interviewing and analysis. *Social Problems, 37*, 96–116.

Duncan, T., Sebar, B., & Lee, J. (2015). Reclamation of power and self: A metasynthesis exploring the process of recovery from anorexia nervosa. *Advances in Eating Disorders: Theory, Research and Practice, 3*(2), 177–190. doi:10.1080/21662630.2014.978804

Eshkevari, E., Rieger, E., Longo, M. R., Haggard, P., & Treasure, J. (2014). Persistent body image disturbance following recovery from eating disorders. *The International Journal of Eating Disorders, 47*, 400–409, doi:10.1002/eat.22219

Farstad, S. M., McGeown, L. M., & von Ranson, K. M. (2016). Eating disorders and personality, 2004–2016: A systematic review and meta-analysis. *Clinical Psychology Review, 46*, 91–105. doi:10/1016/j.cpr.2016.04.005

Fox, J. R. E. (2009). A qualitative exploration of the perception of emotions in anorexia nervosa: A basic emotion and developmental perspective. *Journal of Clinical Psychology and Psychotherapy, 16*, 276–302.

Gilligan, C. (1982). *In a different voice: Psychological theory and women's development.* Cambridge, MA: Harvard University Press.

Jenkins, J., & Ogden, J. (2012). Becoming 'whole' again: A qualitative study of women's views of recovering from anorexia nervosa. *European Eating Disorders Review, 20*, 23–31. doi:10.1002/erv.1085

Kyriacou, O., Easter, A., & Tchanturia, K. (2009). Comparing views of patients, parents and clinicians on emotions in anorexia: A qualitative study. *Journal of Health Psychology 14*, 843–854.

Mertens, D. M. (2015). *Research and evaluation in education and psychology* (4th ed.). Thousand Oaks, CA: SAGE Publications, Inc.

Oldershaw, A., Hambrook, D., Stahl, D., Tchanturia, K., Treasure, J., & Schmidt, U. (2011). The socio-emotional processing stream in Anorexia Nervosa. *Neuroscience and Biobehavioural Reviews, 35*(3), 970–988.

Peltola, H. R., & Saresma, T. (2014). Spatial and bodily metaphors in narrating the experience of listening to sad music. *Musicae Scientiae, 18*, 292–306.

Piran, N., & Teall, T. (2012). The developmental theory of embodiment. In G. McVey, M. P. Levine, N. Piran, & H. B. Ferguson. (Eds.), *Preventing eating-related and weight-related disorders: Collaborative research, advocacy, and policy change* (pp. 169–198). Waterloo, ON: Wilfred Laurier University Press.

Piran, N., & Thompson, S. (2008). A study of the adverse social experiences model to the development of eating disorders. *International Journal of Health Promotion & Education, 46*, 65–71.

Racine, S. E., & Wildes, J. E. (2013). Emotion dysregulation and symptoms of anorexia nervosa: The unique roles of lack of emotional awareness and impulse control difficulties when upset. *International Journal of Eating Disroders, 46*(7), 713–720. doi:10.1002/eat.22145

Rodin, J., Silberstein, L., & Striegel-Moore, R. (1984). Women and weight: A normative discontent. *Nebraska Symposium on Motivation, 32*, 267–307.

Skårderud, F. (2007a). Eating one's words, part I: 'Concretised metaphors' and reflective function in anorexia nervosa – An interview study. *European Eating Disorders Review, 15*(3), 163–174. doi:10.1002/erv.777

Stanghellini, G., Castellini, G., Brogna, P., Faravelli, C., & Ricca, V. (2012). Identity and eating disorders (IDEA): A Questionnaire Evaluating Identity and embodiment in eating disorder patients. *Psychopathology, 45*, 147–158. doi:10.1159/000330258.

Steinhausen, H. C. (2002). The outcome of anorexia nervosa in the 20th century. *American Journal of Psychiatry, 159*, 1284–1293.

Sutton, B. (2011). Playful cards, serious talk: A qualitative research technique to elicit women's embodied experiences. *Qualitative Research, 11*, 177–196.

Woodman, M. (1980). *The owl was a baker's daughter.* Toronto, ON: Inner City Books.

Appendix 1

Sentence Stem Cards

My body reminds me of...	My body allows me to...	My body feels...
My body is...	My body prevents me from...	My body makes me feel...

12 Older Women and the Embodied Experience of Weight

Laura Hurd Clarke

Introduction

Embodiment, or the way we inhabit and experience our bodies as we move through the world, entails a complex interplay between our corporeality and our sociocultural context. In this chapter, I draw upon the extant literature to examine how dominant age, gender, and health norms in western society influence older women's embodied experiences of weight. In particular, I explore how older women perceive and make sense of their weight in a social context in which aging female bodies are considered unattractive and health is simultaneously understood as a moral responsibility and the outcome of individual effort. I further consider the literature which has found that older women reevaluate the importance of appearance in later life. I conclude by discussing the overall implications of the sociocultural research and theorizing concerning older women's embodiment of weight and suggest possible ways forward.

Older Women, Weight, and Disordered Eating: What Do We Know?

Although body image research has historically focused primarily on college-aged women, in recent years, scholars have begun to investigate the perceptions and experiences of more diverse samples. The resultant findings indicate that displeasure with the body is a "normative discontent" (Rodin, Silberstein, & Striegel-Moore, 1984, p. 267) across the life span as middle-aged and older women report body dissatisfaction rates that are similar to their younger female counterparts (Bedford & Johnson, 2006; Runfola et al., 2013). Like younger women, older women often express dissatisfaction with their weight (Allaz, Bernstein, Rouget, Archinard, & Morabia, 1998; Grogan, 2017; Lewis & Cachelin, 2001; Stevens & Tiggemann, 1998). For example, in a study of body image and embodied aging that I conducted with 22 women aged 61–92 (Hurd, 2000; Hurd Clarke, 2002a,b), the participants often pinpointed their weight as their key source of dissatisfaction as they made statements similar to the following: "I'd like to weigh less" (aged 61), "I don't like my fat body" (aged 76), and "Weight has pretty much always been a concern or problem for me" (aged 85). Consequently, many older women attempt to control or alter their weight through the use of restrictive diets, exercise, and herbal supplements (Bedford & Johnson, 2006; Hurd Clarke, 2010).

In addition to a consideration of body image and weight in later life, there is a growing literature that has explored eating disorders among older women. This research suggests that approximately 2%–4% of women aged 60+ have eating disorders (Gadalla, 2008; Mangweth-Matzek et al., 2006), with binge eating disorder and other eating disorders being more common in older women as compared to the higher rates of anorexia nervosa and bulimia nervosa found in younger women (Podfigurna-Stopa et al., 2015). Of particular concern is the evidence that suggests that eating disorder rates may be on the rise among older women as a result of their lifelong struggles with clinical eating issues as well as the onset of disorders after middle age (Midlarksy, Marotta, Pirutinsky, Morin, & McGowan, 2017; Podfigurna-Stopa et al., 2015). Key risk factors for eating disorders in middle age and later life are similar to those experienced by younger women and include body image dissatisfaction, perfectionism, intergenerational patterns of body image dissatisfaction and weight preoccupation, comorbidities such as mood and anxiety disorders, stress, and traumatic life events (Gadalla, 2008; Madowitz, Matheson, & Liang, 2015; Maine, Samuels, & Tantillo, 2015; McLean, Paxton, & Wertheim, 2010; Midlarksy et al., 2017). However, the assumption that eating disorders only occur in young women and the entrenchment of habits over time result in clinical eating issues often going underdiagnosed and remaining untreated in the older population (Maine et al., 2015; Peat, Peyerl, & Muehlenkamp, 2008).

Although many parallels may be drawn between the psychological mechanisms underpinning older women and younger women's body dissatisfaction and presentation of eating disorders, there are some unique sociocultural factors in later life that strongly influence women's embodiment of weight. In the sections that follow, I will explore how age, gender, and health norms and ideals intersect with the social and physical realities of growing older in distinctive ways. In doing so, I will consider how older women may internalize and resist sociocultural norms concerning the aging, female body.

Ageism, Beauty, and Body Dissatisfaction in Later Life

One of the most powerful influences on the ways that older women inhabit and experience their bodies are the primarily negative cultural meanings attributed to growing older in western society. Rather than being esteemed or assumed to be a natural and inevitable process, agedness is reviled and feared, and older adults face progressive social exclusion with the advancement of time. This systematic process of exclusion is referred to as ageism, a term coined by Butler (1975) and defined as "the systematic stereotyping and discrimination against older adults because they are old" (p. 12). Ageist stereotypes depict old age as a time of inevitable poor health, dependency, obsolescence, senility, social disengagement, lack of sexuality, and loss of attractiveness (Hurd Clarke, 2010; Nelson, 2002; Palmore, 1999). These stereotypes underpin a cultural narrative of decline in which later life is devalued and youthfulness is positioned as the ideal to which all must continually strive and by which our social status is gauged (Gullette, 1997). The cultural disparagement of aging has everyday consequences. Indeed, the societal privileging of youthfulness legitimizes discriminatory policies and practices by which older men and women are denied opportunities and resources in the workplace (Harris, Krygsman, Waschenko, & Rudman, 2017; Stypinska & Turek, 2017), the health-care system (Ben-Harush et al., 2016; Chrisler, Barney, & Palatino, 2016; Dobbs et al., 2008), and daily interactions (Hurd Clarke & Griffin, 2008; Ward & Holland, 2011). In this way, ageism poses a serious threat to the quality of life and well-being of older adults.

Although it is a pernicious social problem that we all will experience should we live long enough (Calasanti, 2005), ageism is particularly injurious to older women who must endure the combined oppressions of being old and female (Ginn & Arber, 1995; Itzin & Phillipson, 1995). Women learn from an early age that their social status is linked to their physical appearances, specifically their approximation to the feminine beauty ideal of a young, toned, wrinkle-free, and voluptuous yet slender body (Bordo, 2003). In contrast, men derive social status from their physical and social accomplishments (Calasanti & King, 2005). Consequently, growing older is a gendered process, and there is a double standard of aging for women and men (Sontag, 1997). While women lose social status as they grow older and their appearances increasingly deviate from ageist beauty standards, men may retain their cultural currency in later life insofar as they demonstrate and embody idealized masculine qualities such as strength, productivity, wealth, and power. The centrality of appearance to women's social status is evidenced in the research that has examined interpersonal relationships as well as age-based discrimination in the workplace. For example, heterosexual men, especially those who are higher in social status as a result of being affluent and well educated, have been found to place greater emphasis on the physical attractiveness of their mates than do women (Fales et al., 2016). In particular, Fales et al. (2016) found that wealthy men strongly preferred women who were slender. Similarly, women are more likely to report that they experience discrimination in the workplace as a result of their appearances and sexuality (Duncan & Loretto, 2004; Walker, Grant, Meadows, & Cook, 2007) and to associate looking older with being socially invisible to younger individuals (Hurd Clarke & Griffin, 2008).

Although the beauty ideal for women encompasses various aspects of physical appearance, weight is central to the narrative of the problematic and unattractive older female body. Older women often express a preference for curvier female bodies than current extremes of thinness allow (Hurd Clarke, 2002b). However, older women, like their younger counterparts, also typically rate their bodies as heavier than their internalized beauty ideals (Stevens & Tiggemann, 1998). The discrepancy between their preferred and actual bodies might, in part, be explained by the physical changes that occur with age, including the weight gain and increases in total body fat and abdominal fat that are common in later life, particularly after menopause (Davis et al., 2012; Grogan, 2017). Older women often refer to these physical processes in their accounts of their changing body sizes and shapes. For example, a 76-year-old woman I interviewed stated,

> When you get to around 60, you develop a pot. Like a fat belly. And no matter whether you've had children or whether you're married, most women do...I guess it started a little bit when I was in my mid-fifties...And I found that every year I gained another 10 pounds.
>
> (Hurd Clarke, 2002a, p. 757)

Moreover, many older women report finding it increasingly difficult to remain slim and toned with age, as articulated by a 67-year-old woman I interviewed:

> When I was in my 20s and 30s, I never had any weight problems... Once I got into my 40s, I started to notice I was getting that roll around the waist...I find that the older I get, the easier it is for me to put weight on.
>
> (Hurd Clarke, 2002a, p. 757)

Although they acknowledge that weight gain is common in later life, older women rarely question or challenge western beauty ideals. Rather, to their own detriment, older women suggest that aging and the associated weight gain experienced by most women result in an inevitable loss of physical attractiveness as well as an increasing inability to retain the male gaze. For example, an 87-year-old woman had this to say:

> Women's bodies are ugly. Older women's bodies...I think most people think their bodies are ugly...Even women before 60. Once they start to sag and stuff, there's no beauty in it. If you're looking–if you're looking for beauty as beauty in the–as the bodies we see on T.V., all these lovely, gorgeous girls. If that's beauty, then women over 50 or 60 whose bodies are sagging, their busts are sagging, their bellies are all over, you know, from the baby bearing, and the ass is sagging–they're ugly. There's no beauty in that. No man is going to find beauty in that.
>
> (Hurd, 2000, p. 87)

In this way, older women are acutely aware of the social risks of being old and overweight.

Healthism and Weight in Later Life

In addition to ageist beauty ideals, older women's perceptions and ex-periences of their weight in later life are strongly influenced by societal norms concerning health and health promotion. Healthism entails the as-sumptions that engagement in health promotion is a moral obligation and health is the outcome of individual effort (Crawford, 2006). Healthism is a pervasive cultural norm which constructs poor health and deviation from body ideals as the result of laziness and a failure to adequately disci-pline the body. This is especially evident in the fat phobia or weight-based discrimination that has become prevalent in western society (Brownell, 2005). As appearances are used to judge individual health and morality, healthism leads to victim blaming and diverts attention away from the influence of social position and the accumulation of health inequities over the life course (Crawford, 1980, 2006; Dworkin & Wachs, 2009; Hurd Clarke & Bennett, 2013b).

In later life, healthism is buttressed by ageism as fears of bodily decline and social marginalization underpin individuals' efforts to manage their bodies and optimize their health. Against the backdrop of ageist stereotypes, Rowe and Kahn (1997) have suggested the possibility of what they refer to as suc-cessful aging, which is defined by the presence of three factors, namely low probability of disease and disability, high functioning, and active life en-gagement. Rowe and Kahn (1998) assert that successful aging is attainable "through individual choice and effort" (p. 37), including but not limited to weight control practices. The concept of aging successfully has been fervently taken up by health-care professionals and consumer culture as individuals are strongly urged to properly care for their bodies so as to avoid 'failing' at aging by becoming overweight, unfit, unhealthy, unproductive, and ultimately un-desirable (Higgs, Leontowitsch, Stevenson, & Rees Jones, 2009).

Within this social context, weight is associated with a complex web of moral and health meanings. On the one hand, being overweight is associated with 'indulgence' and a failure to adequately discipline the body through health promotion. A 78-year-old woman I interviewed put it this way:

> I am impatient with my weight gain…I think hormonal change cer-tainly is a factor but the rest of it is lack of suitable exercise and prob-ably indulgence…I don't think weight gain is a natural process…My lack of discipline…is like a thorn in your flesh because it's a weakness that you have to think, 'Oh, I've caused this'.
>
> (Hurd Clarke, 2002a, p. 758)

Although she conceded that hormonal changes associated with menopause influenced her weight, the above woman argued that weight gain was neither 'natural' nor inevitable, a position that underscored her sense of personal failure and inadequacy.

At the same time, being overweight is also equated with poor health and articulated in terms of fears of bodily decline. A 69-year-old woman put it this way:

> I think everybody is concerned about weight! I think especially as you get older. It sounds odd but it's not just for looks. It's because we get into high cholesterol and heart problems and things like that. And you know that you should be taking your weight down...Like I've put on 20 pounds this past year which I don't like. I'm not happy about it but not because of what I look like. It's my health. It's not good for me... and I worry about my health.
>
> (Hurd Clarke, 2002a, p. 764)

In other words, being overweight is both socially and physically risky. Thus, it is perhaps not surprising that many older women suggest that their reasons for trying to lose weight encompass both social and health motivations, which often coexist in an uneasy tension, as articulated by a 72-year-old woman:

> I guess we think that thin, shapely people are beautiful. I suppose that's the real reason [for trying to lose weight]. I mean, there are a lot of people now who are concerned for their health. They should be if they're not. It really does matter. But I guess it's appearance first; it certainly isn't health first. They wouldn't be doing a lot of other silly things if their health was a real concern.
>
> (Hurd Clarke, 2002a, p. 767)

Conceding that health was a growing concern for many older people, the above woman argued that appearance motivations were the primary driver of most women's eating practices.

That said, the onset of health issues and changes to body functionality that are typical of later life often underscore and influence the relationship between health and appearance. One woman I interviewed summarized the relationship between health and appearance in this way: "Keeping well is the thing you worry about when you're 70. Not so much how it looks as how well is it functioning" (Hurd, 2000, p. 89). Tiggemann (2004) articulates this changing understanding of the body as follows: "In simple terms, with age women's bodies deteriorate, they remain equally dissatisfied, but it matters less" (p. 35). While body dissatisfaction remains constant across the life span, health and body functionality become more salient than appearance over time (Baker & Gringart, 2009; Hurd, 2000; Liechty & Yarnal, 2010; Reboussin et al., 2000). As such, the physical realities of growing older result in a reprioritization of health and appearance, particularly in the face of decreasing functional abilities.

Bringing It All Together: Concluding Comments

In this chapter, I have examined the sociocultural norms and bodily ideals that shape and constrain older women's embodiment of weight. While slenderness is equated with beauty, youth, and health, overweight is associated with being ugly, old, and sick. The physical changes that accompany growing older often include weight gain, among other bodily alterations, making it progressively harder for women to approximate the beauty ideal. Losing markers of physical attractiveness results in women experiencing declines in social status, which translates into social invisibility, challenges in finding and retaining romantic partners, and discrimination. Even as they may downplay the importance of appearance, older women are under strong pressure to continue to manage their appearances, especially to control their weights. Collectively, ageism, beauty standards, and healthism heighten the likelihood of older women experiencing body dissatisfaction, a key risk factor for eating disorders.

Moving forward, we must confront and address the impacts of ageism, sexism, and healthism on older women's perceptions of their bodies and experiences of growing older. To do that, we need to foster and promote resilience and positive body image across the life course by reframing aging as a natural, if not desirable, journey, valuing women for qualities other than their appearances, and empowering individuals of all ages to appreciate, respect, and embrace bodily diversity. However, it is not sufficient to simply change the attitudes and perceptions of individuals – we must strive to alter the social context underlying women's experiences of their weight and aging bodies. Thus, we need to disrupt cultural narratives that position beauty as a physical quality or the sole purview of the young, later life as a time of inevitable decline and decay, and health as a moral barometer rather than a human right. Through education and policy initiatives, we can strive to eradicate the often taken-for-granted and insidious assumptions about gender, health, and old bodies that lead to personal suffering, social exclusion, and age- and gender-based discrimination. In doing so, we can move towards the creation of a more equitable and inclusive social world.

References

Allaz, A. F., Bernstein, M., Rouget, P., Archinard, M., & Morabia, A. (1998). Body weight preoccupation in middle-age and ageing women: A general population survey. *International Journal of Eating Disorders, 23*(3), 287–294.

Baker, L. & Gringart, E. (2009). Body image and self-esteem in older adulthood. *Ageing & Society, 29*(6), 977–995.

Bedford, J. L. & Johnson, C. S. (2006). Societal influences on body image dissatisfaction in younger and older women. *Journal of Women & Aging, 18*(1), 41–55.

Ben-Harush, A., Shiovitz-Ezra, S., Doron, I., Alon, S., Leibovitz, A., Golander, H., Haron, Y., & Ayalon, L. (2016). Ageism among physicians, nurses, and social workers: Findings from a qualitative study. *European Journal of Ageing, 14*(1), 39–48.

Bordo, S. (2003). *Unbearable weight: Feminism, western culture, and the body.* 10th anniversary ed. Los Angeles, CA: University of California Press.

Brownell, K. D. (2005). *Weight bias: Nature, consequences, and remedies.* New York, NY: Guildford Press.

Butler, R. N. (1975). *Why survive? Being old in America.* New York, NY: Harper and Row.

Calasanti, T. (2005). Ageism, gravity, and gender: Experiences of aging bodies. *Generations, 29*(3), 8–12.

Calasanti, T., & King, N. (2005). Firming the floppy penis: Age, class, and gender relations in the lives of old men. *Men and Masculinities, 8*(1), 3–23.

Chrisler, J. C., Barney, A., & Palatino, B. (2016). Ageism can be hazardous to women's health: Ageism, sexism, and stereotypes of older women in the health-care system. *Journal of Social Issues, 72*(1), 86–104.

Crawford, R. (1980). Healthism and the medicalization of everyday life. *International Journal of Health Services, 10*(3), 365–388.

Crawford, R. (2006). Health as a meaningful social practice. *Health, 10*(4), 401–420.

Davis, S. R., Castelo-Branco, C., Chedraui, P., Lumsden, M. A., Nappi, R. E., Shah, D., & Villaseca, P. (2012). Understanding weight gain at menopause. *Climacteric, 15*(5), 419–429.

Dobbs, D., Eckert, J. K., Rubinstein, B., Keimig, L., Clark, L., Frankowski, A. C., & Zimmerman, S. (2008). An ethnographic study of stigma and ageism in residential care or assisted living. *The Gerontologist, 48*(4), 517–526.

Duncan, C. & Loretto, W. (2004). Never the right age? Gender and age-based discrimination in employment. *Gender, Work and Organization, 11*(1), 95–115.

Dworkin, S. L. & Wachs, F. L. (2009). *Body panic: Gender, health, and the selling of fitness.* New York, NY: New York University Press.

Fales, M. R., Frederick, D. A., Garcia, J. R., Gildersleeve, K. A., Haselton, M. G., & Fisher, H. E. (2016). Mating markets and bargaining hands: Mate preferences for attractiveness and resources in two national U.S. studies. *Personality and Individual Differences, 88*, 78–87.

Gadalla, T. M. (2008). Eating disorders and associated psychiatric comorbidity in elderly Canadian women. *Archives of Women's Mental Health, 11*(5), 357–362.

Ginn, J., & Arber, S. (1995). 'Only connect': Gender relations and ageing. In S. Arber & J. Ginn (Eds.), *Connecting gender and ageing: A sociological approach* (pp. 1–14). Buckingham, UK: Open University Press.

Grogan, S. (2017). *Body image: Understanding body dissatisfaction in men, women and children.* New York, NY: Routledge.

Gullette, M. M. (1997). *Declining to decline: Cultural combat and the politics of the midlife.* Charlottesville, VA: University of Virginia Press.

Harris, K., Krygsman, S., Waschenko, J., & Rudman, D. L. (2017). Ageism and the older worker: A scoping review. *The Gerontologist.* doi:10.1093/geront/gnw194

Higgs, P., Leontowitsch, M., Stevenson, F., & Rees Jones, I. (2009). Not just old and sick – the 'will to health' in later life. *Ageing & Society, 29*(5), 687–707.

Hurd, L. C. (2000). Older women's body image and embodied experience: An exploration. *Journal of Women & Aging, 12*(3–4), 77–97.

Hurd Clarke, L. (2002a). Older women's perceptions of ideal body weights: The tensions between health and appearance motivations for weight loss. *Ageing & Society, 22*(6), 751–773.

Hurd Clarke, L. (2002b). Beauty in later life: Older women's perceptions of physical attractiveness. *Canadian Journal on Aging, 21*(3), 429–442.

Hurd Clarke, L. (2010). *Facing age: Women growing older in anti-aging culture.* Lanham, MD: Rowman and Littlefield.

Hurd Clarke, L. & Bennett, E. V. (2013b). Constructing the moral body: Self-care among older adults with multiple chronic conditions. *Health, 17*(3), 211–228.

Hurd Clarke, L. & Griffin, M. (2008). Visible and invisible ageing: Beauty work as a response to ageism. *Ageing & Society, 28*(5), 653–674.

Itzin, C. & Phillipson, C. (1995). Gendered ageism as a double jeopardy for women in organizations. In C. Itzin & J. Newman (Eds.), *Gender, culture, and organizational change: Putting theory into practice* (pp. 81–90). London, UK: Routledge.

Lewis, D. M. & Cachelin, F. M. (2001). Body image, body dissatisfaction, and eating attitudes in midlife and elderly women. *Eating Disorders, 9*(1), 29–39.

Liechty, T. & Yarnal, C. M. (2010). Older women's body image: A lifecourse perspective. *Ageing & Society, 30*(7), 1197–1218.

Madowitz, J., Matheson, B. E., & Liang, J. (2015). The relationship between eating disorders and sexual trauma. *Eating and Weight Disorders: Studies on Anorexia, Bulimia and Obesity, 20*(3), 281–293.

Maine, M. D., Samuels, K. L., & Tantillo, M. (2015). Eating disorders in adult women: Biopsychosocial, developmental, and clinical considerations. *Advances in Eating Disorders: Theory, Research and Practice, 3*(2), 133–143.

Mangweth-Matzek, B., Rupp, C. I., Hausmann, A., Assmayr, K., Mariacher, E., Kemmler, G., Whitworth, A. B., & Biebl, W. (2006). Never too old for eating disorders or body dissatisfaction: A community study of elderly women. *International Journal of Eating Disorders, 39*(7), 583–586.

McLean, S. A., Paxton, S. J., & Wertheim, E. H. (2010). Factors associated with body dissatisfaction and disordered eating in women in midlife. *International Journal of Eating Disorders, 43*(6), 527–536.

Midlarksy, E., Marotta, A. K., Pirutinsky, S., Morin, R. T., & McGowan, J. C. (2017). Psychological predictors of eating pathology in older adult women. *Journal of Women & Aging.* doi:10.1080/08952841.2017.1295665

Nelson, T. D. (2002). *Ageism: Stereotyping and prejudice against older persons.* Cambridge, MA: The MIT Press.

Palmore, E. B. (1999). *Ageism: Negative and positive* (2nd ed.). New York, NY: Springer.

Peat, C. M., Peyerl, N. L., & Muehlenkamp, J. J. (2008). Body image and eating disorders in older adults: A review. *The Journal of General Psychology, 135*(4), 343–358.

Podfigurna-Stopa, A., Czyzyk, A., Katulski, K., Smolarczyk, R., Grymowicz, M., Maciejewska-Jeske, M., & Meczekalski, B. (2015). Eating disorders in older women. *Maturitas, 82*(2), 146–152.

Reboussin, B. A., Rejeski, W. J., Martin, K. A., Callahan, K., Dunn, A. L., King, A. C., & Sallis, J. F. (2000). Correlates of satisfaction with body function and body appearance in middle and older aged adults: The activity counseling trial (ACT). *Psychology & Health, 15*(2), 239–254.

Rodin, J., Silberstein, L., & Striegel-Moore, R. (1984). Women and weight: A normative discontent. *Nebraska Symposium on Motivation, 32,* 267–307.

Rowe, J. W. & Kahn, R. L. (1997). Successful aging. *The Gerontologist, 37*(4), 433–440.

Rowe, J. W. & Kahn, R. L. (1998). *Successful aging.* New York, NY: Random House.

Runfola, C. D., Von Holle, A., Trace, S. E., Brownley, K. A., Hofmeier, S. M., Gagne, D. A., & Bulik, C. M. (2013). Body dissatisfaction in women across the lifespan: Results of the UNC-SELF and gender and body image (GABI) studies. *European Eating Disorders Review, 21*(1), 52–59.

Sontag, S. (1997). The double standard of aging. In M. Pearsall (Ed.), *The other within us: Feminist explorations of women and aging* (pp. 19–24). Boulder, CO: Westview Press.

Stevens, C., & Tiggemann, M. (1998). Women's body figure preferences across the life span. *The Journal of Genetic Psychology, 159*(1), 94–102.

Stypinska, J. & Turek, K. (2017). Hard and soft age discrimination: The dual nature of workplace discrimination. *European Journal of Ageing, 14*(1), 49–61.

Tiggemann, M. (2004). Body image across the adult life span: Stability and change. *Body Image, 1*(1), 29–41.

Walker, H., Grant, D., Meadows, M., & Cook, I. (2007). Women's experiences and perceptions of age discrimination in employment: Implications for research and policy. *Social Policy & Society, 6*(1), 37–48.

Ward, R., & Holland, C. (2011). 'If I look old, I will be treated old': Hair and later-life image dilemmas. *Ageing & Society, 31*(2), 288–307.

13 The Neuroscience of Eating Disorders and Embodiment

Jessica Moncrieff-Boyd, Ian Frampton, and Kenneth Nunn

> The mind is its own place, and in itself can make a heaven of hell, a hell of heaven.
>
> John Milton, *Paradise Lost*

Introduction

The mind is the brain in action. The brain has representations of the body sensed and the body in action. The brain is part of the body, and the body is the first and most immediate part of the brain's environment. Body maps include time and meaning, not merely spatial information. "Body image" is a poor descriptor for such a rich experience of the bodily self and for the pathognomonic dissatisfaction with and disownership of the self in anorexia nervosa (AN). Similarly, the term "eating disorder" may keep focus on symptom expression as opposed to brain-based mechanisms that potentially underlie and maintain these conditions. This chapter explores the neuroscience of eating disorders through the lens of a neurobiological theory characterising AN as a condition underpinned by the disturbance of the representation of the body in the brain. This model is discussed with reference to the crucial role of the somatosensory cortex and insula in the construction of embodiment, self-ownership, and emotional responses to the self, including the situation of these structures within wider brain networks. The clinical implications of this model and recent neurobiological findings are considered, including the use of treatment approaches that attempt to address somatosensory integration distortions.

Mind is to brain as flight is to wing (Searle, 1992). Mind is the function, and brain is the structure. Mind might be better thought of as a verb – the thing a brain does. In addition, brain is to body as feather is to wing, a component of a broader system. Birds have trouble being birds without feathers, and humans have trouble being humans without brains (Searle, 1992). The brain is part of the body and, in action, mind is a criterion of our humanity. However, there is an aspect in which these analogies seriously fall short, because brain is to environment as map is to country. The brain maps all that is outside of it, falling beyond its borders.

The brain regards the body as its first and most immediate environment. The brain has maps of the outside world and also of the body, internally (viscerally) and externally (skin). The brain builds dozens of maps representing the self and its world, especially the bodily self. These include maps of detailed point-to-point representations (in the primary sensory cortices) as well as abstract "maps of meaning" in each sensory modality (secondary visual, auditory, kinesthetic and spatial cortices). Then, there are maps of maps in which all the sensory modalities are combined (in the tertiary sensory cortices). Finally, the maps have autobiographical historical, emotional and motivational landmarks highlighted so that final production is something unsurpassed in the universe – except in other brains as they produce minds.

No Puppet Master of the Self

For centuries, scientists and philosophers have sought to understand where in the brain is the "theatre of the mind", to no avail. There is no single brain structure that has an "actor or agent" watching and controlling all the workings. More recently, it has been suggested that the body is the theatre of the mind, as well as its principal actor (Merleau-Ponty, 1964, 2005). Our reception of the world is through the body as experienced by the senses: the receptive self. For "nothing is in the mind that is not first in the senses" (Aristotle, 1907/2007) except the mind itself (Leibniz, 2012). This "feeling of what happens" (Damasio & Dolan, 1999) is an owned feeling – i.e. it is what happens to *me*. A characteristic feature of consciousness is the conviction of ownership – i.e. it is *my* consciousness. Our intention towards our body, our world and our future is expressed through the body as action mediated by the brain to form the expressive self. In the territory between the receptive self and the expressive self is the interpretive self – the body analysed and its brain analysing (Gazzaniga, 1998).

The Three Selves: The Receptive, the Expressive and the Interpretive Selves

To these three aspects of self (the receptive, the expressive and the interpretive selves), mapping is critical to understand what is happening, where it is happening and when it is happening. The self as represented within the brain is part of a larger field of study on homuncular (little human) representation. This chapter aims to outline how the understanding gained in these studies influences our conceptualization of eating disorders and the embodied experience of those who suffer from them.

The Brain as Body, the Brain in the Body and the Body in the Brain

Brains are collections of highly unusual cells that are specialised for sensitivity, connectivity and stability. They have almost completely given up reproduction by the time their owner is born. They are exquisitely vulnerable to toxicity, infection, lack of oxygen and glucose and take up 20% of their bodies' energy needs during wakefulness. They have double layers of protection, an immune system reserved for the brain alone and exquisite repair systems. The activity of brains outstrips their capacity for elimination of waste during the day and only "catch up" by idling during sleep when waste products can be exported to the rest of the body. All of this, so their owners can *receive* by the senses, *interpret* by connecting everything into an orchestrated whole and *respond* through the motor system. Eating disorders are disorders of awareness of the body, disorders of interpreting the body and disorders of connecting those parts of the brain representing different perceptions of the body.

The Body as Experienced by the Senses: The Receptive Self

If all the body were an eye, or ear, or nose and all the world a light, or sound, or rose, we would likely understand the receptive self more easily and clearly. But when we add all senses, combined in place and time, interpreted by past experience, current emotions, impelling motivations and corresponding actions, what we feel, and what we feel about what we feel, becomes an intricate weave and fabric of experience. By the illusion of simultaneous experience, things happening together in our personal time, we have a sense of a single self.

When the emphasis is on being *acted upon*, we can call this *the receptive self*. As we consider parts of this receptive whole, we can be both observer and observed at the same time. This self-reflexivity allows us to experience the body both as subject and as observer (Aron & Aron, 1998; Longo, Azañón, & Haggard, 2010), experienced from within and observed from without. An elegant research exploration of this is captured in the work of Sachdev, Mondraty, Wen and Guillford (2008) in which they identify different brain structures activated in those with eating disorders when observing and experiencing themselves. Their work suggests that people with eating disorders show hypoactivation of regions typically implicated in self-processing, such as the insula and attentional circuits. A disorder in the receiving self, such that the received world, including the world of the body, is not received accurately. What if the received self is disconnected from interpretive or expressive selves? It must feel without understanding and without an ability to express what it is feeling. Sachdev et al. (2008) found just such a defect in insula function where much of the receptive self is instantiated.

The Body as Intention towards Action: The Expressive Self

When the perspective changes and we are *acting upon* and not acted upon, *the expressive self* comes into focus. What we intend, where we are headed, what are our plans and how might we do it all lean towards an inclination, a posture of action, an impulsion to do. The dynamic nature of the expressive self is conveyed by motor neurons, enacted by the muscles on arteries that cause the face to flush, the heart to beat, glands to exude hormones and the hundreds of muscles on bone, in bowels and bladder, heart and lung to do their bidding.

But what if there is disorder in the expressive self? The expressed self, including the body in action, is no longer speaking true to intent, to plan, to action. What if the expressive self is somehow disconnected from the receptive self, the interpretive self, and must act in the absence of accurate and helpful information about the world, especially the world of the body?

The Body as Analysed and Analysing: The Interpreting Self

The brain makes sense of its own body and the world around it. The territory between receiving and responding is the interpretative "space" within the brain and the self that it seeks to explain. Gazzaniga (1998) writes about the specific role for the interpretive self within the left hemisphere. The body is understood at a cognitive level based on structural, topographic and semantic knowledge (Kemmerer & Tranel, 2008) including generalised knowledge of the nature of "bodies" and a specific understanding about one's own body.

Affectively, the body becomes the object of emotional experiences, as well as the container and expresser for these experiences (Damasio, 2006; Longo et al., 2010). These emotions subsequently shape conscious attitudes and beliefs held about one's own body. Both the cognitive and emotional facets of somato–representation are influenced by external factors, including the body as an object to others, and the acquisition of culturally and socially shaped beliefs about the body (Longo et al., 2010).

What are the principles for interpreting bodily experience?

1 *Impact of generic ambient culture:* What do others think of their bodies? How does this affect how I think about mine?
2 *Impact of personalized ambient culture:* What do others think of my body? How does this affect how I think about my body?
3 *Global bodily judgement upon body:* What do I think of my body as a whole?
4 *Particular bodily judgement upon body parts:* What do I think of my body's different parts?
5 *Salience of body parts for survival, progeny and relationships:* What parts of my body are important for my survival, reproduction and relational goals?

6   *Historical salience:* What parts of my body have been important in my history?

7   *Match/mismatch between emotional in-put and body parts:* What parts of my body are receiving, or not receiving, affective in-put?

8   *Match/mismatch between emotional out-put and body parts:* What parts of my body are involved with the expression of affect?

Interpretation is often *post hoc* and surprises the owner just as much as those about. We may be embarrassed, appalled, disgusted and delighted before we know why. It is natural for us to expect that reception should lead to interpretation and the response. However, as Gazzaniga (1998) points out, in much that happens in day-to-day life, the interpretation follows reception and response and must come up with the best explanation possible. This means that when we ask *why* questions, we often get *post-hoc* reconstructions based on the brain's best guess rather than an accurate idea of what was received and in what way it was connected with the response. When there are disconnections in the receptive self, the interpretive self may be left to construct the best story it can from inaccurate incoming data.

The Homuncular Theory of Bodily Experience

The neuroanatomy of homunculi. How is the body represented within the brain? All of the senses converge on a part of the cortex called the somato (bodily) sensory (receiving or incoming) cortex (the outside layer – literally "the bark" – of the brain). The somatosensory cortex is the strip of brain behind the deep ravine (the central sulcus) that goes from ear to ear and that divides the front from the back of the brain. Each part of the body is represented, with the largest sections being face and hand. It looks quite distorted but still constitutes a little version of the owner – a homunculus.

Sensation becomes meaningful perception, and motor intention becomes preparation for action. Each area of representation then refers to a higher area for integration, organisation, comparison with other modalities, past experience, present threats and wishes and long-term goals. We call this the secondary somatosensory cortex. When intention must be mapped onto bodily action, we have the secondary motor areas known as supplementary motor areas.

The body as represented in the brain receives input and signals output from the tertiary cortex cortices. In the case of somato-sensation and somato-motor response, this is located in the insular cortex (Figure 13.1)

The insula is deeply connected to many of the main structures in the brain that have been associated with different key aspects of eating disorders. Its role in connecting these structures makes it a key location for pathology if things go wrong. It is a key location for disconnection and

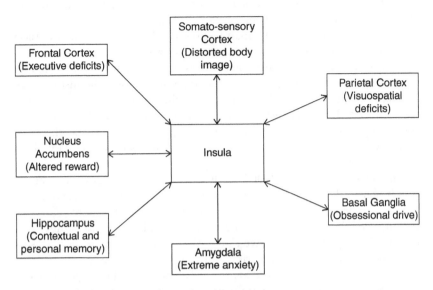

Figure 13.1 Insula neural activity in AN (Nunn, Frampton, & Lask, 2012).

distortion in the awareness of bodily self – which is so critical to eating disorder pathology. The insula is a network hub within the normal bodily awareness system that has been implicated in AN (Nunn, Frampton, Fuglset, Törzsök-Sonnevend, & Lask, 2011).

The Boundary of Homunculi: The Self-Non-Self Distinction and the Centre for Disgust

It is clear that any map has boundaries defined and limits of representation. The most important boundary for the body is the self/non-self boundary. The most obvious boundary of the body is the skin, as well as the mouth and nose for entry and the anus and urethra for departure. These are represented in the anterior insula, especially the ventral anterior insula (front and bottom of the insula). This is also referred to as the disgust centre where decisions are made and reactions are initiated to disown food and anything seeking entry. But sometimes the distinction between self and non-self is confused. Disgust is directed against the self. Self-disgust figures largely in the experience of those with eating disorders.

Disgust as Boundary Emotion

Disgust emerges as a relevant emotion as it is both a pertinent affective experience among those with eating disorders, and an emotion intrinsically connected to embodiment and the experience of self. Disgust is characterised by a visceral experience of revulsion and aversion in response to an elicitor. It has an ideational (feeling) component involving beliefs about an elicitor's potential for contamination, and a visceral (emotion) component (Damasio, 2006) manifesting as an experience of revulsion sometimes accompanied by nausea. Behaviourally, disgust, like fear, results in rejection and avoidance behaviours, and its physiological correlates involve sympathetic and parasympathetic co-activation. The insula is the central brain structure underpinning both the perception and expression of disgust (Phillips et al., 2004) embedded in a neural circuit of emotional processing also involving prefrontal areas and cortico-striatal-thalamic pathways (Phillips et al., 1997, 1998; Sprengelmeyer, Rausch, Eysel, & Przuntek, 1998).

Charles Darwin's (1878/2002) early descriptions of disgust as an emotion intrinsically associated with food are emulated in modern accounts of the phylogenetic origins of disgust in food rejection and distaste (Rozin & Fallon, 1987; Rozin, Fallon, & Mandell, 1984). Thus, disgust is suggested to have developed as an affective elaboration of these adaptive mechanisms designed to prevent contamination by toxins or pathogens.

The directionality of disgust is primarily from the self towards non-self, again reflecting its phylogenetic origins as a method of pathogen avoidance (Rozin & Fallon, 1987). Accordingly, the self emerges as fundamental to the experience of disgust. The distinction between self and non-self can be defined in physical terms in regard to the border or boundary of the body (the skin), with the mouth and other orifices representing portals between self and non-self. Disgust is "the guardian of the mouth" (Haidt, Rozin, McCauley, & Imada, 1997, p. 111), and crossing the physiological border between self and non-self (i.e. saliva in the mouth versus saliva outside the mouth) can also determine the acceptability of a potential disgust elicitor. Disgust can similarly act as the "guardian of the soul", in that it protects the psychological and moral self from external socio-moral contamination.

In this way, disgust can be regarded as a sentinel boundary emotion, facilitating behaviour that maintains the integrity of the self, both physically and morally (in the case of socio-moral disgust). Schaller and Park (2011) conceptualise disgust as part of the *behavioural immune system*, a collection of behavioural mechanisms that identify and respond to external threat. Like the physiological immune system, disgust becomes a method of facilitating identification and rejection of non-self in order to protect the integrity of self.

Self-disgust as boundary disorder. If disgust is an adaptive, sentinel emotion, then self-disgust represents an aberration of disgust that is neither adaptive nor protective. As with externally directed disgust, self-disgust involves a felt sense of revulsion and abhorrence, where the object of revulsion is the bodily self, parts of bodies, thoughts or behaviours (Powell, Simpson, & Overton, 2015a). Concurrently, self-disgust is viscerally engendered and expressed in the body. Self-disgust can be a transitory experience, or in extreme cases, a mood or emotional "schema" (Powell et al., 2015a) with deep and consequential bodily concomitants.

In this way, self-disgust can be constructed as a *behavioural autoimmune disorder*, where self turns on self. In extreme cases (such as in the case of somatoparaphrenia, body identity-integrity disorder or AN), self may be registered as non-self, so that the self is rejected and reviled (Moncrieff-Boyd, Byrne, & Nunn, 2014). In conscious, affective awareness, self-disgust has the potential to create a sense of inescapability from the self and body, leading to a sense of hopelessness. Metaphorically, the body becomes the harness for the person, where the body cannot be avoided or escaped.

The experience of self-disgust engages both our receptive and interpretive selves; it is experienced in the body at a visceral level, as well as a cognitive level where it is consciously directed at the body. Self-disgust also captures the duality of the body being both analysed and analysing, where the body and self are both disgusting and disgusted.

Eating Disorders and the Homunculi

The developing homunculi and the crises of neuroplasticity: Change over time. Small babies have small bodies and large heads containing large brains. The representation in their brains of their small bodies gives weight to the face and hands, and very little to the torso and limbs. As the body grows, the basic proportions remain infantile like, but the compression of information to existing space allocations becomes quite marked. A body that was a few kg grows into 70–80 kg to be represented in essentially the same space. When puberty comes, especially the rapid puberty of girls, thighs lengthening, hips widening, breasts budding and navels rounding are all part of the secondary sexual characteristics that must be accommodated by the brain maps. This process of brain maps changing is called neuroplasticity. Boys change more slowly, more evenly, over more years. The challenge of neuroplasticity is less acute, and the possible confusion between a child's body and adult's is less likely to arise.

The neurochemistry, neurovascularity and neuroanatomy of neuroplasticity. There are many complex chemical changes associated with neuroplasticity, but one of the best characterised is that of noradrenaline (also called norepinephrine). Noradrenaline is involved in regional blood supply regulation in the brain. It is involved with anxiety and stress systems. We know that in eating disorders, overall blood supply is reduced across the brain. Blood supply is increased in the anterior insula region (the disgust and depression centres) of the brain and reduced in the posterior region of the insula (bodily awareness centres). Distortion of bodily awareness is one of the cardinal criteria of restricting eating disorders, and anxiety and sensitivity to stress are commonly dysregulated before the manifest onset of an eating disorder such as AN. The blood vessels and sections of the middle cerebral arteries include the insular branches of the second section (M2) of the middle cerebral artery.

Specificity: The noradrenergic model outline. Impaired neuroplasticity (particularly during puberty when the neural representation of the body in the brain has to change rapidly to accommodate rapid changes in body shape – especially for females) has been implicated in the Noradrenergic Dysregulation (NORA) hypothesis of AN, developed by Nunn and colleagues (Nunn et al., 2011; Nunn, Frampton, & Lask, 2012). In this model, underlying dysregulation of the noradrenergic system is a risk factor for body image disturbance – since the representation of the body in the brain cannot keep pace with actual bodily change, leading to a disturbed sense of body shape and size.

The Three Large-Scale Networks of the Brain and the Critical Role of the Insula

The brain can be helpfully considered to be made of three major systems – the central executive network (CEN), the default mode network (DMN) and the salience network (SN) (Menon, 2011; Raichle et al., 2001; Sridharan, Levitin, & Menon, 2008). The CEN roughly corresponds to the existing notion of executive function and is primarily directed to the outside world (dlPFC and the PPC, plays an important role in working memory and general attention). The DMN roughly corresponds to internal preoccupation and focus on the internal state of the individual in day dreaming, reminiscing, future imaginings and wakeful resting – the gently idling brain (anchored in the PCC and medial PFC, is important for self-referential mental activity; Raichle et al., 2001). The resources of the brain are limited, and the decision to focus on the external world or the internal world must be based on the salient events happening in each. The SN is largely accounted for by the insula and the anterior cingulate gyrus, a structure critical to concentration and selective attention. It can be seen that in even the most basic terms, a failure in the insula means an inefficient use of cognitive resources and a confusion between internal and external priorities. There is a disconnection between and failure of integration of the internal priorities of the body and the external demands upon the body.

The Large-Scale Network Perspective of Eating Disorders

When the CEN is marooned like an island, it can go on trying to inefficiently solve problems with any real connection to understanding them from the past or acting upon them. We call this rumination – or *analysis paralysis*. When the DMN is marooned, self-absorbed preoccupation with the past and the distress of present experience also go on inefficiently and unabated with no problem-solving capacity from the CEN, which we call emotion-focused coping. When the SN is paralysed as in AN, non-essentials become the focus of decision-making, and the disconnection between the CEN and DMN renders the brain inefficient, ruminating ineffectually and self-absorbed with the past and the emotion of the moment. Small-scale disgust networks work against this large backdrop.

Treatment Implications for Eating Disorders

A number of clinical implications arise from our neurobiological model of AN, informed by recent neuroscientific findings. In regard to altered homuncular representations of the body, treatments involving mindfulness-based meditation techniques, particularly body scan-type meditations, may act to enhance mental representations of the body in the brain (Mateos Rodríguez, Cowdrey, & Park, 2014). Ongoing meditation practice is also shown to result in structural and functional changes in insular regions (Hölzel et al., 2008). Neurofeedback may offer another method of modulating the insula. Neurofeedback involves providing visual feedback from real-time imaging (i.e. real-time fMRI) in order to facilitate voluntary modulation of neural activity in cortical areas; emerging research has produced promising results modulating target regions and subsequent symptom expression in stroke rehabilitation, as well as psychiatric conditions including major depressive disorder through amygdala modulation (Young et al., 2014) and insular modulation in schizophrenia (Ruiz et al., 2013). Such approaches have potential promise in the treatment of eating disorders (Bartholdy, Musiat, Campbell, & Schmidt, 2013) and may provide an avenue for directly targeting dysregulation in implicated cortical regions for AN, including the insula.

Knatz et al. (2015) suggested the need for a radically different approach to AN treatment that focuses on underlying neurobiological mechanisms as opposed to expressed symptomatology. The authors proposed Neurobiologically Enhanced With Family Eating Disorder Trait Response Treatment (NEW FED TR) as a new intervention combining family-based approaches with identifying and targeting neurobiological factors in the illness. For example, the treatment includes exercises for patients and their families that demonstrate poor interoceptive awareness as a specific example of insular dysfunction. The research group is currently running a clinical trial for this treatment (Knatz, Wierenga, Murray, Hill, & Kaye, 2015).

Other pathways for treatment may lie in addressing sensory and proprioceptive integration deficits among those with AN, as suggested by Case, Wilson and Ramachandran (2012), who identified such multisensory integration deficits as factors likely underlying weight/size discrepancies experienced towards one's own body in AN. However, it remains unclear how such perspective integration deficits could be specifically be corrected and whether it involves modulating bottom-up (sensory) inputs or top-down cortical integration processes, perhaps though methods such as biofeedback discussed before.

From an emotion processing and regulation perspective, addressing experiences of disgust along with other relevant emotions such as fear may also be an important avenue for treatment. A number of clinicians in the field have pointed to the need for further consideration of broader emotional components in the treatment of both AN and bulimia nervosa (BN). Fox, Federici, and Power (2012) highlighted the role of emotional processing and regulation in eating disorders, as well as the potential utility of emotion-centred treatment options, such as Dialectical Behavioural Therapy (including Radically Open Dialectical Behavior) and Emotion Focused Therapy. In regard to self-disgust, dissonance-based approaches such as compassion- and acceptance-based therapy may also prove to be effective (Powell, Simpson, & Overton, 2015b).

Our emotional responses to our bodies and ourselves are also linked to internalised representations of cultural norms and standards, which in turn shape the experience of our body from the inside out. Disgust is an emotion that is tied to culturally determined standards of acceptability and morality, particularly in the case of moral taboos such as incest, but continues to expand into broader domains such as political ideology and lifestyle choices (Haidt et al., 1997). The progressive moralization of the thin ideal, along with the movement towards condemning obesity and being overweight in the majority of Western cultures, becomes a powerful factor that, when internalised, shapes the experience of the interpretive self. We are similarly witnessing the collective moralization of food choices through the rise of movements such as clean eating and organic produce. These forces then influence our emotional responses to our own body and shape, where bodies (and foods that enter our bodies) deemed unacceptable by this standard can trigger disgust. The interplay between our ambient culture and our interpretive self, situated within and simultaneously perpetuating this context, emerges as an area in eating disorders worthy of continued clinical attention. In particular, clinicians may wish to consider the possibility of the perceived breach of socio-morally determined standards of acceptability as a pertinent trigger of self-disgust, as well as a driver for perceived "morally pro-social" behaviours (i.e. specific dietary restrictions).

Finally, a focus on the potential neurobiological basis for eating disorders has led to the development of neurosurgical approaches including deep brain stimulation (Lipsman et al., 2017). Clearly, such radical treatment approaches raise important ethical issues (Park, Singh, Pike, & Tan, 2017), not least from a psychological perspective in the implications for how people with eating disorders make sense of their experience (Coman, 2014). Above all, we hope that recent advances in the neuroscience of eating disorders and embodiment will lead to the development of novel, effective treatments for these complex and serious disorders (Nunn, 2014).

References

Aristotle. (2007). *The metaphysics* (J. H. McMahon, Trans.). New York, NY: Dover Press. (Original translation published 1907.)

Aron, L. & Aron, L. (1998). The clinical body and the reflexive mind. *Relational Perspectives on the Body, 12*, 3–38.

Bartholdy, S., Musiat, P., Campbell, I. C., & Schmidt, U. (2013). The potential of neurofeedback in the treatment of eating disorders: A review of the literature. *European Eating Disorders Review, 21*(6), 456–463.

Case, L. K., Wilson, R. C., Ramachandran, V. S. (2012). Diminished size-weight illusion in anorexia nervosa: Evidence for visuo-proprioceptive integration deficit. *Experimental Brain Research, 217*(1), 79–87.

Coman, A. (2014). Emerging technologies in the treatment of anorexia nervosa and ethics: Sufferers' accounts of treatment strategies and authenticity. *Health Care Analysis*, 1–13. doi:10.1007/s10728-014-0286-3

Damasio, A. & Dolan, R. J. (1999). The feeling of what happens. *Nature, 401*(6756), 847–847.

Damasio, A. R. (2006). *Descartes' error.* Random House. Retrieved from https://books.google.co.uk/books?hl=en&lr=&id=5aczCwAAQBAJ&oi=fnd&pg=PR15&dq=descartes+error&ots=fNSvWu7W5P&sig=MmL5avHODkddDHYPkTPBPNOj9r0

Darwin, C. (1878/2002). *The expression of the emotions in man and animals.* London, England: Oxford University Press.

Fox, J. R. E., Federici, A., & Power, M. J. (2012). Emotions and eating disorders. In J. R. E. Fox & K. P. Gross (Eds.), *Eating and its disorders* (pp. 167–184). Walden, MA: Wiley.

Gazzaniga, M. S. (1998). The mind's past. University of California Press. Retrieved from https://books.google.com.au/books?hl=en&lr=&id=GC-vDFERkgMC&oi=fnd&pg=PT9&dq=Gazzaniga+(1998&ots=dUvqeZcqIX&sig=bBJ2PHsP4XyGaDqYObIuzwHidg4

Haidt, J., Rozin, P., McCauley, C., & Imada, S. (1997). Body, psyche, and culture: The relationship between disgust and morality. *Psychology & Developing Societies, 9*(1), 107–131.

Hölzel, B. K., Ott, U., Gard, T., Hempel, H., Weygandt, M., Morgen, K., & Vaitl, D. (2008). Investigation of mindfulness meditation practitioners with voxel-based morphometry. *Social Cognitive and Affective Neuroscience, 3*(1), 55–61. doi:10.1093/scan/nsm038.

Kemmerer, D. & Tranel, D. (2008). Searching for the elusive neural substrates of body part terms: A neuropsychological study. *Cognitive Neuropsychology, 25*(4), 601–629.

Knatz, S., Wierenga, C. E., Murray, S. B., Hill, L., & Kaye, W. H. (2015). Neurobiologically informed treatment for adults with anorexia nervosa: a novel approach to a chronic disorder. *Dialogues in Clinical Neuroscience, 17*(2), 229–36.

Leibniz, G. W. (2012). *Philosophical papers and letters: A selection* (Vol. 2). Springer Science & Business Media. Retrieved from https://books.google.com.au/books?hl=en&lr=&id=eWYyBwAAQBAJ&oi=fnd&pg=PA1&dq=(Leibniz,+1702+except+the+mind+itself&ots=EhgRAXE1G2&sig=bHIk4sV5sqHUXsaxF_rdgCPIBcA

Lipsman, N., Lam, E., Volpini, M., Sutandar, K., Twose, R., Giacobbe, P., ... Lozano, A. M. (2017). Deep brain stimulation of the subcallosal cingulate for treatment-refractory anorexia nervosa: 1 year follow-up of an open-label trial. *The Lancet Psychiatry.* https://doi.org/10.1016/S2215-0366(17)30076-7

Longo, M. R., Azañón, E., & Haggard, P. (2010). More than skin deep: Body representation beyond primary somatosensory cortex. *Neuropsychologia, 48*(3), 655–668.

Mateos Rodríguez, I., Cowdrey, F. A., & Park, R. J. (2014). Is there a place for mindfulness in the treatment of anorexia nervosa? *Advances in Eating Disorders, 2*(1), 42–52. https://doi.org/10.1080/21662630.2013.795755

Menon, V. (2011). Large-scale brain networks and psychopathology: A unifying triple network model. *Trends in Cognitive Sciences, 15*(10), 483–506.

Merleau-Ponty, M. (2005). The body as expression and speech. *The Phenomenology of Perception,* (pp. 202–234). New York, NY: Routledge. (Original work published 1945).

Merleau-Ponty, M. (1964). *The primacy of perception: And other essays on phenomenological psychology, the philosophy of art, history, and politics.* Northwestern University Press. Retrieved from https://books.google.com.au/books?hl=en&lr=&id=CMk4mUpjdosC&oi=fnd&pg=PR9&dq=MerleauPonty,+1964+the+primacy+of+perception&ots=dBimTetora&s=FRKTFtZWJrXRFWQK3E3KxxVSoDk

Moncrieff-Boyd, J., Byrne, S., & Nunn, K. (2014). Disgust and anorexia nervosa: Confusion between self and non-self. *Advances in Eating Disorders: Theory, Research and Practice, 2*(1), 4–18.

Nunn, Ken, Frampton, I., Fuglset, T. S., Törzsök-Sonnevend, M., & Lask, B. (2011). Anorexia nervosa and the insula. *Medical Hypotheses, 76*(3), 353–357.

Nunn, K, Frampton, I., & Lask, B. (2012). Anorexia nervosa—a noradrenergic dysregulation hypothesis. *Medical Hypotheses, 78,* 580–584. doi:S0306-9877(12)00044-8 [pii] 10.1016/j.mehy.2012.01.033

Nunn, K. P. (2014). The brain: A family of cooperating, competing and sometimes conflicting systems–Part III. *Advances in Eating Disorders: Theory, Research and Practice, 2*(1), 81–92.

Park, R. J., Singh, I., Pike, A. C., & Tan, J. O. A. (2017). Deep brain stimulation in anorexia nervosa: Hope for the hopeless or exploitation of the vulnerable? The Oxford Neuroethics Gold Standard Framework. *Frontiers in Psychiatry, 8,* 44. doi:10.3389/fpsyt.2017.00044

Phillips, M. L., Williams, L. M., Heining, M., Herba, C. M., Russell, T., Andrew, C., ... others. (2004). Differential neural responses to overt and covert presentations of facial expressions of fear and disgust. *Neuroimage, 21*(4), 1484–1496.

Phillips, M. L., Young, A. W., Scott, S. K., Calder, A. J., Andrew, C., Giampietro, V., ... Gray, J. A. (1998). Neural responses to facial and vocal expressions of fear and disgust. *Proceedings of the Royal Society of London B: Biological Sciences, 265*(1408), 1809–1817.

Phillips, M. L., Young, A. W., Senior, C., Brammer, M., Andrew, C., Calder, A. J., ... Williams, S. C. R. (1997). A specific neural substrate for perceiving facial expressions of disgust. *Nature, 389*(6650), 495–498.

Powell, P. A., Simpson, J., & Overton, P. G. (2015a). An introduction to the revolting self: Self-disgust as an emotion schema. *The revolting self: Perspectives on the psychological, social, and clinical implications of self-directed disgust* (pp. 1–24). London, UK: Karnac Books.

Powell, P. A., Simpson, J., & Overton, P. G. (2015b). Self-affirming trait kindness regulates disgust toward one's physical appearance. *Body Image, 12,* 98–107.

Raichle, M. E., MacLeod, A. M., Snyder, A. Z., Powers, W. J., Gusnard, D. A., & Shulman, G. L. (2001). A default mode of brain function. *Proceedings of the National Academy of Sciences, 98*(2), 676–682.

Rozin, P. & Fallon, A. E. (1987). A perspective on disgust. *Psychological Review, 94*(1), 23.

Rozin, P., Fallon, A., & Mandell, R. (1984). Family resemblance in attitudes to foods. *Developmental Psychology, 20*(2), 309.

Ruiz, S., Lee, S., Soekadar, S. R., Caria, A., Veit, R., Kircher, T., ... Sitaram, R. (2013). Acquired self-control of insula cortex modulates emotion recognition and brain network connectivity in schizophrenia. *Human Brain Mapping, 34*(1), 200–212.

Sachdev, P., Mondraty, N., Wen, W., & Gulliford, K. (2008). Brains of anorexia nervosa patients process self-images differently from non-self-images: An fMRI study. *Neuropsychologia, 46*(8), 2161–2168.

Schaller, M. & Park, J. (2011). The behavioural immune system (and why it matters). *Current Directions in Psychological Science, 20*(2), 99–103. doi:10.1177/0963721411402596

Searle, J. R. (1992). *The rediscovery of the mind.* MIT Press. Retrieved from https://books.google.com.au/books?hl=en&lr=&id=eoh8e52wo_oC&oi=fnd&pg=PR9&dq=searle+mind+is+to+body&ots=tCSMIv_oVP&sig=YzYZhz1F2SCkbBRfH8bd6UTVK_Q

Sprengelmeyer, R., Rausch, M., Eysel, U. T., & Przuntek, H. (1998). Neural structures associated with recognition of facial expressions of basic emotions. *Proceedings of the Royal Society of London B: Biological Sciences, 265*(1409), 1927–1931.

Sridharan, D., Levitin, D. J., & Menon, V. (2008). A critical role for the right fronto-insular cortex in switching between central-executive and default-mode networks. *Proceedings of the National Academy of Sciences, 105*(34), 12569–12574.

Young, K. D., Zotev, V., Phillips, R., Misaki, M., Yuan, H., Drevets, W. C., & Bodurka, J. (2014). Real-time FMRI neurofeedback training of amygdala activity in patients with major depressive disorder. *PloS One, 9*(2), e88785.

14 Ayahuasca and the Healing of Eating Disorders

Marika Renelli, Jenna Fletcher, Anja Loizaga-Velder, Natasha Files, Kenneth Tupper, and Adele Lafrance

Eating disorders (EDs) are complex mental health issues that involve cognitive, physical and emotional symptoms (Golden et al., 2003; Polivy & Herman, 2002). It is widely accepted that the avoidance of challenging emotions is central to the development and maintenance of an ED (Harrison, Sullivan, Tchanturia, & Treasure, 2009). Many have theorized that an individual's focus on and negative view of body image, along with attempts to change their body, are more strongly related to the embodiment or acceptance of emotion, rather than physical weight and shape (Sim & Zeman, 2005). Negative affect is projected onto the body, and engaging in ED behaviors offers temporary relief from unmanageable emotions. EDs also have the highest mortality rate of all the psychiatric disorders (Hoek, 2006) and are considered highly treatment-resistant, especially anorexia nervosa (Waller, 2016). As such, the field has called for innovative treatments to be considered, and as EDs are now a global phenomenon, therapeutic modalities from across cultures must also be explored (Hay, 2013).

Anecdotal reports have indicated that some individuals with EDs have explored the use of the traditional Amazonian plant medicine ayahuasca with positive results. A growing body of research points to promise of its utility in the healing of various mental health issues, including depression, anxiety, substance use disorders and post-traumatic stress disorder (Fábregas et al., 2010; Halpern, Sherwood, Passie, Blackwell, & Ruttenber, 2008; Loizaga-Velder & Verres, 2014; Osório et al., 2015; Sanches et al., 2016; Thomas, Lucas, Capler, Tupper, & Martin, 2013). Recent research has also found ayahuasca to have therapeutic benefit for individuals along the continuum of recovery from EDs, with respect to symptom reduction and embodiment, among other positive outcomes (Lafrance et al., 2017). Researchers from around the globe are working to understand the therapeutic mechanisms of ayahuasca (Labate & Cavnar, 2014). Preliminary results suggest that ayahuasca works in a holistic manner, including the physical, psychological and spiritual. For this reason, ayahuasca is a healing tool that has the potential to assist in moving towards an embodied and integrated sense of self.

The Medicine

Ayahuasca, meaning "vine of the soul" in the Quechua language, is a psychoactive substance that originates from the Amazon. It is a brew prepared by boiling the *Banisteriopsis caapi* vine with other plants, but most commonly with the leaves of the *Psychotria viridis* shrub (Rivier & Lindgren, 1972). The plants contain the short-term reversible monoamine oxidase inhibitor (MAOI) alkaloids harmine, harmaline and tetrahydroharmine (*B. caapi*) and the psychoactive alkaloid dimethyltryptamine (DMT) (*P. viridis*). The typical effects of the brew involve changes in perception and cognition (e.g. vivid visual and auditory sensations), newfound insights, recollections of memories, strong emotional experiences (e.g. happiness, sadness, fear), bodily sensations, and spiritual and transpersonal experiences (Riba et al., 2001; Shanon, 2002; Strassman, Qualls, Uhlenhut, & Kellner, 1994). Certain acute effects of ayahuasca are nausea and purging in the form of vomiting, diarrhea, crying, yawning, sweating and shaking (Barbosa, Giglio, & Dalgalarrondo, 2005).

Archaeological evidence suggests that ayahuasca's ritual use by indigenous Amazonian tribes dates back at least several hundred years (Grob, 2013). Currently, at least 75 indigenous Amazonian tribes use ayahuasca for ritual and medical purposes (Luna, 2011). Ayahuasca has also been used as a sacrament in the Brazilian-based churches of the Santo Daime since the 1930s and the União Vegetal since the 1960s. Over the past 25 years, the use of ayahuasca as a psychotherapeutic and spiritual tool has spread throughout North America, Europe and other parts of the world (Tupper, 2008).

The ritual and contextual uses of ayahuasca vary. In traditional practices, a ceremony can involve setting an intention and ingesting the brew in a group, with experienced leaders, or "ayahuascqueros," presiding (Luna, 1986). Ceremonies normally begin after sunset and last several hours. The ceremony leaders may chant, whistle and sing melodies referred to as "icaros" – believed to assist with the healing process – throughout the ceremony (Luna, 1986). Typically for indigenous-style rituals, dietary and behavioral restrictions are adhered to several days before and after consuming the brew. The restrictions may relate to the consumption of recreational drugs, alcohol, red meat, dairy, salt and sugar and engaging in sexual activity.

The Study: The Role of Ceremonial Ayahuasca Use in the Healing of an Eating Disorder

There has been a recent resurgence in the scientific literature exploring the therapeutic potential of psychedelics, which include ayahuasca, for the treatment of mental health issues such as anxiety, mood disorders and substance use disorders (Tupper, Wood, Yensen, & Johnson, 2015). The low remission rates of ED coupled with anecdotal reports of ayahuasca's positive effects point to a need for further inquiry. In response, Lafrance et al. (2017) conducted interviews with 16 individuals with a history of both an ED and ceremonial ayahuasca drinking. Preliminary data revealed behavioral and psychological improvements, including ED symptom reduction or cessation, improved mood, decreased anxiety and problematic substance use, and improved capacity to process, regulate and embody emotions. Other significant outcomes included insights about the illness and an improved relationship with the body. Some risks were also reported. For example, some participants noted that the preparatory diet resulted in some familiar ED thoughts. Also of note, one participant shared an experience of inappropriate sexual advances by a facilitator – raising the very important issue of personal safety of this indigenous therapeutic practice without adequate regulatory structure. As a whole, this pioneering study opened the door for the exploration of ayahuasca's use as a potential healing modality among those with a history of an ED. Given the breadth of data collected, the purpose of this study is to report on additional outcomes from this sample.

Method

Data Collection

A purposeful sampling strategy was employed using criterion-based sampling to select cases that were information-rich for our specific research (Patton, 2002). Participants were recruited by word of mouth, advertising on online discussion groups, targeted listservs, social media and a project website. To avoid a biased sample, participants who had experienced positive, neutral or negative experiences with ayahuasca were encouraged to participate. Inclusion criteria included participants that had been previously diagnosed with an ED by a medical or mental health professional and who had participated in ayahuasca in a ceremonial context at some point in their adult lives.

Participants

As part of the larger study, participants (14 women, 2 men, M_{age} = 34 years, age range: 21–55 years) meeting the inclusion criteria were interviewed. The sample included 10 participants with a previous diagnosis of anorexia nervosa and 6 with a diagnosis of bulimia nervosa. Many participants ($n = 13$) had at some point received ED treatment in inpatient, day hospital and outpatient settings, where various psychotherapeutic modalities were employed. These included *cognitive-behavioral therapy, dialectical behavior therapy, acceptance and commitment therapy, eye movement desensitization and reprocessing, rational emotive behavior therapy, psychodynamic psychotherapy* and *family-based therapy*. The approximate number of ayahuasca ceremonies in which interviewees participated ranged from 1 to 30. For additional information on participant characteristics, refer to Lafrance et al. (2017).

Procedure

Ethics approval was received from Laurentian University and the University of British Columbia. Informed consent was obtained prior to data collection, and following the interview participants were offered information about ED services in their area. The interview schedule was administered via telephone, and the call was recorded. The interviews were approximately 75–180 minutes in length and were transcribed verbatim. Transcriptions were reviewed for accuracy by a research assistant and/or a study author.

Semi-Structured Interview Schedule

The interview schedule was developed based on the methodology of Loizaga-Velder and Verres (2014) and the Ayahuasca Treatment and Outcome Project (Rush, personal communication). The interview was semi-structured and included questions relating to participants' subjective evaluations of ayahuasca's therapeutic potential. The participants were asked follow-up questions when appropriate.

Qualitative Analysis

The interviews were analyzed for themes and patterns by a three-membered team using the methodology of thematic analysis (Braun & Clarke, 2006). Each theme was reported along with the number of participants who endorsed the specific theme.

Inter-coder reliability was measured using average pairwise percent agreement to determine the accuracy of the application of codes to the transcripts among the three coders. Any subthemes that fell below 80% average agreement were reviewed as a team, and a consensus on the final themes was negotiated (see Lafrance et al. (2017) for a detailed description of the methodology).

Rigor

Rigor was ensured during data analysis by methods of investigator triangulation and member checking (Patton, 2002). To confirm accuracy of the analysis, member checking was completed by providing a summary of the results to all participants. Participants were invited to review the themes and provide feedback regarding the degree to which the results accurately reflected their experiences.

Results

Qualitative Analysis

Following thematic analysis of the qualitative interviews, several themes emerged that related to psychological, physical, relational and spiritual effects perceived to be a result of ceremonial ayahuasca. Table 14.1 provides an overview of the themes and subthemes identified, including those reported in Lafrance et al. (2017).

Psychological Effects

A description and interpretation of the subthemes reflecting the effects of ayahuasca on a psychological level have been described in the exploratory study noted earlier (Lafrance et al., 2017) which include the participants' perceived (1) improvement in their capacity to process and regulate emotions; (2) insight into the cause of their ED; (3) increase in their capacity for self-love, -esteem, -compassion and -forgiveness; (4) addressing the root cause of the ED and/or previously experienced trauma; (5) reduction of thoughts and symptoms of the ED, anxiety, depression, self-harm and suicidality; and (6) decreased use of and cravings for psychoactive substances.

In addition to the published subthemes, participants described an increase in their capacity for mindfulness. This included an improved ability to remain in the present moment as well as the ability to experience a greater sense of contentment (37.5%). A psychology graduate student recounted her experience:

> A kind of happy after effect is that I'm much more able to live in the moment as opposed to kind of always focusing on the future next thing and more able to just accept what comes today. So, it could even be anxiety, for sure the future planning was an anxiety thing, it was always kind of a perfectionist thing you know 'After I get this degree then I'll have fun, eventually I'll have fun', and this summer was the most fun I've had in a very long time.
>
> (P11)

Body Perception and Physical Sensations and Effects

The theme relating to physical effects and well-being is comprised of four subthemes centered around improvements in (1) the relationship with the body, (2) the relationship with food, (3) weight regulation and (4) general physical health. An additional subtheme relates to insight into purging in the context of ayahuasca in comparison to purging as a symptom of the ED.

Table 14.1 Overview and Ranking of Subthemes Identified from Semi-Structured Interviews

Theme	Subtheme	Participant endorsement	
		%	n
Psychological effects	Improved emotion processing and regulation[a]	87.5	14
	Validated or transformed subjective theory of illness[a]	81.25	13
	Developed greater capacity for self-love, -acceptance, -esteem, -forgiveness, -compassion[a]	81.25	13
	Decreased or cessation of ED symptoms[a]	68.75	11
	Discovered insights and/or experienced revelatory visions in ceremony[a]	68.75	11
	Addressed root cause of the ED and/or trauma[a]	62.5	10
	Reduced anxiety, depression/self-harm, suicidality[a]	56.25	9
	Reduced cravings and/or use of psychoactive substances[a]	50	8
	Increased mindfulness	37.5	6
Body perception and physical sensations and effects	Acquired insight into purging in ceremony in comparison to purging as a symptom of the ED[a]	62.5	10
	Improved relationship with the body[a]	50	10
	Improved relationship with food and eating	50	10
	Regulation of weight	31.25	5
	Improved general physical health	18.75	3
Relational effects and experiences	Improved relationships with family, children and/or romantic partners	62.5	10
	Experienced intergenerational or relational visions/insights in ceremony	56.25	9
Spiritual and/or transpersonal effects and experiences	Acquired awareness of spiritual/transpersonal connections	93.75	15
	Experienced spiritual/transpersonal connections in ceremony	62.5	10
	Transformed contemplative spiritual or religious practices	56.25	9

[a]Discussed in Lafrance et al. (2017).

As a result of ayahuasca drinking and in the time period following participation in ceremonies, some individuals experienced their body in a more positive way. This shift was often accompanied with profound feelings of gratitude and honor for their physical body. For some participants, acute visions in ceremony were powerful vehicles for facilitating this transformation.

For example, one participant visualized her body as a "*hollow decaying skeleton*," juxtaposed with visions of herself as a "*beautiful full-bodied woman*," which precipitated a deep desire for healing in that she couldn't wait to "*get back and just start gaining some weight*" (Lafrance et al., 2017).

Similarly, some participants noted a shift towards more balanced food choices and a greater awareness of hunger cues. Others experienced newfound appreciation and respect for food as a form of nourishment, as opposed to a means through which to engage in symptoms. One participant reported a transformation in her ability to engage in mindful eating: "*Now I sit down and every meal I'm able to stop, to chew, to fully be mindful in my meal. I'm not reading, I'm not watching TV, I'm not listening to anything. I really enjoy that moment*" (P16).

Participants also gained insight into the ways in which their body weight had meaning beyond simply being a consequence of restrictive or binge-eating symptomatology. For some participants, this deeper insight resulted in subsequent changes to their actual body weight, in the direction of their natural set point. A life coach gained insight into both her use of food as a strategy for self-soothing and her excess weight as a form of self-protection:

> It feels like to me that the weight had something to do with protecting myself and because of ayahuasca I don't have to protect myself anymore... and so I started working with the medicine in May and I lost weight without any help, all of a sudden it just melted off... I was eating at the hole, which I'm not anymore.
>
> (P4)

Ceremonial ayahuasca drinking was also reported to lead to better physical health. Changes included improvements related to, or resolution of, chronic health issues that had proven difficult to manage using conventional medicine, including polycystic ovarian syndrome (PCOS), chronic fatigue and elevated blood pressure. A registered nurse with a history of PCOS shared that after five years of amenorrhea, her menstrual cycle resumed after two ayahuasca ceremonies and has been regular since that time.

The final subtheme related to purging in ceremony and how it compared to purging as a symptom of the ED (Lafrance et al., 2017). Many participants (62.5%) described purging in ceremony as having a different quality, in that it was perceived as an integral part of the healing process.

Relational Effects and Experiences

Several participants reported improvements in their relationships with friends and loved ones, including parents, siblings, romantic partners and children. They described newfound or deepened capacities for understanding, empathy and acceptance. Following the ceremonies, some participants took action steps towards repairing ruptured relationships. One participant recalled how subsequent to his participation in ceremonies, he engaged in a transformational conversation with his brother, a person with whom he had endured painful childhood experiences. His teaching during the acute ayahuasca experiences allowed him to acknowledge his own suffering and that of his brother's, creating a pathway to compassion and forgiveness:

> One of the first things I did when I returned after experiencing aya-huasca was speak to my older brother, who was one of the biggest sources of trauma growing up. And we spoke and I was really shocked by the results. I was communicating with him based on what I had experienced. One of the main points was that he was only capable of the form of abuse that he engaged in from suffering himself. And that if we were going to have a relationship, he was going to have to acknowledge that he needed to heal and to engage in that healing in whatever form that it took. And upon having this discussion with him I was really shocked to see that he actually began to cry. And that's not something we ever do in front of each other. This is all surreal it ever happened, we hugged it out and we began talking about different forms of treatment.
>
> (P2)

Several participants reported visions and insights related to important relationships and ancestral lines. These experiences included feeling a deep connection with caregivers, moving through pain from family-based trauma and accepting that their loved ones cared for them as best they were able given their own psychological wounds. For example, one participant described an encounter with an ancestor in which she was shown the intergenerational pain fueling the transmission of maltreatment and abuse in her family. Another participant recalled an acute experience during which she was able to connect with her mother's wholehearted and unconditional love for her as well as her pain:

> I had a ceremony where I was a baby and my mom was holding me and I was experiencing the expression of her unconditional love for me which I know was there underneath all of her own conditioning and woundedness. So, the medicine was able to show me that – it really re-patterned that for me - I was able to feel that, like absorb that on a cellular level and to feel a lot of compassion for her as well.
>
> (P7)

Spiritual and/or Transpersonal Effects and Experiences

Nearly every participant commented on powerful spiritual and transpersonal effects both during and after participation in ceremonies. The majority of participants recounted an acute experience during which they felt a deep connection to God, a greater entity and/or nature. One participant shared how this in-ceremony experience led to a deepening of her belief in universal love:

> I know one of my initial ceremonies I had the experience that was really profound... So, I've been raised to think and believe in a God and think that we're all one. So it's hard to really believe it because it's so not tangible and I know when I did that ceremony I felt so connected to God and to that divine presence that there was a beautiful sense of life, like everything was just so beautiful. Life was connected, the birds the trees, everything had a pulse, everything lived. You know shadows came out but there was an abundance of love. So, because my first ceremony was love I believe it now that it does exist and we're all worthy of it because we're all one, we're all loved.
>
> (P8)

Other participants reported that their intense spiritual experiences led to insights into the meaning of life and their role in it. One participant described an acute experience of oneness with nature that also put into perspective the grandeur of life on earth, thus helping to reduce the relative importance of her body weight.

> I felt like I was down and the soil was blanketing me and the branches were wrapping themselves around me. I just felt like there's this super intelligence and I feel like that's something I can't take for granted. It's a life force. I feel like I'm a life force and I feel it's all connected now. I'm connected and I'm part of the earth and when I die, my roots and my energy will become some other life force and I just feel like everything is so much more special and it's beyond the stereotype of weight.
>
> (P1)

Another subtheme that emerged related to an increase in religious, spiritual or contemplative practices post-ayahuasca drinking. More than half of the participants indicated that these increases involved engagement with meditation, yoga, journaling and a deeper appreciation for, or reintegration of, the practice of prayer. One participant described her deepened reconnection with prayer:

> I grew up going to church and then we stopped going to Catholic church when I was like 8 or 9 and we'd go for holidays you know, celebrate Easter and Christmas but I felt really disconnected from that religion and so now I understand more about what prayer is and I do it, and that really helps to anchor me.
>
> (P3)

Member Checks

Member checks sought participant feedback on the accuracy of the research findings. Only one participant provided additional commentary following member checking, sharing that her lengthy struggle with an ED had ended, her weight had increased and her quality of life had improved:

> My 18-year-long eating disorder has stopped. It has been two years since. I was at 95 pounds when I stopped my eating disorder. I am now 110–115 pounds. I had another ceremony telling me to stop tread-milling. I have dramatically reduced my exercise load. I have become a teacher and I have a successful career now!
>
> (P1)

Discussion

In this pioneering study, qualitative analysis was conducted to identify the perceived outcomes of ceremonial ayahuasca use among individuals with a history of a diagnosed ED. In the context of this second study, thematic exploration of the participant interviews resulted in the identification of four major themes relating to improvements in various domains of functioning. Specifically, the findings suggest that ayahuasca facilitates healing in a holistic manner, where psychological, physical, social and spiritual aspects of the self are implicated in healing, in turn promoting an embodied wholeness.

Psychological Outcomes

A wide range of psychological benefits related to ayahuasca drinking were reported and discussed in Lafrance et al. (2017). Highlights include the potential for ayahuasca in (1) supporting the processing of trauma and/or previously avoided emotion underlying ED symptoms; (2) reducing comorbid symptoms of depression, anxiety, self-harm, suicidality and psychoactive substance use; and (3) increasing the capacity to love oneself (Lafrance et al., 2017). In addition to these previously reported findings, participants noted improvements in their capacity for mindfulness, including an ability to observe, tolerate and embody their inner experiences, present-moment thoughts and emotions. This finding is consistent with research that found individuals who had drunk ayahuasca experienced increased capacities for mindfulness according to standardized self-report measures (Sampedro et al., 2017; Soler et al., 2016). They proposed that ayahuasca may facilitate therapeutic change by enhancing an individual's ability to decenter or create distance from maladaptive thoughts and emotions. This is especially relevant for those struggling with an ED who sometimes experience a harsh and even unrelenting inner critic (Dolhanty & Greenberg, 2007). These findings are also in line with brain-imaging studies that have shown that ayahuasca seems to modify the activity of the Default Mode Network (DMN: Palhano-Fontes et al., 2015; Sampedro et al., 2017), an area in the brain linked to self-referential mental activity, emotional processing and memory recollection (Raichle et al., 2001). These researchers propose that ayahuasca attenuates the DMN, which allows for access to meditative states and in turn leads to introspection and changes in self-perception, processes that may facilitate ED recovery.

Body Perception and Physical Effects

Visions in ceremony as well as insights following participation in aya-huasca ceremonies were perceived to facilitate a greater level of respect, love and gratitude for the physical body and food. In some cases, this phenomenon led to reduced ED symptoms, normalization of eating and weight, and more accurate perceptions of the body. Disturbances in eating behavior such as extreme avoidance, restriction or intake of food are defining characteristics of EDs. Ayahuasca may help some in-dividuals to reestablish a healthy and positive relationship with eating, where food is viewed as a source of nourishment for the body important for physiological health. Additionally, a hallmark of an ED is a turning away from and against the physical body in one's thoughts, attitudes and actions (Stice & Shaw, 2002). The way in which the body is expe-rienced, treated and nourished is central to the maintenance and reso-lution of ED symptoms. Therefore, reconciliation with one's physical body in both attitude and action is, in our opinion, a crucial component of ED recovery. It appears from this study that ayahuasca can assist in this process by facilitating a shift – at least for some – towards a more positive relationship with the physical body that supports an integrated and embodied sense of self.

Relational Outcomes

Along with physical and psychological impairments, EDs are known to adversely affect social functioning (Fairburn & Harrison, 2003). This is particularly true for those with anorexia nervosa, in which insecure attachments and a predisposition to obsessive compulsive, anxious and avoidant traits increase the risk and maintenance of the disorder (Treasure & Schmidt, 2013; Ward et al., 2001). Furthermore, as the illness progresses, loved ones may understandably experience and express strong emotional responses (Treasure & Schmidt, 2013). An individual who is anxious and emotionally avoidant may find such responses challenging to process and tolerate and, in turn this amplifies difficulties with social processing and emotion regulation, only to create more distanced and strained interpersonal relationships, and increased reliance on the ED for coping. Many participants in this study noted both transformation of childhood pain relating to attachment injuries or trauma and improvements in current relationships with loved ones. These findings confirm those of other studies of individuals participating in ceremonial ayahuasca, in which participants reported greater feelings of love and empathy for others (Harris & Gurel, 2012; Kjellgren, Eriksson, & Norlander, 2009) as well as improved communication, forgiveness and relationship repair (Harris & Gurel, 2012; Loizaga-Velder & Verres, 2014).

Spiritual and/or Transpersonal Effects

Ayahuasca's effects on participants' deepening of their spirituality occurred through acute in-ceremony experiences of transcendental states, as well as spiritual teachings and insights experienced both in-ceremony and in the time that followed. These findings corroborate reports from individuals with substance use issues who had drunk ayahuasca and attributed their spiritual and transpersonal experiences to have therapeutic value, mainly by reducing drug cravings (Loizaga-Velder & Verres, 2014). Both participants and therapists surveyed hypothesized that these changes may be a result of an enhanced sense of life purpose and meaning, as well as trust in a connection with a higher entity or power. Research with the psychedelic psilocybin also reported that mystical experiences induced while under its effects evoked both personal meaning and spiritual significance, which in turn significantly correlated with reduced tobacco craving and use (Garcia-Romeu, Griffiths, & Johnson, 2015). Although the mechanism of change remains unclear, it has been hypothesized that these positive attitudinal and behavioral changes are the result of powerful spiritual insights and personal meaning interpreted from these acute mystical experiences (Bogenschutz & Pommy, 2012). With this in mind, it is possible that our participants' reported reductions in ED thoughts and symptoms may, in part, be a positive effect of their spiritual and transpersonal experiences induced by ayahuasca. Similarly, the spiritual tenets of 12-step addiction recovery programs, such as Alcoholics Anonymous, consider a spiritual transformation or "spiritual awakening" as a central component in changing addictive behavior (Forcehimes, 2004). Research on spirituality and EDs has also demonstrated that improvements in spiritual well-being correlate with better treatment outcomes, positive changes in attitudes about eating and body shape, and reduced ED symptomatology (Richards, Berrett, Hardman, & Eggett, 2006).

Ayahuasca's Therapeutic Process and Value

Given that our primary outcomes reflect this triad of physical, psychological and social domains of healing, we feel it is critical for the field to consider a biopsychosocial approach to recovery. In fact, and in light of our findings, we would go further to again propose that those affected by an ED might be even better served by a biopsychosocial *and* spiritual approach to recovery, regardless of the modality employed. Although conventional ED modalities rarely incorporate a core spiritual component, preliminary research has suggested that spiritual growth may facilitate ED recovery (Richards et al., 2006), and this is supported by our findings. In summary, ayahuasca appears to facilitate an integrative approach to healing an ED that encompasses simultaneous and integrative changes within the whole person – the physical, psychological, social and spiritual. Moreover, ayahuasca seems to do so by engaging the innate healing resources of the self, promoting the embodiment of the true self.

Additional Considerations

Although the preliminary findings of this study show promise for the ceremonial use of ayahuasca along the continuum of healing from an ED, it is important to delineate some of the risks associated with ayahuasca drinking. Leaders in the field have expressed concern that the dietary restrictions and purging in the context of ayahuasca ritual preparation and participation could trigger or exacerbate ED thoughts and symptoms (Labate, Anderson, & Jungaberle, 2011). While the results of the study by Lafrance et al. (2017) did not validate these concerns, they are based on a relatively small sample, and thus further investigation is warranted. Other considerations include the associated physical complications of EDs and possible contraindications such as electrolyte imbalance, cardiac arrhythmias, low blood pressure and the potential concurrent use of contraindicated selective serotonin reuptake inhibitors (Callaway & Grob, 1998; Riba et al., 2001). These issues may also pose additional risks for those traveling to remote areas of developing countries to access ayahuasca, should complications arise requiring medical attention.

It's important to note as well that some individuals who seek out ayahuasca for mental health issues are desperate for help – especially if conventional treatments have not yielded improvements in symptoms or quality of life. Individuals who seek out ayahuasca for healing purposes may ignore, downplay or hesitate to discuss the associated risks with their loved ones or medical team for fear that they will not be supported or may even be discouraged to seek out this healing modality. It is also not unheard of for individuals to express fear or concern about their loved one's use of ayahuasca, given the limited research on its use of ayahuasca among those with EDs. As such, medical professionals could benefit from education on the uses and mechanisms of action of ayahuasca and other psychedelics. The field also requires drug policy that supports the scientific research of ayahuasca among clinical populations most in need.

Study Limitations

This study is not without limitations. There was potential selection bias in that individuals who agreed to participate may have experienced more positive effects of drinking ayahuasca and/or hold more positive views than individuals who did not volunteer to share their perspectives. Anecdotally, there have been reports of less than positive experiences, although these did not emerge in our study.

The interviews were also limited to individuals who had actively sought out ayahuasca, with no comparison to those who have not. There may be individual differences among those who have felt drawn to and actively sought ayahuasca. This poses challenges to generalizing the results to all those with EDs.

In this study, our sample was also quite homogeneous: English-speaking individuals with current or historical EDs. Most of the participants were Caucasian women, and all but one were from North America. Our participants were a highly educated group, and interestingly, many were employed in helping professions. As such, these individuals may have had greater insight into and theoretical understanding of the psychology of EDs, emotions and trauma, which could have affected their responses. Future research should also investigate the experiences of heterogeneous ayahuasca-drinking ED populations.

Finally, questions and prompts from the semi-structured interview may have influenced some of the participants' responses to support the research questions and outcomes. As such, future research must extend beyond the exploratory (i.e. longitudinal studies, controlled clinical studies) to evaluate the unique therapeutic potential of ceremonial ayahuasca drinking.

Conclusion

We believe that the study results are significant in that they provide new perspectives and opportunities for therapeutic pathways for EDs, especially among Westerners. These findings point to some of the potential therapeutic changes in the healing of EDs, some of which may inspire future innovative and integrative modalities of treatment.

References

Barbosa, P. C., Giglio, J. S., & Dalgalarrondo, P. (2005). Altered states of consciousness and short-term psychological after-effects induced by the first-time ritual use of ayahuasca in an urban context in Brazil. *Journal of Psychoactive Drugs, 37*(2), 193–201.

Bogenschutz, M. P., & Pommy, J. M. (2012). Therapeutic mechanisms of classic hallucinogens in the treatment of addictions: From indirect evidence to testable hypotheses. *Drug Testing and Analysis, 4*(7–8), 543–555.

Braun, V., & Clarke, V. (2006). Using thematic analysis in psychology. *Qualitative Research in Psychology, 3*(2), 77–101. doi:10.1191/1478088706qp063oa

Callaway, J. C., & Grob, C. S. (1998). Ayahuasca preparations and serotonin re-uptake inhibitors: A potential combination for severe adverse reactions. *Journal of Psychoactive Drugs, 30*(4), 367–369.

Dolhanty, J., & Greenberg, L. S. (2007). Emotion-focused therapy in the treatment of eating disorders. *European Psychotherapy, 7*(1), 97–116.

Fábregas, J. M., González, D., Fondevila, S., Cutchet, M., Fernández, X., Barbosa, P. C. R., ..., Bouso, J. C. (2010). Assessment of addiction severity among ritual users of ayahuasca. *Drug and Alcohol Dependence, 111*(3), 257–261.

Fairburn, C. G., & Harrison, P. J. (2003). Eating disorders. *The Lancet, 361*(9355), 407–416.

Forcehimes, A. A. (2004). De profundis: Spiritual transformations in Alcoholics Anonymous. *Journal of Clinical Psychology, 60*, 503–517.

Garcia-Romeu, A., Griffiths, R. R., & Johnson, M. W. (2015). Psilocybin-occasioned mystical experiences in the treatment of tobacco addiction. *Current Drug Abuse Reviews, 7*(3), 157–164.

Golden, N. H., Katzman, D. K., Kreipe, R. E., Stevens, S. L., Sawyer, S. M., Rees, J., ... Rome, E. S. (2003). Eating disorders in adolescents. *Journal of Adolescent Health, 33*(6), 496–503.

Grob. (2013). Foreword. Ancient medicine and the modern world. In B. Labate & C. Cavnar (Eds.), *The therapeutic use of Ayahuasca* (pp. vii–xiv). Berlin: Springer-Verlag.

Halpern, J. H., Sherwood, A. R., Passie, T., Blackwell, K. C., & Ruttenber, A. J. (2008). Evidence of health and safety in American members of a religion who use a hallucinogenic sacrament. *Medical Science Monitor, 14*(8), 15–22.

Harris, R., & Gurel, L. (2012). A study of ayahuasca use in North America. *Journal of Psychoactive Drugs, 44*(3), 209–215.

Harrison, A., Sullivan, S., Tchanturia, K., & Treasure, J. (2009). Emotion recognition and regulation in anorexia nervosa. *Clinical Psychology & Psychotherapy, 16*(4), 348–356.

Hay, P. H. (2013). A systematic review of evidence for psychological treatments in eating disorders. *International Journal of Eating Disorders, 46*(5), 462–469.

Hoek, H. W. (2006). Incidence, prevalence and mortality of anorexia nervosa and other eating disorders. *Current Opinion in Psychiatry, 19*, 389–394.

Kjellgren, A., Eriksson, A., & Norlander, T. (2009). Experiences of encounters with ayahuasca - "the vine of the soul". *Journal of Psychoactive Drugs, 41*(4), 309–315.

Labate, B. C., Anderson, B., & Jungaberle, H. (2011). Ritual ayahuasca use and health: An interview with Jacques Mabit. In B. Labate & H. Jungaberle, (Eds.), *The internationalization of ayahuasca,* (pp. 223–243). Zürich: Lit Verlag.

Labate, B. C., & Cavnar, C. (Eds.). (2014). *The therapeutic use of ayahuasca*. Berlin: Springer.

Lafrance, A., Loizaga-Velder, A., Fletcher, J., Files, N., Renelli, M., & Tupper, K. (2017). Nourishing the spirit: Exploratory research on ayahuasca experiences along the continuum of recovery from eating disorders. *Journal of Psychoactive Drugs*. Retrieved from doi:10.1080/02791072.2017.1361559

Loizaga-Velder, A., & Verres, R. (2014). Therapeutic effects of ritual ayahuasca use in the treatment of substance dependence - qualitative results. *Journal of Psychoactive Drugs, 46*(1), 63–72.

Luna, L. E. (1986). *Vegetalismo: Shamanism among the mestizo population of the Peruvian Amazon.* Stockholm: Almqvist & Wiksell.

Luna, L. E. (2011). Indigenous and mestizo use of ayahuasca: An overview. In R. G. dos Santos (Ed.), *The ethnopharmacology of ayahuasca* (pp. 1–21). Kerala: Transworld Research Network.

Osório, F. L., Sanches, R. F., Macedo, L. R., Santos, R. G., Maia-de-Oliveira, J. P., Wichert-Ana, L., ... Hallak, J. E. (2015). Antidepressant effects of a single dose of ayahuasca in patients with recurrent depression: A preliminary report. *Revista Brasileira de Psiquiatria, 37*(1), 13–20.

Palhano-Fontes, F., Andrade, K. C., Tofoli, L. F., Santos, A. C., Crippa, J. A, Hallak, J. E. C., ... de Araujo, D. B. (2015). The psychedelic state induced by ayahuasca modulates the activity and connectivity of the default mode network. *PLoS One.* doi:10.1371/journal.pone.01181433

Patton, M. Q. (2002). *Qualitative research and evaluation methods* (3rd ed.) Thousand Oaks, CA: Sage.

Polivy, J., & Herman, C. P. (2002). Causes of eating disorders. *Annual Review of Psychology, 53*(1), 187–213.

Raichle, M. E., MacLeod, A. M., Snyder, A. Z., Powers, W. J., Gusnard, D. A., & Shulman, G. L. (2001). A default mode of brain function. *Proceedings of the National Academy of Sciences U S A, 98*(2), 676–682.

Riba, J., Rodríguez-Fornells, A., Urbano, G., Morte, A., Antonijoan, R., Montero, M., ... Barbanoj, M. J. (2001). Subjective effects and tolerability of the South American psychoactive beverage ayahuasca in healthy volunteers. *Psychopharmacology (Berl), 154*(1), 85–95.

Richards, P. S., Berrett, M. E., Hardman, R. K., & Eggett, D. L. (2006). Comparative efficacy of spirituality, cognitive, and emotional support groups for treating eating disorder inpatients. *Eating Disorders, 14*(5), 401–415.

Rivier, L., & Lindgren, J. E. (1972). "Ayahuasca," the South American hallucinogenic drink: An ethnobotanical and chemical investigation. *Economic Botany, 26*(2), 101–129.

Sampedro, F., de la Fuente Revenga, M., Valle, M., Roberto, N., Domínguez-Clavé, E., Elices, M., ... Friedlander, P. (2017). Assessing the psychedelic "after-glow" in ayahuasca users: Post-acute neurometabolic and functional connectivity changes are associated with enhanced mindfulness capacities. *International Journal of Neuropsychopharmacology, 20*(9), 698–711, Retrieved from doi:10.1093/ijnp/pyx036

Sanches, R. F., de Lima Osório, F., dos Santos, R. G., Macedo, L. R. H., Maia-de-Oliveira, J. P., Wichert-Ana, L., ... Hallak, J. (2016). Antidepressant effects of a single dose of ayahuasca in patients with recurrent depression: A SPECT study. *Journal of Clinical Psychopharmacology, 36*(1), 77–81. doi:10.1097/JCP.0000000000000436

Shanon, B. (2002). *The antipodes of the mind: Charting the phenomenology of the ayahuasca experience.* New York, NY: Oxford University Press.

Sim, L., & Zeman, J. (2005). Emotion regulation factors as mediators between body dissatisfaction and bulimic symptoms in early adolescent girls. *The Journal of Early Adolescence, 25*(4), 478–496.

Soler, J., Elices, M., Franquesa, A., Barker, S., Friedlander, P., Feilding, A., ... Riba, J. (2016). Exploring the therapeutic potential of ayahuasca: Acute intake increases mindfulness-related capacities. *Psychopharmacology (Berl), 233*(5), 823–829.

Stice, E., & Shaw, H. (2002). Role of body dissatisfaction in the onset and maintenance of eating pathology: A synthesis of research findings. *The Journal of Psychosomatic Research, 53*, 985–993.

Strassman, R. J., Qualls, C. R., Uhlenhuth, E. H., & Kellner, R. (1994). Dose-response study of N, N-dimethyltryptamine in humans. II. Subjective effects and preliminary results of a new rating scale. *Archives of General Psychiatry, 51*(2), 98–108.

Thomas, G., Lucas, P., Capler, N. R., Tupper, K. W., & Martin, G. (2013). Ayahuasca-assisted therapy for addiction: Results from a preliminary observational study in Canada. *Current Drug Abuse Reviews, 6*(1), 30–42.

Treasure, J., & Schmidt, U. (2013). The cognitive-interpersonal maintenance model of anorexia nervosa revisited: A summary of the evidence for cognitive, socio-emotional and interpersonal predisposing and perpetuating factors. *Journal of Eating Disorders, 1*(1), 13.

Tupper, K. W. (2008). The globalization of ayahuasca: Harm reduction or benefit maximization? *International Journal of Drug Policy, 9*(4), 297–303.

Tupper, K. W., Wood, E., Yensen, R., & Johnson, M. W. (2015). Psychedelic medicine: A re-emerging therapeutic paradigm. *Canadian Medical Association Journal, 187*(14), 1054–1059.

Waller, G. (2016). Recent advances in psychological therapies for eating disorders. *F1000 Faculty Review*, 702. doi: 10.12688/f1000research.7618.1

Ward, A., Ramsay, R., Turnbull, S., Steele, M., Steele, H., & Treasure, J. (2001). Attachment in anorexia nervosa: A transgenerational perspective. *Psychology and Psychotherapy: Theory, Research and Practice, 74*(4), 497–505.

Part III

Prevention and Treatment of Eating Disorders

What is known about eating disorders and embodiment through theory and research serves to facilitate more effective and meaningful interventions for the prevention and treatment of eating disorders. This section presents a variety of approaches to have an impact on both large and small scales, ranging from learning to feel emotions in the body to political resistance through blogging. This section includes a chapter on fat black women blogging as a form advocacy, the use of yoga, an embodiment program for kids in schools, emotions in the body in therapy, and strategies for increasing embodiment. Together these chapters present a vision of how all of us can further develop our own embodiment.

15 "Fat" as Political Disobedience

Black Women Blogging the Resistance

Andrea Shaw Nevins and Jazmyn Brown

Amanda, a size 16/18 white woman, went to Macy's in search of a formal dress for a Christmas party, but she could not find any outfits larger than a size 12. When she approached a store employee to ask for the location of the women's department, Amanda was told that she was standing in it and the sizes did not run any larger than 12. Confounded by how it could be that a women's department did not sell women's sizes, Amanda questioned the sales clerk for more detail on why clothing in the sizes she needed were not available. "It's a demographic thing, ma'am," the clerk explained (Popkin, 2008).

> We do not carry plus sizes of formal wear or business suits. We find, demographically speaking, that most of our upscale clientele is smaller, so we have a really large petites department and just the basics for our plus sized customers. It's nothing against you, ma'am. It's just demographics.
>
> (Popkin, 2008)

Amanda became appalled and even more confused by this response, specifically the employee's effort to couch this unanticipated and upsetting revelation in terms of the logistics of retail management.

The clerk proceeded to explain, just as a simple matter of fact, that Amanda should go to the "Black" Macy's, one of the chain's stores in a neighborhood with "a different demographic," to find the dressy plus-size clothing she wanted. And just in case Amanda was not clear what she meant, the clerk gave Amanda a short lesson in the politics of race and fashion when she broke it down and said, "Women of color tend to be larger, so there is a much bigger plus sized department" at this other store. Amanda was furious over this explanation, and in her account of the experience complains that the clerk, who by the way was black, had "managed to condescendingly call me fat, poor, and low class" in one fell swoop. Well, in effect what the clerk had really called Amanda was "black," situating her large embodiment and full-figured fashion needs as belonging to an alternate and racialized shopping Universe, and perhaps blackness, with all its class-inflected baggage, translates for the clerk and for Amanda into the trifecta of undesirable characteristics (fat, poor, and low class) that Amanda names.

Furthermore, the clerk's analysis of the clientele to which each shopping universe catered offers profound commentary about race and embodiment: "upscale" (read white) women are not meant to be fat, and if you are, tough luck with finding clothing. Ironically, the Macy's employee had quite likely given Amanda very accurate advice about where to find the clothing she wanted, though it was couched in messy and troubling terms of race and class. Additionally, from Amanda's account, she seems extra peeved about the entire episode because the clerk was black. How could a black employee, someone presumably alert to marginalization, be complicit in Macy's decision to locate fat white women as unsuitable customers, deny Amanda access to fashionable clothing in her size, and effectively designate Amanda's embodiment as black?

Amanda's shopping dilemma offers a terribly salient opening for this chapter as it efficiently aligns blackness and fatness as parallel and inextricably yoked states of embodiment. And, with apologies to Amanda, her experience is quite comedic in its critique of Macy's outrageous assumption that white women are not fat – at least not fatter than size 12. "Blogging the Resistance" explores the dynamics inherent in that fateful encounter Amanda had at the "upscale" Macys – the ways in which race, gender, and size intersect on the site of the fat black woman's body to create unique and extreme strains of oppression in the beauty arena where imperatives of whiteness and slenderness render the bodies of large black women subject to dismissal and invisibility, if not evisceration. Furthermore, we aim to establish the ways in which both fat and black women have been deemed a "menace" (Peters, 2014, p. 67) to fashion and consider how the beauty arena functions as a Foucauldian Panopticon in which the bodies of women are policed using powerful surveillance strategies as a means of exerting control.

Lyn Mikel Brown uses the term "corporal colonization" in reference to the Western beauty hegemony's imperatives of slenderness, and it is these colonizing efforts that we seek to expose (Brown, 2011, p. 54). Finally, we address the evolving role of Cyberspace as a site for the exponential expansion of the beauty panopticon but also as the venue where fat black women are striking back and reclaiming their bodies as empire. As it is understood through Piran's Developmental Theory of Embodiment (Piran & Teall, 2012), lack of social power has an influence on the development of disembodiment in women. The devaluation of women through racism in the fashion and beauty arena and the pathologization of fat must be named and explored to identify the sociocultural context within which eating disorders emerge. This is also meaningful phenomenologically; it makes visible both the women who have historically been invisible and those who are seemingly dangerous for taking space and appearing differently from misogynistic appearance ideals.

Black Women's Historical Oppression in the Fashion and Beauty Arena

One black woman's body that may indeed be recognized as signifying an empire is that of performing superstar Beyoncé. She took the stage at the 2017 Grammy's in a luxurious gold gown that took 50 people an entire week to embroider (Lang, 2017). The ensemble also included a halo-shaped head piece, and the outfit referenced both the Madonna (the one from the Bible) and the African Yoruba goddess Oshun, who is often associated with fertility and love (Jeffries, 2017). At some points in American history, a black woman dressed like Beyoncé in fine linens stood the chance of having her clothing legally confiscated by a white person – any white person. Leon Higginbotham explains that according to the South Carolina Negro Act of 1735,

> when a slave managed to obtain clothing that might accord him some dignity or prestige, the act declared that when such clothing was 'above' that which a slave should wear, it could be taken from the slave by 'all and every constable and other persons' to be used for his or their own benefit.
>
> (Higginbotham, 1980, p. 173)

Sumptuary laws such as this one that sought to restrict the access of black bodies to certain types of clothing existed in other parts of the Americas (Buckridge, 2004, p. 31), and in her essay "Born in Chanel, Christen in Gucci," Andrea Shaw Nevins suggests that these laws "were enacted based on hegemonic imperatives to deprive slaves access to the transformative power of fashion" (Shaw, 2012).

The relationship between black women and the Western fashion world has been a long and troubled one that is aptly reflected by the ongoing lack of diversity on the catwalk and on the cover of fashion magazines. A black woman was not featured on the cover of a mainstream fashion magazine all the way until 1968 when Katiti Kironde appeared on the Cover of *Glamour* when she won the "Best Dressed College Girls." Discrimination and deliberate exclusion of black women within the modeling industry abound. The only black models to grace the cover of the *Sports Illustrated Swimsuit* magazine are Tyra Banks in 1997 and Beyoncé in 2007. *Cosmopolitan* magazine published an article with a list of the ten most beautiful women in the world according to science (Mattern, 2016), neglecting to include a single woman of color. Since the first black woman was featured on the cover of *Vogue* in 1974, black women such as Halle Berry, Lupita Nyong'o, Michelle Obama, and Rihanna have been featured on the cover less than 40 times. Since it was founded, the magazine has published 2,833 issues, meaning that a little over one percent of the cover models have been black (Borrelli-Persson, 2017).

Oppression of Fat Women in the Fashion and Beauty Arena

Like black bodies, fat bodies have also been constructed as a threat to fashion. In an August 2012 airing of the fashion design reality show *Project Runway*, the rejection of large bodies as a suitable form for which to create fabulous clothing was made clear when contestant Ven Budhu brought his "real woman" client, Terri Herlihy, to tears on the "Fix My Friend" episode (Chan, 2013). According to Herlihy, Budhu was repeatedly insulting her because of her size; she even goes as far as to describe his behavior as a kind of "bullying." This hesitation about designing for full-figure women is also evident on the fall 2017 season of Project Runway. The fall 2017 season features models in a range of sizes, and according to Project Runway host Heidi Klum, "You have to dress real people, and real people come in different sizes: short, tall, more voluptuous, skinny" (Chan, 2013). However, on several episodes, designers quite openly share their trepidations about designing clothing for fat bodies, as if catering to the average-sized American woman never even crossed their mind.

Fashion icons like designer Karl Lagerfeld and former Vogue editor Anna Wintour have unabashedly claimed the position that fat bodies are not deserving of efforts to style them fashionably and situate these curvier figures as inappropriate symbols of beauty. In Lagerfeld's own words, "What I designed was fashion for slender and slim people" (Vogue, 2004). Wintour holds a similar position and has been described by Andre Leon Talley, former editor at Vogue, as "not liking fat people" (Grove & Morgan, 2005). Furthermore, in a *60 Minutes* interview, Wintour famously referred to Minnesotans as fat when she says, "I had just been on a trip to Minnesota where I can only kindly describe most of the people that I saw as little houses" (Odell, 2009). She proceeds to offer her own medicalized take on fatness when she adds,

> And I just felt like there's such an epidemic of obesity in the United States. And for some reason everyone focuses on anorexia ... We need to spend money, time, and education on teaching people to eat, exercise, and take care of themselves in a healthier way.
>
> (Odell, 2009)

She effectively advocates that efforts directed toward the prevention of the extreme states of slenderness, often associated with anorexia, should be redirected to combat the more meaningful enemy of obesity. In other words, better too skinny than too fat.

Several theorists argue that the sentiments expressed by Lagerfeld and Wintour are quite widespread in the fashion industry, which has a general distaste for dressing fat women. This commitment to robbing fat women of the opportunity to access fashionable clothing is no doubt anchored in the Western disdain toward fatness. As Susie Orbach notes, "Today fat has become not a description of size but a moral category tainted with criticism and contempt" (Orbach, 2012). Daphne Merkin suggests that the recalcitrant designers in the industry are enacting the punishment Western culture sees fit for the "sin" of eating too much and "are merely messengers, delivering up to us our own grotesque parody of religious grace, in which food substitutes for sex and the sinful pleasures of the flesh lead only to the purgatory of size 14" (Merkin, 2010). Lauren Downing sums it all up when she says, "existing well outside of that boundary of both the fashion industry and mainstream commodity advertising, the plus-size woman has effectively been excluded from the sphere of mainstream fashion" (Downing, 2012, p. 7). This marginalization is evident to any fat woman (like Amanda) who has shopped for clothing in a department store, only to find the plus-size department (or in the United Kingdom the outsize section) tucked away at the back of the store.

This hesitation (at best) about designing fashion for fat women resembles in many ways the historical reluctance (also at best) of department stores to carry cosmetics for black women and of designers to sell Eunice and John Johnson their clothes for the adornment of black models who would parade these garments at the Ebony Fashion Show. This exclusion is particularly troubling in an era when bodies are hyper-visible due to all the recent technological innovations such as social media, online magazines, and cable TV with its multitude of viewing opportunities. When fat black women's bodies are restricted from access to some of these spaces or stand to be ridiculed through the power of surveillance, the impact of this exclusion is unsettling. It is also tragic given the pleasurable potential of fashion to shape identity and as a source of empowerment, as huge swaths of women are denied access to the transformative opportunities associated with fashion and beauty.

Beauty Pageants and the Exclusion of Both Fat and Black Women from the Beauty Arena

The Miss America beauty pageant exemplifies the exclusionary thrust of the beauty arena as a space where the intricate connections between the way blackness and fatness restrict admission is apparent. Black women were not allowed to compete in the Miss America contest until 1970, and the first black Miss America, Vanessa Williams, was crowned in 1984 (Banet-Weiser, 1999, p. 127). Contestants have become increasingly slimmer – a reflection of the mounting expectation of slenderness as a foundation for beauty (Wiseman, Gray, Mosimann & Ahrens, 1992, pp. 85–89). It is then no surprise that in 2016 allegations surfaced from former Miss Universe, Alicia Machado, that Donald Trump, who was then an executive producer of the pageant, had referred to her as "Miss Piggy" because she gained weight after receiving the crown (Barbaro & Twohey, 2016). Trump even accompanied the teenaged Machado to the gym where he and a bevy of reporters in an ultimate act of surveillance watched Machado exercise (Barbaro & Twohey, 2016). Beauty pageants exemplify and epitomize the sociocultural phenomenon of erasure of large black women, who occupy a triple consciousness by virtue of their size, gender, and race. Pageants like the Miss America contest reflect larger phenomena that dictate how women view themselves and each other. The policing of women's bodies, which is the basis of dieting crazes and the numberless how-to-get-your-tummy-flat-in-order-to-seduce-your-man articles, among other ideals espoused by various media, encourages a stagnant ideal of thinness.

Beauty pageants function as a microcosmic manifestation of the beauty panopticon, wherein judges survey the competitors, who are the surveyed. The beauty contest pits women against each other for the title of most beautiful, signaling that each woman is surveying herself against her peers and also surveying the other women against certain ideals. The openly voyeuristic nature of beauty competitions reinforces certain ideals in crowning the winner, who becomes the embodiment of the beauty standards used to judge her peers. Beauty pageants are a symptom of a society that emphasizes appearance and encourages constant evaluation of others as well as self-evaluation based on a given set of standards. This type of society forces women to occupy what Berger (1990) calls the dual position of surveyor and surveyed. Berger (1990) argues that, unlike men, whose social presence depends upon their actions and innate power, a woman's presence is intrinsic to her sense of self from the moment she is born, a symptom of the deep-rooted hierarchy in which men are spectators and women are spectated upon by men (p. 46).

Even with the negative repercussions of the beauty panopticon that limits women according to their size, including the disenfranchisement of large black women in particular from the beauty arena, the act of surveillance and self-surveillance allows the marginalized to co-opt the very sociocultural mechanism by which they are excluded. That is to say, large black women benefit from the panoptic gaze that would normally force them to police themselves in order to conform to the thin ideal, using the normally punishing attention to gather interest and challenge beauty norms centered on whiteness and thinness.

The Panopticon

The beauty industry is propelled by the competition espoused in pageants, and the Internet facilitates the judgment of others from the anonymity of behind a screen, facilitating way more expansive acts of body policing. The advent of social media and the "selfie" only exacerbates this phenomenon and facilitates the proliferation of surveillance, allowing women to survey others across a technological space and react with likes, comments, or direct messages, creating an almost anonymous body of surveyors and surveyed. The beauty arena functions as a Foucauldian Panopticon in which women police themselves to conform to white hegemonic beauty standards that insist on whiteness and slenderness as ultimate representations of beauty.

Jeremy Bentham (1791) wrote on his conceptualization of the Panopticon or inspection house in the late 18th century. He designed the structure as a means of keeping all of its prisoners under surveillance simultaneously, placing the inmates under the psychological burden of not knowing exactly when they are being monitored (Bentham, 1791, pp. 1–3). The resulting paranoia forces prisoners to self-police and gauge their actions against what is acceptable to limit punishment. Bentham's blueprint for the structure that would enable continuous surveillance calls for a circular building, with divided cells along the circumference of the building, with the "Inspector's Lodge" occupying the center (Bentham, 1791, p. 5). Rather than applying a coercive force to inmates to deter rebellion, the Panopticon's psychological power over its inmates derives from the looming potential of punishment; prison inspectors could be watching any inmate at any given moment.

Cyberspace itself becomes the Panopticon, which reinforces a reductionist set of beauty ideals that systematically exclude outliers. The reification of white femininity as an ultimate form of female embodiment informs the inspection criteria that women have been acculturated to strive for and what they use as the standard to judge themselves and each other. Germov and Williams (1999) invoke the term "beauty panopticon" in reference to the standards we use to judge beauty and the way self-surveillance is encouraged as part of the policing of our own bodies (p. 117). They argue that women perpetuate the standards by which they judge themselves through constant self-surveillance of their bodies and constant surveillance of the bodies of other women (Germov & Williams, 1999, p. 125). So not only does Western beauty culture reify beauty ideals that celebrate thinness and whiteness, but those who consume these standards also reinforce them. For those who do not fit the ideal, punishment varies and includes self-inflicted dieting. Additionally, most women exist in the torturous state of permanent body dissatisfaction. Punishment also includes the censorship of large bodies and fat bodies from the beauty arena. By excluding both large and black women as viable beauty subjects, traditional white inflected beauty standards become reified.

Fat Black Women Blogging the Resistance and Changing the Nature of the Gaze

Fat black women have a paradoxical relationship with the beauty panopticon. On the one hand, it functions to exclude them from the beauty canon by encouraging self-surveillance and punishing where appropriate; however, on the other hand, the Panopticon has the converse effect when large black women manipulate and harness the sociological/psychological effects that underlie Bentham's original concept. The way that fat black women use social media as a means of both overt and implicit resistance not only humanizes them but also allows them to enter the beauty arena via a less mainstream path. Resistance through social media is also an attempt to reshape and train a new gaze that acknowledges a multiplicity of body types, diversifying the beauty canon from which large black women were excluded.

In regard to humanizing large black women, blogging, especially image-based blogging, relies on visual rhetoric to alter people's perspectives of women, which is defined as the relatively new study of visual imagery within the discipline of rhetoric or persuasive efforts (Foss, 2004, p. 141). The ubiquity of visual imagery within our culture has led to increased study of the effect of images on culture, communicating ideas on the same scope that speeches once accomplished (Foss, 2004, p. 142), sometimes conveying messages that cannot become readily accessible through discourse (p. 143). As a means of communicating, visual rhetoric plays an important role in bloggers' use of social media to post images that challenge the beauty status quo and often involves posing fat bodies in ways that signify confidence and fulfilment, countering the media's consistent portrayal of fat as something shameful that should be hidden from public view. Agnès Rocamora suggests that blogs are intricately connected to the beauty arena and argues that they function

> as a space for the articulation of a panoptic gaze that reproduces women's position as specular objects, but also as a space of empowerment through the control it grants bloggers on their own image, as well as through the alternative visions of femininity it allows them to circulate.
>
> (Rocamora, 2011, p. 410)

By using sites like Tumblr, Instagram, and other image-blogging platforms, large black women commandeer the very system that originally excluded them from the beauty canon, taking advantage of the Internet's ubiquity to actively challenge beauty standards that favor their thin, white counterparts. Rocamora (2011) identifies the surge in popularity of fashion blogs since 2003 as a reflection of the role of the blogosphere as a site of fashion negotiation and trends. Further, Connell (2013) argues that online projects such as blogs increase potential for disrupting normative fashion discourse (p. 210). Fat fashion blogs are examples of what Kargbo identifies as "image-based counternarratives" (Kargbo, 2013, p. 160) that facilitate a shift from the association of fat bodies with shame and disgust to rationalities that offer a healthier sense of embodiment.

Blogging allows women to bypass the erasure that is characteristic of the mainstream media by providing a platform from which images that defy the status quo are directly accessible to anyone with access to the In-ternet, without an intermediary. This phenomenon contrasts sharply with the images presented on magazine covers, which are notorious for being edited to maintain the thinnest standard possible or to outright exclude larger women. Fashion blogging in particular is an interesting niche, since personal blogs differ greatly from the social media accounts of businesses, which seek to maintain a certain image that accentuates their marketabil-ity. According to Kim Cochrane,

> Style blogs are democratizing fashion, offering much more diverse images than we're used to. Fat people are perhaps the least visible group of all in fashion terms, a status that plays out in two related ways. First is the paucity of clothes available to anyone over a certain size, a source of sadness for many fat style bloggers. The other way in which fat women – indeed, almost all women – are marginalized, is in terms of fashion imagery, with an insistence on extremely thin, young, and generally white women in magazines and on catwalks.
>
> (Cochrane, 2010)

Not only does blogging create an avenue for individuals to alter body image discourse as it relates to areas like fashion and health, but blogging platforms also act as a medium that allows the marginalized to counter their historic exclusion from the mainstream that often whitewashes and thins down images of women. By manipulating the function of the beauty panopticon as a method of punishing outliers and utilizing the intrigue that results from divergence from the golden mean of thinness, large black women who utilize the ubiquity of social media to resist the existing status-quo garner attention precisely because they are breaking the rules. The desired effect is increasing the prevalence of narratives of large black women, portraying them as human and just as beautiful as their thin, white counterparts.

The rules or standards of beauty that dictate what is acceptable ver-sus what is taboo are often based on stereotypes. Now that the beauty arena has shifted, beginning to include formerly marginalized women who are black and fat, a new vision of beauty in the Western world is in the nascent stages of emerging. Rather than conforming to the same beauty standards as thin women, fat beauty bloggers often completely refute the standards imposed on them by wearing tight clothing, for example, and embracing styles deemed unfit for larger women. These choices are meant to reject limitations on access to clothing that reveals too much of the fat body. Beauty and fashion blogger Marie Denee on Instagram regularly posts photos in which her outfit is the focus. These types of images, whether they are mirrored or portraits or shots in which she is artfully posed, are typical of the poses common for thinner models. Her images carry a cultural agenda by confronting her viewers with the reality that beauty and fatness are not mutually exclusive.

Another blogger, Chastity Garner Valentine, uses her Instagram account as a self-proclaimed "Digital Influencer," showing an awareness of the power of social media and images. She posts pictures of her in various outfits, including swimsuits and athletic wear, two sartorial options usually off-limits for a woman of her physique. By reclaiming and embracing these types of clothing, which are for the most part only considered appropriate for those with the "right" body, Valentine unabashedly resists marginalization and refuses to have her body policed no matter who is watching. These images, by virtue of them not being socially acceptable, actively challenge beauty norms as they break with the monopoly on beauty and fashion held for generations by thinner women. These bloggers give a human face to larger women, who are automatically disqualified from not just beauty pageants but from the beauty arena as a whole. Their blog posts and image archives entirely resist this belief.

Historically, corpulence has not always been as stigmatized as it is today. The plump female bodies in Classical paintings, as well as older sculptures depicting women with emphasized curves, such as the Venus of Willendorf, speak to the celebration of fatness in previous eras. Stearns (2002) writes that the preoccupation with body image, specifically slimness, in the United States began in the 1900s, becoming engrained in the collective American psyche with the advent of female athleticism and dieting advertisements (p. 3), which contributed to the foundation of an appearance-driven, patriarchal culture in which women are scrutinized by men, each other, and themselves.

Posing corpulence as unhealthy was and still is the means by which capitalist companies target women who are already uncomfortable with their bodies and turn to dieting as a means to alleviate their discomfort and shape themselves to the standard thin mold. Athleticism is associated with being fit and slim, and exercise is generally thought of as for those who wish to lose weight and/or maintain musculature. A 2017 study published in California State University Dominguez Hills Negotiation, Conflict Resolution, and Peacebuilding program's e-journal identified a monopoly on yoga by thin, white, able-bodied, middle- to upper-class women, as well as an appropriation of the original focus of yoga on peace, harmony, clarity, and centering that morphs the practice into something more competitive, sexualized, and exclusive (Sargent, 2017). The climate around yoga is an uninviting one, particularly for large black women.

Thus, the images that Jessamyn Stanley posts to her website are striking; she capitalizes on the initial shock value of a large black woman contorting her body into yoga poses generally thought of as only possible for thin women to make the powerful statement that women can be healthy, fit, and fat, and beautiful while doing so. Her website states that she encourages her students to focus on the question, "How do I feel?" rather than

"How do I look?" This mindset is a response to the emphasis our culture places on appearance, especially for women, as well as how stigmas and mental barriers are purely psychological. Stanley resists the societal pressures to not engage in certain activities – in this case yoga – because of her size, instead garnering a large following on Instagram and her blog and encouraging her students and viewers to break stereotypes. Her atypical approach toward practicing yoga, which includes a body positive attitude that resists the current status quo, is a powerful example of resistance because she actively challenges the marginalization of fat women from the practice of yoga, or more generally from athletics.

Stanley's philosophy of centeredness demonstrates an approach to the issue of body image as it pertains to women called "health at every size," abbreviated HAES (Kasardo & McHugh, 2015, p. 191), because the standard equivalence of a certain weight or body type with health is largely unfounded. Instead of focusing on losing weight – the rapid loss of weight being the obvious focus of diets, fad and otherwise – HAES emphasizes self-acceptance. The positive, holistic approach decouples size/weight from a person's diet, exercise regimen, and psychological state (Kasardo & McHugh, 2015, p. 191). Stanley and other fat bloggers' promotion of self-acceptance through their sites differs from the typical thin, white blogger's emphasis on eliminating belly fat in a week or less, placing emphasis not on other people's perceptions but on one's own self-actualization.

The combined features of blackness and corpulence in women's bodies often signify hypersexuality or render those bodies comedic (Shaw, 2006). However, black female bloggers are working to make themselves visible outside of the context of sex appeal, proving that fat black women can be something other than the woman devoid of any sexual appetite or the woman whose characterization hinges on the number of partners she has. Further, these bloggers offer proof that larger women can do the same things thin women can do and are applauded for, in an everyday context as well as in beauty pageants. Fat black female bloggers offer a means of identification for large women who are aware that their bodies are censored in the beauty and fashion industries and rarely represented as beautiful in various forms of visual media.

Malcolm X's iconic lines from his 1962 speech on protecting black women still have resonance today: the most disrespected person in America is the black woman. The mammy, jezebel, and sapphire archetypes, which are holdovers from slavery that arose from the desire to contain and control black female slaves, have had lasting, damaging effects on society's perceptions of black women through countless repeated dehumanizing images in media (Harris-Perry, 2012). From enslavement to nurturing others' children, fieldwork, sexual exploitation, and producing slave children, and sometimes to medical experimentation deemed too unsafe for whites (Washington, 2006, p. 47), black women in America have never fully owned their bodies.

The use of black female bodies by white slave masters signifies an ethos that black women were to be possessed in every sense of the word, leaving no room for them to acquire a sense of self-ownership. This lack of a means to self-actualize manifests today as negative imagery that reinforces black women's inferiority. King (1988) argues that for a black woman to survive, she must balance her social and domestic roles, performing the tasks of employee, mother, and homemaker simultaneously (pp. 49–50); the triple jeopardy of racism, sexism, and classism that affect black women's multi-faceted identities (p. 47) makes their lives a matter of survival of the fittest. According to West (1999), remaining strong in the face of adversity then becomes a psychological "straightjacket" that inhibits the black woman's right to personhood because it prioritizes perseverance ahead of self-care (p. 77). In spite of the pervasiveness of erasure and demeaning images, black women have not suffered in terms of body image issues compared to their white counterparts. Ironically, a study of body image disturbance, which is an experience of distortion in perception, behavior, or cognition in relation to body weight and appearance, found that black women were less likely to be affected by body image disturbance than white women (Posavac, Posavac, & Weigel, 2001), which may contribute to the increased number of black beauty and exercise bloggers who espouse a body positive attitude.

Conclusion

Numerous studies suggest that the bodies upon which women direct their own gaze play a significant role in how they are affected by the idealization of slenderness evident in mass media. For example, research done by Stice and Shaw (1994) suggests that "exposure to the thin-ideal portrayed in the media resulted in heightened feelings of depression, unhappiness, shame, guilt, and stress, and led to decreased levels of confidence" and to "increased body dissatisfaction" (Stice & Shaw, 1994, pp. 301–302). According to Halliwell and Dittmar (2004), "Women who internalized sociocultural pressures concerning appearance experienced greater anxiety following exposure to thin models than when exposed either to average-size models or landscapes" (Halliwell & Dittmar, 2004, p. 117). The research findings of Groesz, Levine, and Murnen (2002) "support the sociocultural perspective that mass media promulgate a slender ideal that elicits body dissatisfaction" (p. 1).

However, research has shown that discontent with one's body is less prolific among African American women who generally indicate a greater degree of satisfaction with their body than white women and hold more supple visions of beauty that imagine a less rigid beauty boundary in which their black and sometimes fat bodies can be included. One study concludes that "Generally, the data suggest that among girls, Black female adolescents are the least likely to practice weight control, and White female adolescents are the most likely to practice weight control" (Chao et al., 2008,

p. 131). Another study that even in comparison to Latina culture, African American women display a greater degree of body confidence: "In summary, African Americans expressed a higher level of comfort with their body image. More than half of these respondents were comfortable with their weight, and nearly three-quarters were satisfied with their figure" (Kraeplin, 2011, p. 64). Aside from the historical acceptance of fat bodies within the African American community and indeed throughout the diaspora, studies indicate that the mass media to which African Americans expose themselves may have a protective impact on them against the onslaught of admonitions to lose weight and the beauty hegemony's idealization of whiteness and slenderness as ultimate states of feminine beauty (Shaw, 2006).

For example in "Who's that girl: Television's role in the body image development of young white and black women," the authors explain that when black women watch "black-oriented TV," it resulted in "healthier body image" (Schooler, Ward, Merriwether, & Caruthers, 2004, p. 38). Undoubtedly, the experience of viewing blogs and other social media featuring the bodies of large black women has a similarly protective effect. Clay Shirky states,

> Opinions are transmitted by the media, and then they get echoed by friends, family members, and colleagues. It is in this second, social step that political opinions are formed. This is the step in which the Internet in general, and social media in particular, can make a difference. The Internet spreads not just media consumption but media production as well. It allows people to privately and publicly articulate and debate a welter of conflicting views

(2011, p. 34)

While this chapter situates the social networking activities of fat black women as a form of resistance against the "colonization" of their bodies and the implanting of white and Western beauty ideals, we think it is important to acknowledge the limitations of this resistance since so many of the images of fat black women circulating in the blogosphere are of hyper-feminized bodies, creating the ongoing marginalization of not just slender but fat women's bodies that are not designed in response to the patriarchal male gaze. While blogging offers an opportunity to resist beauty norms, this gerrymandering of beauty boundaries to include primarily hyper-feminized bodies is problematic and creates further exclusion within a historically marginalized rejected group.[1]

Note

1 For further discussion of this, see Millimen, S. K. (2015). *All made-up: the hyperfeminization of fat women.* The University of Toledo.

References

Banet-Weiser, S. (1999). *The most beautiful girl in the world: Beauty pageants and national identity.* Berkeley, CA: University of California Press.

Barbaro, M., & Twohey, M. (2016, September 27). Shamed and angry: Alicia Machado, a Miss Universe mocked by Donald Trump. *New York Times.* Retrieved from www.nytimes.com/2016/09/28/us/politics/alicia-machado-donald-trump.html?mcubz=0

Bentham, J. (1791). *Panopticon; Or, the Inspection-House.* Dublin: Paynes.

Berger, J. (1990). *Ways of seeing.* London, UK: Penguin Books.

Borrelli-Persson, L. (2017, March 7). Vogue fun facts by the numbers. *Vogue.* Retrieved from www.vogue.com/article/vogue-covers-models-facts-history

Brown, L. M. (2011). We're taking back sexy: Girl bloggers spark a movement and create enabling conditions for healthy sexuality. *Girlhood Studies, 4*(2), 47–69.

Buckridge, S. O. (2004). *The language of dress: Resistance and accommodation in Jamaica, 1760–1890, 31.* Mona, Jamaica: University of West Indies Press.

Chan, A. (2013). Project Runway's real-sized model: Show was adult bullying at its best. *Today, February.* Retrieved from: www.today.com/popculture/project-runways-real-size-model-show-was-adult-bullying-its-966526.

Chao, Y. H., Pisetsky, E. M., Dierker, L. C., Dohm, F. A., Rosselli, F., May, A. M., & Striegel-Moore, R. H. (2008). Ethnic differences in weight control practices among US adolescents from 1995 to 2005. *International Journal of Eating Disorders, 41*(2), 124–133.

Cochrane, K. (2010). Young, fat and fabulous: Marginalized by the style world they love, big women have fought back online with fashion blogs of such popularity and influence that even the industry is starting to take notice. *The Guardian* January, 30. Retrieved from: http://frocksandfroufrou.com/wp-content/uploads/2011/10/Young-fat-and-fabulous-From-the-Guardian-The-Guardian.pdf

Connell, C. (2013). Fashionable resistance: Queer "fa (t) shion" blogging as counterdiscourse. *WSQ: Women's Studies Quarterly, 41*(1), 209–224.

Downing, L. (2012). *Fashionably fatshionable: A consideration of the fashion practices of self-proclaimed fat women.* Doctoral dissertation, Parsons The New School for Design.

Foss, S. K. (2004). Theory of visual rhetoric. In G. Barbatsis, S. Moriarty, K. Kenney, & K. L. Smith (Eds.), *Handbook of visual communication : Theory, methods, and media* (pp. 141–152). London, UK: Routledge.

Germov, J. & Williams, L. (1999). Dieting women: Self-surveillance and the body panopticon. In D. Maurer & J. Sobal (Eds.), *Weighty issues: Fatness and thinness as social problems* (pp. 117–129). New York, NY: Aldine De Gruyter.

Groesz, L. M., Levine, M. P., & Murnen, S. K. (2002). The effect of experimental presentation of thin media images on body satisfaction: A meta-analytic review. *International Journal of Eating Disorders, 31*(1), 1–16.

Grove, L., & Morgan, H. (2005). Vogue editor rouses the fat and the furious. *NY Times,* September, 19. Retrieved from: www.nydailynews.com/archives/gossip/

Halliwell, E., & Dittmar, H. (2004). Does size matter? The impact of model's body size on women's body-focused anxiety and advertising effectiveness. *Journal of Social and Clinical Psychology, 23*(1), 104–122. doi:10.1521/jscp.23.1.104.26989.

Harris-Perry, M. (2012). Black women are standing in a crooked room. *Jezebel*, January, 19. Retrieved from: https://jezebel.com/5873870/black-women-are-standing-in-a-crooked-room

Higginbotham, A. L. (1980). *In the matter of color: Race and the American legal process. The colonial period* (vol. 608). New York, NY: Oxford University Press.

Jeffries, B. S. (2017). Oshun Yoruba Deity. *Encyclopedia Britannica*, September 3. Retrieved from: www.britannica.com/topic/Oshun

Kargbo, M. (2013). Toward a new relationality: Digital photography, shame, and the fat subject. *Fat Studies*, 2(2), 160–172.

Kasardo, A. E. & McHugh, M. C. (2015). From fat shaming to size acceptance: Challenging the medical management of fat women. In M. C. McHugh & J. C. Chrisler (Eds.), *The wrong prescription for women: How medicine and media create a "Need" for treatments, drugs, and surgery* (pp. 179–201). Santa Barbara, CA: ABC-CLIO.

King, D. K. (1988). Multiple jeopardy, multiple consciousness: The context of a Black feminist ideology. *Signs: Journal of Women in Culture and Society*, 14(1), 42–72. Retrieved from: www.jstor.org/stable/3174661

Kraeplin, C. R. (2011). Minority females & the thin ideal: Ethnic versus mainstream fashion magazines and their effects on acculturation & body image in young black & latino women. *Journal of Research on Women and Gender*, 2(1), 50–82.

Lang, C. (2017). Only Beyoncé could pull off a dress with her own face on it. *Time*, February, 13. Retrieved from: http://time.com/4668868/beyonce-grammys-2017/

Mattern, J. (2016). The 10 most beautiful women in the world, according to science. *Cosmopolitan Middle East*, August, 25. Retrieved from: www.cosmopolitanme.com/content/474-the-10-most-beautiful-women-in-the-world-according-to-science

Merkin, D. (2010). The F word. *New York Times Fashion Magazine*, August, 11. Retrieved from: www.nytimes.com/2010/08/22/t-magazine/22face-merkin-t.html

Odell, A. (2009). 60 Minutes Outtakes: Anna Wintour on fur, photoshop, and obese people. *The Cut*, May, 18. Retrieved from: www.thecut.com/2009/05/60_minutes_outtakes_anna_winto.html

Orbach, S. (2012). Fat is a prejudice issue. *The Guardian*, May, 3. Retrieved from: www.theguardian.com/commentisfree/2012/may/03/fat-prejudice-issue

Peters, L. D. (2014). You are what you wear: How plus-size fashion figures in fat identity formation. *Fashion Theory*, 18(1), 45–71.

Piran, N., & Teall, T. (2012). The developmental theory of embodiment. In G. McVey, M. P. Levine, N. Piran, & H. B. Ferguson, *Preventing eating-related and weight-related disorders: Collaborative research, advocacy, and policy change* (pp. 171–199). Waterloo, ON: Wilfred Laurier Press.

Popkin, B. (2008). Go to the black Macys if you want a plus-sized formal dress. *Consumerist*, December, 17. Retrieved from: https://consumerist.com/2008/12/17/go-to-the-black-macys-if-you-want-plus-sized-formal-dresses/

Posavac, H. D., Posavac, S. S., & Weigel, R. G. (2001). Reducing the impact of media images on women at risk for body image disturbance: Three targeted interventions. *Journal of Social and Clinical Psychology*, 20(3), 324–340. Retrieved from: www.deepdyve.com/lp/guilford-press/reducing-the-impact-of-media-images-on-women-at-risk-for-body-image-qko8DP0fz6. Accessed 15 February 2017.

Rocamora, A. (2011). Personal fashion blogs: Screens and mirrors in digital self-portraits. *Fashion Theory, 15*(4), 407–424.

Sargent, K. (2017). Fat shaming: Bias and hiring in the yoga and fitness industry? February, 2017. Retrieved from: http://imsweb.csudh.edu/ejournalncrp/index.php/fat-shaming-bias-and-hiring-in-the-yoga-and-fitness-industry/

Schooler, D., Ward, M. L., Merriwether, A., & Caruthers, A. (2004). Who's that girl: Television's role in the body image development of young white and black women. *Psychology of Women Quarterly, 28*(1), 38–47.

Shaw, A. E. (2006). *The embodiment of disobedience: Fat black women's unruly political bodies.* Lanham, MD: Lexington Books.

Shaw, A. E. (2012). "Born in Chanel, Christen in Gucci": The rhetoric of brand names and haute couture in Jamaican Dancehall. *Fulani, archipelagos of sound transitional caribbeanities, women, and music* (part 2, ch. 7). Kingston, Jamaica: University of the West Indies Press.

Shaw, H., Ramirez, L., Trost, A., Randall, P., & Stice, E. (2004). Body image and eating disturbances across ethnic groups: More similarities than differences. *Psychology of Addictive Behaviors, 18*(1), 12.

Shirky, C. (2011). The political power of social media: Technology, the public sphere, and political change. *Foreign Affairs, 90,* 28–41.

Stearns, P. N. (2002). *Fat history: Bodies and beauty in the modern west.* New York, NY: NYU Press.

Stice, E., & Shaw, H. E. (1994). Adverse effects of the media portrayed thin-ideal on women and linkages to bulimic symptomatology. *Journal of Social and Clinical Psychology, 13*(3), 288–308.

Vogue. (2004). Lagerfeld's High Street split. *Vogue Daily,* November, 18. Retrieved from: www.vogue.co.uk/article/lagerfelds-high-street-split

Washington, H. A. (2006). *Medical apartheid: The dark history of medical experimentation on Black Americans from colonial times to the present.* Doubleday Books.

West, T. C. (1999). *Wounds of the spirit: Black women, violence, and resistance ethics.* New York, NY: NYU Press.

Wiseman, C. V., Gray, J. J., Mosimann, J. E., & Ahrens, A. H. (1992). Cultural expectations of thinness in women: An update. *International Journal of Eating Disorders, 11*(1), 85–89.

16 Yoga as Pathway to Positive Embodiment in the Prevention and Treatment of Eating Disorders

Catherine Cook-Cottone

Introduction

Yoga can be a pathway to positive embodiment and support the prevention and treatment of eating disorders (Cook-Cottone, 2015a, 2015b; Douglass, 2011). Many treatment programs are adding the practice of yoga to their mental health programs (Douglass, 2011). There is a growing body of theory and research that supports this practice (Cook-Cottone, 2015a, 2015b; Klein & Cook-Cottone, 2013; Mahlo & Tiggemann, 2016). There is also a theoretical foundation for this practice (Cook-Cottone, 2006, 2015a). A healthy yoga practice can address three seemingly separate, yet deeply intertwined aspects of self that play a role in positive embodiment and eating disorder risk and prevention: (a) the mind and body relationship, (b) a sense of meaning, and (c) loving-kindness. The first, the mind and body relationship, is *what* we are in the world. That is, what we are is embodied beings. The second, meaning, is *why* we are in the world. This includes intentions, goals, and/or reasons for being. The third, loving-kindness, is the *how* we are in the world. Loving-kindness is the way that you are embodied. It is the way you pursue your mission, your intentions, and/or your reason for being. This chapter will address positive embodiment, meaning, and yoga as a pathway to an embodied and meaningful life. Theoretical underpinnings will be reviewed as well as the research conducted to date exploring yoga and eating disorder prevention and treatment. Each of the key themes (i.e., what, why, and how) is integrated throughout the chapter to provide a sense of theoretical and practical continuity (see Figure 16.1).

This exploration of positive embodiment begins with the big question, "*What* does it mean to be a human being?" There is tension and overwhelm in the question and the answer. I believe risk for and prevention of eating disorders lies here. First, and perhaps foremost, phenomenologically we are our bodies (Cook-Cottone, in press, 2015a, 2015b; Douglass & Bottrill, 2017; Svenaeus, 2013). Second, existentially we long for meaning (Douglass, 2011; Frankl, 1962; Heintzelman & King, 2014). The tension lies in the flesh and bones of being in this world and the seemingly ethereal

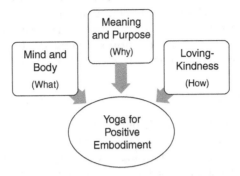

Figure 16.1 Yoga as a Pathway to Positive Embodiment.

and external nature of meaning. To be human is to live this tension. In the same way, eating disorders are a uniquely human struggle. The tension between what is authentically present and one's sense of meaning and aspiration can split a person, pressuring them to abandon who and what they really are for what they wish they could be (Cook-Cottone, 2006).

Eating Disorder

Over the many years, through private practice and research, I have witnessed young men and women struggle to connect with their bodies while simultaneously experiencing an absence, displacement, or loss of meaning in their lives (Cook-Cottone, 2015a). They often feel they have no road map for how to be with, and in, their bodies in a positive manner while finding the seemingly meaningless, meaningful (e.g., calories, pounds, inches, and the illusion of perfection; Cook-Cottone, 2015a; Douglass, 2011). The attempt to resolve the tension between material and aspirational is apparent within the eating disorder struggle. Despite the very human intention inherent in these efforts, both a healthy and authentic experience of the physical and emotional self and a truly meaningful sense of purpose are lost (Cook-Cottone, 2006).

Moving from risk toward engagement in clinical-level eating disorder involves two contradictory things (Cook-Cottone, 2016a, 2016b). Psychologically, a person is working very hard to leave themselves by avoiding the authentic experience of their bodies, thoughts, and/or feelings (Cook-Cottone, 2016a, 2016b). Ironically, engagement in eating-disordered behavior actively employs those who struggle in an intense, unremitting, cognitive, emotional, and pathological engagement with their bodies (Cook-Cottone, 2016a). In fact, at clinical levels, individuals think of almost nothing else; they are continually distracted by and engaged in thoughts about and the sensations of the body (Cook-Cottone, 2016a). Positive embodiment provides a safe passageway to recovery. They need not abandon themselves to get better. There is an old self-help term that gets close to what is happening, "The way out is through." To effectively prevent and treat disordered eating, one must learn how to negotiate life and its challenges without leaving oneself or turning against the body. To maintain positive embodiment, "*The way out is in*" (Cook-Cottone, 2016a, p. 99).

Positive Embodiment

As Western culture has evolved, our relationships with our bodies have taken on a cognitive emphasis, or priority, with body image often driving body-directed behaviors such as eating, exercise, and self-harm (or self-care; Cook-Cottone, 2015a, in press). Given the cultural emphasis on appearance (i.e., form over function), a media propagating primarily unrealistic beauty standards with social media amplifying these images, and a dieting industry circulating the belief that losing weight will make you happy, many have internalized these images and conceptual narratives about the body. Negative body image and body dissatisfaction are epidemic (Fiske, Fallon, Blissmer, & Redding, 2014). All sense of loving-kindness (the *how*; see Figure 16.1), gratitude, and compassion for the body is lost in the media noise filled with dieting ads and underweight runway models.

For many years, researchers looking to prevent or treat eating disorders focused on reducing body dissatisfaction (Cook-Cottone 2015a). More recently, researchers have been looking for a positive body image and its role in the prevention and treatment of eating disorders. Tylka and Wood-Barcalow (2015) contend that positive body image is a construct distinct from body dissatisfaction or negative body image; they have embedded the *how* of loving-kindness within their definition of positive body image (see Figure 16.1: Pathway to Positive Embodiment). According to Tylka and Wood-Barcalow (2015), positive body image includes body appreciation, body acceptance and love, a broad conceptualization of beauty, adaptive appearance investment (i.e., engaging in appearance-related self-care that projects one's sense of style and personality), inner positivity, filtering information in a body protective manner, holistic, and both stable and malleable at the same time.

Body image is inextricably linked to and interdependent on how we live and are in *action* in our bodies, our embodiment (Cook-Cottone, in press, 2016a). The effects are bidirectional. That is, how we think affects how we experience our embodiment, and how we experience our embodiment affects how we think (Cook-Cottone, in press, 2016a; Siegel, 2009). Despite cultural trends and practices, we are embodied beings. The everyday way of being with your body is "being as a body" (Svenaeus, 2013, p. 83). It is theorized that how you are *as a body* is reflected in how you think about your body, your body image (Cook-Cottone, in press). In this manner, your cognitive sense of your body comes from your embodiment (Cook-Cottone, in press, 2016a; Piran & Teall, 2012). An individual who understands his or her body is part of their essential nature lives in a way that honors and cares for the body. Further, the way the body is cared for and plays a role in the accomplishment of goals is as important as the goals themselves (Cook-Cottone, in press).

According to researchers, those who are positively embodied feel a sense of connection with their bodies, experience agency and functionality as related to their bodies, have their bodies available to them to experience and express desire, inhabit the body as a subjective (rather than objective) site, and practice attuned self-care (Cook-Cottone, in press; Piran, 2015). Positive embodiment means to be in subjective, embodied action (Cook-Cottone, in press). That is, connection, agency, functionality, the experience and expression of desire, subjective inhabitation, and attuned self-care are all things a person does with and for their body. According to Cook-Cottone (2016a), Piran (2015), and Piran and Teall (2012), the more you positively inhabit your body in nourishing and nurturing behaviors, the more likely it is that you will think about your body in a positive manner. The inverse appears to be true as well. That is, when an individual is not positively embodied, they may experience a sense of disconnection from their body, disturbance of body image or body dissatisfaction, substance-use problems, and disordered eating and others forms of dysregulation (Cook-Cottone, in press, 2015a; Homan & Tylka, 2014).

For those at risk, something changes as they develop. Piran (2015, 2016) describes how girls going through puberty normatively sometimes miss vital embodied experiences of engaging in the world in a positive manner. As detailed in an extensive qualitative study of the female embodiment across the lifespan, for some, there is a disconnection from the body and a sense of discomfort in the body sets in (Piran, 2016). The shift away from positive embodiment is manifested as they begin to dress for appearance rather than comfort, evaluate their bodies by form not function, and struggle to maintain relationships that reflect a valuing of self-worth over acceptance by others (Cook-Cottone, in press; Piran, 2015, 2016). In a paradigm shifting manuscript, Frederickson and Roberts (1997) proposed the self-objectification theory describing a process by which the body is separated out from the person, reduced to the status of a mere instrument, and regarded as if it was capable of representing the person. Rather than part of the essential self, the body is alienated and seen as an obstacle or problem that needs to be remedied (Cook-Cottone, in press; Svenaeus, 2013). The self is no longer unconsciously, or pre-consciously, embodied as the individual interacts with the world, and body image now reflects internalized distortions and iconic ideals of the culture, and the consequences are substantial (Cook-Cottone, in press; Fredrickson & Roberts, 1997).

Positive embodiment arises from inhabiting, living in, the body in a positive manner (Piran, 2015). Described in more detail in the chapter addressing the Developmental Theory of Embodiment (Piran & Teall, 2012), there are three domains of protective factors that maintain or enhance positive embodiment: physical (physical freedom), mental (mental freedom), and social (social power). Positive embodiment gets to the physical "what" of being human. As human beings, we have the cognitive capacity to be intentional about our inhabitation of our bodies. We can simultaneously honor our physical nature while pursing our sense of purpose or meaning in relationships, communities, and perhaps even our world, From a place of positive embodiment comes sustainability, health, well-being, and re-duced risk for eating-disordered thoughts and behaviors.

Embodiment and Emotions

The research on emotions places them squarely within the mind and body connection, a central aspect of the pathway to positive embodiment (the *what*; see Figure 16.1: Yoga as a Pathway to Positive Embodiment). It is a complex process. Emotions are felt in the body, and somatosensory feedback has been proposed to trigger conscious emotional experiences (Nummen-maa, Glerean, Hari, & Hietanen, 2013). Emotional regulation involves in-tegrated activity through the whole brain (Cook-Cottone, 2016a; Koelsch et al., 2015). Conscious cognitive activity involving rational thought and language can help regulate and moderate actively of affect and effector sys-tems including emotional, motor, peripheral arousal, attention, and mem-ory systems (Koelsch et al., 2015). Siegel (2009) argues that self-regulation occurs in two directions. There is another oft-cited yoga affirmation that I find quite compelling, "In order to heal, you need to feel." In an interesting series of five experiments with 701 participants, Nummenmaa et al. (2013) revealed maps of bodily sensations associated with different emotions using a unique topographical self-report method (see Nummenmaa et al., 2013 for the illustrated maps). Further, Nummenmaa et al. (2013) hypothesized that perception of emotion-triggered bodily changes may play a key role in generating consciously felt emotions. That is, emotions live in the body and, perhaps, the body is a key place to experience and manage them.

To be embodied means that you are aware of, feel, and respond to your emotions (Cook-Cottone, 2015a). Generally, researchers agree that eating disorder behaviors may function as maladaptive methods for regulating af-fective states (Lavender et al., 2015). In a review of the research, Lavender et al. (2015) conclude that both anorexia nervosa (AN) and bulimia nervosa (BN) are characterized by broad emotion regulation deficits, with diffi-culties in emotion regulation across the four dimensions found to charac-terize both AN and BN: (1) the flexible use of adaptive and situationally appropriate strategies to modulate the duration and/or intensity of emo-tional responses; (2) the ability to successfully inhibit impulsive behavior and maintain goal-directed behavior in the context of emotional distress; (3) awareness, clarity, and acceptance of emotional states; and (4) the will-ingness to experience emotional distress in the pursuit of meaningful activ-ities. To facilitate positive embodiment, an intervention for eating disorders needs to address the experience of feeling emotions in the body.

Embodied experiences may help with emotion regulation. Neurologically speaking, how we think affects how we experience our feelings and bodies (Cook–Cottone, 2015a). The inverse is also true. How we experience our feelings and bodies affects how we think (Cook–Cottone, 2015a). Siegel (2009) purports that we can change how we experience our emotions and our world through our embodied actions. Ideally, the interventions would provide active practice choosing and applying emotion regulation skills in various situations, maintaining goal-directed behaviors while managing emotions, and developing an awareness of felt experience and emotions. Further, embodied practice feeling and managing emotions may clear a path for the processing for authentically meaningful experiences. Research suggests that an individual's struggle with felt emotions may interfere with pursuit of meaningful activities (Lavender et al., 2015); perhaps the inverse is also true, that positive embodiment marked by emotional competency could facilitate pursuit of meaning.

Embodiment and Meaning

Meaning is fundamental to positive embodiment (the *why*; see Figure 16.1: Pathway to Positive Embodiment). At birth, we are all granted a body with which we are charged to carry out our life paths. In yoga, the life path is referred to as dharma, your reason for being. We spend the first years embodied and deeply dependent on those around us to help us manage cognitively, emotionally, and physically. As we develop our own cognitive independence, the body becomes increasingly less a place from which we engage with the world and more of a conceptually separate entity. That is, rather than living through and from our bodies, we see our bodies as something with which we have a relationship. As we develop, we move through understanding toward meaning. As we develop, one's own understanding of a life path or reasons for being emerges and is intertwined with cultural practices and narratives, the hopes and dreams of our parents, or is lost. In fact, a review of the research on well-being suggests that meaning in life plays a role in positive adaptation (Heintzelman & King, 2014).

In her seminal work, "*Eating disorders: Obesity anorexia nervosa, and the persons within*," Hilde Bruch (1973) describes how patients diagnosed with AN demonstrated a profound sense of infectiveness and propensity toward perfectionism, or a rigid set of other-prescribed standards. In her 1962 paper, Bruch described the core feature of ineffectiveness as manifesting in the body and extending into the girls' relationships and lives. Personal empowerment was described as not occurring through developing a sense of connection with the body and to meaning in the girls' lives; rather, it was found through "negativism and stubborn defiance" (Bruch, 1962, p. 191). Bruch (1962) described "…an insoluble conflict, with their childhoods of robot-like obedience and with their lack of awareness of their own resources and initiative, and of their thoughts and feelings, not to speak of their own bodily sensations" (p. 192).

It was believed that the interwoven aspects of the self – the relationship with the body and our own sense of purpose and meaning – are disrupted for those at-risk for disordered eating (Cook-Cottone, 2006).

This relationship with our bodies is developmental, multifaceted, and complex, manifesting in the cognitive, physical, emotional, and relational domains (Cook-Cottone, in press, 2016a; Fredrickson & Roberts, 1997; Piran, 2015, 2016). Perhaps correspondingly, so is our relationship with our reason for being, sense of purpose, and meaning. Interestingly, disordered eating patients attribute great meaning to ideas such as pounds, inches, calories, and grams which inevitably become self-confirmed, critical issues as they careen toward physical frailty and mortality (Cook-Cottone, 2015a, 2016a). As meaning is shifted to ideas and obsessions that hold little to value to most healthy and engaged people, there is also a correspondingly pathological and intense engagement with the body (Cook-Cottone, 2016a).

Might this be a misguided attempt to engage in the very source of their search for meaning? Vohs and Baumeister (2002) theorize that in order to reduce negative affect and aversive self-attention, some individuals may engage in a process called *cognitive deconstruction*. Cognitive deconstruction involves a narrowing attentional process to relatively concrete, less meaningful stimuli theoretically cutting off the high levels of meaningful interpretation that might give rise to self-evaluation and emotion (Vohs & Baumeister, 2002). In this way, a focus on body shape or size, calories, food portions, and weight may function as cognitive deconstruction narrowing attention and distributing meaning to relatively concrete experiences rather than more abstract and perhaps overwhelming experiences of emotions and the search for a sense of meaning or purpose.

Yoga

Yoga is a form of positive embodiment. Yoga sees the body as a modality of healing (Boudette, 2006; Douglass, 2011). Yoga practice provides active practice in being with and for the body and the self (Cook-Cottone, 2015a; Douglass, 2011). It offers a freedom from the way we habitually understand the world (Douglass, 2011). It does this by raising the practitioner's awareness of the patterns in his or her mind as they move through postures, breath work, relaxation, and meditation techniques (Douglass, 2011). Yoga can be a very powerful tool through which practitioners can encounter their inner lives and begin to notice and understand its effect on his or her embodied experience (Douglass, 2011). The physical cues guide students inward to interceptive awareness and outward through proprioceptive awareness (Cook-Cottone, 2017). As practitioners move through poses and hold poses, they can move from body awareness to choice, noticing the effects of their actions and breath work on the body (Cook-Cottone, 2015a). In practice, yoga students learn tools for distress tolerance and emotion relegation as they notice thoughts and feelings in movement and rest (Cook-Cottone, 2015a). Ultimately, yoga practitioners may move from an experience of thinking about the body to "embodying new ways of thinking" (Douglass, 2011, p. 85). It may also be a pathway from authentic self-knowing to a grounded sense meaning or purpose (Ivtzan & Papantoniou, 2014). Overall, research suggests that yoga may be in effectiveness in the prevention of eating disorder symptoms and correlates as well as a helpful adjunct in eating disorder treatment.

Yoga for Positive Embodiment

Yoga allows those with eating disorders to be in their bodies in a new way (Boudette, 2006). Rather than having all of the senses focused on the external and ideal, awareness is turned inward to internal sensations, "Where am I open? Where am I tight? Where do I hold tension? How is my breathing? How does it change when I hold this posture?" (Boudette, 2006, p. 168). Those who struggle have an opportunity to shift from objectifying the body, to experiencing the body (Boudette, 2006). There is a small set of studies that have explored yoga as a pathway to positive embodiment. These studies get to the benefits of the mind and body connection, the *what* we are in the world (i.e., embodied; see Figure 16.1: Yoga as a Pathway to Positive Embodiment).

In 2006, Impett, Daubenmier, and Hirschman examined the potential of yoga to buffer against the harmful effects of self-objectification as well as to promote embodiment (i.e., body awareness and responsiveness) and well-being in a sample of 19 participants enrolled in a two-month yoga immersion program. According to researchers, participants completed a short survey at six time points during the yoga immersion. Results indicated that the women in the study objectified their own bodies less after participation in the program (Impett, Daubenmier, & Hirschman, 2006). Furthermore, researcher indicated that among both men and women, more frequent yoga practice was associated with increased body awareness, positive affect, and satisfaction with life, as well as decreased negative affect (Impett et al., 2006).

Finally, in 2016, Mahlo and Tiggemann studied 193 yoga practitioners (124 Iyengar, 69 Bikram) and 127 university students (non-yoga participants). Results showed that yoga participants scored higher on positive body image and embodiment and lower on self-objectification. There was also no difference between the types of yoga practiced. The authors concluded that yoga is an embodying activity that can provide individuals an opportunity to cultrate a positive relationship with their body.

Yoga as a Pathway to Self-Knowing and Meaning

It is theorized that an authentic experience of self, a deep mind and body connection, gives rise to meaning, to the *why* (see Figure 16.1; Yoga as a

Pathway to Positive Embodiment). A positive and consistent yoga practice can help get you to your *why,* your reason for being. Yoga is a pathway to self-knowing that begins with a positive relationship with the body characterized by awareness, loving-kindness, self-regulation, self-compassion, and self-validation (Cook-Cottone, 2015a). Through self-awareness of the physical, emotional, and cognitive aspects of self experienced during repeated yoga practice, practitioners may be able to better access an authentic sense of self (Cook-Cottone, 2015a, 2015b, 2016a, 2016a; Douglass, 2011; Kidd & Eatough, 2017).

Deep mind and body connection is believed to facilitate an authentic pathway to finding meaning in one's life. In fact, in a 2014 study of 124 yoga practitioners, Ivtzan and Papantoniou found that the number of years practicing corresponded with measures of meaning in life and gratitude. The authors concluded that yoga may contribute to the development of eudaimonic as well as hedonic happiness (Ivtzan & Papantoniou, 2014).

Yoga as an Act of Loving-Kindness

According to Douglass (2011), underlying the presence of yoga in clinical settings is the 21st-century discourse that holds the individual self as stressed and imagines therapeutic spaces in which stress is handled. Yoga is seen as a form of stress management or self-care within this context (Douglass, 2011). In the practice of yoga, a practitioner can sense the muscles tension, reactivity, heart rate, and breath rate associated with stress as well as the release, downregulation, and deep breathing associated with deep relaxation (Cook-Cottone, 2015a). Through yoga practice, the practitioner becomes emotionally and physically literate in what stress is and is not and what relaxation is and is not (Boudette, 2006). This awareness is prerequisite to an active practice of self-care (Cook-Cottone, 2015a). That is, you must know how your body is feeling to respond to your body. Mindful awareness, noticing, and responsiveness are all done with the attitude of loving-kindness – a radical departure from the harshly critical, highly attuned judgment, and gaze of the internalized objectification that fuels body dissatisfaction and disordered eating. Rather, self-love is a daily engagement in acts of self-care that are response to the felt needs of the body.

Yoga for Disordered Eating

Research on yoga for the prevention and treatment of eating disorders is a slowly evolving field that is still in its youth. Often these studies are difficult to fund as eating disorders are not viewed as a priority for many funding institutions. Further, yoga often does not meet the innovation criteria as it is a practice that spans thousands of years. Research on the combination of yoga and eating disorders is particularly difficult to fund. Unfunded research teams have done much of the research. In the section, a brief overview of the findings is provided along with specific studies in the area of yoga for prevention and treatment of eating disorders.

In 2013, Klein and Cook-Cottone published the first review of the effects of yoga on eating disorder symptoms and correlates. At that time, there were 14 articles that specifically addressed eating disorders and yoga. Of the 14 articles, 40% used a cross-sectional design to look at risk and protective factors for eating disorders among yoga practitioners, and 60% used a design that explored the effectiveness of yoga interventions for preventing and treating eating disorders. Overall, they found that yoga practitioners were reported to be at decreased risk for eating disorders, eating disorder behaviors, and eating disorder risk. Interestingly, although most of the interventions found reduced eating disorder risk or behaviors, there was one study that found no effects (e.g., Mitchell, Mazzeo, Rausch, & Cooke, 2007). Upon further review of the studies, the dosage of yoga presented as important. Other studies identified positive results in reduced risk factors and correlates such as body dissatisfaction, drive for thinness, media influence, and poor interception (Klein & Cook-Cottone, 2013). Also, research indicated positive findings such as higher level of protective factors including competence, positive physical and social self-concept, and emotion regulation. Finally, studies indicated a decrease in eating-disordered behaviors such as bulimic behaviors, binge eating, and food preoccupation.

Overall, the review suggests that much more rigor and funding are needed in this area of research. Ultimately, findings indicate that yoga may play a positive role in the prevention of eating disorders. Specific studies are detailed in the following to illustrate the range of the quality and findings of the current state of the research.

Yoga for the Prevention of Eating Disorders

The use of yoga in the prevention of eating disorders is a fairly recent practice. In 2006, Scime, Cook-Cottone, Kane, and Watson published the first eating disorder prevention intervention utilizing yoga. The Girls Growing in Wellness and Balance (GGWB) program (Cook-Cottone, Kane, Keddie, & Haugli, 2013) is now a manualized 14-week program for preventing eating disorders within a group, for girls at the middle school setting. The program integrated psychoeducational content addressing coping skills, breath work, boundary setting, assertiveness, feelings identification, emotion regulation, and media literacy. The program also includes a creative, constructivist aspect within which the girls in the program create their own healthy magazine and distribute it at the end of the program. Each of the sessions includes 45 minutes of yoga, relaxation, and meditation as well as a journal work to help the girls process the psychoeducational content (see Cook-Cottone, Kane, Keddie, & Haugli, 2013, for the full curriculum).

The first noncontrolled study of this program found that those fifth-grade girls who participated (N = 45) reported reduced body dissatisfaction, drive for thinness, and media influence (Scime, Cook-Cottone, Kane, & Watson, 2006). In 2008, Scime and Cook-Cottone published a controlled study of the program comparing fifth-grade yoga participants (N = 75) and controls (N = 69), finding that those who participated in the GGWB yoga program showed significant decreases in body dissatisfaction and measures of eating disorder symptoms and a significant increase in social self-concept. In 2010, Cook-Cottone, Jones, and Haugli published a matched sample repeated measures study of the GGWB yoga program. In this study of fifth grade, minority participants (N = 25) were matched with Caucasian participants (N = 25) based on body mass index (BMI) and socioeconomic status. Findings indicated that minority and Caucasian participants were equally responsive to program showing significant decreases in drive for thinness, bulimia, and body dissatisfaction. A significant increase was found for both groups in physical self-concept, competence, and social self-concept. No effects were found for either group in perceived stress. Researchers indicated that perhaps participants learned tools to handle stress, yet still perceived that they had stress in their lives.

Most recently, Norman, Sodano, and Cook-Cottone (2014) explored the role of interpersonal styles in outcomes of the GGWB yoga program among fifth-grade girls. They found that drive for thinness and body dissatisfaction were both significantly reduced when compared to controls. Further, the eating disorder symptoms measure was related to lower interpersonal affiliation only for the treatment group. The authors hypothesized that perhaps a group format is effective for some (e.g., those with higher interposal affiliation) than others who may benefit from one-on-one prevention interventions. Overall, the program is considered empirically supported as a prevention intervention for disordered eating.

In 2007, Mitchell, Mazzeo, Rausch, and Cooke randomly assigned 93 college women to either a dissonance group (N = 30), a yoga group (N = 33), or a control group (N = 30). The yoga and dissonance groups met once per week for 45 minutes over a six-week period. The yoga groups were taught by a psychology graduate student who was certified and registered as an Integral Yoga instructor. The dissonance group was taught by another psychology graduate student with group therapy experience. Hierarchical regression analyses revealed that there were no significant post-intervention differences between the yoga and control groups (Mitchell et al., 2007). Dissonance group participants had significantly lower scores than the scores of both other groups on measures of disordered eating, drive for thinness, body dissatisfaction, alexithymia, and anxiety. The authors concluded that the findings have important implications for interventions on college campuses. In particular, dissonance interventions appear to be an efficient and inexpensive approach to reducing eating disorder risk factors. Limitations of this study include the low dosage of yoga offered. However, the study did raise the question of the efficiency of delivering a yoga program as compared to a dissonance program, which showed effects with the same dosage. Further attendance, treatment integrity, and a detailed descript of the yoga and dissonance interventions were not provided.

Yoga for the Treatment of Eating Disorders

Yoga as an adjunct of the treatment of eating disorders has only recently emerged in the field of research on eating disorders. Specific programs include Cook-Cottone, Beck, and Kane's (2006) yoga program, which integrated cognitive behavioral (i.e., functional behavioral analysis), dialectic behavioral techniques (mindfulness, distress tolerance, and interpersonal effectiveness), and dissonance induction for media content along with a 45-minute yoga class administered weekly for six weeks. The theme of each weekly class was woven into the yoga class and closing relaxation and meditation. The sessions also included a reflective journaling component. Participants ($N = 24$) were all actively struggling with a diagnosed eating disorder (e.g., AN and BN) and were also receiving care from an eating disorder specialist. This noncontrolled study found that participants showed decreased drive for thinness and body dissatisfaction. A nonsignificant decrease was for bulimic symptoms at posttest. Limitations of this study include low yoga dosage, low power, and lack of control group.

In 2009, McIver, O'Halloran, and McGartland examined the efficacy of a 12-week yoga program aimed at reducing binge eating. In a randomized trial, researchers assigned community-based participants who identified with diagnostic criteria for binge eating disorder (age 25–63 years) to yoga ($N = 45$) or wait-list control ($N = 45$). Yoga was offered for 45 minutes for 12 weeks. The researcher did not specify the type of yoga practiced. Although data were only analyzed for 25 in each group, researchers reported significant self-reported reductions in binge eating and increased physical activity among the yoga group members. Further, also for the yoga group, they found small and significant reductions in BMI and waist measurement. No changes were found in the wait-list controls. Limitations include small sample size, no description of yoga practice, and no treatment integrity measures.

Also in 2009, Dale, Mattison, Greening, Galen, Neace, and Matacin studied a six-day yoga-based workshop among women with a history of disordered eating. Participants self-reported a history of eating disorder symptoms. Over the six-day program, the participants engaged in 1,170 minutes of Forrest Yoga. Researcher reported improvements in interoception, emotion regulation, and affective problems with improvement maintained at one-month follow-up. This was a very small study of only five participants. There were no control group and limited information about the yoga program and treatment integrity.

In 2010, Carei, Fyfe-Johnson, Breuner, and Brown conducted a randomized controlled trialof yoga in the treatment of eating disorders (i.e., AN, BN, and Eating Disorder Not Otherwise Specified [EDNOS]). The group studied 50 girls and 4 boys, aged 11–21 years, randomized into an eight-week trial of standard care versus individualized yoga plus standard care. Specifically, 27 of the participants were randomized to standard care (i.e., every other week physician/dietician appointments) and 26 to yoga plus standard care. The authors reported an attrition of four. Participants received one hour of yoga semi-weekly for eight weeks using one-on-one instruction. The same registered yoga teacher (at the 200-hour level; RYT-200) was used for all sessions for each of the participants. Yoga sessions followed a treatment manual that can be found in the lead author's dissertation. All sessions were audio-taped, and a random selection of 20% of the audio recordings were assessed for inter-instructor reliability to the protocol.

Outcomes that were evaluated at baseline, end of trial, and one-month follow-up included Eating Disorder Examination (EDE), BMI, Beck Depression Inventory, State Trait Anxiety Inventory, and Food Preoccupation questionnaire. Findings indicated that the yoga group demonstrated greater decreases in the EDE scores over time, while the control group showed some initial decline but then returned to baseline EDE levels at week 12. Further, food preoccupation was measured before and after each yoga session, and dropped significantly after all sessions. Authors reported that both groups maintained current BMI levels and decreased in anxiety and depression over time. The authors concluded that individualized yoga therapy holds promise as adjunctive therapy to standard care.

In 2017, Pacanowski, Diers, Crosby, and Neumark-Sztainer investigated the effect of yoga on negative affect on 38 individuals in a residential eating disorder treatment program. Participants were randomized to a control or yoga intervention (i.e., one hour of yoga before dinner for five days). Negative affect was assessed pre- and post-meal. Mixed-effects models compared negative affect between groups during the intervention period. Findings indicated that yoga significantly reduced pre-meal negative affect compared to treatment as usual (Pacanowski, Diers, Crosby & Neumark-Sztainer, 2017). Notably, researchers found that the effect was attenuated post-meal. The article provided a detailed description of the yoga sequence. Limitations include the small sample size.

Conclusions

Overall, there is nearly as much theory is written on the therapeutic implications of yoga in the prevention and treatment of eating disorders as there is on the research exploring its efficacy. Research and research finding are needed to support the continued exploration of yoga in the prevention and treatment of eating disorders. Nevertheless, many eating disorder treatment centers integrate yoga into their treatment programs, and outpatient service providers recommend yoga for their patients. The theoretical framework is sound, and the research suggests first that yoga appears to be a safe practice for those with eating disorders and may in fact support treatment. Yoga may also help prevent eating disorders, with the bulk of the evidence showing efficacy in the middle school years. The mechanisms of action have yet to be fully understood and appear to lie in positive embodiment. This chapter has provided a framework in which the mind and body connection (*what* we are in this world, embodied), a sense of purpose and meaning (*why* we are in this world), and an overarching attitude and practice of loving-kindness (*how* we are in the world) are essential features of positive embodiment that can be found in yoga practice (see Figure 16.1; Yoga as a Pathway to Positive Embodiment). This framework was placed in juxtaposition with physical, emotional, and cognitive features of eating disorder symptoms. Last, the extant research in the area was reviewed within theoretical framework and then specific to the prevention and treatment of eating disorders. Much more research is needed that incudes carefully controlled randomized trials and those with specific risk factors, symptom patterns, and diagnosis. More needs to be known about the types of spaces and studios are best for teaching yoga for those at risk for and struggling with eating disorders (Cook-Cottone & Douglass, 2017). Further, there is much more that needs to be known about the trainings of the yoga teacher, the type of yoga delivered, the components and ratios of components (e.g., poses, breath work, meditation, and relaxation), the dosage of yoga offered, and the importance of continuous practice. In sum, this chapter serves as an organizing space for what is currently known and perhaps a springboard for what is yet to be explored.

Recommendations for Practice

Practice a Team Approach

The yoga teacher should work as part of a treatment team when working with those who have active eating disorders. If yoga is a prevention intervention, have a list of referrals for assessment and treatment prepared. If in schools, consider using a consultation model and partner with school counselor, social worker, or psychologist.

Encourage a Mind and Body Connection

When teaching yoga, use words that bring a sense of connection to the body and do not overly focus on correcting the body. Continually bring awareness to the yoga practitioner's physicality, breath, and emotional presence. Encourage presence, embodiment, and growth through cues and verbal support. Communication should be specific to the yoga practitioner's physical and emotional states. The yoga teacher's awareness of the student will inform the student's own self-awareness.

Model Positive Embodiment and Self-Love

As the yoga teachers, have a regular yoga proactive and a steady practice of self-care. You can't give what you do not have. Have a no-negative body talk policy in class. Hire teachers with a wide range of body types. Do not promote dieting or food restriction and offer yoga as a way to celebrate the body, not change size or shape.

Work to Create and Experience of Compassion, Support, and Choice

As a yoga teacher, present as a positive and compassionate coach. Teach yoga with a commitment to present moment awareness, openness, acceptance, and loving-kindness. Acknowledge, accept, and allow a wide range of emotions. Encourage an awareness of the embodied nature of feelings and they arise and pass during the yoga practice. Prioritize the lesson or learning inherent in each pose above the form of the pose. Offer both individual and group yoga experiences. Offer accommodations, extensions and challenges, and choice for each of the poses.

Other Considerations

See Neumark-Sztainer (2014) for an extensive list of research recommendations exploring the potential for yoga in the preventions and treatment of eating disorders (p. 143).

References

Boudette, R. (2006). Question & answer: Yoga in the treatment of disordered eating and body image disturbance: How can the practice of yoga be helpful in recovery from an eating disorder? *Eating Disorders, 14,* 167–170.

Bruch, H. (1962). Perceptual and conceptual disturbances in anorexia nervosa. *Psychosomatic Medicine, 24,* 187–194.

Bruch, H. (1973). *Eating disorders: Obesity, anorexia nervosa, and the person within* (vol. 5052). New York, NY: Basic Books.

Carei, T. R., Fyfe-Johnson, A. L., Breuner, C. C., & Brown, M. A. (2010). Randomized controlled clinical trial of yoga in the treatment of eating disorders. *Journal of Adolescent Health, 46,* 346–351.

Cook-Cottone, C. P. (in press). Mindful self-care and positive body image: Mindfulness, yoga, and actionable tools for positive embodiment In E. A., Daniels, M. M., Gillen, & C. H., Markey (Eds), *The body positive: Understanding and improving body image in science and practice.* New York, NY: Cambridge University Press.

Cook-Cottone, C. (2006). The attuned representation model for the primary prevention of eating disorders: An overview for school psychologists. *Psychology in the Schools, 43,* 223–230.

Cook-Cottone, C. (2013). Dosage as a critical variable in yoga therapy research. *International Journal of Yoga Therapy, 23,* 11–12.

Cook-Cottone, C. P. (2015a). Incorporating positive body image into the treatment of eating disorders: A model for attunement and mindful self-care. *Body Image, 14*, 158–167.

Cook-Cottone, C. P. (2015b). *Mindfulness and yoga for self-regulation: A primer for mental health professionals.* New York, NY: Springer.

Cook-Cottone, C. P. (2016a). Embodied self-regulation and mindful self-care in the prevention of eating disorders. *Eating Disorders, 24*, 98–105.

Cook-Cottone, C. P. (2016b). Yoga for the re-embodied self: The therapeutic journey home. *Yoga Therapy Today*, Winter, 40–48.

Cook-Cottone, C. P., & Douglass, L. L. (2017). Yoga communities and eating disorders: Creating safe space for positive embodiment. *International Journal of Eating Disorders, 27*(1), 87–93. doi: 10.17761/1531-2054-27.1.87.

Cook-Cottone, C. P., Beck, M., & Kane, L. (2006). Manualized-group treatment of eating disorders: Attunement in mind, body, and relationship (AMBR). *The Journal for Specialists in Group Work, 33*, 61–83.

Cook-Cottone, C. P., Jones, L. A., & Haugli, S. (2010). Prevention of eating disorders among minority youth: A matched-sample repeated measures study. *Eating Disorders, 18*, 361–376.

Cook-Cottone, C. P., Kane, L., Keddie, E., & Haugli, S. (2013). *Girls growing in wellness and balance: Yoga and life skills to empower.* Stoddard, WI: Schoolhouse Educational Services, LLC.

Douglass, L. (2011). Thinking through the body: The conceptualization of yoga as therapy for individuals with eating disorders. *Eating Disorders, 19*, 83–96.

Douglass, L. L., & Bottrill, S. (2017). Yoga as a tool for emotional regulation in individual with eating disorders. In H. Mason & K. Birch (Eds), *Yoga practices for psychiatric disorders.* Scotland, UK: Handspring Publishing.

Fiske, L., Fallon, E. A., Blissmer, B., & Redding, C. A. (2014). Prevalence of body dissatisfaction among United States adults: Review and recommendations for future research. *Eating behaviors, 15*, 357–365.

Frankl, V. E. (1962). *Man's search for meaning: An introduction to Logotherapy: a newly revised and enlarged edition of from death-camp to Existentialisme.* New York, NY: Beacon Press.

Fredrickson, B. L., & Roberts, T. (1997). Objectification theory: Toward understanding women's lived experiences and mental health risks. *Psychology of Women Quarterly, 21*, 173–206.

Heintzelman, S. J., & King, L. A. (2014). Life is pretty meaningful. *American Psychologist, 69*, 561.

Homan, K. J., & Tylka, T. L. (2014). Appearance-based exercise motivation moderates the relationship between exercise frequency and positive body image. *Body Image, 11*, 101–108.

Impett, E. A., Daubenmier, J. J., & Hirschman, A. L. (2006). Minding the body: Yoga, embodiment, and well-being. *Sexuality Research and Social Policy, 3*(4), 39–48.

Ivtzan, I., & Papantoniou, A. (2014). Yoga meets positive psychology: Examining the integration of hedonic (gratitude) and eudaimonic (meaning) wellbeing in relation to the extent of yoga practice. *Journal of Bodywork and Movement Therapies, 18*, 183–189.

Kidd, M., & Eatough, V. (2017). Yoga, well-being and transcendence: An interpretative phenomenological analysis. *The Humanistic Psychologist, 45*, 258–280.

Klein, J., & Cook-Cottone, C. P. (2013). The effects of yoga on eating disorder symptoms and correlates: A review. *International Journal of Yoga Therapy, 23*, 41–50.

Koelsch, S., Jacobs, M., Menninghaus, W., Liebal, K., Klann-Delius, G., Von Scheve, C., & Gebauer, G. (2015). The quartet theory of human emotions: An integrative and neurofunctional model. *Physics of Life Review, 13*, 1–27.

Lavender, J. M., Wonderlich, S. A., Engel, S. G., Gordon, K. H., Kaye, W. H., & Mitchell, J. E. (2015). Dimensions of emotion dysregulation in anorexia nervosa and bulimia nervosa: A conceptual review of the empirical literature. *Clinical Psychology Review, 40*, 111–122.

Mahlo, L., & Tiggemann, M. (2016). Yoga and positive body image: A test of the Embodiment Model. *Body Image, 18*, 135–142.

Mitchell, K. S., Mazzeo, S. E., Rausch, S. M., & Cooke, K. L. (2007). Innovative intervention for disordered eating: Evaluating dissonance-based and yoga interventions. *International Journal of Eating Disorders, 40*, 120–128.

Norman, K., Sodano, S., & Cook-Cottone, C. P. (2014). An exploratory analysis of the role of interpersonal styles in eating disorder prevention outcomes. *Journal for Specialists in Group Work, 34*, 301–315.

Neumark-Sztainer, D. (2014). Yoga and eating disorders: Is there a place for yoga in the prevention and treatment of eating disorders and disordered eating behaviours? *Advances in Eating Disorders: Theory, Research and Practice, 2*, 136–145.

Nummenmaa, L., Glerean, E., Hari, R., & Heitenan, J. K. (2013). Bodily maps of emotions. *Proceedings of the National Academy of Sciences.* doi:10.1073/pnas.1321664111

Pacanowski, C. R., Diers, L., Crosby, R. D., & Neumark-Sztainer, D. (2017). Yoga in the treatment of eating disorders within a residential program: A randomized controlled trial. *Eating Disorders, 25*, 37–51.

Piran, N. (2015). New possibilities in the prevention of eating disorders: The introduction of positive body image measures. *Body Image, 14*, 146–157.

Piran, N. (2016). Embodied possibilities and disruptions: The mergence of the experience of embodiment construct form the qualitative studies with girls and women. *Body Image, 18*, 43–60.

Piran, N., & Teall, T. (2012). The developmental theory of embodiment. In G. McVey, M. P. Levine, N. Piran, & H. B. Ferguson (Eds), *Preventing eating-related and weight-related disorders: Collaborative research, advocacy, and policy change* (pp. 169–198). Waterloo, ON: Wilfred Laurier University Press.

Scime, M., Cook-Cottone, C., Linda, K., & Watson, T. (2006). Group prevention of eating disorders with fifth-grade females: Impact on body dissatisfaction, drive for thinness, and media influence. *Eating Disorders, 14*(2), 143–155. doi:10.1080/10640260500403881

Scime, M., & Cook-Cottone, C. P. (2008). Primary prevention of eating disorders: A constructivist integration of mind and body strategies. *International Journal of Eating Disorders, 41*, 134–142.

Siegel, D. J. (2009). Mindful awareness, mindsight, and neural integration. *The Humanistic Psychologist, 37*, 137–158.

Svenaeus, F. (2013). Anorexia nervosa and the body uncanny: A phenomenological approach. *Philosophy, Psychiatry, and Psychology, 20*, 81–91.

Tylka, T. L., & Wood-Barcalow, N. L. (2015). What is and what is not positive body image? Conceptual foundations and construct definition. *Body Image, 14*, 188–129.

Vohs, K. D., & Baumeister, R. F. (2002). Escaping the self consumes regulatory resources: A self-regulatory model of suicide. In T. E. Joiner & M. D. Rudd (Eds), *Suicide Science* (pp. 33–41). Boston, MA: Springer.

17 Emotion-Based Psychotherapies in the Treatment of Eating Disorders

Meris Williams and Natasha Files

The authors extend their deep thanks to Dr. Diana Fosha, Dr. Beth Haverkamp, Dr. Karen Kranz, Dr. Adèle Lafrance, and Dale Trimble for their valuable feedback on earlier drafts of this chapter.

Introduction

Emotions are multifaceted, embodied phenomena (Mauss, Levenson, McCarter, Wilhelm, & Gross, 2005), with neuromuscular response and arousal patterns that are integral to how we experience them (Zajonc, 1985). Feeling a "'lump in the throat', 'heavy heart', or [that] 'my blood was boiling'" (Fosha, 2000, p. 25) are some of the palpable, bodily manifestations of emotions. Emotion theory (Darwin, 1965; Lazarus, 1991; Tomkins, 1962–3) posits that emotions play a critical role in adaptation and survival by conveying information through the individual's appraisal of the environment, focusing attention on what is important, and then motivating action in the self (and responses in others) (Damasio, 1999). Disruptions in this process have been proposed to underpin many psychological problems, including eating disorders (EDs) (e.g., Aldao, Nolen-Hoeksema, & Schweizer, 2010; Berenbaum, Raghavan, Le, Vernon, & Gomez, 2003; Gross & Jazaieri, 2014). Among individuals with EDs, one such disruption is the displacement of negative affect onto "feeling fat," as well as bodily nonacceptance and self-loathing; thus, efforts to control and change the body through ED behaviors can be seen as attempts to control and change affect (Kearney-Cooke & Striegel-Moore, 1997). These symptoms produce short-term relief – "starving numbs, bingeing soothes and vomiting provides relief" (Dolhanty & Greenberg, 2007, p. 98) – but interfere with healthy affective processing and give rise to long-term negative physical and emotional health consequences.

After decades of research and treatment focused on the cognitive and behavioral aspects of EDs, there is now wider acknowledgment of the role of emotion in all phases of EDs (i.e., development, maintenance, and relapse) (Fox & Power, 2009; Treasure, 2012). This has been accompanied by a recent burgeoning of conceptual and empirical literature (e.g., Lavender et al., 2014; Oldershaw, Lavender, Sallis, Stahl, & Schmidt, 2015), including findings suggesting that EDs are broadly associated with significant impairments in affective functioning, including heightened negative emotionality, lack of emotion acceptance (e.g., Engel et al., 2005; Waller et al., 2003), difficulties with emotion-based impulse control, and diminished access to helpful emotion regulation strategies (e.g., Brockmeyer et al., 2014; Svaldi et al., 2012). Alexithymia is also common, in particular among those with AN (see Nowakowski et al., 2013 for a review). New emotion-focused treatment models have been generated, including Radically Open Dialectical Behaviour Therapy for anorexia nervosa (AN) (Lynch et al., 2013) and Integrative Cognitive-Affective Therapy for bulimia nervosa (BN) (Wonderlich et al., 2014).

The purpose of the current chapter is to acquaint clinicians and researchers in the EDs field with three additional, emotion-based psychotherapies: Accelerated Experiential Dynamic Psychotherapy (AEDP), Emotion-Focused Therapy (EFT), and Emotion-Focused Family Therapy (EFFT). Consistent with the embodiment focus of this volume, these therapies aim to facilitate adaptive, transformational, bodily-rooted emotional experiences, whereby emotion is both the target and agent of change (Fosha, 2008). When feelings in the body are received (rather than rejected) as in-the-moment cues, clients can glean meaningful knowledge about themselves and situations in order to adaptively respond to their emotional needs (Greenberg, 2012). With this increased emotional self-efficacy, the ED becomes less necessary for affect management (Treasure, Schmidt, & Troop, 2000). As per best practices in ED treatment, emotion-based psychotherapies (as with any psychotherapies) are offered in the context of multidisciplinary care (e.g., medical, psychiatric, dietetic).

AEDP and EFT have been previously discussed jointly in their application to complex trauma (Fosha, Paivio, Gleiser, & Ford, 2009). Using a similar format in the current chapter, we (1) describe key concepts in AEDP (MW), EFT, and EFFT (NF) as applied to ED treatment; (2) offer a clinical case vignette, followed by annotated transcripts designed to illustrate selected interventions from the respective modalities; and (3) compare and contrast the therapies.

Overview of Accelerated Experiential Dynamic Psychotherapy

Originated by Diana Fosha (2000), AEDP proposes a three-factor theory of psychological change, comprised of affect, relatedness, and transformation. Change occurs through "the visceral experience of core affective phenomena within an emotionally engaged dyad" (Fosha, 2003, p. 230) and then working experientially with the positive emotions associated with the experience of transformation itself (Fosha, 2009). Accordingly, AEDP is informed by emotion theory and neuroscience (e.g., Damasio, 1999; Darwin, 1872/1965; Panksepp, 2009; Schore, 2009; Siegel, 1999), attachment theory and research (e.g., Bowlby, 1988;

Main, 1999), and psychodynamic theory (e.g., Winnicott, 1960/1965) and employs experiential, relational, and integrative interventions (Fosha, 2000; Fosha et al., 2009). AEDP helps clients resume impeded growth and reconnect with their core (i.e., authentic, true, essential) selves by focusing on the transformation of bodily-felt affective states and experiences of self, which leads to the liberation of adaptive action tendencies (Fosha, 2000, 2009; Russell, 2015). AEDP posits a theory of psychotherapy based in naturally occurring change mechanisms, foremost of which is an innate, universal, and bodily-rooted drive toward healing and self-repair, named in AEDP as *transformance* (Fosha, 2005, 2008; Yeung & Fosha, 2015).

AEDP holds promise for helping with key aspects of ED recovery: On the basis of a secure therapeutic relationship, clients can be helped to (1) undo aloneness, and de-pathologize and regulate the shame and anxiety often accompanying EDs; (2) more generally develop their abilities in regulating affect; (3) connect with, and engage, their innate capacities for growth and healing in an embodied way, even when ambivalence about recovery is present; (4) regain the adaptive action tendencies associated with defended-against emotions and other affective experiences, while developing self-compassion for having employed experiential defenses/self-protections; (5) reprocess and reintegrate traumatic experiences that may have contributed to the emergence and/or maintenance of the ED; and (6) recognize and begin to operate more fully from their core selves (as distinct from the identity – and any other helpful/protective functions – often provided by an ED). AEDP may also pose challenges for clients with EDs, primarily because they will be invited to attend to bodily, affective, and relational experiences they have avoided in order to function (e.g., Lamagna, 2015).

In the remainder of this section, interwoven with a summary of AEDP's foundational concepts, potential applications of AEDP to EDs and their treatment are offered, and special considerations are highlighted therein. Specific interventions are presented in a later section. For more complete descriptions of AEDP, please refer to Fosha (e.g., 2000, 2003, 2009 and the AEDP website at www.aedpinstitute.org.

Key Concepts in AEDP

AEDP proposes that psychopathology reflects an individual's best efforts at adapting to an environment that didn't match her/his emotional style or needs for self-expression (Russell & Fosha, 2008). When resources in the environment are insufficient to help regulate the individual's affective experiences that are adaptive by nature (including primary emotions such as anger, sadness, fear, disgust, and joy; self-experiences and states such as feeling vulnerable, lonely, or proud; and relational experiences such as feeling close, distant, rejected, and suffocated), core affect becomes associated with highly aversive and nonadaptive states (e.g., anxiety, pathogenic shame) (Fosha, 2001). Navigating and surviving such overwhelming affects in the context of *unbearable aloneness* (Fosha, 2000) necessitate the development of self-protections/defenses, which, when chronically relied upon to defend against affective experience, engender psychological problems (e.g., Fosha, 2000, 2001, 2010). Applied to EDs, this conceptualization suggests that the disorders may develop and/or be maintained as short- or long-term self-preserving/defensive/safety-enhancing strategies to cope with anxiety, shame, and/or other toxic affective states, as well as with intense core emotions that were beyond the individual's capacity to regulate on her/ his own.

In AEDP, focusing on remedying psychopathology, however, is considered insufficient. Fosha (e.g., 2000) therefore embedded AEDP in transformational theory, which proposes that transformation (i.e., growth, development, healing) is a fundamental, biologically wired-in human need and process that is "fundamentally different and separate from the process involved in repairing psychopathology" (Fosha, 2009, p. 13). This assumption lies at the core, and is a distinguishing feature, of AEDP (Fosha, 2010). It informs AEDP therapists' consistently non-pathologizing, moment-by-moment efforts to mobilize their clients' inherent healing and self-righting tendencies and resources, key aspects of what Fosha has termed *transformance* (e.g., Fosha, 2008, 2009, 2010). *Transformance* – an overarching motivational force, guided by a bodily-rooted felt sense of recognition, rightness, and truth – engenders feelings of vitality and energy, as well as core (i.e., authentic) self-experiences. It can be potentiated and activated in safe, secure, relational conditions, such as in a therapy relationship. The centerpiece of AEDP's foundational concepts, *transformance* explicitly guides AEDP therapists to help clients recognize, deepen, and process any glimmers of curiosity, openness to experience, learning, and/ or growth (e.g., Russell, 2015), by encouraging clients to notice, turn toward, and deepen these experiences in a bodily-felt manner (e.g., "Where in your body are you feeling that curiosity?" "What's it like to feel into those sensations?").

Clients with EDs may experience the AEDP therapist's working with *transformance* as an unusual and/or provocative experience, given the tendency of EDs to suspend growth (emotional, cognitive, and/or spiritual, and even physical), sometimes to a significant degree. Despite the drawbacks of having an ED (e.g., time-consuming, narrowed life, isolation, shame), the "known" benefits it offers (e.g., confidence, pride, being better at something than others [Serpell et al., 2004]; providing a sense of selfhood and purpose; affective modulation and safety; and/or secondary gains afforded, such as intensified care and concern from loved ones) may be preferable to the "unknown" and untested benefits of healing and recovery. Furthermore, the extreme emotional, cognitive, and behavioral rigidity and/or chaos associated with EDs may make clients hesitant to participate in *transformance*-facilitating interventions that invite them to deepen even faint experiences of being open, mindful, curious, or hopeful. Even when transformation/change is deeply desired (let alone being considered ambivalently, or not being considered at all, as seen frequently in pre- or early-recovery phases of EDs), "it is also frightening, for it challenges established identity" (Fosha, 2013, p. 498). Finally, with the highest mortality rates of any psychiatric condition, EDs are powerful, health-damaging, and sometimes life-threatening phenomena that usually take years to resolve. Taken together, these factors suggest that *transformance* will be most fruitfully engaged and nurtured by the AEDP therapist in a conscientious and titrated manner, within each ED client's window of affective and relational tolerance.

A second foundational concept of AEDP is its *attachment* orientation (see Lipton & Fosha, 2011; Pando-Mars, 2016 for thorough discussions). AEDP therapists aim, from the first session, to develop secure therapeutic attachments, regardless of the client's presenting attachment style (i.e., secure, insecure, disorganized) (e.g., Fosha, 2010; Russell, 2015). This is fostered by explicitly affirming clients (e.g., for their courage, vulnerability, honesty) and demonstrating caring, appreciation, empathy, and emotional engagement (Fosha, 2010). The *attachment* orientation also prompts therapists to engage in moment-to-moment tracking of clients' *receptive affective experiences* (e.g., Fosha, 2000, 2010), meaning clients' subjective, bodily-based sense of receiving care, empathy, and validation, and thus experiencing being seen, felt, helped, affirmed, recognized, cared for, and empathized with. Therapist self-disclosures are considered essential, attachment- and affect-regulation-promoting interventions, and include self-involving or self-revealing disclosures, and those addressing affect, process, and the client's impact on the therapist. These are intended, among other functions, to establish client-therapist mutual affective resonance, undo aloneness, increase safety, soften defenses, offer emotional attunement, and convey that the client exists in the therapist's heart and mind (Fosha, 2000; Prenn, 2009).

Clients with EDs will present with various attachment styles and experiences in relationships. Secretiveness, feeling possessive of/guarded about the ED, and/or shame often lead individuals with EDs to withdraw, and, consequently, they experience the ED alone. Hence, the AEDP therapist's *attachment* orientation, with its respectful, affirming, empathic, validating, gentle, self-disclosing, and explicitly relational stance, may be experienced by ED clients in a range of ways, including as surprising, unfamiliar, or "weird"; or, something to quickly and intensely grab onto because it feels so good; or, profoundly threatening. Therapists' careful pacing and "dosage" of presence and interventions, informed by tracking and trusting ED clients' moment-to-moment experiences, are important for avoiding relational overwhelm with some individuals, whose experiences of emotional aloneness may be profound and/or whose relationship with the ED may be their most satisfying relationship. If the primary identity the client is bringing into the therapy relationship is the ED, this may also pose challenges for developing a secure therapy attachment. With the client seemingly overridden by the fixed and invariant sense of self offered by the ED, the AEDP therapist's attuning and attaching to the client's core self (which is always there, even if in fractal form [Fosha, 2013]), versus the ED identity, may be discombobulating for the client. This suggests that therapists cultivate relationships with both the ED identity and the core self, while helping to differentiate these two parts (Karen Kranz, personal communication, May 1, 2017). Such complexities regarding attachment will prompt AEDP therapists to be particularly diligent in obtaining consultation, supervision, and/or personal therapy to help them understand their personal attachment style, personal ED history (if relevant), preferred therapy pace, interpersonal intensity, and comfort with self-disclosure, so that they can maximize the possibility of creating secure attachments with their ED clients.

Closely linked to AEDP's *attachment* orientation is the centrality accorded to *dyadic affect regulation*. This concept is based on research suggesting that humans develop the capacity for self-regulating their affect through experience-dependent development that occurs within the caregiver-infant relationship via mutual adaptation and affect coordination (e.g., Schore, 2009). *Dyadic affect regulation* can occur in any dyad (including therapist-client) and is characterized by mutual emotional openness and responsiveness, as well as continued engagement when inevitable relational disruptions or ruptures occur (Fosha, 2003; Russell, 2015). To engage the benefits of *dyadic affect regulation*, AEDP therapists offer a relationship in which clients can feel safe enough to feel, as well as a neurobiological, right-brain to right-brain, "emotional helping hand" to clients' coping repertoires. This is facilitated through dyadically focused, body-based interventions such as coordinating voice tone, gaze, and postures/movements, which enhance clients' capacities to regulate intense and/or previously unregulatable emotions without triggering overwhelm and defensive exclusions of experience. This enables clients to become more capable of self-regulating (Fosha, 2003).

In clients with EDs, given the presence of high anxiety, toxic (versus adaptive) fear (e.g., of food, losing control, deviating from regimens), and shame (e.g., regarding body shape and size, having needs, being seen and/ or deserving of care), and in light of the powerfully protective function(s) of an ED to quell these aversive states, gains in affective regulation may be slow and incremental. Clients are invited to participate in mutual affective resonance and attachment with the therapist – throughout the attunement, rupture, and repair cycles – rather than with their ED (Karen Kranz, personal communication, May 1, 2017). Signs of progress may include phenomena such as clients beginning to receive the therapist's care, leading to increased toleration of core emotions; with more access to core emotions, an increasing sense of a core self as separate from the ED can emerge, accompanied by more genuine self-expression in the therapy relationship; and these developments then serve to scaffold curiosity, courage, and/or skill regarding behavioral changes. To maximize the benefits of *dyadic affect regulation*, therapists using AEDP with ED clients are urged to work at cultivating their own affective competence, thereby laying the foundation for helping clients to cultivate theirs.

Next, AEDP involves helping clients attend to, and articulate, their affective *subjective experiences* (Fosha, 2001; Russell, 2015). The client's affective experience informs the therapy dyad about the state of the client, the relationship, and the therapy process, and, therefore, the interventions employed by the therapist. AEDP therapists' familiarity with affective phenomena (that mark both pathogenic/defensive and healing/core affective processes) keeps clients' phenomenological experiences centralized. Markers may include (but are not limited to) client verbalizations, prosody, para-verbals, eye contact, postures and other body language/movements/positions, breathing rate, and skin flushing or paling (e.g., Fosha, 2009).

Relatedly, and fundamental to AEDP, *emotion and other affective change processes* are centralized. AEDP offers a description (see Figure 17.1) of the transformation possible when emotions are processed to completion and when authentic/true self experiences with authentic/true others are recognized and responded to. Consisting of four states and three state transformations, the model illustrates that when State 1 affects (characterized by stress, distress, symptoms, and defenses) can be regulated and defenses softened or bypassed, State 2 core affective experiences are able to be processed, leading to an affective shift commonly characterized by feeling relief or "lighter," as well as the release of adaptive action tendencies. With *metaprocessing* (see as follows), this shift frequently gives rise to State 3's transformational affects, which are experienced as positive and "right," whether they are joyful or painful, and as "sensory experiences of energy, vibrations, or oscillation in the body in response to change" (Russell & Fosha, 2008, p. 173). Repeated cycling through these first three states can lead to State 4 (core state), in which emerge calm, ease, flow, a "truth sense," and a coherent, cohesive narrative. Bodily-based markers (e.g., facial expressions, prosody, body postures, breathing changes, skin tone changes) in transitions between states alert the therapist that a shift is occurring (e.g., Fosha, 2009). For detailed discussions of the diagram, see Fosha (2009, 2010) and Russell (2015). AEDP also privileges attending to and processing clients' *positive affects and interactions*, which are thought to promote conditions for neurological growth toward exploration and experience-seeking, unleash and build internal resources, and facilitate resilient adaptation (see Russell, 2015, for a summary of positive emotions and AEDP).

Accelerated Experiential Dynamic Psychotherapy
THE PHENOMENOLOGY OF
THE TRANSFORMATIONAL PROCESS
4 States and 3 State Transformations

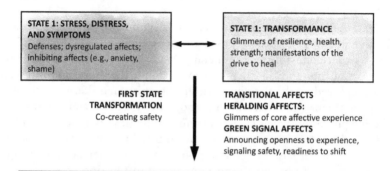

STATE 1: STRESS, DISTRESS, AND SYMPTOMS
Defenses; dysregulated affects; inhibiting affects (e.g., anxiety, shame)

↔

STATE 1: TRANSFORMANCE
Glimmers of resilience, health, strength; manifestations of the drive to heal

FIRST STATE TRANSFORMATION
Co-creating safety

TRANSITIONAL AFFECTS HERALDING AFFECTS:
Glimmers of core affective experience
GREEN SIGNAL AFFECTS
Announcing openness to experience, signaling safety, readiness to shift

STATE 2: THE PROCESSING OF EMOTIONAL EXPERIENCE
Categorical emotions; attachment experiences; coordinated relational experiences; receptive affective experiences; somatic "drop-down" states; intersubjective experiences of pleasure; authentic self states; embodied ego states and their associated emotions; core needs; attachment strivings.

SECOND STATE TRANSFORMATION
The emergence of resilience

ADAPTIVE ACTION TENDENCIES POST-BREAKTHROUGH AFFECTS:
Relief, hope, feeling stronger, lighter, etc.

STATE 3: THE METAPROCESSING OF TRANSFORMATIONAL EXPERIENCE
THE TRANSFORMATIONAL AFFECTS
The mastery affects (e.g., pride, joy); emotional pain associated with mourning-the-self; the tremulous affects associated with the experience of quantum change; the healing affects (e.g., gratitude, feeling moved) associated with the affirmation of the self; the realization affects (e.g., the "yes!" and "wow" affects; the "click" of recognition) associated with new understanding

THIRD STATE TRANSFORMATION
The co-engendering of secure attachment and the positive valuation of the self

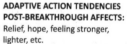

Energy, vitality, openness, aliveness

STATE 4: CORE STATE AND THE TRUTH SENSE
Openness; compassion and self-compassion; wisdom, generosity, kindness; clarity; calm, flow, ease; the sense of things feeling "right" ; capacity to construct a coherent and cohesive autobiographical narrative

Figure 17.1 The Phenomenology of Transformational Experience: This figure describes the four states and three–state transformation of AEDP. Figure created by and used with permission of Diana Fosha.

For clients with EDs, AEDP's centralization of their *subjective experiences, emotions, and other affective change processes* is likely to be challenging. Research indicates that people with EDs tend to experience emotions and sensations in the body in a relatively undifferentiated manner (Barrett, Gross, Christensen, & Benvenuto, 2001; Harrison, Tchanturia, & Treasure, 2010). Furthermore, Selby and colleagues (2014) reported that low differentiation of *positive* emotions specifically was predictive of engaging in more ED behaviors. Their findings suggest that helping ED clients develop emotion differentiation and regulation skills (the very processes AEDP attempts to entrain, so that core affect can be processed), as well as finding positive reinforcers alternative to ED behaviors, may be helpful in recovery. In addition, because people with EDs demonstrate difficulty with expressing facial and nonverbal emotion (Davies, Schmidt, Stahl, & Tchanturia, 2011; Davies, Swan, Schmidt, & Tchanturia, 2012), AEDP therapists will need finely tuned radar to pick up on the faintest affective markers of ED clients' subjective experiences. Mars's (2011) incorporation into AEDP of the "seven channels of experience" may be useful in helping ED clients to notice, tolerate, and turn toward their affective experiences through a variety of bodily-based experiential channels, including sensation, emotion, energy, motor movements, auditory, visual, and/or imaginal. Clinical anecdotal experiences of using AEDP for clients with EDs suggest that *transformance* is inherently rewarding, for example when clients feel pride in processing anger for the first time without shame, anxiety, and/or urges to restrict or binge.

Rounding out AEDP's foundational concepts is *metaprocessing*, wherein the therapist facilitates clients' reflecting on and processing the experience of change and transformation itself, in order to consolidate, deepen, and expand any healing emerging from the session. This intervention is considered unique to AEDP. Five meta-therapeutic processes (*mastery, mourning the self, traversing the crisis of healing change, affirming recognition of the self and its transformation, and taking in and "getting" the magnitude of the change*) are associated, respectively, with five transformational affects: (1) *mastery affects* (e.g., pride, joy), (2) *emotional pain* (i.e., grief and/or pained empathy for the self – referred to as mourning the self – regarding the losses incurred due to defense mechanisms and/or others' limitations), (3) *tremulous affects* (i.e., reacting to healing change with feelings of fear/excitement, positive vulnerability, startle/surprise, curiosity/interest, "this is weird/different/unfamiliar"), (4) *healing affects* (including gratitude and tenderness toward the therapist, as well as feeling moved or touched within oneself), and (5) the *realization affects* (the "yes" of recognition and the "wow" of wonder, awe, and amazement at the emergent realization of the change) (e.g., Russell, 2015). See Iwakabe and Conceicao (2016) for a comprehensive discussion of *metaprocessing*.

For the client with an ED who experiences feeling proud after processing a feeling of anger to completion without shame, anxiety, and/or urges to engage in ED behaviors, the *mastery affect* of pride ("I did that!") would be *metaprocessed* (e.g., "Where do you experience that pride feeling, physically?" "Is it OK to hang out with it for a bit?" "What's that like?" "How is it to be feeling pride here with me?"). For many clients with EDs, *metaprocessing* the transformational affects may be associated with afore-described challenges regarding differentiating and describing affective states (plus potentially dismissing, disowning, or feeling anxiety, guilt, and/or pathogenic shame regarding any positive affects and changes – experiences which must, in turn, be regulated and/or undone). However, clinical experience suggests that cycling iteratively through States 1 and 2 helps ED clients become more receptive to, and adept at, the transformational experience.

Overview of Emotion-Focused Therapy

EFT is an evidenced-based, process-experiential therapy widely recognized for its use with depression (American Psychological Association [APA], Division 12; Angus, Goldman, & Mergenthaler, 2008; Greenberg & Watson, 1998, 2005) and trauma (APA, Division 56; Courtois & Ford, 2009; Greenberg, 2010; Paivio & Greenberg, 2001; Paivio & Nieuwenhuis, 2001). The application of EFT has also been explored with sufferers of EDs in both individual and group settings and has been identified as a therapeutic fit for this population (Brennan, Emmerling, & Whelton, 2014; Dolhanty & Greenberg, 2007, 2009; Greenberg, 2010) due to its focus on under- and overregulated affects (Dolhanty & Greenberg, 2009).

Similar to AEDP, EFT assumes that emotion avoidance is a common presentation in individuals with an ED (Dolhanty & Greenberg, 2009; Lavender et al., 2014; Lavender et al., 2015). Rather than responding to their bodily-felt affective experiences, ED sufferers tend to focus on food, weight, and body image in order to avoid emotional pain. As such, the essence of EFT is to support clients to reconnect with their internal experience, including their bodily-felt sense of emotion, in order to increase their self-efficacy to accept, regulate, and move through emotional experiences (Greenberg, 2010). As clients gain mastery in feeling and expressing emotion, the therapist facilitates interventions to support the transformation of maladaptive emotion schemes. In the remainder of this section, key concepts in EFT are described, and its application to EDs and their treatment is discussed, with special considerations highlighted therein. Specific EFT markers and interventions are presented in a later section. For comprehensive descriptions of EFT, please refer to Greenberg (1996, 1999, 2008, 2014).

Key Concepts in EFT

Emotion schemes are complex internal organizations that combine wired-in emotional responses with cognition and include nonverbal and affective experiences (Greenberg, 2012). Emotion schemes can be interpreted based on the experiences they evoke, and the therapist can use a variety of interventions to help clients make sense and evaluate the impact of their emotion schemes on their well-being. When clients are supported to make sense of these schemes, they begin to understand the narrative around their emotion avoidance (for example, fear of abandonment or core feelings of being unworthy) (Greenberg, 2012). McNally, Timulak, and Greenberg (2014) describe the process of transforming schemes through supporting clients to embody the series of emotions that arise, in order to feel, make sense of, and shift the presentation. Individuals are supported to connect with both the physical and neurobiological experiences of emotion in order to bring their whole body into alignment; as they learn to make sense of and accept their real-time experience, as well as symbolize this experience in words or images, there is a decreased need for symptoms to deflect the sometimes painful reality of being embodied (Elliot et al., 2004).

PRINCIPLES OF EMOTIONAL CHANGE

Dolhanty and Greenberg (2009) have suggested that overcoming avoidance of emotion is not necessarily straightforward when working with ED clients. Anxiety can arise at the thought of connecting with the body and previously avoided emotional pain, and the therapist may also feel apprehension at the idea of "diving in" with the client – therapists are not exempt from the experience of evocative emotion and may find themselves worried about diving in deep and not knowing what to do (particularly if they are new to EFT or concerned that the client may become too overwhelmed) (Dolhanty & Greenberg, 2009). The focus of EFT is on the development of self-efficacy with emotion – that is, the client's belief in her ability to successfully feel and navigate emotion – in order to gain a sense of mastery of emotional experience, rather than simply tolerating emotional pain. Greenberg (2010) outlines six principles of emotional change and describes what occurs when a client is able to transform core maladaptive emotions and find relief from seemingly overwhelming pain:

1   Awareness: More than just noticing, emotional awareness means that the client can feel the emotion in her body as it presents. If needed, the therapist will invite the client to identify the physical cues that present with emotion, which can help clients who are particularly blocked and initially unable to make sense of their emotional experience (Greenberg, 2010). As the client becomes more skilled at attending to her emotion – including its bodily-felt sense – she will be able to better understand the action tendency necessary to meet the associated need. The therapist supports the individual to further connect and listen to the emotion through empathic conjecture, which invites the client to connect to her internal world through focusing with sensory language.

2   Expression: Rather than focusing on the expression of emotion in therapy, the EFT therapist is more interested in supporting the client to identify and connect with the unexpressed emotion that she has learned to avoid. As the client develops awareness and attunes to her current emotional experience, she needs to be supported to integrate her thoughts and feelings (Greenberg, 2010). Research has shown that emotional arousal alone does not produce a good outcome for clients; rather, it is the processing of the aroused emotions that leads to beneficial outcome (Greenberg, Auszra, & Hermann, 2007).

3   Regulation: It is important that the client learns to regulate emotion, as a pathway to transformation. Emotion regulation skills include "identifying and labelling emotion, allowing and tolerating emotions, establishing a working distance, increasing positive emotions, reducing vulnerability to negative emotions, self-soothing, breathing, and distraction" (Greenberg, 2010, p. 3). The EFT therapist also helps the client regulate emotionally via the relationship through ongoing attunement and validation. Regulation is particularly important when there are identified risks related to emotional arousal (such as suicidality) and when the client is becoming overwhelmed when experiencing painful emotion (Dolhanty & Greenberg, 2009).

4   Reflection: The client is supported to make further sense of, and create new meaning around, her emotional experience. Making sense of the events that provoke maladaptive emotional experiences is an important process toward self-knowledge, which is needed for sustainable change. The process of reflection helps identify "feelings, needs, self-experience, thoughts and aims of different parts of the self" (Greenberg, 2010, p. 4). This deep understanding helps the client create new stories to explain her experiences.

5   Transformation: Emotion can change emotion, and the EFT therapist supports the client to transform her primary maladaptive emotions with adaptive emotion states, for example by "the activation of an incompatible, more adaptive experience that undoes or transforms the old response" (Greenberg, 2010, p. 5). Only when an individual is present with her current emotion can she move on to another. For example, deeply attending to hopelessness permits the healthy self to rise with assertion.

6   Corrective Emotional Experience: The therapist can offer the client a new lived experience with the expression of emotion, in relationship. In-session interactions offer corrective experiences, as the therapist empathically leads and follows the client's process of experiencing and working through painful emotion (Greenberg, 2010, p. 6). These experiences are also important as they help the client to develop a sense of mastery over previously avoided – and possibly feared – emotions, in the context of relationship.

CASE FORMULATION

Dolhanty and Greenberg (2009) adapted a process for case formulation based on the application of EFT to AN. Case formulation involves evaluating the following: the client's capacity to focus on, and connect with, their bodily-felt sense; the ongoing, in-session diagnosing of markers and associated interventions; collaborative rapport development; and identification of core themes (Goldman & Greenberg, 1997). The eight steps (originally outlined in Greenberg and Goldman, 2007) are described below, along with wording and considerations from Dolhanty and Greenberg (2009) for working with individuals who have EDs.

1   Identify the presenting problem: using empathic responding, the therapist coaches the client to describe her presenting problem.
2   Listen to, and explore, the client's narrative about the problem: the therapist supports the client to make sense of how she relates to the problem and how she perceives the problem to be impacting her life.
3   Gather information about the client's attachment and identity histories, and current relationships and concerns: the therapist is assessing the client's level of functioning and outside support.
4   Observe and attend to the client's style of processing emotions: the therapist assesses for under- or overregulation, as well as the degree of emotional arousal and the extent to which the client's emotional processing is productive and experiential.
5   Identify and respond to the painful aspects of the client's experience: the therapist attunes to verbal and nonverbal cues of pain to understand the client's history of painful events, which are clues to the development of core maladaptive emotion schemes that manifest in the personal and interpersonal levels. This process offers insight into the client's ability to feel and tolerate emotion, and/or whether the emotion is evoking avoidant coping.
6   Identify markers and, when they arise, suggest tasks appropriate to resolving problematic processes: the assessment of markers and associated tasks helps the client process their experience and integrate previously avoided information and emotion. Markers and interventions are described in detail as follows.
7   Focus on thematic intrapersonal and interpersonal processes: the therapist ensures that ongoing attention is paid to themes that represent disruptions to healthy intra- and interpersonal functioning.
8   Attend to the client's moment-by-moment processing to guide interventions within tasks: the therapist responds to the client's immediate presentation. Rather than rigidly following an intervention through to completion, the therapist makes note of presenting emotions and applies interventions that will support transformation of the immediate pain. For example, if the client is working through a self-critical

marker and an emotion emerges regarding her mother, the therapist shifts to the unfinished business intervention in order to follow the emotion as it presents (Dolhanty & Greenberg, 2009; Greenberg & Goldman, 2007).

MARKERS AND INTERVENTIONS

As noted before, moment-by-moment assessment of emotion directs the therapist to select interventions that fit the immediate presentation, based on interpretation of the client's painful experience and the identification of specific markers. As follows are some of the key markers and interventions in EFT, as outlined in Greenberg (2010). Importantly, when working with clients who have EDs, conflict splits, self-critical splits, and unfinished business are key markers (Dolhanty & Greenberg, 2009):

1   Problematic reactions: If the client is unable to make sense of an emotional or behavioral reaction, the therapist supports the process of systematic evocative unfolding (Watson & Greenberg, 1996). This intervention supports the client to share and deepen the puzzling experience, in order to develop understanding through connecting the event, thoughts, and emotions.

2   Unclear felt sense: If the client is uncertain about how to describe her bodily-felt sense, the therapist helps through focusing (Gendlin, 1996). With focusing, the therapist supports the client to be as curious and open as possible as she describes her physical experience. This helps the client locate herself within the realm of emotional and physical sensations, as she must learn how to make sense of her felt sense experience in order to move through it.

3   Conflict splits/self-critical splits: This marker appears frequently with the ED population. High levels of shame and self-loathing leave the client in a painful cycle, characterized by the voice of criticism (ED sufferers often refer to the "ED voice," known as the "inner critic" in EFT). Unlike an auditory hallucination, the "ED voice" is internal and reflects unprocessed maladaptive emotions and thoughts. Two-chair work (a key intervention in EFT) is the appropriate intervention for this marker, and it focuses on two parts of the self (i.e., the healthy voice and the critical voice). The individual switches between two chairs, speaking the dialogue of the inner critic and healthy part. This process facilitates the softening of the critic and the integration of the two sides (Greenberg, 2010). The critic represents old, unprocessed pain and exists to "rescue" the client from further pain (although its intent seems otherwise due to its advocating for emotion avoidance, rather than for emotion processing).

4   Self-interruptive splits: Another common marker in ED clients (due to both under- and overregulation), this split occurs when part of the

self "interrupts," blocks, or attempts to minimize emotional feeling and expression (i.e., choking back tears or fighting to keep them in). Two-chair work is also employed here, but the client is invited to enact the blocker, often via physical representation (narrowing of the eyes, constricting the voice), metaphor (caged), or verbal statements ("don't let yourself feel," "you must not go there," "you won't be able to handle this") (Greenberg, 2010, p. 7). This process fosters the client working through and overcoming the interruptive part of self, in order to move forward with the therapeutic work.

5   Unfinished business: The empty-chair intervention is introduced when the client presents with intense, unresolved feelings toward a significant other. The client connects to her internalized perspective of the other and her experience and begins to make sense of her emotional reactions. This helps shift views of both self and other.

(Greenberg, 2010, p. 8)

From EFT to EFFT

Influenced by Family-Based Treatment (FBT) and EFT, Dr. Adele Lafrance and Dr. Joanne Dolhanty developed EFFT, a family-based, emotion-focused psychotherapy specifically for use in the context of ED treatment (Lafrance Robinson, Dolhanty, & Greenberg, 2013). Acknowledging that limitations exist in supporting a client to process and regulate her emotions when there is a lack of direct contact with her home supports, the authors propose that family involvement can be highly beneficial in the treatment of all ED cases, for the following reasons:

1   The client's emotional presentation displays strong similarities to, and appears to have been shaped by, their environment. Whether under- or overregulated, adaptively or maladaptively expressed, the emotional patterns of the client and family can mirror one another.

2   Most ED clients, even married adults, have a high degree of family involvement, whether recovery specific, emotional, or more general in the day-to-day.

3   Highly involved parents are sometimes unsuccessful in their supporting roles. For example, the very typical reactions of parental fear and self-blame have been shown to interfere with supportive caregiving efforts in the context of treatment (Stillar et al., 2016), and specialized support is needed.

Overview of Emotion-Focused Family Therapy

Rooted in the deep and unwavering belief of the healing power of families, EFFT was initially developed for individuals with EDs and their families, both as a stand-alone treatment and as an adjunct when standard treatments do not yield desired outcomes. Research has been conducted on EFFT with caregivers of child, adolescent and adult individuals suffering with an ED. A pilot study was completed on the Two-Day Caregiver Workshop intervention, and outcomes showed a significant increase in parental self-efficacy, a decrease in parental self-blame, a positive shift in parents' attitudes regarding their role of emotion coaching, and a reduction in the fears associated with their involvement in treatment (Lafrance Robinson, Dolhanty, Stillar, Henderson, & Mayman, 2014). A follow-up study to the pilot study demonstrated that EFFT targeted and transformed parental fear and self-blame, which led to increased caregiver self-efficacy regarding their active involvement in their child's treatment, regardless of age (Stillar et al., 2016). Furthermore, increased caregiver self-efficacy predicted an increase in behavioral intentions congruent with those targeted throughout the intervention in the domains of meal support, symptom interruption, and emotional support (Strahan et al., 2017). The application of EFFT has since expanded to include general mental health issues, including substance use problems and behavioral issues, with research currently in progress. EFFT can be delivered in the context of therapy sessions with parents only, parent-child dyads, family sessions, and multi-parent workshops.

A fundamental assumption underpinning EFFT is that, regardless of age, all children want to be supported by their parents, and all parents want to support their child in their recovery. Expressions of resistance toward parental involvement from either the parent(s) or child are thought to be motivated by fears of judgment, conflict, and/or that involvement won't go well. Understanding resistance in this way permits the therapist to explore and work through these fears with child and parents alike, such that the deep wish of both the child and her parents to collaborate in the recovery process is uncovered. As noted before, preliminary research has shown that when parental fear and self-blame were targeted for transformation, caregivers experienced a significant increase in caregiving self-efficacy (i.e., their confidence in their ability to support their child's recovery), as well increased intentions to engage in specific behavioral and emotion-focused interventions to do so (Stillar et al., 2016). When the therapist communicates belief in the parents and their role in their child's recovery, parents and children feel more hopeful about the process.

EFFT Interventions

RECOVERY COACHING

The EFFT therapist supports parents to become their child's recovery coaches and to help with meal support and symptom interruption (with monitoring of a physician, if necessary). Recovery coaching varies depending on the presenting symptoms, whether the child lives at home, and where the child is in the recovery process. Overall, the goals are to help the child weight restore/become re-nourished and to interrupt and/or cease use of ED symptoms such as restricting, bingeing, purging, and compulsive exercising (Lafrance & Dolhanty, 2013). This occurs through meal support training (via education, video demonstrations, and role-plays), with the simultaneous use of other EFFT interventions (e.g., emotion coaching).

EMOTION COACHING

The therapist coaches parents to take on the role of emotion coaches, using the following steps of emotion coaching: attend to their child's emotion, label the emotion, validate the emotion/content, meet the emotional need, and if necessary, fix it/problem solve (Robinson et al., 2013). In the short term, emotion coaching helps the ED sufferer obtain the support needed to regulate her emotion in the moment, rendering ED symptoms less necessary for coping. This can be particularly helpful when parents are supporting their child in meal support or when interrupting symptoms, both of which usually produce high emotional arousal. Over time, emotion coaching leads to the child's increased self-efficacy with emotion: parental support to process emotional experiences in the moment offers a foundation for the child to begin internalizing the steps of emotion coaching, consequently increasing her capacity to self-regulate. An individual who believes in her capacity to attend to and move through emotions does not require ED symptoms to avoid or suppress emotional pain. Parents are also taught about emotion basics (i.e., sociocultural history of emotion avoidance, impact of miscues and emotion avoidance, and that each emotion has a label, bodily-felt sense, action tendency, and associated need) to facilitate their understanding of the importance of emotion coaching (Lafrance & Dolhanty, 2013).

RELATIONSHIP REPAIR

Relationship repair is a key EFFT intervention used to increase self-efficacy with emotion and shift patterns of avoidance. It was developed to heal family relationships in cases, for example, where the child or parent is paralyzed by self-blame or when there is unprocessed historical pain that is interfering with the child's ability to accept parental support with recovery and/or emotion coaching. Relationship repair involves supporting parents to facilitate conversations with their child about any lingering hurts, anger, or painful memories (Lafrance Robinson et al., 2014). When parents are supported to facilitate this process, they are able to model to their child that they can "handle" emotional pain, which makes the child more likely to share current emotional struggles without the apprehension of overburdening their parent. The therapist helps parents to brainstorm and process any past hurts or ruptures that could be preventing their child from allowing parental support. Memories that evoke deep shame in the parents are targeted, because a parent who is overcome with shame is not able to fully attune to their child's pain. As parents release themselves from crippling self-blame, they are better able to hear their child's anger without buckling. Relationship repair helps families move beyond emotional hurts (especially if either the parent or child blames a specific event as having contributed to the development or struggle with the ED), leaving the past in history. Discussing these events is the opposite of emotion avoidance, and models to the child that difficult emotions and conversations are manageable, and, more importantly, that the parent is someone with whom they can practice this.

EFFT describes five steps for a successful repair (Lafrance & Dolhanty, 2013). Optimally, the therapist reviews and practices the steps with the parents in order to prepare them for whatever the outcome:

1   Acknowledge to the child the unique impact of the injury and how it may have contributed to a style of emotion avoidance,
2   Express appreciation for "what it must have been like" for the child – both regarding the event itself and the reluctance to share pain (label and validate),
3   Apologize and communicate authentic remorse to the child ("I'm sorry"),
4   State what could have been done instead (even if nothing could have been done, say "I should have found a way") and what will change from now on,
5   Wait for the blast/denial/silence (Lafrance & Dolhanty, 2013).

After the therapeutic apology is executed, there are three possibilities regarding the child's response: silence, blast, or denial. It is important to prepare parents for all three, since the child's reaction may convey that the apology did not work, when it actually signals the opposite. The silence can happen if the child has deep levels of anger and is uncomfortable sharing it, or if the conversation feels highly vulnerable. The blast occurs when the child feels understood and validated, and comfortable enough to share more about the impact of their experience. It may appear as though her anger has increased because she is connecting to and expressing it more freely than usual. The denial may occur if the child feels worried about hurting her parents by acknowledging her pain. Parents are coached and prepared for all outcomes in order to avoid falling into their own anger or shame and disconnecting from the process (Lafrance Robinson et al., 2014). Parents are coached to avoid starting the repair conversation with "I'm sorry" and to focus on deepening through expression of what they realized in reflection of the specific event; a worksheet is provided with step-by-step directions when possible.

WORKING THROUGH PARENTAL FEARS

A significant part of the EFFT process lies in supporting parents to acknowledge and work through any fears and emotional obstacles that surface. These emotional blocks are an expected target of therapy; however, they need to be identified and processed, or they inhibit the offering of optimal support. These fears are the primary reason caregivers are ineffective in refeeding, symptom interruption, and emotion coaching (Robinson et al., 2013). Parental fear, shame, hopelessness, helplessness, and feelings of resentment can be transformed as clinicians employ the steps of emotion coaching to validate the parents' experience.

There are numerous interventions used to address these blocks, and in some cases, bringing these blocks into awareness and offering validation can significantly shift the parents' ability to follow through with the behavior and emotion coaching strategies. By joining with parents in the depths of their blocks (i.e., feeling resentment toward their child or lacking confidence in capacity to support their child's recovery in the home), the clinician can help parents to move through the blocks and have renewed hope and anticipation for continuing the process. Parents are also offered paper measures to help identify their specific fears (e.g., of pushing their loved one too far, their loved one running away or dying by suicide, or losing control over their own emotions), in order to process and create safety plans when needed. They are also presented with the New Maudsley's Animal Models (Treasure, Schmidt, & Macdonald, 2009). Skills training is used to deepen parents' confidence and, when needed, experiential work is offered (specifically targeted to resolving blocks regarding refeeding, symptom interruption, emotion coaching, and relationship repair). The experiential work is a scripted form of chair work that allows the parent to connect to their own inner critic and then to their child (a shortened variation of self-critical split and unfinished business). Similar to EFT, the clinician follows moment-by-moment emotion (or lack of emotion) as it presents, and proceeds with interventions accordingly.

CLINICIAN BLOCKS

Therapists are not exempt from the powerful impact of emotion and, just as carers are supported to work through the blocks that stop them from optimally supporting their child, so are EFFT clinicians expected, and supported, to identify and work through the impact of strong emotions that manifest as therapy-interfering behaviors, known as "clinician blocks." Research suggests that clinicians' own fear and shame can impact decision-making and recommendations (e.g., not including parents in care, discharging a family earlier than is optimal, or backing off on behavioral interventions despite the need) (Lafrance Robinson & Kosmerly, 2015).

The EFFT model involves providing supervision for clinicians to help them identify and experientially work through these blocks in order to foster clinician self-efficacy in the treatment process. Individual and group supervision can take place in-person, over the phone, or through web-based videoconferencing. Peer supervision groups are recommended – and even supported through a Facebook group – and clinicians are encouraged to find ways to reflect upon how their emotion is impacting their work with families.

Applications to a Clinical Case Vignette

In this section, a brief clinical case vignette is presented as a basis for illustrating how selected interventions specific to AEDP, EFT, and EFFT are employed. The case represents a composite of several ED clients.

> Holly self-referred to therapy at age 23 because she felt distressed by, and wanted to stop, bingeing. She reported a 10-year history of ED behaviours and intermittent treatment. She described a current pattern of restrictive eating, compulsive exercise, and bingeing and purging approximately four times per week. In the initial session, Holly said she neither wished to stop restricting her food intake nor decrease her exercise regimen.
>
> In session 4, Holly reports wanting to be honest with her parents about the ED, because she wants their support to not binge at family dinners. She also reports feeling worried about burdening them with this request, given they are concerned about her maternal grandfather's health. She reports considering not approaching her parents for this reason.

AEDP Transcript

There are no pre-set scripts when employing AEDP interventions. In each moment, while carefully tracking markers of the client's affective experience, the therapist draws from a number of intervention possibilities, choosing one based on timing and titration, and aligning with the overarching goals, which are to help clients process core affective experiences to completion and connect with their core selves. The unit of intervention is what the therapist does, plus how the client responds, which then suggests next intervention(s) (Fosha, 2000). The therapist's moment-to-moment tracking informs moment-by-moment interventions that are intended to help soften, bypass, or even preempt the activation of clients' ingrained self-protections/defenses, increasing the likelihood that clients can co-create a safe relationship with the therapist, and then turn toward, and process to completion, avoided affective experiences so that associated adaptive action tendencies can be unleashed.

In this transcript snippet, the therapist helps the client counteract the shame that is preventing her from asking her parents for help and facilitates her moving into and beginning to process a core emotion (sadness) (i.e., State 1 to State 2 progression). From deeply-felt sadness emerge adaptive action tendencies (reaching out for help; comfort-seeking), leading to affective experiences of courage and resolve to ask her parents for help.

HOLLY: (smiling incongruently; brittle look in eyes) I don't think I could ask them right now, and that's OK. They are way too busy with helping Grandad. **[State 1 defenses present]** (pauses, eyes start to tear up) **[State 1 defenses softening]** I do want to ask them to help me, you know, but they don't even know I'm still doing the ED. They think I'm fine now. (pauses, looks down **[possible pathogenic affect emerging]**) I should be over this.

THERAPIST: (says gently with compassion in eyes) Would it be OK to look at me for a moment? Holly: Uh-huh. (glances up briefly) Therapist: What do you see in my face? **[aiming to undo shame]**

HOLLY: (pausing, looking searchingly at therapist's face for a few seconds, eyes still red) I…uh…I see no judgement. Caring. **[client's receptive affective capacities are online]**

THERAPIST: [metaprocessing] How is it for you to see my caring and acceptance of you? [changing language from absence of judgment, to presence of acceptance; helping to further engage client's receptive affective capacities]

HOLLY: It's good. [undifferentiated, but positive affect description] (sighs; facial muscles soften) [markers of positive parasympathetic activation]

THERAPIST: (conveying interest, curiosity) What lets you know it feels 'good?' Is there a sensation in your body, or an energy, or maybe a movement your body wants to make…? **[helping client to experience a positive affect with increased bodily-rooted granularity, to maximize experience of positive affect]**

HOLLY: I guess I feel a bit lighter here (moves hands back and forth across upper chest) **[motoric and sensation channels of experience identified]**

THERAPIST: **[metaprocessing; attempting to help client deepen positive affect]** What's that like, to feel that 'bit lighter here'? (mimics client's hand movements)

HOLLY: It's good (smiles). I already said that, didn't I? (face flushes, head dips down **[shame re-emerging]**).

THERAPIST: (warmly, gently, and playfully) Yep! And that's OK (sincere, smiling) **[counteracting shame]**. We're **["we" = building attachment]** helping you get specific with your emotions. Emotions give us so much important information about ourselves and about what we want and need **[offering psychoeducation, which can be regulating]**. I know this is hard, and you're doing a great job **[affirming]**.

HOLLY: (smile gets bigger, facial muscles relax) **[green signal affect emerging]** (pauses; a more serious facial expression emerges) You know, my parents have no idea how long I've been living with this (eyes begin to get glassy) **[glimmer of core emotion]**

THERAPIST: (gently) **[wanting to deepen this glimmer of core emotion]** Your eyes just got glassy. There's an emotion stirring inside...

HOLLY: (tears starting to well up in eyes) **[core emotion continuing to emerge]** I'm just so tired of doing this on my own. I want to tell them I need their help, but I don't know if I can. (tears disappearing, starting to talk faster) **[signaling possible emergence of anxiety...]** Because Grandad is so sick right now and they have their hands full, and I don't want to worry them **[...and then defense]**, and I...

THERAPIST: (gently interrupting) Holly...would it be OK if we just take a breath together? **[to regulate anxiety]**

HOLLY: OK (looks at therapist; takes two diaphragmatic breaths with the therapist; tears well up) **[with anxiety more regulated, core emotion re-emerges]**

THERAPIST: (softly) What's this emotion, right now?

HOLLY: I feel sad. Like, in my heart, it feels like wringing out a dishtowel (hand curls into a fist at heart level; tears running down face) **[bodily-rooted, core affective experience described with granularity including image of dishtowel, motor movements, and emotion accurately labeled]**

THERAPIST: Would it be OK for us **[explicit acknowledgment of attachment, dyadic emotion regulation]** to make some space for the sadness that's in your heart? (mirroring client's clenched fist at heart level) **[attempting to deepen core affect with body-focused experiencing, to help client process sadness to completion]**

HOLLY: (nods, tears continue to flow, with breath hitching) **[client is in a core affective, State 2, experience]**

THERAPIST: (gently) You're doing an amazing job being with this sadness **[affirming]**. Can you feel me here with you? **[undoing aloneness, making explicit the dyadic affect regulation process and secure attachment]** (Holly: "Uh huh") Is that heart-wringing feeling still there? (Holly: "Uh huh") What else do you notice, as you really inhabit this sad feeling? **[helping client stay in State 2 so that sadness can be felt to completion]**

HOLLY: There's not much energy. It feels heavy... (another wave of tears emerges)

THERAPIST: (kindly and with feeling) I'm so feeling that sadness with you. **[explicit acknowledgment of dyadic affect regulation]**... What's that like, to be feeling the sadness, here with me? **[undoing aloneness; explicitly highlighting the attachment bond]**.

HOLLY: It's hard. (long pause) But it's good **[a 'feels- right'-even-if-painful transformation moment]**. (begins to wipe her eyes with a tissue; hitching sigh) It's actually a relief that someone understands me **[signaling the completion of a wave of sadness; post-breakthrough affect emerging: Second State Transformation]**

THERAPIST: Where are you feeling the relief in your body? [helping client to deepen the visceral experience of post-breakthrough affect]

HOLLY: In my shoulders.

THERAPIST: Let's see if we can stay with that relief feeling a little. What does the relief feel like in your shoulders? **[facilitating the client staying with the bodily experience of relief]**

HOLLY: Just, lighter...kind of like, a bit tingly.

THERAPIST: What's that like, to be with that lighter feeling, that tingliness? **[metaprocessing]**

HOLLY: It's cool (smiles uncertainly)....I can't believe I just let myself feel sad! [State 3 realization and mastery affects emerging: the 'wow' of the emergent realization of change, surprising of self, pride]

THERAPIST: Wow, yes. How cool is that? **[affirming, showing delight in the client]** It looks like you surprised yourself!

HOLLY: Holy cow...I sure did! (giggles)

THERAPIST: (smiling, matching client's non-verbals) What's that like to have done that? **[metaprocessing]**

HOLLY: It's weird! But, you know, 'good weird,' if that makes sense (client's head is tilting, eyes moving from side to side) **[signaling newness, potential tremulous affect]**

THERAPIST: That makes total sense! What would it be like, I wonder, to really lean into that 'good-weird' feeling? **[wanting to somatically deepen this new affective experience]**

HOLLY: OK (eyes widening). (pause) Wow, that's so cool. And still weird! ["weird-cool" is a realization affect, suggesting transformational experience occurring]

THERAPIST: (smiling) I feel so proud of you, like my heart is all bursty! **[genuine therapist self-disclosure, affirming and delighting in the client]** (pausing) What's it like for you to hear that I feel proud of you? **[helping to build client's receptive affective capacities]**

HOLLY: It feels...kind of...warm...and settled...here (points to torso) **[client is authentically receiving the therapist, experienced bodily by the client]**...(long pause), which is also weird. And different.

THERAPIST: Just take a moment to feel into that warm, settled feeling, here with me **[grounding this in body-focused and also relational experience]** (client nods)

HOLLY: (long pause) You know, I know my parents love me. I feel like they would probably want to know I was struggling even if they have a lot going on right now. They've told me, like, a million times, to let them know if I need help. It feels a bit scary to ask, but, right now, if they were here in the room, I think I could do it **[harnessing of adaptive action tendencies of sadness including reaching out,**

help- and comfort-seeking; feeling pride in self; courage and resolve emerging; Third State Transformation, positive valuation of the self].

From this point, the exchange could proceed in many different directions, depending on what emerges in the client's experience and what the therapist chooses to facilitate based on tracking the client. Another wave of core sadness could emerge, or mourning of the self for having believed she was burdensome for such a long time (State 3: emotional pain), or moving into State 4 (core state), as examples.

EFT Transcript

EFT interventions are based on in-session markers identified through moment-to-moment assessment. Holly's concern about being honest with her parents brings up the markers of self-criticism, "I should be over this," and behavioral self-interruption, "I shouldn't ask them for help." Although she wants their support, there is a part of her that is interrupting her from getting this need met. In this transcript, the therapist helps the client to identify and work through the blocker with the two-chair intervention. Classic EFT self-interruptive splits are focused on a blocked emotion or expression; however, chair work can also be adapted to other behavioral issues that are recovery-interfering (e.g., "don't eat" and "don't have your parents involved"). The transcript that follows illustrates how EFT interventions are fluid; the outlined intervention focuses on self-interruption, but the final line opens opportunity to shift to unfinished business as Holly connects with feelings regarding her mother.

HOLLY: (eyes redden) I want to ask them to help me, you know, but they don't even know I'm still doing the ED. They think I'm fine now. (pauses, looks down) I should be over this.

THERAPIST: (speaking as the client) It's almost like on the one hand "I want to tell them everything and would love their support," but on the other hand "I'm so afraid of making them worried, that I'd rather just stay quiet." **[empathic conjecture]**

HOLLY: (nods head in agreement) I'm so lost... I just want to be honest about how hard it is. I hate pretending to be OK when I'm freaking inside.

THERAPIST: Um-hm, it's like there's something that stops you though. And that's so frustrating. **[identifying self-interruptive marker]**

HOLLY: Um-hm.

THERAPIST: Can we connect to that part? The part that always seems to stop you from asking for help?

HOLLY: OK.

THERAPIST: (faces a chair in front of Holly for two-chair intervention) OK, so come over here (to the 'critic/blocker' chair) and I want you to be the part of yourself that stops you from telling them. Picture yourself there (in the self-chair) and command her. Is it like: 'Don't say anything, don't open your mouth, don't go there...' **[exploratory]**

HOLLY: OK, yeah, it's like. 'You should be over this, you don't need help. You're being so weak.'

THERAPIST: And speak the command...you know, it's like 'don't...'

HOLLY: Yeah, it's like, 'Don't go there, grandad is sick, and even if he wasn't, there's a reason why you haven't gone there.'

THERAPIST: 'You don't have the strength to go there, I don't believe you can handle it.' **[evoking the blocker]**

HOLLY: 'You can't handle it. You've proven that. You just can't handle it.'

THERAPIST: And tell her what it is...that she can't handle it...like is it psychiatric hospitalization? **[naming the fear]**

HOLLY: No, it's just...I snap when people try to help me.

THERAPIST: Snap? **[clarification]**

HOLLY: Yeah, I get really mean to my parents.

THERAPIST: Oh...remind her. Remind her what happened last time she let them in.

HOLLY: 'You get evil, you yell and throw things.'

THERAPIST: 'So you need to listen to me because if you don't, things will get out of hand.'

HOLLY: 'Yeah, you get crazy.'

THERAPIST: Not get, tell her 'You are crazy.'

HOLLY: 'You are crazy.'

THERAPIST: 'And so I'm protecting you. I don't want you to overwhelm your parents with all this crazy.'

HOLLY: 'Yeah, you would scare them away.'

THERAPIST: 'The shame would be too much, you would lose too much, and then you would be all alone... because they can't handle it.'

HOLLY: Yeah.

THERAPIST: 'And so I'm protecting you. I don't want you to overwhelm your parents and lose them. I don't want you to hurt anyone else in the process.'

HOLLY: I don't want anyone else to have to deal with this and so...

THERAPIST: 'So keep your crazy mouth shut. Keep stuff really deep.'

HOLLY: 'Yeah, keep it inside.'

THERAPIST: 'You owe it to them to keep it together.'

HOLLY: (overwhelmed, sad) Yeah.

THERAPIST: OK, come over here? **[gives a moment for Holly to switch to the "self" or "experiencing" chair (Dolhanty & Greenberg, 2009)]** Take a breath, ok? What's that like to hear that? (breathe to regulate)

HOLLY: It makes sense.

THERAPIST: It does make sense. Tell her (pointing at the critic/blocker chair).

HOLLY: It makes sense.

THERAPIST: And tell her what it's like to make sense.

HOLLY: (tears welling) It's so hard. I feel so alone.

THERAPIST: It is so lonely. It's unbearable. What else? Tell her.

HOLLY: I'm so tired. I always have to perform. It's so much work.

THERAPIST: It is so much work. And tell her what it's like, to not be able to handle it.

HOLLY: It's just exhausting.

THERAPIST: It is. And so tell her: 'I am just so exhausted.'

HOLLY: (deep sigh) I am so exhausted.

THERAPIST: Speak the sigh.

HOLLY: I'm exhausted and, I don't want to be exhausted, but I don't know what to do because I feel like because, yeah, I just don't know what to do because if I…

THERAPIST: Um-hm, so tell her, what do you need?

HOLLY: I need help, but I'm afraid to ask.

As Holly attends to the "blocker" voice, she is able to understand its impact and identify her healthy needs. The therapist continues the work by asking her to express gratitude to the "blocker" for its function of protecting her from fear of abandonment (through deep validation) and supports her to express gratitude for its protective function. It is important to note that until the blocker has been deeply validated and appreciated, it is unlikely to transform. In the following, the therapist helps Holly to offer compassion and reassurance to this part of herself, in order to help integrate it.

THERAPIST: Right, and so there's still this part. I can hear her. I think she is terrified. She's protecting you. And so can you tell her 'thank you'?

HOLLY: Thank you.

THERAPIST: 'Thank you for protecting me because I really needed you.'

HOLLY: Yeah, I needed you and you've helped me.

THERAPIST: You've brought me through so much.

HOLLY: Yeah, you help me do so much.

THERAPIST: And so it's almost like you need to tell her, like 'I love you. You have saved me from so much.'

HOLLY: You have saved me from so much, but I'm so exhausted.

THERAPIST: It's so exhausting. 'So I need you to help me bring in some more help. And don't worry, I'm not going to kick you out. I want you to stay, I really do.' She's your identity drive and she has saved you. 'And so when I say thank you, it's not empty.' We are genuinely loving her up. She is a gift. But I also hear you saying 'I can't keep going this way, and I am yearning for more support.'

HOLLY: (nodding, tears welling) I do want my parents involved.

THERAPIST: Speak the tears, tell her.

HOLLY: You make it so scary, but I feel so lonely living this lie. I need more support.

THERAPIST: And so it's like 'I hear you want to protect me, and I'm grateful for that, but I also want to find a way for my parents to be involved.'

HOLLY: (hesitant, then nods in agreement)

THERAPIST: What's bigger? The pause or the nod?

HOLLY: The nod.

THERAPIST: The nod. You do want your parents involved. You need them. Tell her again.

EFFT Transcript

After working through her fear and shame with two-chair work followed by empty-chair work for the unfinished business intervention (see before), Holly agreed it would be helpful to allow her therapist meet with her parents. Holly sent her parents a text explaining that she had been struggling and would rather not go into detail with them right now, but that she wanted them to meet with her therapist so that they could learn how to better help her. Her parents responded with concern and immediately made an appointment with Holly's therapist. Holly's therapist did not have consent to share specific information, which is of no concern in the context of EFFT given the treatment target of attending to and working through emotion and its avoidance within the family, with parents regarded as experts on their child and leading this process.

After brief introductions, the therapist validates Holly's parents' feelings about their having received the text about her struggle: fear, shame, and sadness. They admit that they had wondered if things were spiraling due to a significant increase in her food intake, but they didn't want to comment on their observations for fear of causing their daughter further distress. The therapist attends to and validates the parents' emotions and provides them with psychoeducation about the EFFT model, with a focus on emotion coaching as an adjunct to meal support and symptom interruption.

THERAPIST: It can be hard to know what to say in those moments. The ones where she's clearly struggling with a meal, but also trying to keep a smile. It's the internal battle like 'Honey, I see that you need something, but I don't know if I should approach or retreat because I'm scared of saying the wrong thing or making it worse!' **[validation]**

MOM: Oh my goodness, that's where I get myself into trouble! I've tried to help in the past, but it always ends up exploding, so now I'm afraid to open my mouth or even be in the room.

DAD: It's true. Whatever we say is likely to be the wrong thing. We can't look at her sideways without a wall going up.

THERAPIST: Um-hm, it can sometimes feel like speaking another language. Some individuals with ED are overly attuned to others' experiences with emotion, and feel their own emotions quite deeply. Oftentimes, they lack the resources to regulate and ED symptoms become a way to manage stress. This means that reactions can seem out of proportion with events, and this is further exacerbated by the rigidity of a starved brain.

MOM: So what do we do?

THERAPIST: I'm going to help you learn how to speak her language. Over the next couple of sessions, we will review how to apply the steps of emotion coaching, but for today, let's focus on validation. This is both the most profound, and hardest, part of the work! And I am going to work with you until you feel comfortable with it. **[unconditional positive regard for the parents' capacity]**

The therapist proceeds to review what validation is and is not (is putting yourself in your loved one's shoes, is not placing judgment or trying to make the uncomfortable emotion/content go away). After the parents have the basics, they practice validating some of the statements that Holly says where they feel stuck, such as: when Holly says, "I feel fat."

PREVIOUS RESPONSE: You are beautiful, and besides, remember that you need to focus on things other than appearance.

NEW RESPONSE (VALIDATION): Ugh, that is such an uncomfortable feeling, it's the worst feeling in the world! Like you want to hide under a blanket, deep in the basement and not show your face until you feel better. I'm so sorry honey.

Comparing and Contrasting EFT, EFFT, and AEDP for Use in ED Treatment

In considering AEDP, EFT and EFFT as applied to the treatment of EDs, all three psychotherapies privilege emotional transformation through bodily-based emotional experiencing. Additionally, they share the following: they aim to help individuals with EDs (and, in EFFT, also their families) (1) increase their awareness and utilization of core adaptive emotions; (2) experience and process emotions to completion; and (3) experience and benefit from healthy, genuine relationships – all in service of diminishing the need for ED behaviors to regulate affect. Furthermore, each of the modalities employs moment-by-moment, in-session assessment/tracking of clients' subjective experiencing, which guides interventions with clients and parents alike. Each modality also emphasizes individuals' and/or families' strengths, resilience, adaptations, and resources and explicitly affirms these. In AEDP and EFT, the relationship between client and therapist is assumed to be fundamental to the change process (Fosha et al., 2009; Greenberg, 2014). In EFFT, the client is seen as the bond between the parents and child; therefore, the therapist's role is integral in offering positive regard and supporting parents to work through blocks. While the therapy relationship is central to all three therapies, AEDP differs in its more explicit focus on the experiential processing of the therapist-client attachment. The intervention of *metaprocessing* also appears to be unique to AEDP, wherein the experience of transformation itself is processed (Fosha et al., 2009).

Prevention Considerations

The commonalities between EFT, EFFT, and AEDP suggest that one aspect of preventing EDs (as situated within the complex, multifactorial nature of EDs, including biological, psychological, and social components) is helping children become efficacious with their emotions. If an individual experiences mastery in feeling and processing emotions and believes that her support people can offer attuned responses, she will be less likely to rely on ED symptoms for emotion regulation.

Summary and Conclusions

Emotion-based psychotherapies offer myriad interventions for helping individuals with EDs. In this chapter, we have provided overviews of the theory and practice of three such therapies: AEDP, EFT, and EFFT. Many similarities exist among the modalities, most notably that, if individuals can be supported to be connected to their bodies, they will be more able to navigate emotional pain without using ED symptoms to help them escape these experiences.

References

Aldao, A., Nolen-Hoeksema, S., & Schweizer, S. (2010). Emotion-regulation strategies across psychopathology: A meta-analytic review. *Clinical Psychology Review, 30*, 217–237. doi:10.1016/j.cpr.2009.11.004

Angus, L., Goldman, R., & Mergenthaler, E. (2008). Introduction. One case, multiple measures: An intensive case-analytic approach to understanding client change processes in evidence-based, emotion-focused therapy of depression. *Psychotherapy Research, 18*(6), 629–633. doi:10.1080/10503300802430673

Barrett, L. F., Gross, J., Christensen, T. C., & Benvenuto, M. (2001). Knowing what you're feeling and knowing what to do about it: Mapping the relation between emotion differentiation and emotion regulation. *Cognition & Emotion, 15*(6), 713–724. doi:10.1080/02699930143000239

Berenbaum, H., Raghavan, C., Le, H. N., Vernon, L. L., & Gomez, J. J. (2003). A taxonomy of emotional disturbances. *Clinical Psychology: Science and Practice, 10*(2), 206–226. doi:10.1093/clipsy.bpg011

Bowlby, J. (1988). *A secure base: Parent-child attachment and healthy human development.* New York, NY: Basic Books.

Brennan, M. A., Emmerling, M. E., & Whelton, W. J. (2014). Emotion-focused group therapy: Addressing self-criticism in the treatment of eating disorders. *Counselling and Psychotherapy Research*, 1–9. doi:10.1080/14733145.2014. 914549

Brockmeyer, T., Skunde, M., Wu, M., Bresslein, E., Rudofsky, G., Herzog, W., & Friederich, H. C. (2014). Difficulties in emotion regulation across the spectrum of eating disorders. *Comprehensive Psychiatry, 55*(3), 565–571. doi:10.1016/j. comppsych.2013.12.001

Courtois, C. A., & Ford, J. D. (Eds). (2009). *Treating complex traumatic stress disorders: An evidence-based guide.* New York, NY: Guilford.

Damasio, A. R. (1999). *The feeling of what happens: Body and emotion in the making of consciousness.* New York, NY: Harcourt Brace.

Darwin, C. (1965). *The expression of emotion in man and animals.* Chicago, IL: University of Chicago Press. (Original work published 1872).

Davies, H., Schmidt, U., Stahl, D., & Tchanturia, K. (2011). Evoked facial emotional expression and emotional experience in people with anorexia nervosa. *International Journal of Eating Disorders, 44*(6), 531–539. doi:10.1002/eat.20852

Davies, H., Swan, N., Schmidt, U., & Tchanturia, K. (2012). An experimental investigation of verbal expression of emotion in anorexia and bulimia nervosa. *European Eating Disorders Review, 20*(6), 476–483. doi:10.1002/erv.1157

Dolhanty, J., & Greenberg, L. S. (2007). Emotion-focused therapy in the treatment of eating disorders. *European Psychotherapy, 7*(1), 97–116. Retrieved from www. drjoannedolhanty.com/wordpress/wp-content/uploads/2017/02/06-Eating_ DolhantyK.pdf

Dolhanty, J., & Greenberg, L. S. (2009). Emotion-focused therapy in a case of anorexia nervosa. *Clinical Psychology & Psychotherapy, 16*(4), 336–382. Retrieved from www.drjoannedolhanty.com/wordpress/wp-content/uploads/2017/02/ EFT.AN_.case_.pdf

Engel, S. G., Wonderlich, S. A., Crosby, R. D., Wright, T. L., Mitchell, J. E., Crow, S. J., & Venegoni, E. E. (2005). A study of patients with anorexia nervosa using ecologic momentary assessment. *International Journal of Eating Disorders, 38*(4), 335–339. doi:10.1002/eat.20184

Fosha, D. (2000). *The transforming power of affect: A model for accelerated change.* New York, NY: Basic Books.

Fosha, D. (2001). The dyadic regulation of affect. *Journal of Clinical Psychology/In Session. 57*(2), 227–242. http://dx.doi.org.ezproxy.library.ubc. ca/10.1002/1097-4679(200102)57:2<227::AID-JCLP8>3.0.CO;2-1

Fosha, D. (2003). Dyadic regulation and experiential work with emotion and relatedness in trauma and disorganized attachment. In M. F. Solomon & D. J. Siegel (Eds), *Healing trauma: Attachment, mind, body, and brain* (pp. 221–281). New York, NY: Norton.

Fosha, D. (2005). Emotion, true self, true other, core state: toward a clinical theory of affective change process. *Psychoanalytic Review, 92*(4), 513–552. doi:10.1521/prev.2005.92.4.513

Fosha, D. (2008). Transformance, recognition of self by self, and effective action. In K. J. Schneider (Ed.), *Existential-integrative psychotherapy: Guideposts to the core of practice* (pp. 290–320). New York, NY: Routledge.

Fosha, D. (2009). Emotion and recognition at work: Energy, vitality, pleasure, truth, desire & the emergent phenomenology of transformational experience. In D. Fosha, D. J. Siegel & M. F. Solomon (Eds.), *The healing power of emotion: Affective neuroscience, development, clinical practice* (pp. 172–203). New York, NY: Norton.

Fosha, D. (2010). Wired for Healing: Thirteen ways of looking at AEDP. *Transformance: The AEDP Journal, 1*(1). Retrieved from www.aedpinstitute.org/transformance/wired-for-healing/content/uploads/2015/09/2013_Fosha_Emergence_Neuropsychotherapist.pdf

Fosha, D. (2013). A heaven in a wild flower: Self, dissociation, and treatment in the context of the neurobiological core self. *Psychoanalytic Inquiry, 33*, 496–523. doi:10.108007351690.2013.815067

Fosha, D., Paivio, S. C., Gleiser, K., & Ford, J. (2009). Experiential and emotion-focused therapy. In C. Courtois & J. D. Ford (Eds), *Complex traumatic stress disorders: An evidence-based clinician's guide* (pp. 286–311). New York, NY: Guilford.

Fox, J. R., & Power, M. J. (2009). Eating disorders and multi-level models of emotion: An integrated model. *Clinical Psychology & Psychotherapy, 16*(4), 240–267. doi:10.1002/cpp.626

Gendlin, E. T. (1996). *Focusing-oriented psychotherapy: A manual of the experiential method.* New York, NY: Guilford. Retrieved from www.focusing.org/gendlin/docs/gol_2144.html

Goldman, R., & Greenberg, L. (1997). Case formulation in process experiential psychotherapy. In T. Eells (Ed.), *Handbook of psychotherapy case formulation* (pp. 402–429). New York, NY: Guilford.

Greenberg, L. (1996). Allowing and accepting emotional experience. In R. Kavanaugh, B. Zimmerberg-Glick, & S. Fein (Eds), *Emotion: Interdisciplinary perspectives* (pp. 315–336). Mahwah, NJ: Erlbaum.

Greenberg, L. (1999). Ideal psychotherapy research: A study of significant change processes. *Journal of Clinical Psychology, 55*, 467–1480. doi:10.1002/(SICI)1097–4679(199912)55:12<1467::AID-JCLP5>3.0.CO;2-2

Greenberg, L. (2006). Emotion-focused therapy: A synopsis. *Journal of Contemporary Psychotherapy, 36*(2), 87–93. doi:10.1007/s10879-006-9011-3

Greenberg, L. S. (2008). Emotion and cognition in psychotherapy: The transforming power of affect. *Canadian Psychology/Psychologie canadienne, 49*(1), 49. doi:10.1037/0708-5591.49.1.49

Greenberg, L. S. (2010). Emotion-focused therapy: A clinical synthesis. *Focus, 8*(1), 32–42. doi:10.1176/foc.8.1.foc32

Greenberg, L. S. (2012). Emotions, the great captains of our lives: Their role in the process of change in psychotherapy. *American Psychologist, 67*(8), 697–707. doi:10.1037/a0029858.

Greenberg, L. (2014). The therapeutic relationship in emotion-focused therapy. *Psychotherapy, 51*(3), 350. doi:10.1037/a0037336

Greenberg, L. S., & Goldman, R. (2007). Case formulation in emotion-focused therapy. In T. D. Eells (Ed.), *Handbook of psychotherapy case formulation* (2nd ed.; pp. 379–411). New York, NY: Guilford Press. Retrieved from http://shadowsgovernment.com/shadows-library/Eells/Handbook%20of%20psychotherapy%20case%20formulation%20(524)/Handbook%20of%20psychotherapy%20case%20formulation%20-%20Eells.pdf#page=3960

Greenberg, L., & Watson, J. (1998). Experiential therapy of depression: Differential effects of client-centered relationship conditions and process experiential interventions. *Psychotherapy Research, 8*(2), 210–224. doi:10.1093/ptr/8.2.210

Greenberg, L. S., & Watson, J. C. (2005). *Emotion-focused therapy of depression*. Washington, DC: American Psychological Association.

Greenberg, L., Auszra, L., & Herrmann, I. (2007). The relationship between emotional productivity, emotional arousal and outcome in experiential therapy of depression. *Psychotherapy Research, 2*, 57–66. doi:10.1080/10503300600977800

Gross, J. J., & Jazaieri, H. (2014). Emotion, emotion regulation, and psychopathology: An affective science perspective. *Clinical Psychological Science, 2*(4), 387–401. doi:10.1177/2167702614536164

Harrison, A., Tchanturia, K., & Treasure, J. (2010). Attentional bias, emotion recognition, and emotion regulation in anorexia: state or trait? *Biological Psychiatry, 68*(8), 755–761. doi:10.1016/j.biopsych.2010.04.037

Iwakabe, S., & Conceicao, N. (2016). Metatherapeutic processing as a change-based therapeutic immediacy task: Building an initial process model using a task-analytic research strategy. *Journal of Psychotherapy Integration, 26*(3), 230–247. doi:10.1037/int0000016

Kearney-Cooke, A., & Striegel-Moore, R. (1997). The etiology and treatment of body image disturbance. In D. M. Garner & P. E. Garfinkel (Eds), *Handbook of treatment for eating disorders* (2nd ed.; pp. 295–306). New York, NY: Guilford.

Lafrance, A., & Dolhanty, J. (2013). *Emotion-focused family therapy for eating disorders*. Two day caregiver workshop manual.

Lafrance Robinson, A., & Kosmerly, S. (2015). The influence of clinician emotion on decisions in child and adolescent eating disorder treatment: A survey of self and others. *Eating Disorders, 23*(2), 163–176. doi:10.1080/10640266.2014.976107

Lafrance Robinson, A., Dolhanty, J., Stillar, A., Henderson, K., & Mayman, S. (2014). Emotion-focused family therapy for eating disorders across the lifespan: A pilot study of a 2-Day transdiagnostic intervention for parents. *Clinical Psychology & Psychotherapy, 23*(1), 14–23. doi:10.1002/cpp.1933

Lamagna, J. (2015). Making good use of suffering: Intra-relational work with pathogenic affects. *Transformance: The AEDP Journal, 6*(1). Retrieved from www.aedpinstitute.org/transformance/making-good-use-of-suffering-intra-relational-work-with-pathogenic-affects/

Lavender, J. M., Wonderlich, S. A., Peterson, C. B., Crosby, R. D., Engel, S. G., Mitchell, J. E., …, & Berg, K. C. (2014). Dimensions of emotion dysregulation in bulimia nervosa. *European Eating Disorders Review, 22*(3), 212–216. doi:10.1002/erv.2288

Lavender, J. M., Wonderlich, S. A., Engel, S. G., Gordon, K. H., Kaye, W. H., & Mitchell, J. E. (2015). Dimensions of emotion dysregulation in anorexia nervosa and bulimia nervosa: A conceptual review of the empirical literature. *Clinical Psychology Review, 40*, 111–122. doi:10.1016/j.cpr.2015.05.010

Lazarus, R. S. (1991). *Emotion and adaptation*. New York, NY: Oxford University Press.

Lipton, B., & Fosha, D. (2011). Attachment as a transformative process in AEDP: Operationalizing the intersection of attachment theory and affective neuroscience. *Journal of Psychotherapy Integration, 21*(3), 253. doi:10.1037/a0025421

Lynch, T. R., Gray, K. L., Hempel, R. J., Titley, M., Chen, E. Y., & O'Mahen, H. A. (2013). Radically open-dialectical behavior therapy for adult anorexia nervosa: Feasibility and outcomes from an inpatient program. *BMC Psychiatry*, *13*(1), 293. doi:10.1186/1471-244X–13–293

Main, M. (1999). Epilogue. Attachment theory: Eighteen points with suggestions for future studies. In J. Cassidy & P. R. Shaver (Eds), *Handbook of attachment: Theory, research and clinical applications* (pp. 845–888). New York, NY: Guilford.

Mars, D. (2011). AEDP for couples: From stuckness and reactivity to the felt experience of love. *Transformance: The AEDP Journal*, *2*(1). Retrieved from www.aedpinstitute.org/transformance/aedp-for-couples/

Mauss, I. B., Levenson, R. W., McCarter, L., Wilhelm, F. H., & Gross, J. J. (2005). The tie that binds? Coherence among emotion experience, behavior, and physiology. *Emotion*, *5*(2), 175. doi:10.1037/1528-3542.5.2.175

McNally, S., Timulak, L., & Greenberg, L. S. (2014). Transforming emotion schemes in emotion focused therapy: A case study investigation. *Person-Centered & Experiential Psychotherapies*, *13*(2), 128–149. doi:10.1080/14779757.2013.871573

Nowakowski, M. E., McFarlane, T., & Cassin, S. (2013). Alexithymia and eating disorders: A critical review of the literature. *Journal of Eating Disorders*, *1*(1), 21. doi:10.1186/2050–2974-1–21

Oldershaw, A., Lavender, T., Sallis, H., Stahl, D., & Schmidt, U. (2015). Emotion generation and regulation in anorexia nervosa: A systematic review and meta-analysis of self-report data. *Clinical Psychology Review*, *39*, 83–95. doi:10.1016/j.cpr.2015.04.005

Paivio, S. C., & Greenberg, L. S. (2001). Introduction: Treating emotion regulation problems. *Journal of clinical psychology*, *57*(2), doi:153–155.10.1002/1097–4679 (200102)57:2<153::AID-JCLP2>3.0.CO;2-F

Paivio, S. C., & Nieuwenhuis, J. A. (2001). Efficacy of emotion focused therapy for adult survivors of child abuse: A preliminary study. *Journal of Traumatic Stress*, *14*(1), 115–133. doi:10.1023/A:1007891716593

Pando-Mars, K. (2016). Tailoring AEDP interventions to attachment style. *Transformance: The AEDP Journal*, *6*(2). Retrieved from www.aedpinstitute.org/transformance/tailoring-aedp-interventions-to-attachment-style-pg1/

Panksepp, J. (2009). Brain emotional systems and qualities of mental life: From animal models of affect to implications for psychotherapeutics. In D. Fosha, D. J. Siegel, & Solomon, M. F. (Eds), *The healing power of emotion: Affective neuroscience, development, & clinical practice* (pp. 1–26). New York, NY: Norton.

Prenn, N. (2009). I second that emotion! On self-disclosure and its metaprocessing. In A. Bloomgarden & R. B. Mennuti (Eds), *Psychotherapist revealed: Therapists speak about self-disclosure in psychotherapy* (pp. 85–99). New York, NY: Routledge.

Robinson, A. L., & Dolhanty, J. (2013). Emotion-focused family therapy for eating disorders across the lifespan. *Bulletin*, *28*(3), Toronto, ON: National Eating Disorder Information Centre. Retrieved from www.drjoannedolhanty.com/wordpress/wp-content/uploads/2017/02/NEDIC.EFFT_.pdf

Robinson, A. L., Dolhanty, J., & Greenberg, L. (2013). Emotion-focused family therapy for eating disorders in children and adolescents. *Clinical Psychology & Psychotherapy*, *22*(1), 75–82. doi:10.1002/cpp.1861

Robinson, A. L., Strahan, E., Girz, L., Wilson, A., & Boachie, A. (2013). 'I know I can help you': Parental self-efficacy predicts adolescent outcomes in Family-based

Therapy for Eating Disorders. *European Eating Disorders Review, 21*(2), 108–114. doi:10.1002/erv.2180

Russell, E. (2015). *Restoring resilience: Discovering your clients' capacity for healing.* New York, NY: Norton.

Russell, E., & Fosha, D. (2008). Transformational affects and core state in AEDP: The emergence and consolidation of joy, hope, gratitude and confidence in the (solid goodness of the) self. *Journal of Psychotherapy Integration, 18*(2), 167–190. doi:10.1037/1053-0479.18.2.167

Schore, A. N. (2009). Right brain affect regulation: An essential mechanism of development, trauma, dissociation, and psychotherapy. In D. Fosha, D. J. Siegel, & M. F. Solomon (Eds), *The healing power of emotion: Affective neuroscience, development, clinical practice.* Chapter 5. New York, NY: Norton.

Selby, E. A., Wonderlich, S. A., Crosby, R. D., Engel, S. G., Panza, E., Mitchell, J. E., ..., & Le Grange, D. (2014). Nothing tastes as good as thin feels: Low positive emotion differentiation and weight-loss activities in anorexia nervosa. *Clinical Psychological Science, 2*(4), 514–531. http://dx.doi.org.ezproxy.library.ubc.ca/10.1177/2167702613512794

Serpell, L., Teasdale, J. D., Troop, N. A., & Treasure, J. (2004). The development of the P-CAN, a measure to operationalize the pros and cons of anorexia nervosa. *International Journal of Eating Disorders, 36*(4), 416–433. doi:10.1002/eat.20040

Siegel, D. J. (1999). *The developing mind* (vol. 296). New York, NY: Guilford Press.

Stillar, A., Strahan, E., Nash, P., Files, N., Scarborough, J., Mayman, S., ..., & Marchand, P. (2016). The influence of carer fear and self-blame when supporting a loved one with an eating disorder. *Eating Disorders, 24*(2), 173–185. doi:10.1080/10640266.2015.1133210

Strahan, E., Stillar, A., Files, N., Nash, P., Scarborough, J., Connors, L., ..., & Lafrance, A. (2017). Increasing self-efficacy with emotion-focused family therapy for eating disorders: A process model. *Person-Centered and Experiential Psychotherapies,* 1–14. doi:10.1080/14779757.2017.1330703

Svaldi, J., Griepenstroh, J., Tuschen-Caffier, B., & Ehring, T. (2012). Emotion regulation deficits in eating disorders: A marker of eating pathology or general psychopathology? *Psychiatry Research, 197*(1), 103–111. doi:10.1016/j.psychres.2011.11.009

Tomkins, S. S. (1962–3). *Affect, imagery, and consciousness: Vols. 1 & 2.* New York, NY: Springer.

Treasure, J. (2012). Emotion in eating disorders. *European Eating Disorders Review, 20*(6), 429–430. doi:10.1002/erv.221

Treasure, J., Schmidt, U., & Macdonald, P. (Eds.). (2009). *The Clinician's guide to collaborative caring in eating disorders: The new Maudsley method.* London, UK: Routledge.

Treasure, J., Schmidt, U. H., & Troop, N. A. (2000). Cognitive analytic therapy and the transtheoretical framework. In K. J. Miller & S. J. Mizes (Eds), *Comparative treatments for eating disorders* (pp. 283–308). New York, NY: Springer.

Waller, G., Babbs, M., Milligan, R., Meyer, C., Ohanian, V., & Leung, N. (2003). Anger and core beliefs in the eating disorders. *International Journal of Eating Disorders, 34*(1), 118–124. doi:10.1002/eat.10163

Watson, J. C., & Greenberg, L. S. (1996). Pathways to change in the psychotherapy of depression: Relating process to session change and outcome. *Psychotherapy Theory Research & Practice, 33*(2), 262–274: doi:10.1037/0033-3204.33.2.262

Winnicott, D. W. (1960/1965). Ego distortion in terms of true and false self. In *The maturational processes and the facilitating environment* (pp. 140–152). New York, NY: International Universities Press.

Wonderlich, S. A., Peterson, C. B., Crosby, R. D., Smith, T. L., Klein, M. H., Mitchell, J. E., & Crow, S. J. (2014). A randomized controlled comparison of integrative cognitive-affective therapy (ICAT) and enhanced cognitive-behavioral therapy (CBT-E) for bulimia nervosa. *Psychological Medicine, 44*(3), 543–553. doi:10.1017/S0033291713001098

Yeung, D., & Fosha, D. (2015). Accelerated experiential dynamic osychotherapy. In *The sage encyclopedia of theory in counseling and psychotherapy*. New York, NY: Sage.

Zajonc, R. B. (1985). Emotion and facial efference: A theory reclaimed. *Science, 228,* 15–22. Retrieved from www.communicationcache.com/uploads/1/0/8/8/10887248/emotion_and_facial_efference-_a_theory_reclaimed.pdf

18 "Free To Be"

An Embodiment Program for Youth

Renae Y. Regehr and Rhea L. Owens

Jean Kilbourne, a pioneer advocate for media literacy, states that

> The advertisers have an enormous amount of money and power. But we can use their weight against them. We can use their very images to educate about their real messages. We can redefine the crucial concepts – love, rebellion, sexuality, friendship, freedom – that advertising has corrupted, and take them back for our own health, power, and fulfillment.
>
> (1999, p. 32)

Similarly, Tracy Tylka, a prominent body image researcher, suggests that "Removing negative [and] maladaptive characteristics but not teaching positive [and] adaptive characteristics will likely create intermediate health characterized by lack of pathology but the absence of vitality" (2011, p. 57). These quotes capture the goals of many body image programs: to improve health, instill power, and nurture vitality and fulfillment in individuals' lives. Generally, body image programs are designed to address many challenges adolescents face, such as social pressures and cognitive, social, and physical changes that impact their body image (e.g., Frisen & Holmqvist, 2010; Ricciardelli & McCabe, 2011; Wertheim & Paxton, 2011). Even though the majority of adolescents will not develop eating disorders, their lives may be characterized by a lack of self-actualization, underdeveloped talents, or floundering (Piran, 2015; Tylka, 2011). Recently, recommendations have been made to develop programs that address positive body image and related factors that contribute to growth and vitality in both boys and girls (Bucchianeri & Neumark-Sztainer, 2014; Tylka, 2011). In this chapter, we discuss positive body image and identify factors that increase or maintain positive body image. After, we explore how embodiment theory can inform eating disorder prevention and nurture positive body image in adolescents. Lastly, we briefly review existing body image programs and specifically describe Free To Be (FTB), a new positive body image program designed for adolescent boys and girls that was guided by embodiment theory (Piran, 2015; Piran & Teall, 2012).

Positive Body Image

Body image is a multidimensional construct that permeates biophysical, behavioral, affective, and cognitive domains (Smolak & Cash, 2011) and influences how a person positively or negatively experiences their life (Tylka, 2011). Based upon the research of Wood-Barcalow, Tylka, and Augustus-Horvath (2010), Holmqvist and Frisén (2012), and Frisén and Holmqvist (2010), the authors define positive body image as a predominant feeling of appreciation and respect for the body. Positive body image has been understood to be a separate, complex, and multidimensional construct that is not anchored on one end of a spectrum with negative body image anchored on the other (Tylka & Wood-Barcalow, 2015a). In other words, to have a positive body image does not necessarily mean that a person has low body dissatisfaction or low body preoccupation (Tylka, 2011).

Factors That Increase and Maintain Positive Body Image

To understand body image holistically, it is important to recognize that not everyone espouses a negative body image. Wood-Barcalow and Tylka (2010) have identified factors that are likely to increase positive body image: being media literate, environments that provide unconditional acceptance and support, environments that broadly conceptualize attractiveness, and the belief that a higher power has created each person to be inherently unique. Characteristics that coincide with having a positive body image include engaging in self-care, mentoring others, protectively filtering information, seeking out positive environments, appreciating and respecting the body, minimizing exposure to harmful media, emphasizing inner attributes as important, and having flexible standards of beauty (Frisén & Holmqvist, 2010; Holmqvist & Frisén, 2012; Tylka, 2011; Wood-Barcalow & Tylka, 2010). It is important to note that the precursors and outcomes of positive body image work in a reciprocal and cyclical manner to maintain a high level of positive body image (Tylka, 2011).

Increasing Positive Body Image through Positive Embodiment

More recently, there has been an increase in understanding positive body image through the lens of embodiment (Hefferon, 2015; Menzel & Levine, 2011; Piran & Teall, 2012). No firm consensus has been reached on the definition of embodiment. Therefore, to build on previous conceptualizations (e.g., Impett, Daubenmier, & Hirschman, 2006; Meier, Schnall, Schwarz, & Bargh, 2012; Piran & Teall, 2012) and for the purposes of this chapter and the FTB program, we defined embodiment as (a) being aware of thoughts, emotions, behaviors and bodily sensations, and (b) an overarching feeling of being present (as opposed to disconnected) within one's own physical body. As Young (1992) described, a person's identity and sense of self is "experienced in and through the body" (p. 90); the body is a vessel through which we experience life. Additionally, humans exist in a social world with others; therefore, it is important to recognize that social and cultural contexts are highly influential in shaping our sense of self (Piran & Teall, 2012).

Characteristics that express positive embodiment are (a) feeling attuned to one's states/needs/rights/desires; (b) feeling confident and assertive to move about and express one's states/needs/rights/desires and individuality; (c) feeling joy, comfort, connection, and other positive feelings about oneself and with others; and (d) actively engaging within the world (Piran & Teall, 2012). The developmental theory of embodiment examines and delineates factors within social, mental, and physical contexts that protect or hinder the development of negative and positive body image (Piran & Teall, 2012), which in turn can protect or hinder the onset of eating disorders (Piran, 2015). Such an integrated etiological model significantly extends positive body image research and the prevention of eating disorders and body dissatisfaction, because although oppressive discourse exists, exposure to negative or oppressive experiences will not necessarily lead to a negative body image if a person is able or taught to challenge, reframe, or reject negative messages (Piran, 2015). Further, if a person has a high level of positive embodiment, they are more likely to have higher levels of positive body image (Menzel & Levine, 2011). Thus, FTB is situated as a primary prevention program to eating disorders, and this chapter will focus on factors that promote positive body image. The goal of FTB is to increase positive body image through activities that increase characteristics of positive embodiment, such as developing media literacy awareness, cultivating individual strengths, building resilience to social pressures that impact body image, and nurturing a positive social environment.

Existing Positive Body Image Programs

To date, nearly all body image programs have focused on reducing body dissatisfaction and surrounding symptoms related to eating disorders among adolescent females (Yager, Diedrichs, Ricciardelli, & Halliwell, 2013). Yager and colleagues (2013) recently conducted a review of school-based body image programs for adolescents. They concluded that there is still a great need for universal-selective prevention programs targeting adolescent boys and girls. They stated that although programs thus far have been largely unsuccessful, there are promising interventions that demonstrate improvement in body image variables. In the 18 programs reviewed in developing FTB, including those from Yager et al.'s (2013) review (Dunstan, Paxton, & McLean, 2016; Golan, Hagay, & Tamir, 2013; Halliwell & Diedrichs, 2014; Halliwell, Jarman, McNamara, Risdon, & Jankowski, 2015;

McCabe, Ricciardelli, & Karantzas, 2010; O'Dea & Abraham, 2000; Richardson & Paxton, 2010; Richardson, Paxton, & Thomson, 2009; Sharpe, Schober, Treasure, & Schmidt, 2013; Stanford & McCabe, 2005; Steiner-Adair et al., 2002; Stewart, Carter, Drinkwater, Hainsworth, & Fairburn, 2001; Wade, Davidson, & O'Dea, 2003; Weiss & Wertheim, 2005; Wilksch, Tiggemann, & Wade, 2006; Wilksch & Wade, 2009; Wilksch, Durbridge, & Wade, 2008; Wiseman, Sunday, Bortolotti, & Halmi, 2004), aside from decreasing body dissatisfaction for high-risk participants only (O'Dea & Abraham, 2000; Weiss & Wertheim, 2005), five out of the 18 programs found a decrease in body dissatisfaction for the entire sample at post-intervention (Dunstan et al., 2016; Halliwell & Diedrichs, 2014; Halliwell et al., 2015; Richardson & Paxton, 2010; Wilksch & Wade, 2009), five did not find a significant decrease in body dissatisfaction (Golan et al., 2013; McCabe et al., 2010; Richardson et al., 2009; Wade et al., 2003; Wiseman et al., 2004), and six did not explicitly target body dissatisfaction (Sharpe et al., 2013; Stanford & McCabe, 2005; Steiner-Adair et al., 2002; Stewart et al., 2001; Wilksch et al., 2006; Wilksch et al., 2008).

This review suggests that current programs utilizing a combination of cognitive dissonance, peer-based, and media literacy approaches may be beneficial in improving body image. Additionally, there is an increasing call for negative body image prevention programs for groups other than white adolescent girls and that include both boys and girls (Smolak & Cash, 2011; Yager et al., 2013). Existing programs that have included adolescent boys and girls (Dunstan et al., 2016; Golan et al., 2013; O'Dea & Abraham, 2000; Richardson et al., 2009; Wade et al., 2003; Wilksch et al., 2006; Wilksch & Wade, 2009) resulted in inconsistent improvements at post-intervention. Programs designed specifically for boys (McCabe et al., 2010; Stanford & McCabe, 2005) also revealed minimal to no changes in body image variables.

Free To Be

FTB is a six-session positive body image program designed for adolescent boys and girls. FTB, informed by the developmental theory of embodiment (Piran & Teall, 2012), focuses on increasing positive body image by targeting positive predictors of positive embodiment. These positive predictors, or protective factors, can be grouped into three domains: physical, mental, and social contexts (Piran, 2015; Piran & Teall, 2012). Within the physical domain, FTB aims to foster experiences of positive bodily attunement through interventions that increase appreciation for one's body. Within the mental domain, FTB aims to increase critical thinking skills against constraining appearance and behavior pressures through interventions that increase media literacy and highlight personal internal characteristics. Within the social domain, FTB aims to foster experiences of equity and connection to one's community that will forge connections and relationships not premised on appearance or social identity. FTB clearly addresses two important aspects of the Tripartite Influence Model, including body image development and media and peers; however, it lacks parental involvement. A future version of FTB could include a parental component; however, the focus of this particular program was on the adolescent.

Effective eating disorder prevention programs tend to be multisession, interactive, and utilize a combination of approaches (Stice, Shaw, & Marti, 2007; Yager et al., 2013). Accordingly, in addition to applying the developmental theory of embodiment (Piran & Teall, 2012) as a guide, FTB involves six 55-minute, mixed-sex, interactive sessions for adolescents involving empirically supported peer-based (Dunstan et al., 2016; Richardson & Paxton, 2010; Sharpe et al., 2013), media literacy (Wilksch & Wade, 2009), and cognitive dissonance (Halliwell & Diedrichs, 2014; Halliwell et al., 2015; Stice, Mazotti, Weibel, & Agras, 2000; Stice, Rohde, & Shaw, 2013) approaches. See Table 18.1 for a summary of the aims and content of each session.

Table 18.1 FTB Program Outline: Purpose of Session, Interventions/Activities Used, and Goals of Activities

	Interventions/Activities	*Goals of Activities*
Purpose of Session 1: Shifting perspectives of appearance pressures	I Explanation of program (*psychoeducation*)	To introduce the program, develop expectations, and create a safe environment
	II Appearance pressures through history (*visual PowerPoint/group discussion*)	To increase awareness of appearance pressures as in flux and that no objective standard of beauty exists
		To broaden conceptualizations of standards of attractiveness
	III "What are appearance pressures?" (*interactive activity followed by large group discussion*)	To increase understanding of current appearance pressures
	IV "Problem with appearance pressures" (*interactive activity, sharing, large group discussion*)	To expand awareness of the problems with pursuing appearance pressures/ ideals
		To maximize dissonance and shift perspectives that appearance pressures are problematic and costly
	V Memory exercise	To reinforce the notion that appearance should not be the basis of one's self-worth and self-esteem

Interventions/Activities	Goals of Activities

Purpose of Session 2: Media images uncovered

I Debrief homework (*sharing in front of large group*)
: To increase internalization of material learned

II "Becoming a critical consumer of media" (*individual activity and large group discussion*)
: To increase media literacy and encourage a critical stance towards advertising and media images
: To increase awareness that the majority of media is digitally altered
: To develop healthy strategies for protecting oneself and others when they are dissatisfied after viewing media

III "Your voice matters: Letter to magazine editor" (*small group discussion and individual activity*)
: To increase a critical stance towards digitally altered media in mass media
: To promote positive agency and empower students to advocate for change

Purpose of Session 3: Increasing body appreciation and gratitude

I Debrief homework (*sharing in front of large group*)
: To create an environment of critical thinking towards mass media
: To promote positive agency and social power unrelated to appearance

II "What I like about you and myself" (*small group and individual activity, followed by large group discussion*)
: To increase body appreciation and body image flexibility
: To increase positive views about oneself
: To broaden conceptualizations of attractiveness standards
: To develop coping strategies for body image threats

III "Gratitude exercise" (*individual activity followed by large group sharing*)
: To increase awareness and gratitude of positive characteristics and strengths
: To increase body appreciation and body image flexibility
: To create a positive social environment premised on validating others' internal strengths and not appearance

IV "Take action: Creative encouragement" (*interactive individual activity/homework*)
: To decrease self-worth as contingent on appearance
: To reinforce positive internal characteristics and strengths
: To develop healthy and practical coping strategies for body image threats

Purpose of Session 4: Countering constraining stereotypes

I "Identifying constraining stereotypical behavior ideas" (*small group activity followed by large group discussion*)
: To increase critical questioning of engrained beliefs about constraining stereotypical behaviors and pressures

(*Continued*)

	Interventions/Activities	Goals of Activities
	II Problems with constraining stereotypical behavior ideas" (*small group activity*)	To develop awareness of limitations that exist when abiding by constraining stereotypical behavior pressures of what it means to be a boy or girl
		To decrease internal pressures to abide by constraining stereotypical behaviors
	III "Role-play: constraining stereotypes" (*small group activity followed by large group discussion*)	To recognize different ways appearance and behavior stereotypes can manifest in real life
		To learn and practice healthy alternatives to deal with constraining stereotypes about appearance and behavior
		To create a positive social environment not premised on constraining stereotypical behavior pressures of what it means to be a boy or girl
		To increase positive agency
Purpose of Session 5: Positive activism for change	I "Create positive change: Be an activist" (*small group activity followed by large group discussion*)	To inspire students to create positive change in the world surrounding positive body image
		To have students create their own healthy, social environments
		To increase appreciation and respect for the body
		To develop healthy coping strategies against body image threats
		To increase media literacy surrounding body image
		To maximize dissonance and shift perspectives that appearance pressures, constraining behavior, and appearance stereotypes are problematic and costly
Purpose of Session 6: Moving towards a positive body image	I Debrief project (*sharing in front of large group*)	To increase students' assertive voice surrounding positive body image
		To decrease internalization of appearance pressures, constraining behavior, and appearance stereotypes
		To develop healthy coping strategies against body image threats
	II "My best possible self" (*individual activity*)	To increase positive views about oneself
	III Final debrief and closure (*large group discussion*)	To review the important themes from each session

Implementing FTB

Materials

A leader manual, student activity booklet, and PowerPoint have been created for FTB. The leader manual outlines the content and materials needed for each session, as well as timing guidelines for each activity. A detailed instructional description and rationale are provided for each activity. Students are given their own FTB student activity booklet where they complete activities and exercises.

Ongoing Development

Currently, 119 boys and girls have received FTB programming as research participants to evaluate the program, led by a counseling psychology graduate student and social worker. An additional 600 students have participated in FTB as non-research participants, facilitated by teachers, graduate students, or professionals. Given the gendered nature of body image concerns, we are still learning how to effectively address the specific and different concerns boys and girls may have in a co-ed context. The following description of the FTB sessions outlines the activities and aims of the program.[1]

Session One

The overall focus of session one is to bring awareness to appearance pressures, understand who benefits from appearance standards, and develop a critical stance towards appearance pressures. The session begins with students viewing images of males and females of different ages throughout discrete periods in history. As students view the images, they record in their booklets what they believe the people in the images felt pressured to look like. The program begins with this activity to demonstrate how, what, and who is considered attractive has changed over time. The focus then shifts to students brainstorming as a group what current appearance pressures are and problems that can arise when pursuing or abiding by appearance pressures (adapted from McClean & Paxton, 2011). The goal of having students brainstorm interactively and write down their ideas is to maximize dissonance, shifting towards a perspective that abiding by appearance pressures is problematic and costly. Students then write a short reflection describing a memory when they felt happy, special, or valued not based on their appearance. Finally, they brainstorm how they can make their friends feel valued or special irrespective of their appearance. The take-home messages from session one are (a) that appearance pressures are in flux, (b) appearance pressures are comprised of a narrow range of criteria that the overwhelming majority of people cannot adhere too, (c) there is no objective standard of who or what is attractive, and (d) feeling special or happy should not be based on appearance.

Session Two

The overall focus of session two is to increase awareness of the "smoke-screen" behind mainstream media, enhance critical thinking skills towards media images, and understand the impact media manipulation has on the viewer. Session two begins with students watching two videos of different images being digitally manipulated. After, students view a series of digitally manipulated images on the PowerPoint and are instructed to write down all of the characteristics that they think have been altered. They then view and compare the unedited version of the images, side by side with the digitally manipulated photo. Students then brainstorm problems that can occur from seeing unrealistic and altered photos. The purpose of supporting discussion surrounding digitally manipulated photos is to increase their awareness that the majority of media is digitally manipulated, hopefully encouraging a critical stance towards advertising and media images. Students then brainstorm and share healthy strategies for protecting others from body dissatisfaction. The last activity of session two promotes positive personal agency and aims to empower students to advocate for change. Students write a letter to a magazine editor about media manipulation, providing reasons as to why it is important to not have digitally manipulated images in their magazines, social media, and websites. The take-home messages of session two are as follows: (a) the majority of mass media has been manipulated, which ultimately impacts a person's perception of what is normal; (b) although people sometimes feel down about themselves, there are healthy strategies that can be used to help people feel better; and (c) each person has the power to advocate for positive social change.

Session Three

The overall goal of session three is to increase appreciation, gratitude, and joy for one's body and internal characteristics. Session three begins by having several students read their letters they wrote to magazine editors aloud. After, in small group discussions, students complete a body appreciation activity involving stories of characters with differing bodies and abilities. Once students have completed the activity, they are asked how they can help their friends feel joy that is not tied to their physical being or help their friends know that they matter when they feel their body image is threatened. The purpose of having students repeatedly think about ways to support their friends is to increase the likelihood of internalizing and adopting some of these healthy practices into their lives and promoting them with others. The next activity is completed individually; students fill in the endings of sentences about personal attributes that they are grateful for and are later asked to share these sentences. The goal of writing and sharing their gratitude lists is to increase positive feelings about oneself and their body and to create a positive social environment premised on validating others' positive qualities rather than on appearance. The take-home messages of this session are (a) that each person's body is capable of doing amazing things regardless of what their bodies look like; (b) each person has multiple positive internal characteristics and strengths that they can be grateful for; and (c) body image challenges are normal, but it is beneficial to protect ourselves and others by developing healthy coping strategies.

Session Four

The focus of session four is countering constraining stereotypes and learning healthy alternatives to dealing with constraining appearance and behavior pressures. The session begins with a group discussion about what stereotypes are. After, students generate a list of gender-related appearance and behavior stereotypes that they have seen in the media. Through small and large group discussions, students explore problems that may arise from stereotyping others. The last activity involves a role-play where students are guided to recognize the different ways constraining stereotypes can manifest in real life, with the purpose of learning positive, alternative ways of addressing them. In small groups, students complete example alternate endings for a script that contains a constraining stereotype about appearance or behavior and are then given time to write and present their own role-plays. The take-home messages of session four are as follows: (a) it is important to think critically about stereotypes because it can negatively impact a person, and (b) there are a variety of healthy alternatives for coping or combating constraining stereotypes in real life.

Session Five

The focus of session five is for the students to teach positive body image lessons to others (adapted from Stice et al., 2013). Students engage in an activism project that aims to reinforce the information they have learned and simultaneously increase personal agency, positive social power, and connection to their community. Students work in small groups and develop a plan of how to promote positive body image for community environments. The students present this project to the larger group during the final session. The take-home messages of session five are as follows: (a) developing a positive body image requires intentional action, and (b) there are a multitude of ways they can help others develop a positive body image.

Session Six

The overall focus of the sixth session is to review the important themes covered previously, have the small student groups share their positive body image projects with the larger group, and increase positive views about oneself. The session begins with each small group sharing their project with the larger group. This activity has several aims: (a) to inspire students to create positive change in the world surrounding positive body image, (b) to further develop students' own assertive voice and sense of personal agency, (c) to increase media literacy surrounding body image, and (d) to increase students' internalization of the material. The final activity of FTB is a "best possible self" activity (see Markus & Nurius, 1986; Owens & Patterson, 2013). Students write a description about their future selves, where their appearance looks the same and they are happy and engaged in life. Next, students generate a list of specific ways they can achieve this best possible future self. The take-home messages of session six are as follows: (a) students can create and elicit positive change related to positive body image in a variety of ways, and (b) well-being and hope can be cultivated regardless of our appearance.

Program Evaluation

Two preliminary quantitative evaluations of FTB have occurred with grade 7 and 10 students. In the first evaluation, a similar version of FTB described in this chapter was implemented in a four-session, 75-minute, co-ed class setting with students in grade 10 ($N = 46$). Students completed the following measures: Body Image Coping Strategies Inventory's Positive Rational Accepting Coping subscale (body image coping strategies; Cash, Santos, & Williams, 2005), Sociocultural Attitudes Towards Appearance Questionnaire-4 (SATAQ-4), Internalization of Thin Ideal subscale, and Pressure From Media subscale (internalization of thin ideal and pressure from media; Schaefer et al., 2015). From pre- to posttest, results revealed that for both boys and girls, participants in FTB reported increased positive body image coping strategies, decreased internalization of the thin ideal, and decreased pressure from the media (Regehr, Owens, Cox, & Cheung, 2016). At one-month follow-up, these gains were not sustained. A second evaluation, using the six-session program described in this chapter, was conducted with boys and girls in grade 7 ($N = 76$). This program evaluation used the following measures: Body Appreciation Scale-2 (positive body image; Tylka & Wood-Barcalow, 2015b), Body Image Coping Strategies Inventory's Positive Rational Accepting Coping subscale (body image coping strategies; Cash, Santos, & Williams, 2005), and Eating Disorder Inventory's Body Dissatisfaction subscale (body dissatisfaction; Garner, Olmsted, & Polivy, 1983). Media literacy was assessed using items adapted from Richardson and Paxton (2010). Results showed from pre- to posttest that positive body image, positive body image coping strategies significantly, and media literacy increased, and body dissatisfaction decreased significantly (Regehr, 2017). Program feedback, using items adapted from Richardson and Paxton (2010), from the grade 7 participants also revealed students found FTB to be enjoyable, interesting, and informative and that they would recommend it to others (Regehr, 2017). While these preliminary results are encouraging, further research with additional participants with greater diversity, a control group, and longitudinal follow-up assessment will be helpful. Further, while it is helpful to have a program designed for both boys and girls, given the lack of research in this area with boys and the co-ed nature of a large number of classroom settings, additional studies examining gender differences or gender as a moderating variable are warranted.

Conclusion

As a Western culture, body image has become an increasing topic of interest in both the scholarly literature and media. There has been heightened awareness of the powerful influences that are impacting adolescents' body image: parental attitudes (Hart, Cornell, Damiano & Paxton, 2014), attractive celebrity culture (Brown & Tiggemann, 2016), body comparison behaviors (Tiggemann & Slater, 2004), and pornography (Dines, 2010). To combat the rise of negative body image, communities of women have announced their "body positivity" (Okwodu, 2017; Silverton, 2017), petitions against the use of digitally manipulated media have been signed by thousands of people (Sauers, 2012; Stewart, 2015), ads deemed to be "body shaming" or billboards that had considerable digital alterations have been banned in London (Tapsfield, 2016) and Norway (Off & Douglas, 2016), and a number of media literacy and body image programs have been developed (e.g., Dunstan et al., 2016; Halliwell & Diedrichs, 2014; Halliwell et al., 2015; Richardson & Paxton, 2010; Sharpe et al., 2013; Wilksch & Wade, 2009).

The emerging research on embodiment and positive body image (e.g., Piran et al., 2006; Piran & Teall, 2012) points to a holistic way of conceptualizing negative and positive body image; physical, mental, and social factors are intricately interwoven into a person's body image experience. While embodiment and body image literature have primarily focused on girls and women (Piran & Teall, 2012), promising preliminary results of FTB suggest that adolescent girls *and* boys benefit from body image activities guided by a theory of embodiment. By teaching students to recognize and attempt to understand our current cultural ideals and practices, we can empower them to think critically about the messages they are receiving and believing. As research and practice involving embodiment theory and body image grows, we can continue to explore and understand how to prevent eating disorders, promote positive body image, and nurture growth and vitality in both boys and girls during adolescence.

Note

1 To receive the most up-to-date version of the program, please contact the program developer at renae@freetobetalks.com.

References

Brown, Z. & Tiggemann, M. (2016). Attractive celebrity and peer images on Instagram: Effect on women's mood and body image. *Body Image, 19,* 37–43. doi:10.1016/j.bodyim.2016.08.007

Bucchianeri, M. M., & Neumark-Sztainer, D. R. (2014). Body dissatisfaction: An overlooked public health concern. *Journal of Public Mental Health, 13*(2), 64–69. doi: 10.1108/JPMH-11–2013–0071

Cash, T. F., Santos, M. T., & Williams, E. F. (2005). Coping with body-image threats and challenges: Validation of the body image coping strategies inventory. *Journal of Psychosomatic Research, 58*(2), 191–199. doi:10.1016/j.jpsychores.2004.07.008

Dines, G. (2010). *Pornland: How porn has hijacked our sexuality.* Boston, MA: Beacon Press.

Dunstan, C. J., Paxton, S. J., & McLean, S. A. (2016). An evaluation of a body image intervention in adolescent girls delivered in single-sex versus co-educational classroom settings. *Eating Behaviors.* doi: 10.1016/j.eatbeh.2016.03.016

Frisén, A., & Holmqvist, K. (2010). What characterizes early adolescents with a positive body image? A qualitative investigation of Swedish girls and boys. *Body Image, 7*(3), 205–212. doi:10.1016/j.bodyim.2010.04.001

Garner, D. M., Olmsted, M. P., & Polivy, J. (1983). Development and validation of a multidimensional Eating Disorders Inventory for anorexia nervosa and bulimia. *International Journal of Eating Disorders, 2*(2), 15–34.

Golan, M., Hagay, N., & Tamir, S. (2013). The effect of "In Favor of Myself": Preventive program to enhance positive self and body image among adolescents. *PLoS ONE, 8*(11), e78223. doi:10.1371/journal.pone.0078223

Halliwell, E., & Diedrichs, P. C. (2014). Testing a dissonance body image intervention among young girls. *Health Psychology: Official Journal of the Division of Health Psychology, American Psychological Association, 33*(2), 201–204. doi:10.1037/a0032585

Halliwell, E., Jarman, H., McNamara, A., Risdon, H., & Jankowski, G. (2015). Dissemination of evidence-based body image interventions: A pilot study into the effectiveness of using undergraduate students as interventionists in secondary schools. *Body Image, 14,* 1–4. doi:10.1016/j.bodyim.2015.02.002

Hart, L. M., Cornell, C., Damiano, S. R., & Paxton, S. J. (2014). Parents and prevention: A systematic review of interventions involving parents that aim to prevent body dissatisfaction or eating disorders. *The International Journal of Eating Disorders,* 9–11. doi:10.1002/eat.22284

Hefferon, K. (2015). The role of embodiment in optimal functioning. In S. Joseph (Ed.), *Positive psychology in practice: Promoting human flourishing in work, health, education, and everyday life* (2nd ed., pp. 792–805). Hoboken, NJ: John Wiley & Sons. doi: 10.1002/9781118996874.ch45

Holmqvist, K., & Frisén, A. (2012). "I bet they aren't that perfect in reality:" Appearance ideals viewed from the perspective of adolescents with a positive body image. *Body Image, 9*(3), 388–395. doi:10.1016/j.bodyim.2012.03.007

Impett, E. A., Daubenmier, J. J., & Hirschman, A. L. (2006). Minding the body: Yoga, embodiment, and well-being, *3*(4), 39–48. doi:10.1525/srsp.2006.3.4.39

Kilbourne, J. (1999). *Can't buy my love: How advertising changes the way we think and feel.* New York, NY: Simon & Shuster.

Markus, H., & Nurius, P. (1986). Possible selves. *American Psychologist, 41*, 954–969. doi:10.1037/0003–066X.41.9.954

McCabe, M. P., Ricciardelli, L. A., & Karantzas, G. (2010). Impact of a healthy body image program among adolescent boys on body image, negative affect, and body change strategies. *Body Image, 7*(2), 117–123. doi:10.1016/j.bodyim.2009.10.007

McClean, S. A., & Paxton, S. J. (2011). *Happy Being Me: Co-educational body image program student activity book.* Melbourne: La Trobe University.

Meier, B. P., Schnall, S., Schwarz, N., & Bargh, J. A. (2012). Embodiment in social psychology. *Topics in Cognitive Science, 4*(4), 705–716. doi:10.1111/j.1756-8765.2012.01212.x

Menzel, J. E., & Levine, M. P. (2011). Embodying experiences and the promotion of positive body image: The example of competitive athletics. In R. M. Calogero, S. Tantleff-Dunn, & J. K. Thompson (Eds), *Self-objectification in women: Causes, consequences, and counteractions* (pp. 163–186). Washington, DC: American Psychological Association.

O'Dea, J., & Abraham, S. (2000). Improving the body image, eating attitudes, and behavoirs of young male and female adolescents: A new educational approach that focuses on self-esteem. *International Journal of Eating Disorders, 28*(1), 43–47.

Off, C., & Douglas, J. (2016, May 13). Norweigan city bans "Photoshopped" billboard models, citing body image concerns. *Canadian Broadcast Corporation Radio.* Retrieved from www.cbc.ca/radio/asithappens/as-it-happens-friday-edition-1.3581291/norwegian-city-bans-photoshopped-billboard-models-citing-body-image-concerns-1.3581299

Okwodu, J. (2017, January 30). The All Women's Project's founders on pushing for diversity and fashion as protest. *Vogue.* Retrieved from www.vogue.com/article/all-woman-project-series-two-body-diversity-fashion

Owens, R. L., & Patterson, M. M. (2013). Positive psychological interventions for children: A comparison of gratitude and best possible selves approaches. *Journal of Genetic Psychology, 174*, 403–428. doi:10.1080/00221325.2012.697496

Piran, N. (2015). New possibilities in the prevention of eating disorders: The introduction of positive body image measures. *Body Image*, 1–12. doi:10.1016/j.bodyim.2015.03.008

Piran, N., Antoniou, M., Legge, R., McCance, N., Mizevich, J., Peasley, E., & Ross, E. (2006). On girls' disembodiment: The complex tyranny of the 'ideal girl'. In D. L. Gustafson & L. Goodyear (Eds), *Women, health, and education: CASWE 6th bi-annual international institute proceedings* (pp. 224–229). St. John's, NL: Memorial University.

Piran, N., & Teall, T. (2012). The developmental theory of embodiment. In G. L. McVey, M. P. Levine, N. Piran, & H. B. Ferguson (Eds), *Preventing eating-related and weight-related disorders: Collaborative research, advocacy, and policy change* (pp. 169–198). Waterloo, ON: Wilfried Laurier University Press.

Regehr, R., Owens, R., Cox, D., & Cheung, W. (2016, June). *Evaluating More To You: A media literacy, peer-based, and cognitive dissonance intervention for increasing positive body image among adolescents.* Poster session presented at the Canadian Psychological Association in Victoria, B.C., Canada.

Regehr, R. (2017). *Evaluating Free To Be: A positive body image program for adolescents.* Unpublished master's thesis, University of British Columbia, Vancouver.

Ricciardelli, L. A., & McCabe, M. P. (2011). Body image development in adolescent boys. In T. F. Cash & L. Smolak (Eds), *Body Image: A handbook of science, practice, and prevention* (2nd ed., pp. 85–91). New York, NY: Guilford Press.

Richardson, S. M., & Paxton, S. J. (2010). An evaluation of a body image intervention based on risk factors for body dissatisfaction: A controlled study with adolescent girls. *The International Journal of Eating Disorders, 43*(2), 112–122. doi:10.1002/eat.20682

Richardson, S. M., Paxton, S. J., & Thomson, J. S. (2009). Is BodyThink an efficacious body image and self-esteem program? A controlled evaluation with adolescents. *Body Image, 6*(2), 75–82. doi:10.1016/j.bodyim.2008.11.001

Sauers, J. (2012, May, 2). Aweomse 14-year-old delivers 25,000 anti-Photoshop signatures to Seventeen Magazine. *Jezebel.* Retrieved from http://jezebel.com/5907048/awesome-14-year-old-delivers-25000-anti-photoshop-signatures-to-seventeen-magazine

Schaefer, L. M., Burke, N. L., Thompson, J. K., Dedrick, R. F., Heinberg, L. J., Calogero, R. M., …, Swami, V. (2015). Development and validation of the sociocultural attitudes towards appearance questionnaire-4 (SATAQ-4). *Psychological Assessment, 27*(1), 54–67. doi:10.1037/a0037917

Sharpe, H., Schober, I., Treasure, J., & Schmidt, U. (2013). Feasibility, acceptability and efficacy of a school-based prevention programme for eating disorders: Cluster randomised controlled trial. *The British Journal of Psychiatry, 203*(6), 428–35. doi:10.1192/bjp.bp.113.128199

Silverton, L. (2017, January 25). Meet the women using Instagram to fight their eating disorders. *Refinery29.* Retreived from www.refinery29.uk/eating-disorders-instagram-body-positive

Smolak, L., & Cash, T. F. (2011). Future challenges for body image science, practice, and prevention. In T. F. Cash & L. Smolak (Eds), *Body Image: A handbook of science, practice, and prevention* (2nd ed., pp. 471–478). New York, NY: Guilford Press.

Stanford, J. N., & McCabe, M. P. (2005). Evaluation of a body image prevention programme for adolescent boys. *European Eating Disorders Review, 13*(5), 360–370. doi:10.1002/erv.654

Steiner-Adair, C., Sjostrom, L., Franko, D., Pai, S., Tucker, R., Becker, A., & Herzog, D. (2002). Primary prevention of risk factors for eating disorders in adolescent girls: Learning from practice. *International Journal of Eating Disorders, 32*(4), 401–411. doi:10.1002/eat.10089

Stewart, D., Carter, J. C., Drinkwater, J., Hainsworth, J., & Fairburn, C. G. (2001). Modification of eating attitudes and behavior in adolescent girls: A controlled study. *The International Journal of Eating Disorders, 29*(2), 107–118.

Stewart, N. (2015, February 8). Vancouver organization launches petition to slim down Photoshop use. *Global News.* Retrieved from http://globalnews.ca/news/1818185/vancouver-organization-launches-petition-to-slim-down-photoshop-use/

Stice, E., Mazotti, L., Weibel, D., & Agras, W. S. (2000). Dissonance prevention program decreases thin-ideal internalization, body dissatisfaction, dieting, negative affect, and bulimic symptoms: A preliminary experiment.

International Journal of Eating Disorders, 27(2), 206–217. doi:10.1002/ (SICI)1098–108X(200003)27:2<206::AID-EAT9>3.0.CO;2-D

Stice, E., Rohde, P., & Shaw, H. (2013). *The body project: A dissonance-based eating disorder prevention intervention.* New York, NY: Oxford University Press.

Stice, E., Shaw, H., & Marti, C. N. (2007). A meta-analytic review of eating disordes prevention programs: Encouraging findings. *Annual Review of Clinical Psychology, 3,* 207–231. doi:10.1146/annurev.clinpsy.3.022806.091447

Tapsfield, J. (2016, June 13). Body-shaming ads will be BANNED from London's transport network, new mayor Sadiq Khan declares. *Daily Mail.* Retrieved from www.dailymail.co.uk/news/article-3639069/Body-shaming-ads-BANNED-London-s-transport-network-new-mayor-Sadiq-Khan-declares.html

Tiggemann, M., & Slater, A. (2004). Thin ideals in music television: a source of social comparison and body dissatisfaction. *The International Journal of Eating Disorders, 35*(1), 48–58. doi:10.1002/eat.10214

Tylka, T. L. (2011). Positive psychology perspectives on body image. In T. F. Cash & L. Smolak (Eds.), *Body Image:A handbook of science, practice, and prevention* (2nd ed., pp. 56–65). New York, NY: Guilford Press.

Tylka, T. L., & Wood-Barcalow, N. L. (2015a). What is and what is not positive body image? Conceptual foundations and construct definition. *Body Image,* 1–12. doi:10.1016/j.bodyim.2015.04.001

Tylka, T. L., & Wood-Barcalow, N. (2015b). The Body Appreciation Scale: Item refinement and psychometric evaluation. *Body Image, 12,* 53–67. doi:10.1016/j. bodyim.2005.06.002

Wade, T. D., Davidson, S., & O'Dea, J. A. (2003). A preliminary controlled evaluation of a school-based media literacy program and self-esteem program for reducing eating disorder risk factors. *International Journal of Eating Disorders, 33*(4), 371–383. doi:10.1002/eat.10136

Weiss, K., & Wertheim, E. H. (2005). An evaluation of a prevention program for disordered eating in adolescent girls: Examining responses of high-and-low-risk girls. *Eating Disorders, 13,* 143–156. doi:10.1080/10640260590918946

Wertheim, E. H., & Paxton, S. J. (2011). Body image development in adolescent girls. In T. F. Cash & L. Smolak (Eds), *Body Image:A handbook of science, practice, and prevention* (2nd ed., pp. 76–82). New York, NY: Guilford Press.

Wilksch, S. M., Durbridge, M. R., & Wade, T. D. (2008). A preliminary controlled comparison of programs designed to reduce risk of eating disorders targeting perfectionism and media literacy. *Journal of the American Academy of Child and Adolescent Psychiatry, 47*(8), 937–947. doi:10.1097/ CHI.0b013e3181799f4a

Wilksch, S. M., Tiggemann, M., & Wade, T. D. (2006). Impact of interactive school-based media literacy lessons for reducing internalization of media ideals in young adolescent girls and boys. *International Journal of Eating Disorders, 39*(5), 385–393. doi:10.1002/eat.20237

Wilksch, S. M., & Wade, T. D. (2009). Reduction of shape and weight concern in young adolescents: A 30-month controlled evaluation of a media literacy program. *Journal of the American Academy of Child and Adolescent Psychiatry, 48*(6), 652–661. doi:10.1097/CHI.0b013e3181a1f559

Wiseman, C. V., Sunday, S. R., Bortolotti, F., & Halmi, K. A. (2004). Primary prevention of eating disorders through attitude change: A two country comparison. *Eating Disorders, 12,* 241–250. doi:10.1080/10640260490481447

Wood-Barcalow, N. L., Tylka, T. L., & Augustus-Horvath, C. L. (2010). "But I Like My Body": Positive body image characteristics and a holistic model for young-adult women. *Body Image*, 7(2), 106–116. doi:10.1016/j.bodyim.2010.01.001

Yager, Z., Diedrichs, P. C., Ricciardelli, L. A., & Halliwell, E. (2013). What works in secondary schools? A systematic review of classroom-based body image programs. *Body Image*, 10(3), 271–281. doi:10.1016/j.bodyim.2013.04.001

Young, L. (1992). Sexual abuse and the problem of embodiment. *Child Abuse and Neglect*, 16(1), 89–100. doi:10.1016/0145-2134(92)90010-O

19 Lifespan Integration Therapy for Eating Disorders

A Case Study of Anorexia Nervosa

Cindy Wuflestad and Peggy Pace

Lifespan Integration (LI) therapy offers an embodied therapeutic approach to facilitate integration of the body-mind system in eating disorder treatment and recovery. Because our bodies hold experiences of oppression, violation, and trauma, it can become unbearable to be in one's own body. This results in a protective splitting off from one's body, which perpetuates body objectification and loss of unity of the mind-body whole. Because pain is located in our bodies, our bodies logically hold the clues for healing toward body-self unity or embodiment. "Talking therapies" often fall short in touching the body-mind system. For example, even though talking therapies can offer clients insight and tools for changing dysfunctional patterns, primitive feeling states are still activated by situations that are triggering. LI therapy integrates current understandings about body memory and treatment methods (Ogden, Minton, & Pain, 2006; Rothschild, 2000; van der Kolk, 2015) into an innovative therapeutic approach that directly targets neurophysiological processes through an implicit, body-based process (see Pace, 2012).

In LI therapy, one's sense of self becomes coherent and integrated within a cohesive autobiographical narrative through repetitions of the client's memory cues in the presence of an emotionally attuned therapist. This process results in clients experiencing an increased sense of connection to themselves, others, life, and the present. LI accesses the innate ability of the body-mind system to heal itself by combining active imagination, the juxtaposition of ego states in time, and a timeline of memories to facilitate neural integration and rapid healing. Memory cues from each year of the client's life are used during the integrating phase of LI protocols. These cues allow memories related to the targeted emotional theme to spontaneously surface during the LI timeline process (Pace, 2012). LI therapy was initially used with adult survivors of childhood abuse or neglect. However, it soon became apparent in LI practice that LI therapy facilitates rapid healing in people of all ages and is effective with a wide range of therapeutic issues. For a more thorough introduction to LI therapy, see Pace (2012), *Lifespan Integration Therapy: Connecting Ego States through Time*. Since 2004, over 2,000 therapists throughout the US, Canada, and Western Europe have been trained in LI.

Symptoms associated with eating disorders (including Anorexia Nervosa, Bulimia Nervosa, and Binge Eating Disorder) that are often targeted in LI therapy include irregular eating patterns, hyper-focus on body image, rigid thinking patterns, depression, high levels of anxiety, feeling "out of control", fatigue, sleeplessness, addictions, emotional outbursts, racing thoughts, racing nervous system, numb body, lack of initiative and motivation, poor concentration, dissociation, trouble with relationships, and feelings of hopelessness. In order to help an individual with an eating disorder, the clinician needs to be competent in creating a holistic treatment plan. Often, there are also high-risk physical issues occurring in the body which require monitoring by a multidisciplinary treatment team. As each client is unique, their lived experience is unique, and it is the clinician's responsibility to give effective, attuned, and timely attention aimed both toward greater mental health and well-being as well as toward a reduction of the significant physical risks of eating disorders.

Affect Regulation and the Window of Tolerance

The focus of this chapter is to describe a therapeutic case utilizing LI for Anorexia Nervosa. In this chapter, I (CW) will explain how I worked with Beth, a client struggling with Anorexia Nervosa, moving her toward balanced self-regulation using specific LI protocols. These protocols facilitated Beth's own embodiment of compassion and acceptance within her self-system. Louis Cozolino states, "our ability to enjoy being inside of ourselves, successfully engaging with others and managing life's day-to-day stressors depends on the attainment of affect regulation" (Cozolino, 2006, p. 86). I have treated over a thousand clients in my career and, no matter the diagnosis, we are always working together to address their ability to manage their own emotions and actions while staying positively connected with family, friends, and coworkers.

In order to build this type of emotional balance in our clients, we as therapists must be able to regulate our own emotions. The old saying goes, "you can't lead someone somewhere you haven't gone yourself". It is the LI clinician's ability to self-regulate and attune with the client, and then intentionally direct the movement of the client's activated system (sympathetic and parasympathetic nervous system) using the LI protocol-specific structure, that makes this possible; the therapist needs to keep the therapeutic frame of "window of tolerance" (WOT) in mind during the LI experience. For clients with eating disorders, they have learned to operate outside their WOT to move away from the reality of their emotional discomfort. LI integrates the maladaptive hypo- or hyperarousal and allows their body and mind to release and reconsolidate old neural firing patterns.

So, what is healthy emotional regulation? Healthy emotional regulation occurs when we are able to engage our brains on many levels in a given situation. We are considered regulated or stable emotionally when we can be present in a current experience, aware and grounded in our bodies, feeling our emotions, and able to stay mindful of the actual situation externally before us. It requires brain complexity and flexibility to move between primal, subcortical brain regions where fight, flight, freeze, and collapse are activated (limbic system-emotional brain, and brain stem) to midbrain and frontal cortex activations where mindful appraisal of the situation and consequences of actions are determined (executive brain function or pre-frontal cortex). Dan Siegel refers to this psychophysiological brain complexity as functioning in our "window of tolerance" (Siegel, 2011, p. 87).

"Window of tolerance" is now used broadly within the mental health community and is an important idea to keep in mind when using LI protocols. The assumption is that the human brain develops its own "window of tolerance" over time, where it regulates emotional, nervous system responses and stays mindfully present in a situation, *homeostasis*. Some windows are wider, and some are narrower than others. This window is developed by recurring experiences in which the person moves from regulation to dysregulation and back again to regulation. These recurring experiences are stored in networks of sensory, motor, and emotional memory. Positive emotional rebound, neural growth, and affect regulation are optimized in the brain in a context of positive parent-child interactions. This process is what we are reinforcing or creating when attuning with the client by going through their narrative in the timeline. When they visualize the cue, their body activation is triggered. Once the nervous system is engaged with the primitive activation, we engage the client in moving from dysregulation to regulation or "rebound" (Siegel, 1999).

This process of rebounding occurs several times within an LI session, resulting in higher levels of emotional regulation. Early emotional regulation, established via mother-infant, contributes to the organization and integration of neural networks and the eventual development of self-regulation in the child; this continues into adulthood. According to clinical psychologist David Wallin,

> In the new attachment that the therapist is attempting to generate, the patient's emotions are central and their affect regulation – which allows them to be felt, modulated, communicated, and understood ... (this is) the heart of the process that enables the patient to heal and to grow.
>
> (Wallin, 2007, p. 64)

Beth's Story: A Case Study of LI for Anorexia Nervosa

Beth's naturopath had referred her to me and informed me that she was being treated for Anorexia Nervosa at a local Eating Disorder Clinic where she was under the care of several doctors and specialists. I was asked to treat the emotional aspects of her disorder using LI.

Beth and her mom, Sue, came to the first appointment together. Beth, 27 years old, had just moved back to her home town a few weeks before to live with her parents, who were "very caring and supportive". Being the oldest and only daughter, Beth and Sue had a close relationship; they described themselves as "best friends" and very attached to each other. Beth's two single, adult brothers still lived at home. The whole family was "very close".

Beth's goals for therapy were to work on "health issues, past issues, loss of self-identity, loss of direction, depression, and stress". When I asked Beth about her Anorexia Nervosa, she had determined that her past two romantic relationships had caused her eating disorder: one relationship that ended in divorce and the current engagement that was on rocky ground. In an effort to align with Beth's presenting problem and the underlying cause of PTSD from two abusive relationships, I explained that LI could help her with her rigid, obsessive eating patterns and with the intrusive thoughts around her abusive, oppressive relationships.

Beth and Sue explained the most recent events. Beth had been living in Arizona for the past six months with her fiancé until last week when Sue drove down to pick Beth up. Beth and her fiancé had been fighting every day, and she had stopped eating due to all the anxiety of the turbulent relationship. Her body was shutting down. She was losing weight: going from 130 lbs to below 100 lbs. Menstruation had stopped several months earlier, and she was in medical crisis. Once she returned to her home town with her mother, Beth was evaluated by her naturopath and referred to the doctors at the clinic. The result of the medical assessments and tests from the previous week showed critically low liver functioning, heart concerns, and bone mass issues. Beth's anorexia symptoms were serious. The small amount of food she consumed daily was not supporting her body. I found the severity of her condition to be very incongruous to the goals she had written on her intake: "increase her confidence and self-esteem, get more energy, be happier and healthier".

Conceptualization and Treatment Planning

Though Beth and Sue fully believed that the abusive love relationships were the problem, it was clear that there were underlying attachment issues that had allowed Beth to enter into her romantic relationships initially and had caused her to tolerate the abusive behavior. Our attachment with our primary caregiver(s) is the foundation for our adulthood connection. Though there was certainly love in the family, I was curious what we would find once we focused attention on Beth's early years. I gave Beth the assignment of developing a timeline of her life based on the LI parameters, and I anticipated that it would provide more information regarding early trauma. It did.

I considered several LI protocols in formulating a treatment plan for Beth that would meet her goals and address the underlying issues that were apparent in our first session. It would include a protocol that addresses Anorexia specifically to focus on getting Beth eating again and a PTSD protocol to address the trauma and relationship issues with her ex-husband and current fiancé; once those were addressed, we would use other LI preverbal protocols to work on the attachment issues that had created the underlying dysregulation in her, causing the incongruence I was witnessing between what she reported and what was actually happening in her internal and external world. Since the time I worked with Beth, there are newer LI protocols that specifically address dysregulation.

The first session. Beth's rigid eating was at a critical stage. If she didn't start eating, then she would not be able to address the other issues. She would have died. The day after her intake appointment, we met for our first LI session and used a protocol that worked with the part of Beth that was "Afraid to Eat". It had manifested when she was 18 years old and felt "out of control" and "didn't know what normal felt like". She had quit school and moved in with her boyfriend. Working and living away from her family for the first time, she was overwhelmed. Through the coaching work of LI, Beth was able to help herself move from the hyperaroused state of being anxious, scared, and ashamed for not feeling successful in school or in her relationship with her boyfriend. She felt more compassion for herself. She understood that her emotions were important and that restricting food was actually adding to her anxious feeling, rather than helping. She explained that the shameful feeling had caused her to "punish herself". The urge to be responsible for everything and rigidly manage eating shifted toward an attitude of having more "fun" instead of managing the eating.

At the end of the session, I took note of her high level of self-contempt. Self-contempt often is a result of not being able to express anger outwardly, so it is turned inward toward self. I did not discuss this with Beth at the time. Other LI protocols allow for the client to release rage and anger toward the perpetrator in their active imagination, which clears the brain-firing pattern. Bessel Vander Kolk's research has shown that the brain will not release the firing pattern unless it is focused on the actual perpetrator. That is what makes LI so effective to regulate the strong emotions of rage. Beth had some obvious people to rage about, but my hunch was there would be more under her own roof. I love that in LI, we do not have to just talk about it; we can efficiently target it with coaching during the LI process.

By the next day, Beth reported eating more calories and eating several times a day as prescribed in her nutrition plan from the clinic. She reported being fearful that she would gain too much weight, but she was willing to continue eating. Beth said she felt that after the first session, she "decided to choose life and health", "she deserved it", even though she was impatient to get feeling better. From that point forward, she continued to eat and add foods to her diet, as her digestive system was able to handle more. It would take two years before some of her body organs were back functioning in "normal" ranges, though. After one LI session, she was willing to eat. That's success.

Addressing adult relationship trauma. The next step was using a protocol to focus on the trauma that surrounded her first marriage at 19 years of age. We developed the timeline together. It all began nine years earlier when she started dating Ben. Ben was 21 and a good friend of her 15-year-old brother. Ben would hang out at Beth's home; "he was like family". As their relationship turned sexual, her parents let them be together at the house; "No questions asked". Her parents believed that it was safer under their roof. Beth decided to quit school and moved in with Ben. Her parents didn't like the idea, but "if that's what you want to do?" is how they responded. Beth was working long hours, and Ben couldn't seem to keep a job. They got married, and for the first year, they got help financially from her parents. Ben continued to struggle with keeping a job and became very depressed. His anger and yelling and threats escalated, as he spent more time home drinking during the day while Beth was at work. He would barrage her with questions when she walked in the door from work. Why did it take you so long to get home from work? Why can't you figure out how to fold my shirts right? He would go out with his friends and then rage when she wanted to go out with her friends. Her anxiety continued to build, as she worked harder to please him and live up to his constant demands. His demands grew more violent over the next year of marriage. When she finally left him to move back home, he chased her car and smashed the window out with his bare hand. She took him to the hospital before leaving him.

In our LI session, as she released the trauma of the violence in the relationship, the panic feelings and anger grew stronger. By mid-session, the sensations of heaviness and sadness were coming up in her body. During a check-in, she reported, "I gravitate towards taking care of people. He always got his way". We used a few different protocols over the next few appointments to process this relationship. By the end of the third session, she was able to look back with relief that it was over. She said smiling at me, "I have choices now". She also reported feeling stronger, more connected to herself, and she noticed more of her own emotions.

At the beginning of our next appointment, she reported increased self-awareness, continued commitment to eating healthily and according to the plan she developed with her nutritionist, and a growing realization of how anxious she was when her family or others didn't support her. Beth was angry that her parents had acted more like "friends, than parents" when she was dating and married to Ben. Though these new feelings and thoughts were uncomfortable and "scary" for her to experience for the first time, it was a good sign that she was beginning to connect more fully to her true embodied experience. To self-soothe is one of the primary components of healthy self-regulation. Instead of the hyper-focus on food management, she was finding healthier alternatives to soothe herself, like making her bedroom a "safe, comfortable, private hangout" away from the rest of her family. The compassionate care she gave to everyone else in her life was beginning to be self-directed.

Targeting attachment and developmental experiences. Between sessions more childhood memories began to emerge. As she would report these, I would add them to the possible target list for later LI work. It had become clear that Beth's "caring and supportive" parents had failed her by being her "best friends" and not creating safe boundaries for her. I started with a protocol called Cell Being to assess her connection to herself and facilitate greater differentiation from the enmeshed relationships between her and the others in life. After a few sessions, she was able to see how she had focused on everyone else and lost herself. She defined her "essence" or Cell Being as a "sparkler" and that was congruent with what I was noticing in her: bright, funny, smart, and engaging. Her self-image continued to improve as she became more differentiated from what others wanted her to be and she began to connect more deeply with who she believed herself to be. "I'm pretty amazing", she said at one point.

Then, we focused on other protocols that address preverbal attachment ruptures. These protocols allow the LI clinician to externally bring a focused, calm, and caring presence to the client. The objective is to create an embodied sense in the client of being safely held, cared for, and delighted in.

In the first few sessions, Beth liked connecting with her preverbal experience. Yet, it was difficult for her to let me show care and nurturance toward her in our session. She told me at the end of one session,

> It feels scary for me to trust you when I feel this vulnerable, even though I know I trust you. It's weird. I know I'm safe with you here, but I feel nervous like I'm too much for you to handle.

The more I focused caring, patient, and loving attention toward her using the protocol, the more the entanglement with her mother's neediness was exposed. I used specific phrasing, which would address her feelings of being "too much" for me. "I want to bring all my attention towards whatever you need". "Your needs are important here". "You don't have to do one thing for me."

Beth's ability to receive had been entangled with her mom's inability to regulate her own anxiety, insecurity, and loneliness. As we went through the timelines, Beth's anger grew toward not only her parents but also her brothers. In order to address Beth's anger and enmeshment with her family members, we moved to other LI protocols.

We worked at the stage when Beth's brother was added to the family. When Beth was less than a year old, her father began commuting to another State to develop his commercial fishing business. He would leave

Sue and Beth home for weeks and months at a time. Sue, Beth's mom, grew more resentful and anxious in his absence but was able to handle the single parenting well enough. Then, when Beth was 18 months old, her brother Tom was born. It grew more difficult for Sue to manage or regulate her emotions with the lack of sleep and without support from other adults. She would be anxious and have anger outbursts during the day as she tried to take care of her newborn baby and toddler alone. Toddler Beth would often "get to sleep with mommy" to keep her company, and Beth would often hear her mommy cry herself to sleep. This created the perfect environment for toddler Beth to become mommy's "little helper", "best friend", and confidant. Parentification occurs when children are put into adult roles of caregiving when they do not have the mental or physical resources to help like an adult. A toddler will work hard to please mommy or daddy, and so it was for Beth with her mother.

In the therapy process, as Beth connected with those early experiences through LI, she felt immediate love and joy in the connection. As she began to give herself attention, she realized how distracted she was and noticed a strong desire to encourage her mother. The thought came to her about her mom, "you were doing the best that you could for being all alone" and "I'm sorry dad made it so hard for you". While she focused on her mother, she lost the connection with herself. I had anticipated that this would happen. Beth was more focused on her mother's needs and not on her own toddler needs. It was critical in this part of Beth's work to not engage her empathy toward her mom.

The adult client will often present with messages they heard or experienced in that earlier time from their primary caregiver. It does not have to be the mother's intention to elicit this response from the child. A capable child interprets the mother's needs as being more important. When that becomes the primary mode of relating and continues through time, it becomes the client's brain default or coping mechanism.

In LI, the client is always advocating for the younger self-experience, because we are building in new neurological structure and repairing what did not exist for the client in their early-life brain mapping. In Beth's case, she had already been the one who helped her mom regulate her emotions. Her mother's anxiety had elicited Beth's toddler level of resourcefulness, help, and comfort. Our work together was to stop that adapted brain pattern and refocus the care back toward the one who should have been the focus, which was Beth.

These are the clinical moments when coaching is needed. I'll often use phrases like,

> Your mother is a grown up. You are too little to help her with all of her grown up problems. You show lots of love to her and it is never a toddler's job to take care of her mommy. It is a mommy job to take care of you, help you, and play with you.

These interventions create the language that enables differentiation and redirects the responsibility for caregiving back to the parent and away from the child brain adaptation within the client.

Through several sessions, Beth became more focused on herself. She connected with her own loneliness for losing her mother's attention when her brother was born. Beth also advocated for herself imaginally by releasing anger toward her mom for not having boundaries and using Beth as a comfort and confidant, rather than finding other adults who could help. She released anger toward her father by holding him responsible for not creating a healthy plan for his wife and family, but instead leaving them "abandoned" for such long periods of time. As her work deepened, she was able to express that she had been angry with them throughout her life, and she was noticing more incidents through the timeline repetitions. This release is always done imaginally toward the perpetrator and will reduce the brain-firing pattern in a session or within a few.

We followed up with other protocols for some of the situations in her youth where she had been put into a parentified role between her father's absences for work and her mother's loneliness and anxiety. As a result of this work over the next few months, Beth experienced a greater empathy for herself, her mother, and her father, while still holding them responsible for their problems and poor parenting. At the beginning of one session, she reported to me,

> It was hard for everyone when my dad got into his *work-aholic* mode. It was even hard for him. But now I know that's a problem he has and it doesn't have anything to do with me. I don't have to fix him or help my mom fix him. Or make her feel okay anymore.

It was during this time in Beth's work that she asked for therapy referrals for her mom, Sue, and for her brothers. Beth was speaking up for herself at home and making boundaries. She was able to say "No" when her boundaries were being violated. When her brother's girlfriend and their baby moved into the house, Beth made clear boundaries around the privacy she wanted for her bedroom and the parameters around when she was willing to help and not help with the baby. She was staying present in the moment of her home life to access her best thinking and tools. Her WOT was widening.

Beth continued to progress over the next few months using a variety of LI protocols. We addressed the events where she took care of her parents, younger brothers, and friends in her childhood. We addressed some of the themes she lived into during her life: "I have to make everyone happy", and "I have to be in crisis to get attention". Beth came to one appointment reporting that she had figured something out. "Dad is a risk taker and gets people excited, while mom is a people drainer. Maybe my relationship with my mom isn't so great." She was getting clarity around the thoughts and beliefs that had been entangled in her dysregulated emotional responses. She was aware of the impact of her caregiving on her emotions and nervous system, and she understood the beliefs that were part of the problem. Her body and mind were becoming congruent. By using a variety of LI protocols, her system was regulating better and her WOT was increasing.

Current relationship focus. Next, we focused on her relationship with her then current fiancé. It only took one session for her to see how she had started and developed the relationship by overriding her own needs and emotions to focus on his. She realized that she always felt "out of control" in the relationship, either "shut down" or hyper-focused on "trying to make him happy". Over the next few appointments, we continued to focus on her relationship with her fiancé. After several sessions, she said she was "ready to face the present", and even though she felt "vulnerable and alone, she needed to break up with him". This was greater evidence that she was increasing her ability to regulate her own emotions and advocate for herself.

Summary of gains and therapy termination. At the same time, she was making other advancements. Her body was strong enough to handle more physical activity like longer walks and yoga. Her thinking cleared. She continued to gain weight. She graduated from her Eating Disorder Group. She started to work part-time, which eventually turned to full-time. Her rigid rules were replaced by a more flexible way of making decisions for herself. "What do I want; what is right for me, now" had replaced "what do they need or want from me? Will this make them happy?" She continued to stay more balanced in the relationships in her life with family and coworkers at work. She began building new friendships with people and tested her ability to have healthier boundaries. She had even begun a college-level art class.

Beth came to her final appointment. We had been working together for 26 months. She was calm, relaxed, and excited as we talked about her leaving for San Francisco to start her new life in an art studio. She talked about how proud she was of herself for all she had accomplished over the past two years. She was disciplined, but flexible and not rigid. She was maintaining a healthy weight and had started her menstrual cycle a month before. Her body felt stronger, and the doctors had taken her off all the medications she had been on over the past few years. She felt confident with people but not afraid to be alone. She was able to be patient and present with her family, while expressing herself and maintaining good boundaries.

Beth had experienced every LI protocol we had developed at that time. She had been open and focused to get help as we journeyed together. She sat in front of me attuned to herself, differentiated from her family, and ready to launch into the life ahead of her. My treatment plan for Beth had been to get her eating and then get her to be self-regulated and "rebounded" emotionally. I couldn't help but remember her goals for therapy, "increase confidence and self-esteem, get more energy, be happier and healthier". We reached our goals together.

Conclusion

In this chapter, we have attempted to give several examples of how LI is able to address emotional regulation in eating disorder clients effectively and efficiently. When using LI, we have the privilege of not only clearing trauma but also directly facilitating in each session increased emotional regulation as the client addresses the body arousal firing pattern developed in their past. Helping clients widen their WOT is successful client care. Health comes when we are able to engage in our life experience in a way that acknowledges the embodiment of the emotions that fit the truth of our life experience. The LI protocol structure allows clients to connect and attune to themselves and, therefore, manage their body/mind/spirit world and connect with the external world around them in a balanced way. Informed by current understandings about how trauma is stored in body-based neural networks, LI provides an embodied therapeutic method for facilitating eating disorder recovery.

References

Cozolino, L. (2006). The *neuroscience of human relationships: Attachment and the developing social brain.* New York, NY: W.W. Norton & Company.

Ogden, P., Minton, K., & Pain, C. (2006). *Trauma and the body: A sensorimotor approach to psychotherapy.* New York, NY: W. W. Norton & Co.

Pace, P. (2012). *Lifespan integration: Connecting Ego states through time.* La Vergne, TN: Eirene Imprint.

Rothschild, B. (2000). *The body remembers: The psychophysiology of trauma and trauma treatment.* New York, NY: W. W. Norton & Company.

Siegel, D. J. (1999). *The developing mind: Toward a neurobiology of interpersonal experience.* New York, NY: The Guilford Press.

Siegel, D. J. (2011). *Mindsight: The new science of personal transformation.* New York, NY: Bantam Books.

van der Kolk, B. (2015). What happens when a traumatic memory is triggered? In The Trauma Treatment Revolution (video presentation). Psychotherapy networker, traumanetworker.kajabi.com

Wallin, D. J. (2007). *Attachment in psychotherapy.* New York, NY: The Guilford Press.

20 Bringing the Body Back into "Body Image"

Body-Centered Perspectives on Eating Disorders

Adrienne Ressler and Susan Kleinman

Introduction

The body itself must be regarded as a core element in the treatment of body image disturbance with eating disorder clients. How can we not recognize the importance of the body and the knowledge it holds? The body cries with pain or sorrow, trembles in anger, jumps for joy, leaps with excitement, slumps in defeat, and yearns for connection.

> The body and mind are interrelated parts that form a cohesive whole. They operate in a reciprocal manner. Body movements are influenced by our thoughts, attitudes and feelings; our thoughts, attitudes and feelings are influenced by the rhythm and the movements of the body.
> (Rice, Hardenberg, & Hornyak, 1989, p. 258)

We, as well as our clients, benefit from working within a holistic frame that reflects the powerful synchrony between body and mind. When we invite opportunities for creativity and spontaneity to emerge, this synchrony is maximized. In this chapter, we will put forth the premise that practice-based evidence, in conjunction with evidence-based practice, can impart valuable information to allow practitioners to incorporate body-focused techniques into their everyday working style.

The Complexity of Body Image

To date, body image continues to be one of the most complex of the core issues associated with eating disorder treatment. It follows, then, that bringing the body back into body image treatment is surely a consideration for our work with eating disorder clients. In 2006, Berkman et al. reported that the literature on the treatment of all eating disorders is "of highly variable quality" and recommended that "future studies should address novel treatments for the disorder, optimal duration of intervention and optimal approaches for those who do not respond to medication or CBT [cognitive behavioral therapy]" (p. 5). Methods considered novel in 2006—such as meditation, mindfulness, massage, and yoga—are now considered to be standard healing interventions. In 1998, May (cited in Wylie, 2004) reviewed the literature for empirical studies of the effectiveness of body psychotherapy. He found only 20 such studies (not including Eye Movement Desensitization and Reprocessing [EMDR] or Gendlin's technique, Focusing), 15 of which showed beneficial results (Wylie, 2004, p. 7). Pert devoted her career to conducting research to study the science behind mind-body medicine. "Mind doesn't dominate body, it *becomes* body—body and mind are one," she stated (1997, p. 187). Pert concluded that the process of communication, the flow of information throughout the whole organism, is evidence that the body is the actual outward manifestation, in physical space, of the mind (p. 187). Like Charles Darwin, who reported, "repressed emotion almost always comes to the surface in some form of body motion" (as quoted in Deaver, 2009, pp. 43–44), Pert wrote that

> When emotions are repressed, denied, not allowed to be whatever they may be, our network pathways get blocked, stopping the flow of the vital feel-good, unifying chemicals that run both our biology and our behavior. When emotions are expressed—which is to say that the bio-chemicals that are the substrate of emotion are flowing freely—all systems are united and made whole. Separation of mind and body is a false dichotomy.
>
> (p. 273)

The Development of Body Image

Our search of literature written prior to 1980 yielded only a few pioneers devoted to examining body image, for example Fisher, Schilder, Cleveland, and Bruch. Their speculations set the stage for a plethora of commentaries reflecting that the construct of body image is complex, inherently multidimensional, and difficult to define. Thompson, Heinberg, Altabe, and Tantleff-Dunn (1999) found defining body image to be "tricky" (pp. 9–10). Fisher (1990) pronounced,

> Body image is turning out to be an exceedingly complex affair. There is no such entity as 'The Body Image.' [...] The inexhaustible list of behaviors that has turned out to be linked with measures in the body-experience domain, documents the ubiquitous influence of body attitudes. Human identity cannot be separated from its somatic headquarters in the world.
>
> (p. 18)

Fisher and Stark (cited in Kearney-Cooke & Steichen-Asch, 1990) proposed that even before birth, body image development is influenced by how close the match is between the parents' expectations and the actual reality of the baby's looks, sex, and temperament. Montagu (1986) stressed the importance of the stimulation of the skin, particularly through nurturing touch, as a critical element along with mutual gaze transaction, mirroring, and affirming language in setting the stage for body image development. Krueger (2002) credited Damasio for noting "the core of the self is developmentally grounded in body experience" (p. 178). The term *embodiment* has become widely used within the holistic community to describe any reference to body connection, but few may realize that the word, used by Winnicott in 1965, was used as being synonymous with *in-dwelling*, "a seamless linkage of self, body functions, and the limiting membrane of the skin" (Krueger, 2002, p. 177). We found that the descriptions that follow, authored by Krueger and Damasio, separately capture the true intent of Winnicott's meaning:

> Body image is integral to the sense of self and self-organization. The self, as well as emotional processes, are always and inherently embodied, co-created and inter-subjectively constructed and revised. There is no realm of thought, feeling or action that can be conceived without bodily engagement and expression.
>
> (Meissner, 1998, as quoted by Krueger, 2002, p. 116)

Damasio's words concur, "All experience, thought and feelings are embodied feelings, first and foremost about the body, they offer us the cognition of our visceral and musculo-skeletal states [...] feelings let us mind the body" (Krueger, 2002, p. 177).

Since 1980, the interest in research on body image has increased among researchers. Brownell (2012) wrote, "The field has grown to a critical mass of investigators who are studying this issue from multiple viewpoints... This has led to a richness of discourse, multidisciplinary work and impressive advances in understanding body image problems" (p. xxi). In addition to early theories put forth to lay the groundwork for the study of body image, the expanded understanding of the factors contributing to body dissatisfaction now is known to include cultural definitions of attractiveness, anxious temperament, perfectionistic traits, dieting, and compartmentalization of the body into separate, unrelated parts. Eating disorder clients often struggle to make known the emotions and experiences embedded deep within. Many repeat and reinforce a litany of punishing words and/or phrases that become imprinted in their minds and bodies. Negative self-talk examples we hear often include "I am gross," "I am fat," "I am disgusting," and "I am ugly and unlovable." It is rare that our clients demonstrate a capacity for self-compassion, instead returning to their habitual default mode of self-judgment, isolation, and being consumed with their negative thoughts and feelings.

Body Image Disturbance

Despite the fact that there may not be agreement regarding a singular, all-encompassing definition of body image, there is agreement that the body itself and body image are core to eating disorder treatment. Psychoanalyst Hilde Bruch left a legacy highlighting the pivotal role of body image in the treatment of eating disorders. Bruch (1965) states, "The complex nature of body image is manifested in disturbances of perception, an inability to recognize signals and sensations in the body and delusional-like distortions of size and weight" (p. 555). To expand this definition, we have included the concept that body image identity involves differentiating "who I am" from "how I look."

We have found it is essential that the clinician and client define body image in the same manner so as to ensure a common ground for effective and clear communication. Ressler (2000) provides the following working definition of body image that many practitioners find useful.

Body image can be defined as encompassing three dimensions:

- The picture you have in your mind's eye of how you look to yourself
- How you believe others perceive you
- How you feel "living" in your body

(p. 35)

An example of therapeutic body image work as follows embraces this definition. Kleinman developed the Body Image Experiential (BIE) format in 2001 in order to provide an opportunity for clients to explore body image issues from their own internal experiential perspective. The BIE format combines psychoeducational, experiential, and psychodynamic methods, which lend themselves to the exploration of this important subject (Kleinman, 2002, p. 5). The format challenges clients to recognize that their distortions are signals representing conflict from within and, once they accept this premise, preparing them for the increased likelihood they will be able to understand and replace their negative default mode with more positive options.

The BIE sessions always begin with an exploration of the working definition of body image (earlier)—how each client sees herself, believes others see her, and feels living in her body. I then ask the group to identify actions they take when they experience these specific perceptions and feelings. Most clients provide examples that reveal their use of negative emotionally driven behaviors to cope with overwhelming or uncomfortable situations. These might include restricting food, overexercising, or self-harm. I follow this step by sharing a quote I've selected that provides a tangible way for them to explore the feelings that underlie their negative body image perceptions.

On one particular day, I chose this quote to address the vulnerability inherent in change: "Because transitions require adapting, shifting gears and changing the lens from which we function, they have the potential to disturb our emotional balance and leave us without a familiar sense of security" (Russo, Nardozzi, & Kleinman 2004, pp. 5–6). The group discussed the quotation's relevance, after which I introduced the experiential component of the format to embody the process further. "Identify a safe space in the room, move to that space and notice what it feels like to be there," I instructed. "Now identify a different space and notice what it's like to move from your familiar space to the new one. Try it first with eyes open and repeat with eyes closed." This experience shifted the focus from a cognitive process to an internal process to capture vulnerable feelings and sensations. Participants were then able to directly express their bodily experiences by responding to the following questions on a worksheet:

1   What was your safe space in the room?
2   How did it feel to leave that space?
3   How did it feel to be in the new space?
4   What did you find interesting about this experience?

Their responses indicated how or why the experience had been important:

- "I was a little surprised that I reached the new space because I don't trust myself. Once there, I didn't know what to do. That's typical for me."
- "I was so sure I was going in the right direction, but I really wasn't. I ended up way far away and I felt lost."
- "I held my breath and walked very slowly; I felt scared and confused. Sometimes I get panic attacks and I wonder if they are related to being scared like this."
- "I really wanted to get to my new place and when I couldn't find it, I got upset with myself because I failed."
- "My safest space in the room was near an exit. I always stay near the edges of a room or where I can see anyone leave or enter."
- "I looked outside of myself for direction rather than trusting myself and I didn't know what to do. My leg began to shake-that happens all the time but this time I noticed it. Do you think it's related?"
- "I felt tense, tightness in my chest, my breathing slowed down. I felt like I was suffocating. My choice to use the corner of the room as a starting point and the opened door/exit as an ending point may signify an easy way for me to escape from me."

All of the group members identified somatically related experiences that connected them to their body. Several were able to be consciously aware of how their observations related metaphorically in their lives. These insights would eventually make it possible for them, over time, to explore their body responses on a deeper level, leading them to a stronger sense of connection and wholeness. Embodied experiences such as this represent a touchstone to the needs of eating disorder clients who struggle to articulate and make known the emotions and experiences embedded deep within. "Although talk therapy is widely recognized as valuable, it may not always allow for a holistic approach, directly engaging the deep emotional issues accessed through the right hemisphere of the brain" (Wylie, 2004, p. 3).

Embodiment: Communication from Within

The very nature of embodiment (embodyment) implies that body behavior should be a strong aspect of the therapeutic process, weaving together the essence of the self as a whole being—emotions, thoughts, actions—in harmonious synchrony (Kleinman & Ressler, 2017). Clinician's own experience of embodiment, ability to access unconscious material and sense of being in the body, is part of their own identity and plays an important role in the therapeutic relationship [attunement] (Ressler & Kleinman, 2006, p. 4). Although many tend to think of attunement in relation to others, attunement also reflects a connection to self. When clinicians connect with and utilize their own feelings creatively as part of the therapeutic process, they are better able to help their clients decode their own inner experiences and transform these experiences into opportunities for growth. We have found that "developing an attuned therapeutic relationship promotes client insight, trust, validation, and connection to feelings. It embodies qualities inherent in a healing relationship" (Ressler & Kleinman, 2012, p. 419).

Embodied clinicians are able to spontaneously use creative processes, such as metaphorical expression, to develop meaning in their work. Jung referred to metaphor as *the healing symbol*. "It affects the person on three levels: the mental level on which we interpret meaning, the imaginative level, where the actual transforming power resides, and the emotional level connected to the feelings embodied in the metaphor" (Woodman, 1988/1993, p. 54). In our terms, metaphor works simultaneously on the cognitive level, interpreting the meaning; the imaginative level, creating the image internally (living pictures seen in the eye of the mind); and the emotional level, connecting the feelings embodied in the metaphor.

Montross (2013) provided a powerful metaphor that touched upon all three levels referenced by Jung. Her mentor, Mary Weatherton, used this metaphor when Montross was debating whether to devote her psychiatric practice to working with severely disturbed patients:

> The patients we work with have fallen through the ice in the middle of a frozen lake", she [Mary] began, "My job—your job should you take this path—is to go out to them, to be with them on the thin ice, and to work with them to get them out of the frigid water.

But you must know that if you go out to them on that thin ice, there's a real danger that you'll fall in, too. So, if you go into this work, you've got to be anchored to the shore. You can reach out one hand to the person in the water, but your other hand needs to have a firm grip on the people and things that connect you to the shore. If you don't, you lose your patients and you lose yourself.

(p. 212)

Clinical Intuition

The winter 2015 issue of the Renfrew Center Foundation's professional journal, *Perspectives*, focused on intuition from various points of view. Laura Weisberg's contribution came from her experience as a psychotherapist:

Clinical intuition is reflected in the music and dance within the therapeutic relationship, one of the most powerful agents of therapeutic change. [...]We utilize our intuitive capacities to sense when to support and when to challenge, when to lean in and when to allow space, when to increase the level of activation in the room and when to help soothe and calm things down.

(2015, pp. 11–12)

Weisberg's lyrical words underscore the work of Marks-Tarlow (2012), "Clinical intuition involves implicit processes that lead us to know, feel, and sense things without knowing how we know" (p. 55). Marks-Tarlow's intent regarding the efficacy of clinical intuition follows:

My aim is to elevate clinical intuition to its rightful position as the central ingredient for putting clinical theory into practice, for perceiving and responding to complex interpersonal patterns, and for effecting deep change in patients and ourselves along the way.

(2014, p. xxxii)

Our belief on the efficacy of incorporating body-focused methods to body image treatment mirrors Marks-Tarlow's position on elevating clinical intuition to its rightful place.

Practitioners utilizing the intricate interplay between brain, body–mind, and beliefs work through the use of the senses, which serve as antennae or receptors. Sharing the feeling states of others appears to be intimately linked to the functioning of mirror neurons, allowing individuals to grasp the mindset of others kinesthetically (Pallaro, 2007). Many concepts from experiential methods can be incorporated readily into any meaningful therapeutic relationship; a keen awareness of clients' energy, breathing, gestures, body positioning, use of space, and language cues all provide valuable data for clinicians to acquire a deeper understanding of the body's signals and to resonate with those states of being.

Accessing Clinical Intuition through Dance/
Movement Therapy Concepts

Dance/movement therapists weave together nonverbal dialogues that transform everyday movements into expressive communication (Kleinman, 2014). As a process, the use of dance/movement therapy (DMT) opens a pathway to reestablish connection with the client's abandoned body. The patterns that emerge are then explored through both nonverbal and verbal reflection, allowing clients to experience and express feelings and, in collaboration with the therapist, identify how emerging awareness parallels and reflects their unique behavioral patterns. Clients are encouraged to be "detectives", viewing their embodied experiences and cognitive perceptions as clues to help them recognize and decode their own emotional issues. According to Dulicai (2016), "*spontaneous* gestures of clients are clues to dance/movement therapists and with creativity we have the freedom necessary to do our work well. Take care lest we miss them" (p. 34).

Overview of concepts. Concepts such as *rhythmic synchrony* (RS), *kinesthetic awareness* (KA), and *kinesthetic empathy* (KE), which underlie the process of DMT, lend themselves beautifully for incorporation into any practitioner's therapeutic style (Ressler, Kleinman, & Mott, 2010, p. 414).

RS manifests in clinicians' ability to attune to their clients' pace and timing in order to address the distress that lies beneath the surface. When therapists are not in rhythm with their clients, pacing and timing are compromised.

KA represents the ability of clinicians to experience their own feelings and sensations inwardly. If clinicians are detached from listening to their own body, it is likely that their clients will respond with the same degree of detachment.

KE is the ability, on a body level, to understand and sometimes experience what others are feeling. It has significant relevance to the therapeutic relationship and the journey clients and clinicians undertake together.

Case example. The incorporation of these DMT concepts by a non-DMT practitioner is evidenced in the example that follows. It is important to mention that within the confines of the actual treatment session, in real time, there is fluidity in moving between these concepts; rather than being concrete and finite, they are states of being and, thus, difficult to identify precisely.

Sheila (pseudonym), a 43-year-old married woman diagnosed with binge-eating disorder, came for treatment regarding problems in her marriage. She explained that her husband insisted she lose weight and recorded her progress, or lack thereof, on a chart in their bedroom after her daily weigh-ins. His goal was for Sheila to lose enough weight to look like one of *Charlie's Angels*, three fantasy crime-fighting beauties featured in a popular television series. If Sheila did not lose weight each day, he would take away her car keys. When I asked Sheila if she wanted to lose weight, she replied she wouldn't mind but, "I'll be damned if I give him the satisfaction!" Leaning in, I gently asked Sheila why she accepted this abusive behavior from her husband (KE). She responded by speaking of her childhood in a straightforward, toneless manner. She revealed a horrific trauma background of sexual abuse by her foster father after being abandoned by her family at age seven. At age 16, deciding to tell her foster mother what had transpired, she found herself thrown out of the house and called a liar. As Sheila spoke, I became aware of uneasiness in my own center (KA) as well as a feeling of being drawn towards her (KE). Edging slightly closer and sensing Sheila's fragility, I spoke softly (RS, KE). "That's a terrible story", I empathically responded (KE). "How do you feel about what happened to you?" Sheila, continuing in her soft monotone, said, "I'm really angry." "Would you like to get some of the angry feelings out?" I asked. She nodded. My clinical intuition (KE) informed me that Sheila needed to tap into her physical energy reserve in order to access the unexpressed emotions that were literally weighing her down in both her body and in life. Picking up a *bataka* (padded bat), I stacked some large pillows on the floor. "Let's try an experiment. Why don't you hit the pillows with the bat and we'll see what happens." Sheila pounded weakly on the pillows and then looked up beseechingly, "I'm so sorry. I want to feel something, but I don't." I assured her there was no right or wrong way to do this exercise. She sighed in relief, and we both laughed (KE), lightening the atmosphere and releasing Sheila from her default mode of pleasing others. Something in her face and her body indicated to me that she was in touch with her own tempo and timing (RS, KE). I responded in kind (KE), "Sheila, forget the *bataka*—what does your body want to do?" Without pause, she twisted her hands together and what came out of her was almost a snarl, "I'd like to wring his neck!" This outburst was a clear indication of what Sheila's body needed to do in order to move further into experiencing and understanding what she had uncovered. As a result, the next sessions consisted of Sheila wringing out wet dishtowels as she verbally wrung out from her body the anger and sadness that had been buried deep inside her for over 30 years (RS, KA, KE).

Because I had used the DMT concepts as guides to attune to Sheila, I was able to empathically reflect and validate her unconscious and unspoken needs. This allowed Sheila to access previously closed pathways to her "true self" (Ressler, 2009, p. 154).

All Clinicians Are Researchers: Treatment-Based Practice

Presently in the field of eating disorders, a chasm exists between those who adhere to evidence-based practice and those who support the efficacy of treatment-based practice. Clinicians are daily collecting impressions, grouping together likenesses, differentiating differences, and tailoring their clinical efforts, both on empirical and experiential evidence to best meet the needs of their clients. A visionary, the social worker, Virginia Satir (2014), was known as *the mother* of family therapy. She began her own research early in life, writing,

> When I was five... I decided that when I grew up I'd be a 'children's detective on parents.' I didn't quite know what I would look for, but I realized a lot went on in families that didn't meet the eye.
>
> (Virginia's Education, n.d.)

We believe there may be something to this concept of the clinician as detective. Many a detective novel contains elements of this type of approach, the authors utilizing methods that closely parallel criterion for data collection and often calling for the detective to utilize clinical intuition and operate within the parameters of a therapeutic alliance (real or imagined) with the person being pursued. In his book *The First Deadly Sin*, Lawrence Sanders' (1980) protagonist, Captain Delaney, retired chief of the New York Police Department, has written a series of training monographs for his homicide team. One of the monographs argued that

> [...] In spite of the great advances in laboratory analysis, the forensic sciences, computerized records, and probability percentages, the new detective disregarded his hunches and instinct at his peril, for frequently they were not a sudden brainstorm, but were the result of observation of physical evidence and experience of which the detective might not even be consciously aware. But stewing in his subconscious, a rational and reasonable conclusion was reached, thrust into his conscious thought, and should never be allowed to wither unexplored, since it was, in many cases, as logical and empirical as common sense.
>
> (p. 406)

Delaney introduces the idea of an *adversary concept*, which examines the affinity between hunter (detective/clinician) and hunted (suspect/client). He explores how, in certain cases, "it was necessary for the detective to penetrate and assume the physical body, spirit and soul of the criminal in order to bring him to justice" (Sanders, 1980, p. 406). This latter strategy comes curiously close to echoing the words of Margaret Little (1986), psychoanalyst and author of *Transference Neurosis and Transference Psychosis: Toward Basic Unity*. She writes,

> The analyst has to be willing to feel about his patient, with his patient, and sometimes even for his patient, the sense of supplying feelings which the patient is unable to find within himself and in the absence of which no real change can happen.
>
> (p. 58)

Pathways from the Past Generate Springboards to the Future

Powerful forms of expression have been with us since the beginning of time—ancient Greek drama, tribal dances, drawings of cave dwellers, religious rituals. The experiential and somatic methods in use today are built upon the practices, beliefs, and findings of innovators from the past, each one laying the groundwork for new discoveries. Carl Jung planted seeds with his *active imagination theory* so that Mary Whitehouse was able to create *Authentic Movement*. Wilhelm Reich's theories of energy yielded to the development of *Bioenergetic Analysis*, which was made popular by Alexander Lowen and John Pierrakos. Fritz Perls and his wife Laura, influenced by Rank, developed *Gestalt Therapy*, which Ilana Rubenfeld later integrated with her own work in *Alexander Technique* to create *Rubenfeld Synergy*. Jacob Moreno, best known for creating *group therapy* and *psychodrama*, developed training methods that were sustained and passed on by countless clinicians (including his wife Zerka Moreno). And, Harry Stack Sullivan and Frieda Fromm Reichmann each influenced Marian Chace, known as the mother of *Dance/Movement Therapy* (Ressler & Kleinman, 2012, pp. 418–424).

These early innovators have each been so influential in terms of their creative legacy. The following statement by David Treadway (2014) captures a perfect rendering of the path taken by those of us who were influenced by these great thinkers and whose work in the 1970s and 1980s resurrected and ignited an awakening of the body-mind psychotherapy in use today. "I know I practice an often intuitive craft, not an exact and predictable science. I bring my therapeutic models, repertoire of techniques, previous clinical experience and my all too limited personality to my encounter with the clients I see" (2014).

Conclusion

Creative healers and artists have long known intuitively what scientists have just begun to discover in recent years. "The body is merely the visibility of the soul, the psyche", Jung wrote, "and the soul is the psychological experience of the body. So it is one and the same" (Krueger, 2002, p. 77). As the field of eating disorders has matured, we, as seasoned clinicians, have concluded that embracing body-focused interventions must become an essential element of comprehensive and effective treatment of body image. Building on Herbert, Neeren, and Lowe's (2007), work to bring science and practice into dialogue with each other, Main, McGilley, & Bunnell (2010) state,

> The need to bridge the science/practice gap does not devalue either domain's distinct and relative merits, nor does it negate the necessity for interdisciplinary debate. It is no longer acceptable to rely on

research that does not reflect clinical realities.... Nor is it acceptable for clinicians to base their treatment approaches solely on their own clinical intuition

(p. xxv)

It follows that the gap within the eating disorder professional community, in relation to art and science, might benefit from that perspective. It is clear that no winners emerge when an issue as complex and core to eating disorders, namely body image, is not fully explored—practitioners must be able to use a variety of modalities delivered with enough clinical wisdom, empathy, and clinical intuition to form an authentic attachment relationship for healing. There is to date no known exact recipe for recovery. What we do know, however, is that leaving the body out of the ingredients needed for effective body image treatment leads to, in Bruch's (1962) words, improvement that is "apt to be only a temporary remission" (p. 189).

References

American Psychiatric Association. (2006). Practice guideline for the treatment of patients with eating disorders: Third edition. *American Journal of Psychiatry,* 163(Supp. 7), 1–128.

Berkman, N. D., Bulik, C. M., Brownley, K. A., Lohr, K. N., Sedway, J. A., Rooks, A., & Gartlehner, G. (2006). *Management of eating disorders. Evidence Report/Technology Assessment No. 135* (AHRQ Publication No. 06-E010). Rockville, MD: Agency for Healthcare Research and Quality. Retrieved from http:// archive.ahrq.gov/downloads/pub/evidence/pdf/eatingdisorders/eatdis.pdf

Brownell, K. D. (2012). Foreword. In T. Cash (Ed.), *Encyclopedia of body image and human appearance: Vol. 1. A-F* (pp. xxi–xxii). Waltham, MA: Academic Press.

Bruch, H. (1962). Perceptual and conceptual disturbances in anorexia nervosa. *Psychosomatic Medicine, 24*(2), 187–194.

Bruch, H. (1965). Anorexia nervosa and its differential diagnosis. *Journal of Nervous &Mental Disease, 141*(5), 555–566. doi:10.1097/00006254–196612000-00007

Deaver, J. (2009). *Roadside crosses.* New York, NY: Simon & Schuster.

Dulicai, D. (2016). In S. Kleinman, J. W. Cathcart, A. Lohn, & S. Chaiklin (Eds.), *Movement reflections* (pp. 3–4). Columbia, MD: Marian Chace Foundation.

Fisher, S. (1990). The evolution of psychological concepts about the body. In T. F. Cash & T. Pruzinsky (Eds.), *Body images: Development, deviance, and change* (pp. 3–20). New York, NY: Guilford Press.

Herbert, J. D., Neeren, A. M., & Lowe, M. R., (2007). Clinician intuition and scientific evidence. What is their role in treating eating disorders. *Perspectives,* Winter, 15–17.

Kearney-Cooke, A., & Steichen-Asch, P. (1990). Men, body image, and eating disorders. In A. E. Andersen (Ed), *Males with eating disorders* (pp. 54–74). New York, NY: Brunner/Mazel.

Kleinman, S. (2002). Challenging body image distortions through the eyes of the body. Paper presented at Roots and revelation: dance/movement therapy forging new collaborations, innovations and freedom, 37th *Annual Conference of the American Dance Therapy Association*, Burlington, VT (No longer in print).

Kleinman, S. (2014). Eating disorder hope. Dance/movement therapy in the treatment of eating disorders: Re-claiming authentic connection with the self. Retrieved from www.eatingdisorderhope.com/recovery/self-help-tools-skills-tips/dancemovement-therapy-in-the-treatment-of-eating-disorders-re-claiming-authentic-connection-with-the-self

Kleinman, S., & Ressler, A. (2017, February 18). Personal communication.

Krueger, D. (2002). *Integrating body self and psychological self: Creating a new story in psychoanalysis and psychotherapy*. New York, NY: Brunner-Routledge.

Little, M. I. (1986). *Transference neurosis and transference psychosis: Toward basic unity*. New York, NY: Aronson.

Marks-Tarlow, T. (2012). Implicit processes. In *Clinical intuition in psychotherapy: The neurobiology of embodied response* (pp. 31–56). New York, NY: W.W. Norton.

Marks-Tarlow, T. (2014). Introduction. In *Awakening clinical intuition: An experiential workbook for psychotherapists* (pp. xvii–xxxvi). New York, NY: W.W. Norton.

Main, M., McGilley, B. H., & Bunnell, D. W. (2010). *Introduction. Treatment of eating disorders: Bridging the research-practice gap* (pp. xxi–xxv). Burlington, MA: Academic Press.

Montagu, A. (1986). *Touching: The human significance of the skin* (3rd ed.). New York, NY: Perennial Library.

Montross, C. (2013). Epilogue. In *Falling into the fire: A psychiatrist's encounters with the mind in crisis* (pp. 207–216). New York, NY: Penguin Press.

Pallaro, P. (2007). Somatic countertransference: The therapist in relationship. In P. Pallaro (Ed.), *Authentic movement: Vol. 2. Moving the body, moving the self, being moved: A collection of essays* (pp. 176–193). London, UK: Jessica Kingsley.

Pert, C. B. (1997). *Molecules of emotion: Why you feel the way you feel*. New York, NY: Scribner.

Ressler, A. (2000, September–October). A body to die for: Rethinking weight, wellness and body-image. *Pulse*, pp. 34–37.

Ressler, A. (2009). BodyMind treatment: Connecting to imprinted emotions and experiences. In M. Maine, W. N. Davis, & D. J. Shure(Eds.), *Effective clinical practice in the treatment of eating disorders: The heart of the matter* (pp. 145–163). New York, NY: Routledge.

Ressler, A., & Kleinman, S. (2006). Reframing body-image identity in the treatment of eating disorders. In W. Davis & S. Kleinman (Eds.), *Fostering body-mind integration* (Vol. 1, pp. 1–19). Philadelphia, PA: Renfrew Center Foundation.

Ressler, A., & Kleinman, S. (2012). Experiential and somatopsychic approaches to body image change. In T. Cash (Ed.), *Encyclopedia of body image and human appearance: Vol. 1. A-F* (pp. 418–424). Waltham, MA: Academic Press. doi:10.1016/B978-0-12-384925-0.00067-5

Ressler, A., Kleinman, S., & Mott, E. (2010). The use of holistic methods to integrate the shattered self. In M. Maine, B. H. McGilley, & D. W. Bunnell (Eds.), *Treatment of eating disorders: Bridging the research-practice gap* (pp. 404–425). London, UK: Academic Press.

Rice, J., Hardenberg, M., & Hornyak, L. (1989). Disturbed body image in anorexia nervosa: dance/movement therapy interventions. In L. Hornyak & E. Baker (Eds.), *Experiential therapies for eating disorders* (p. 258) New York, NY: Gilliford Press.

Russo, D., Nardozzi, J., & Kleinman, S. (2004). The challenge of making transitions: A central issue of recovery (Renfrew Center Working Paper, Vol. 2, summer). Available from The Renfrew Center Foundation, 475 Spring Lane, Philadelphia, PA 19128.

Sanders, L. (1980). *The first deadly sin*. New York, NY: Berkley.

Satir, V. (2014). FamousPsychologists.org. Retrieved from www.famouspsychologists.org/virginia-satir

Thompson, J. K., Heinberg, L. J., Altabe, M. N., & Tantleff-Dunn, S. (1999). *Exacting beauty: Theory, assessment and treatment of body image disturbance*. Washington, DC: American Psychological Association.

Treadway, D. (2014, September/October). Transgender counseling: A therapist struggles with his clinical choices. *Psychotherapy Networker*. Retrieved from www.psychotherapynetworker.org/daily/posts/couples-therapy/transgender-counseling-a-therapist-struggles-with-his-clinical-choices

Virginia's Education. (n.d.). Retrieved from http://satirglobal.org/about-virginia-satir

Weisberg, L. J. (2015, Winter). Intuition in psychotherapy. *Perspectives*, pp. 11–12. Retrieved from http://renfrewcenter.com/sites/default/files/2015%20WINTER%20PERSPECTIVES%202.4.15_0.pdf

Woodman, M. (1993). Healing through metaphor. In *Conscious femininity: Interviews with Marion Woodman* (pp. 53–55). Toronto, ON: Inner City Books (Written by Ralph Earle and reprinted from *Common Ground*, Summer 1988).

Wylie, M. S. (2004). Somatic therapy: Using the mind–body connection to get results. *Psychotherapy Networker, 28*(4), 1–7. Retrieved from www.psychotherapynetworker.org/daily/freereports/somatic-therapy-using-the-mind-body-connection-to-get-results

21 Practical Strategies for Promoting Embodiment in Eating Disorder Prevention and Treatment

Janelle L. Kwee and Mihaela Launeanu

Do you, the reader, know what you are feeling right now? What is your body telling you? Is it a feeling you enjoy or do not enjoy? Do you feel something more vividly or do you feel numb? Imagine pointing to wherever you feel something in your body. What is it that you feel? Do you have any idea what this means for you? It is good to stop and check in with ourselves in our bodies about what we are feeling and how we are doing, not just when there is a sense of major significance but even as we read the paper, check our e-mail, watch a movie, or have coffee with a friend. Perhaps you are bored in reading this book, weighed down by facts and citations. What does boredom feel like? Perhaps you are feeling angered about eating disorders or inspired or energized to do something about it. How do these feelings show up for you? Do you feel lightness, heaviness, warmth, or a movement of some sort? Checking in and listening to our embodied existence is not something that is valuable only when we feel tears and grief, but to identify any feeling or when we are aware of a numb disconnection. When do you notice yourself feeling anger, awe at beauty, a sense of truth or rightness, a sense of clarity, awareness of a valuable possibility, or peace and contentment? How do you sense these things? As you engage these questions, pay attention to your embodied sensing; this is not just a cognitive thought exercise but an opportunity to be connected to your whole self. We open this chapter with an invitation for you to enter in dialogue with your body as a "warm up" to considering the simple and practical ways in which we engage our clients toward greater embodied awareness.

Embodiment offers the perspective of an integrated self, which not only cannot exist without the body but also exists *as* a body. The mind and body are inextricably connected and reciprocally influence each other (Allan, 2005). Struggles with the body, prominent for all who suffer with eating disorders, are also existential struggles with the very pain of being a person living in a finite body (Heidegger, 1962; Merleau-Ponty, 2012). The mind cannot effectively work *against* or *outside of* the body because one's very self as a person is materially embodied. Reclaiming agency in and through the body is necessary for reclaiming and reintegrating the self in the world.

Notwithstanding these existential realities, the focus of the current definition and categorization of eating disorders emphasizes external body aspects such as weight, shape, and Body Mass Index (BMI), as well as food and eating behaviors (American Psychiatric Association, 2013). The role of subjective emotional or embodied experience in the conceptualization of eating disorders is lacking in the way eating disorders are currently conceptualized in the DSM 5 (Beyer, Chan, Kwee, Launeanu, & McBride, 2016). Similarly, the current standard of care for eating disorders maintains a focus on externalized physical behaviors and measurements including weight, distorted cognitions, body image, and eating behaviors. In the current medical behavioral model, multiple hospitalizations are the norm, reported rates of recovery are devastatingly low (46.9%; Steinhausen, 2002), and rates of chronicity and relapse range from 20.8% (Steinhausen, 2002) to 35% (Carter, Blackmore, Sutandar-Pinnock, & Woodside, 2004). Mainstream therapies may, in fact, collude with the client's over focus on the external aspects of their bodies and may further contribute to objectification.

Given the dynamics of submission and compliance common in eating disorder treatment focused primarily on weight restoration, we believe that it is essential to support women in the journey of integration and expression of the unity of their mind-body whole, in order to reclaim voice and power in their embodied existence in this world. Specifically, the purpose of this chapter is to offer practical approaches for promoting holistic and healthy embodied experiences in eating disorder prevention and treatment. Embodiment-focused efforts at prevention and treatment of eating disorders are situated at the crossroads of a variety of disciplines. Although we write from a perspective informed by our own clinical experiences as practicing psychotherapists, it is our intent to share practical strategies that will be useful for equipping practitioners of multiple disciplines working together to support all of our clients' journeys toward greater embodiment. From a feminist lens, promoting embodiment as the central strategy in preventing and treating eating disorders represents cultural resistance to the objectification of women.

Moving Past BMI Charts and Eating Logs

Eating disorders reflect not only individual vulnerabilities but also social systemic dysfunction that eventually may give rise to individual suffering. For instance, the social construction of gender and body with its emphasis on objectified body appearance disconnected from one's embodied experience provides the fertile context for the onset and high prevalence of eating disorders. The preoccupation with dieting and counting calories as a means to attain the socially prescribed body appearance leads to an obsession with food and eating behaviors (Sáenz-Herrero & Díez-Alegría, 2015).

Most of the current models of preventing and treating eating disorders perpetuate these systemic tendencies as they continue to see the body as an object that needs to have a certain weight and shape, and, consequently, as a passive recipient of food and forced feeding. However, attending to emotional starvation for wholeness, not just to food and eating, is equally important and needs to become a distinct and intentional focus in eating disorder prevention and treatment. "Who I am" as embodied self is just as important as shape and weight. With an embodiment focus, what one does *to* her body in the form of dieting, exercising, and eating is less salient than how she feels and lives *in* her body as a person. In this section, we offer a brief summary of our critique of the current standard of care and propose alternate goals for eating disorder prevention and treatment that move beyond weight restoration and promote embodiment. We conclude this section with a discussion about the ethical tensions in eating disorder care.

Critique of the current standard of care. Current treatments of eating disorders in hospital settings support a behavioral or medical model in which weight restoration is primary. These models are least time intensive, allowing more and more patients to circulate through much needed "beds," but without providing effective "healing" treatment (Galsworthy-Francis & Allan, 2014; Kass, Kolko, & Wilfley, 2013). This can often lead to multiple hospitalizations, where individuals have their "weight restored" but become further disembodied, dehumanized, and powerless in the process (Beyer et al., 2016) These models of care neglect the common concern of "voicelessness" or lack of agency experienced by individuals struggling with an eating disorder. In doing so, they reinforce the oppression of women, and the patriarchal values in which the patient must "behave well" in order to "get better." Our critique of the current standard of care is summarized by the following assertions:

- Weight restoration focus does not support embodied healing and may in fact work against the journey to embodied healing;
- There is a cycle of "voicelessness" or lack of agency in the treatment of eating disorders, which emphasizes compliance to others' demands over one's body;
- Patriarchal values and oppression of women are perpetuated by treatment strategies that maintain a dualistic focus of body as separate from the self;
- Health should be measured more broadly than BMI and organ functioning; and
- Treatment approaches should not reinforce the source of the wounds associated with the development of eating disorders in the first place (e.g., the excessive preoccupation with feeding and external body characteristics).

In summary, the current standard of care reflects an emphasis on body as object rather than body as self. While the immediate survival of the physical body may be rightfully defended, the body as self remains further uninhabited. This disconnection between behaviors and embodied experience maintains a fundamental split between mind and body that further constitutes a significant vulnerability toward relapse in individuals struggling with eating disorders.

Embodiment-focused goals for eating disorder recovery. In order to effectively restore individuals to health, treatment approaches need to work against the source of their struggle rather than to reinforce it. Individuals who suffer from eating disorders must be supported in becoming *more* themselves, experiencing being alive, embodied, and agentic in the world. Because the self is not divided dualistically between mind and body, the experience of being more fully a self in the physical sense directly influences one's experience of being more fully oneself spiritually, emotionally, and relationally. Here, we summarize several embodied goals for eating disorder recovery:

- To become more fully one's self;
- To experience oneself in and through one's body as being alive, being embodied, and being an agent in the world;
- To experience *being one's body* as a key part of identity;
- To feel access to one's emotions in the body; and
- To experience strength and voice in one's body.

In summary, embodiment-focused goals for eating disorder recovery focus on integration and wholeness, toward becoming more of oneself within oneself and in taking up literal and symbolic space in the world.

Ethical tensions. The high mortality rate of eating disorders is often cited as a rationale for more forceful methods of refeeding. Without food, the person with a severe eating disorder such as Anorexia Nervosa will not survive. There is an obvious ethical tension between refeeding and focusing on the development of the person's agency when the person suffering from the eating disorder refuses food. We acknowledge and respect these real tensions while maintaining that there is always a place for promoting dialogue with the person with an aim to increase their sense of freedom and agency within their embodied existence. Related to this, the unique vulnerabilities and needs according to each stage of eating disorder recovery (see Beyer & Launeanu, Chapter 11) are essential to consider for making intervention decisions.

Applying Embodiment Principles in Eating Disorder Prevention and Treatment

Cognitive and behavioral models of treatment have been commonly used for the treatment of disordered eating (Kass et al., 2013; Lipsman, Woodside, & Lozano, 2014; Thompson, 1990). While accessing thoughts and behaviors are undoubtedly pathways for accessing the self, they do not fully capture the phenomenological experience of being embodied. Rather, we aim to help clients not only recognize and reflect on their embodied selves but to experience embodiment in sessions. Leading clients into embodied experiences can include exploration of somatic experiencing, and noticing implicit affective states made known through corporeal sensations. Making use of the body in therapy, particularly listening to the self in the body during session (for example, "where did you feel that in your body when you told me about that?"), can act as a way of giving voice to the person by listening to the body as well as to the content of what is said. This conveys tacitly that the body is good and deserves to be experienced.

In the same way that our clients as people are not disembodied minds floating around having conversations about eating disorder treatment, we as therapists are fully embodied and present in and through our physical selves. In our own embodied presence, we have an important responsibility and opportunity to model body awareness and respect in our encounters with clients. One important way we can do this is through countertransference self-disclosure about our own experience of a client in session by saying, for example, "my chest got tight when you described...". The therapist's ability to name somatic cues as they listen to a client empathically can become a bridge for the client to more fully encounter themselves and their own emotional experience. Therapists can also model awareness and freedom of expression of the somatic nature of affect by describing how they experience emotions, for example by describing feeling hot or tight with the feeling of anger, and how this is a cue that they are needing to protect themselves somehow. It is essential to be in touch with our bodies as persons first, but also specifically as healers. Our embodied awareness often tells us things that our minds would take far longer to grasp or may never "see." Essentially, the body sees things we otherwise miss.

In earlier chapters, specific examples of various approaches to prevention and treatment are described in detail. These include (a) yoga (see Cook-Cottone, Chapter 16); (b) emotion-based psychotherapies including Advanced Experiential Dynamic Psychotherapy (AEDP), Emotion-Focused Therapy (EFT), and Emotion-Focused Family Therapy (EFFT) (see Williams & Files, Chapter 17); (c) Lifespan Integration (LI; see Wuflestad & Pace, Chapter 19); (e) a school-based health promotion program "Free to Be" talks (see Regehr & Owens, Chapter 18); and (f) using dance and movement therapy (see Ressler & Kleinman, Chapter 20). Other body-based psychotherapies relevant to eating disorder treatment include Hakomi Body Mindfulness (Kurtz, 1990), Sensorimotor Psychotherapy (Ogden, 2015), and Somatic Experiencing (SE; Levine, 2014). In addition, earlier chapters have described research identifying the relevance of intergenerational experiences (see McBride & Kwee, Chapter 2), sexuality (see Siemens & Kwee, Chapter 9), tracing body poems through eating disorder recovery (see Beyer & Launeanu, Chapter 11), embodiment through the lifespan (see Hurd Clarke, Chapter 12), neuroscience and embodiment (see Moncrief-Boyd, Nunn, & Frampton, Chapter 13), using plant medicine and traditional healing (see chapter about Ayahuasca; Renelli et al., Chapter 14), and using media to express resistance to disembodiment (see Shaw & Brown, Chapter 15). In this chapter, we will add to these strategies that promote embodiment by elaborating some practical ways of living in one's body inspired by the therapeutic framework of Existential Analysis (Längle, 2012).

Existential Analysis as a framework for promoting embodiment. While we draw on principles that overlap with these other contributions, in this chapter, we aim to describe exercises that are accessible to a variety of practitioners who may not be specifically trained in the specific therapeutic modalities described earlier. We will draw specifically on principles informed by Existential Analysis (see Launeanu & Kwee, Chapter 2) for providing a holistic framework for understanding embodiment and conceptualizing treatment within its dialogical framework and the structural model of the four Fundamental Motivations (FMs), including restoring physical space and safety, cultivating body sensuality and emotion, reclaiming an embodied self, and nurturing creativity and spirituality in and through the body. Although aspects of the suggested exercises are relevant to all four FMs, we will elaborate prompts to promote dialogue with one's body in the first section, under the heading "restoring physical space and safety."

Restoring physical space and safety. The process of restoring physical space and safety corresponds to the first FM in which we understand the body as the physical structure of human existence. The relevant questions are *Can I exist as a human being in this physical world with my own physicality?* or *Can I exist as a body in the world?* To answer affirmatively to these questions, one must experience space, protection, and support in one's embodied existence. As the experience of the body as supportive and safe is deeply disrupted in the experience of eating disorders, an intentional exploration of these areas represents an important step in restoring a sense of embodied experience. The body provides a firm, solid, stable ground for existence, and it holds and carries the person in this world. By experiencing being "held" and supported by one's body, we can bring the person into dialogue with her own body. The aim of this dialogue is to listen to the body and to experience what our body has to offer for being in the world. *Where do I feel supported in my body? Where does it hurt? Can I lean into my body? How does my body hold me? How do I experience my body as my home? Can I come home to my body?* The body also creates space, inwardly and outwardly. The body provides our first experience of space in the world. Restoring the experience of having space through our bodies is essential. We are visible to the world through the space we take up in it. We also take space inside, which we particularly experience through breath. Breath work that prompts a client to be aware of taking in air, holding it, and exhaling it can enhance a sense of inner space. *Can I breathe in fully? Can I feel space on the inside? Can I allow myself to take up space in this room (even for this moment)?* Together with breath work, stretching, progressive muscle relaxation, therapeutic movement or dance, and yoga, all cultivate the experience of being in the space of one's body and taking up space in the world. Even if not a central therapeutic intervention, helping clients to stop at the beginning of a session, to be aware of their breath, to be mindful of taking up space in the room (and perhaps consciously allowing their posture to reflect this taking up space), and giving themselves the time and space just for themselves are powerful ways to stimulate an inner sense of being in the space of one's body. The body also provides protection, a container in which we feel protected from the outside world. In this sense, it is helpful to encourage clients to ask themselves, *What is my body able to do? How does my body protect me?*

Body visualization. To promote a more engaged and intentional dialogue with the body as our source of physical space and safety, we encourage using visualization exercises for talking to one's body, listening to one's body, noticing it, and being mindfully aware of inhabiting it. We ask what the body is saying as we enter in dialogue with it. The alienation from one's body that is experienced in eating disorders makes this exercise threatening and nearly impossible without having sufficient external support at the beginning. This external support and prompting for body visualization and dialogue is what the therapist or other eating disorder practitioner offers. In dialogue with their bodies, we help our clients ask if they can allow their bodies to hold them and if they can surrender to the support and reliability (even if it feels limited) of their bodies. We are receptive beings and as such, "things" talk to us, touch us, and move us. Hence, we need to let our bodies talk to us, to listen carefully to them, and also to use our bodies to listen to the world, and to speak on our behalf to the world. We support clients in sensing the body from within, helping them to ask, *What sensations do I experience now in my body?* Clients may be aware of experiencing a variety of sensations such as tingling tightness, pressure, warmth or coldness, twitching or numbness, and disconnect.

Psychosomatic sensing and feeling helps us to see things that we would otherwise miss. A body visualization exercise takes a client through each part of their body, perhaps starting with the head and moving through the whole body ending in the toes. The focus is on allowing the body to speak to them and on imagining being in each part of the body. It gives the client and therapist a sense of how much contact the client has with her body, how much she relies on it, and how well she lives in it. It gives a sense of which parts of one's body the person may not be in good contact with, and perhaps which parts of the body are holding trauma and pain. Some question prompts that may be used in a body visualization exercise include the following:

- How do I experience my body in this moment?
- What physical sensations am I aware of? What do I sense in my body? What is my body telling me?
- How close is my body to me? How close am I to my body?
- How well do I live inside my body? Do I take up every part of my body, or do I only live in some of them?
- How much sensitivity do I have for my body? How can I show care for my body in this moment?
- Do I feel gratitude to have this body? Would I rather have a different one? Is there any part of my body that I feel grateful for in this moment?
- What is my body providing for me right now? How do I receive this?
- Do I notice my body when it feels pleasure or only pain? Can I feel it when it is well? Can I feel it when it is sick?

Biographical exploration of the body. Biographical exploration of one's relationship with her body can provide clues for a client to understand their current experience of their bodies. The following are questions that can help a client explore their "body story" and increase a sense of dialogue with her body:

- How have I experienced my body over the course of my life? Has my relationship with my body changed? How and when did it change?
- Have I experienced my body as a sick body that hindered me or didn't support me in doing the things I wanted to do? Have I experienced disabilities in my body? Have I been prone to sickness?
- What has my family taught me about my body and bodies in general? Are physical bodies valued as important in my family? Were bodies allowed to take up space, to be loud, to have needs, and to be cared for in my family? Were bodies valued as tools to work? Were bodies valued for their beauty? Did my family see bodies as "dirty," belonging to the back alleys of existence, or were bodies important and precious? How did my family deal with sickness and injuries?
- How did my family physically express care and tenderness? Was there cuddling, hugging, kissing, and holding? Was there physical abuse or punishment? Were there contradictions in physical and verbal expressions about my body?
- What role did food have in my home growing up? What were our eating habits? Did we eat together as family? Did we enjoy food? Did people diet? Were some foods seen as "bad"?
- What were attitudes toward sports, fitness, and health in my family?
- How did I learn about hygiene? Was hygiene merely executed for cleanliness or was it a way to nurture and love my body? How do I exercise hygiene now? Do I just take a bath to be clean, or do I take it to relax and care for my skin? Do I put on sunscreen quickly just to prevent burning, or is this a way to nurture and care for my body?

- What were my family's attitudes toward sexuality? How was this seen, felt, and talked about? Could I show myself naked in my family? When was this no longer acceptable? Was my body or sexuality sometimes taken advantage of? Was sexuality seen as threatening?
- How did my family teach me to take care of my clothes and hair?

Body attitudes. Deepening further a client's dialogue with her body, the following prompts explore one's attitudes in relationship with her body:

- What is my attitude about having a body?
- What is the relationship of distance and closeness that I have in my body?
- Is my relationship with my body a loving one? Can I touch or stroke my own body? What is it like to look at myself naked? Can I see beauty in my body?
- Do I live *in* my body?
- How do I feel about *being* my body?
- How do I take care of my body well and when do I neglect it?
- Does my body feel too big or too small for me? What kind of space do I feel I need in my body to be me?

Personal evaluation. In dialogue, we not only listen and talk, but we also consider, reflect, seek to understand, and make personal judgments. This is particularly important in restoring agency in the full embodied person. It is not just what *is* that matters, but the person is invited to show up and take a position toward what is. The following prompts can be used for stimulating the inner evaluation about one's relationship with one's body:

- Is my relationship with my body OK the way it is?
- What would I like to change about my relationship with my body?
- In what physical rhythms is my relationship with my body good (consider habits such as warm baths, brushing hair, sexuality, massage, and food)?
- In what areas would I like to have a different relationship with my body?

Movement exercises can also give clues to both the client and therapist about how the client's relationship with her body is. Does she enjoy movement in her body? Is it straining or does something feel painful or awkward?

Cultivating body sensuality and emotion. The body is also the source of life and is experienced as being alive or as "lived body" (Sartre, 1943). In our lived bodies, we experience emotionality, sensuality, and inner awareness of vitality. The relevant existential questions of the second

FM with respect to one's lived body are *Do I experience pleasure and goodness in and through my body? Do I like my body/living in my body?* Answering yes to these questions requires access to sensuality, emotionality, and relationality. People with eating disorders often experience inner numbness or deadness with limited emotionality and scarce connections with others and with life itself. Allowing emotions, including negative emotions, to be felt and expressed are pathways toward connecting with life again. For example, asking questions such as *Have grief and rage been silenced? With whom does the client have relationships? Does she experience closeness and warmth with others? When does she experience pleasure?* may bring to the fore fertile areas of exploring one's experience and connection with the lived body.

Avenues for cultivating the sensual body include artistic appreciation and expression, poetry, dance and movement, enjoyment of nature, gardening, and sexuality. If appropriate in the context of your role as an eating disorder practitioner, consider the role of nature walks or observation of nature or suggesting these to the client. Through our senses, we experience beauty, value, and goodness. To cultivate the sensual body, we help clients slow down to savor beauty and pleasure in everyday activities and interactions that are not just food related. Savoring beauty and pleasure that is not food related is a less threatening place to begin with people suffering from eating disorders. Eventually, being able to taste and thoroughly enjoy food is a major sensual accomplishment.

The relational body is experienced through spending time with others, eye contact, closeness, and physical touch. An openness to emotions and to life is paralleled by the openness to the other. The capacity for relational experiencing of closeness can also be cultivated in the psychotherapeutic relationship. Can the client experience the warmth of being cared for, attuned to, given time and undivided attention?

As explored earlier (see Siemens & Kwee, Chapter 9), sexual embodiment or the experience of being one's whole self through and within one's body has been identified as an avenue for reclaiming body-self unity and a sense of pleasure in one's body. Encouraging clients to explore subjective connection to their bodies and sexuality appears to be a pathway toward embodied wholeness. This represents a movement from objectification to 'subjectification' of one's own experience as a whole person, from within one's own senses and physicality. Becoming attuned to one's whole self in and through one's senses (i.e., sexual, emotional, relational) facilitates awareness as a body.

Reclaiming embodied sense of self. The most subjective, intimate, and personal side of one's experience with the body is being one's body. In other words, experiencing that my body is my physical identity: I am my body. Without this experience of the body-self unity, the person only experiences having a body and, thus, a constant distance or separation between one's sense of self and one's body. If I only have a body, then my body is the object of my consciousness and I am separated from it. The experience "I am my body" restores the essential unity of psyche and matter, and the most intimate connection with one's lived physicality.

The existential questions pertaining to the body in the third FM include *May I be my body? Am I allowed to be myself in my body? Does my body show or express authentically who I am?* We express ourselves through our body; our bodies reveal our persons to the world. The uniqueness of who we are shines through the materiality of our bodies. We each realize our existence in and through our bodies.

As therapists, we may use various prompts to invite clients to reflect on these themes more intentionally: *Do I feel that my body corresponds to who I am? Do I feel that my body is carrying and expressing my person, my unique essence in this world? How do I experience this? Do I feel that my body is indeed my body, or is this a foreign body to me? Are there any particular activities or perhaps other people who help me feel myself in my body?*

A very important area of exploration related to FM3 is that of personal physical boundaries that delimitate one's self from others in order to protect one's own. Research has indicated that people suffering from eating disorders had experienced significant violations of their personal boundaries and, thus, may experience boundary confusion or difficulties setting boundaries (Piran, 2016). Hence, therapists working with these individuals may want to focus on exploring this area more intentionally by inviting clients to experiment and reflect on how they set interpersonal boundaries: *Do I set physical boundaries with my body? How is it for me to do that? How do I do that?* (For example, do I cross my arms, sit higher in the chair, move away or lean forward, etc.?) *What is the comfortable physical distance between me and another person? What is it too close or too far away for me? Can I use my body to delineate my physical space that allows me to be myself? Am I aware of my physical boundaries?*

In order for someone to experience "I am my body," one needs to receive attention and respect, justice, and appreciation toward one's body. In therapy, the following prompts may be used to explore whether clients have experienced enough of these conditions for the development of their embodied self-worth: *Who respects and appreciates my body? Do I feel respected, appreciated, and taken seriously with respect to my body? Do I pay attention to my body? How?* (For example, do I soothe and relax my body after an extenuating workday or after exercising? Do I sleep enough to rest my body as a way to showing respect to myself?) *Do I respect myself in how I treat my body? Do I take my body cues seriously? Do I pay attention to what my body needs? What do I appreciate or value about my body?* Therapists may encourage clients that in between therapy sessions, they deliberately engage in activities that show respect and appreciation for their bodies such as getting a massage, sleeping in over the weekend, and eating their favorite food.

Building self-acceptance of one's physicality as embodiment of one's self is crucial for individuals suffering from eating disorders. At the worst of their eating disorder, these people vehemently reject and hate their bodies, and describe them as ugly, clumsy, heavy, and disgusting (Beyer &

Launeanu, Chapter 11). Developing a sense of acceptance of one's body in the course of recovery from eating disorders represents a very difficult task, usually accomplished imperfectly and in small increments. Here are some suggestions for reflecting on this theme of self-acceptance of one's body: *What can I accept about my body? Do I accept myself in my body? Do I accept my flaws as well as what I value about my body?*

An important dimension of FM3 is that of the moral conscience and related self-conscious emotionality (e.g., shame, guilt). Our moral sense is essentially embodied, and we experience embodied moral agency through our bodies as we experience a felt, embodied sense of right and wrong in a given situation. Individuals struggling with eating disorders are significantly more prone to discount this felt sense of what fits with themselves and to feel ashamed or guilty as a result (Racine & Wildes, 2013). Hence, it is helpful for the therapist to encourage clients to attend to the felt sense of what fits or does not fit with one's self: *Does it feel right to do this with or to my body? Does this fit with who I am? Does this food fit with my body? Do I feel right about eating this or about doing this kind of exercise? How does this sit with me?*

Finally, FM3 is not exclusively about one's self in isolation but rather about one's self in personal encounters with the others. Some of these encounters involve the body to a significant degree and expose one's embodied self (e.g., intimate touch, sexuality). Often, individuals affected by eating disorders experience difficulties in their physical intimate encounters with others. Hence, therapists may invite these clients to reflect on the following: *With whom do I feel comfortable to share a hug or even a more intimate embrace? May I be myself in my sexual encounters? Do I enjoy intimate touch? Do I feel ashamed of my body?*

Nurturing freedom, creativity, and spirituality in and through the body. Finally, we ask the existential questions of the fourth FM: *What do I find meaningful in being and having this body? What valuable possibilities can come through my body? Where or for what is my body needed? How can I contribute to my life and even to the world through my body?* After considering what can I do in and through my body, what do I like to do in my body, and what is me in my body, one is now free to consider what one wants and ought to do with one's body. For instance, in our bodies, we have opportunity for freedom and movement, creativity, belonging to a larger context, and, thus, experiencing our spirituality.

Therapeutically, from the fourth FM perspective, we support our clients in listening to what is meaningful and valuable for them. *Where do they experience meaningful belonging? For what can their bodies be useful and purposeful? What is meaningful for them with respect to their embodied existence?* For example, do they find meaning in their body capacity to experience pleasure or pain, to feel one's strength and resistance in interacting with the world, or to connect intimately with another person through their body? Or do they rather experience meaninglessness, lack of purpose, and even a sense of burden in these opportunities?

Discovering and cultivating one's embodied agency, sense of freedom, capacity to move one's body, and creativity by engaging in physical activities that may lead to creating valuable existential possibilities are critical in preventing and recovering from eating disorders (see Beyer & Launeanu, Chapter 11). Typically, individuals who struggle with their bodies or with eating disturbances tend to experience their bodies as a prison, feel trapped in their bodies, and experience their bodies as useless and burdensome. They also tend to lose their capacity to engage flexibly and spontaneously in physical activities but rather perform these in a mechanical, repetitive manner (see Beyer & Launeanu, Chapter 11). Hence, it is particularly important that therapists explore these themes intentionally in working with these clients.

With respect to one's sense of agency, therapists may invite their clients to explore the following themes: *What does my body want to do in this moment? If I allowed my body to do that, how would that be? May I allow my body to do what I want? May I choose freely what to do with my body?* Being aware of what one's body wants or desires and learning how to express one's will through one's body are critical milestones in the process of recovery from an eating disorder (see Beyer & Launeanu, Chapter 11) because they allow the person to restore their embodied sense of agency and control.

Often, recovering one's embodied agency goes hand in hand with experiencing an increased sense of freedom in one's body. Having become aware of what one's body wants, the person can now explore her capacity to choose and her freedom to do so. Closely related to freedom is one's responsibility for one's choices. In this sense, therapists may invite clients to reflect on the following themes: *Do I feel free in my body? Do I experience my body as free? Do I experience my will in my body actions or attitudes? If I made this choice regarding my body, what are the consequences? Can I take responsibility for these consequences?* Addressing freedom and responsibility together as they relate to one's body may be a powerful therapeutic tool for discussing some difficult or sensitive topics such as "if I made the choice to starve myself, could I face the consequences of my choice, and is this choice truly reflecting my freedom or the compulsive voice of the eating disorder?" These explorations contribute to restoring one's sense of agency and voice that leads to further empowerment.

A special way through which embodied freedom can be fully experienced is through engaging in spontaneous and pleasurable body movement. Restoring the capacity to delight in one's body capacity to move was described as a key moment in recovery from anorexia (see Beyer & Launeanu, Chapter 11). Here are some prompts to explore and promote this capacity in psychotherapy: *Do I enjoy moving my body, or do I exercise compulsively in order to burn calories and stay thin? Am I mindful of my body movements? Am I aware that my body movements allow me to go places, to explore and accomplish what I want? What movements do I enjoy and want to do?*

Eventually, experiencing an increased sense of agency and freedom allows the person to become creative in and through her body. The theme to explore in this area is: *What can I create with or through my body?* For example, if I am a woman and I choose so, my body could bring a human being into this world. Or, I can create beautiful movements and enchanting choreographic stories by moving my body to the music in dancing. Or, I could bring forth the strength and gracefulness of the human body by enjoying a sport or any physical activity. All these activities are possibilities through which the body expresses the deep creative spark of the person and contributes to the creation of values such as beauty, gracefulness, and strength.

A key question related to experiencing creativity through one's body is *What good or valuable possibility could come into this world through my body?* For example, I can delight others by performing a beautiful dance, or I can inspire someone to start a sport because of my passionate engagement in that sport. In order to experience embodied creativity, one needs to engage in physical activities that are freely chosen and enjoyed, and that reflect one's wants and preferences. Hence, the therapist may want to encourage clients to reflect on the following questions: *Do I regularly engage in physical activities such as dancing, sports, and yoga? Do I enjoy these activities? Do I choose these, and do I feel free while doing them? What do these activities bring that's valuable in my life? Do they contribute to my life and my well-being, or do I do them as a means to a goal (e.g., not to gain weight)?*

Conclusion

Our bodies provide our first space to live in; they provide reliability and support. Health gives us the experience of the continuity of life. The body provides support to our existence, and we also experience our bodies being supported in the physical world that we belong to. We experience regularities in our bodies through the rhythms of sleep, hunger, eating and being satisfied, and menstruation. The body provides the vital ground and foundation for our existence. It carries and nourishes our spiritual and psychological life. Without our bodies, we cannot feel. Without our bodies, we cannot think. Without our bodies, we cannot love or receive love. Our bodies are the spaces through which each of our lives is realized and through which we dedicate ourselves to a sense of purpose. True recovery from eating disorders must integrate self within body.

As practitioners working with people suffering from eating disorders, we encourage you to think inclusively and creatively about how to promote embodied experiencing in your clients. Do this with the aim to see them become more as people, not just to weigh more as bodies. Do this with the risk that it is not nearly as "safe" as implementing a treatment plan based on eating logs, weigh-ins, and BMI calculations. Many useful body meditations and visualizations exist. See, for example, the work of Tara

Brach (www.tarabrach.com), whose meditations for cultivating embodied presence are available online. We encourage you to pursue more training in the therapeutic modalities and preventive approaches described in earlier chapters in this book. In order to effectively support people who suffer from eating disorders to full health, we need to stand against the objectification prevalent in our society and in treatment that perpetuates mind-body dualism. Embodiment-focused goals for eating disorder recovery focus on mind-body integration and wholeness with an aim for the client to become more of oneself within oneself and in taking up space in the world.

References

Allan, H. T. (2005). Gender and embodiment in nursing: The role of the female chaperone in the infertility clinic. *Nursing Inquiry, 12,* 175–183.

American Psychiatric Association. (2013). *Diagnostic and statistical manual of mental disorders* (5th ed.). Washington, DC: American Psychiatric Association.

Beyer, C., Chan, E., Kwee, J., Launeanu, M., & McBride, H. (2016). *Seeking the body electric: Understanding eating disorders through embodiment and feminist-existential lenses.* Presentation, CPA Convention.

Beyer, C., & Launeanu, M. (in press). Poems of the past, present and future: Becoming a more embodied self in recovering from anorexia nervosa. In H. L. McBride & J. K. Kwee (Eds.), *Healthy embodiment and eating disorders: Theory, Research, Prevention and treatment.* New York, NY: Routledge.

Carter, J. C., Blackmore, E., Sutandar-Pinnock, K., & Woodside, D. B. (2004). Replase in anorexia nervosa: A survival analysis. *Psychological Medicine, 34,* 671–679. doi:10.1017/S0033291703001168

Galsworthy-Francis, L., & Allan, S. (2014). Cognitive behavioural therapy for anorexia nervosa: A systematic review. *Clinical Psychology Review, 34,* 54–72. doi:10.1016/j.cpr.2013.11.001

Heidegger, M. (1962). *Being and time.* Oxford, UK: Blackwell Publishers Ltd.

Kass, A. E., Kolko, R. P., & Wilfley, D. E. (2013). Psychological treatments for eating disorders. *Current Opinion Psychiatry, 6,* 549–555. doi:10.1097/YCO.0b013e328365a30a

Kurtz, R. (1990). *Body-centered psychotherapy: The Hakomi method.* Mendecino, CA: LifeRhythm.

Längle, A. (2012). The Viennese School of Existential Analysis. The search for Meaning and Affirmation of Life. In L. Barnett & G. Madison (Eds.), *Existential therapy: Legacy, vibrancy, and dialogue* (pp. 159–170). New York, NY: Routledge.

Levine, P. (2014). *Somatic experiencing.* Astrolabio: Ubaldini.

Lipsman, N., Woodside, D. B., & Lozano, A. M. (2014). Trends in anorexia nervosa research: An analysis of the top 100 most cited works. *European Eating Disorders Review, 22,* 9–14.

Merleau-Ponty, M. (2012). *Phenomenology of perception* (D. L. Landes, Trans.). New York, NY: Routledge (Original work published 1945).

Ogden, P. (2015). *Sensorimotor psychotherapy: Interventions for trauma and attachment.* New York, NY: WW Norton.

Piran, N. (2016). Embodied possibilities and disruptions: The emergence of the experience of embodiment construct from qualitative studies with girls and women. *Body Image, 18,* 43–60. doi:10.1016/j.bodyim.2016.04.007

Racine, S. E., & Wildes, J. E. (2013). Emotion dysregulation and symptoms of anorexia nervosa: The unique roles of lack of emotional awareness and impulse control difficulties when upset. *International Journal of Eating Disroders, 46*(7), 713–720. doi:10.1002/eat.22145

Sáenz-Herrero, M., & Díez-Alegría, C. (2015). Gender and corporality, corporeality, and body image. In M. Sáenz-Herrero (Ed.), *Psychopathology in women: Incorporating gender perspective into descriptive psychopathology* (1st ed., pp. 113–142). Switzerland: Springer International Publishing. doi:10.1007/978-3-319-05870-2-6

Sartre, J. P. (1943). *Being and nothingness.* New York, NY: Washington Square Press.

Steinhausen, H. C. (2002). The outcome of anorexia nervosa in the 20th century. *American Journal of Psychiatry, 159,* 1284–1293.

Thompson, J. K. (1990). *Body image disturbance: Assessment and treatment. Psychology practitioner guidebooks.* Elmsford, NY: Pergamon Press.

Concluding Thoughts

22 Embodiment and Eating Disorders

An Emergent Vision for Theory, Research, and Practice

Janelle L. Kwee and Hillary L. McBride

It is a painful reality that eating disorders are hugely prevalent, have the highest mortality rate of any psychiatric diagnosis (Arcelus, Mitchell, Wales, & Nielsen, 2011; Jáuregui-Garrido & Jáuregui-Lobera, 2012) and represent a gendered and culturally situated phenomenon (Bordo, 1993). Women and girls receive between 90% and 95% of eating disorder diagnoses (Levine & Piran, 2004, Wilson, Becker, & Heffernan, 2003). And, while the number of women with eating disorders is rising, globally (Pike & Dunne, 2015), the risk of developing an eating disorder increases with time spent in Westernized cultures (Franko, 2007). Eating disorders have appropriately received significant attention in the academic and clinical literature in recent years; however, external body characteristics and behaviors have normally been emphasized, including weight, food and eating behaviors, and Body Mass Index (BMI), and these treatments have limited effectiveness (Wilson, Grilo, & Vitousek, 2007). In contrast, embodiment refers to the inextricable connection between mind and body in the unity of the self (Allan, 2005). The common thread among all of the contributions in this book is a focus on embodiment in eating disorder theory, research, prevention, and treatment.

Embodiment and eating disorders are situated at the crossroads of a variety of disciplines, and together they represent an integration of developmental, counseling, and clinical psychology, philosophy, medicine, politics, literature, culture, and neuroscience. While not all of these perspectives are integrated with equal representation, it has been our intent with this book to engage a broad dialogue about eating disorders and embodiment from a variety of disciplines. In this chapter, we attempt to bring together salient insights from the preceding chapters as they inform a future-oriented vision for what we need to better understand, prevent, and treat disordered eating.

Theoretical Perspectives of Embodiment and Eating Disorders

The first section of the book introduces the importance of embodiment for understanding eating disorders, situates eating disorders as a problem of gender-based oppression resulting from women's value existing in their bodies, explores phenomenological theories of embodiment and Existential Analysis, introduces the developmental theory of embodiment, presents the challenges in conceptualizing and measuring embodiment, and highlights the need for embodied approaches to research. In considering what is needed for conceptualizing embodiment and eating disorders as we move into the future, we address the need for a macro-system lens, a holistic conceptualization of the embodied self, and embodied research and measurement.

Macro-System Lens

While individualistic factors are normally used to describe and predict health and illness, the epidemic of disordered eating and normative body dissatisfaction is a product of a sociocultural context in which women's bodies are objectified, their worth is measured by appearance, and appearance standards are largely unattainable (Bordo, 1993; Levine & Piran, 2004; Piran & Cormier, 2005). Being female is itself a risk factor for developing eating disorders in Westernized patriarchal societies (Bordo, 1993; Levine & Piran, 2004). It has even been suggested that women and girls who suffer from eating disorders represent compliance and adherence to sociocultural values, making them the symptom bearers of the social disease of objectification and silencing of women's bodies and selves (Piran & Teall, 2012). Causality of eating disorders needs to be understood at multiple levels, with a significant shift toward a cultural macro-system lens. Only with this understanding going into the future will clinicians and all advocates of women and girls be equipped to target the broader problems that influence disordered eating behaviors. Moving forward, we suggest that it is dangerous and irresponsible for diagnostic conceptualizations of eating disorders to neglect contextual factors. Patriarchal objectification of women's bodies needs to be acknowledged as the source of the illness and addressed in programs designed to prevent and treat eating disorders.

Holistic Conceptualization of the Embodied Self

While related, embodiment represents a distinct concept from that of body image with embodiment being the lived experience of self as a body and body image representing more of a cognitive appraisal of one's body. The experience of embodiment is critical in understanding eating disorders, given the body-related struggles that persons suffering with eating disorders experience (Stanghellini, Castellini, Brogna, Faravelli, & Ricca, 2012). Disorders of food and eating represent existential struggles of the self, related to how to exist as a living body-being in the world. Future conceptualization, practice and research related to eating disorders need to maintain a holistic conceptualization of the self as inextricably connected to the lived body experience. We suggest that, when theorizing about eating disorders, academics think critically about how to center the body, and the lived experience of the body, in theory.

Embodied Research and Measurement

The challenge of capturing the messiness of lived human embodied experience in research is no more salient than it is in the field of eating disorder research. To maintain a feminist and transformative approach, we must maintain a vision to move past survey methods, and scaling questions representing a post-positivist paradigm, to capture the complexities and experiences of affect, sensuality, and psychic energy. Chan (Chapter 7) suggests that embodied methodologies should center around ways of accessing the "living energies" of storytelling. Further exploratory research is needed to continue to enhance our current understanding of embodiment, and ways to use embodiment for the prevention of eating disorders, and as an existential intervention for the treatment of eating disorders. Stanghellini et al.(Chapter 8) advocate overcoming simplistic behavioral assessments, and Launeanu et al.(Chapter 6) propose a phenomenologically grounded theoretical-methodological framework for conceptualizing and measuring embodiment. The future of eating disorder scholarship requires methods of inquiry that honor and give voice to embodied experience.

Research

Research in this volume relevant to embodiment and eating disorder addresses sexual shame and disordered eating as parallel manifestations of body objectification, hopeful evidence that the cycle of disembodiment can be interrupted intergenerationally, embodiment as experienced in stages of eating disorder recovery, the experience of (dis)embodiment as a product of ageism and healthism among older women, the neuroscience of eating disorders, and the use of plant medicine and traditional healing ceremonies in eating disorder treatment. As we reflected on these contributions and what we hope to see in the research literature related to eating disorders and embodiment moving forward, we identified several priorities. These include (a) greater inclusion of non-Western narratives and broader multidisciplinary perspectives of embodiment, (b) the use of transformative research paradigms, (c) outcome research of holistic embodiment-focused eating disorder interventions, and (d) research addressing men's experiences of eating disorders.

Non-Western Narratives and Broader Multidisciplinary Perspectives

Advancing research about eating disorders and embodiment will benefit from broader multidisciplinary dialogue and inclusion of more non-Western perspectives than we have been able to include in this book. For example, ethnographic research in the anthropology of the senses explores culturally distinct ways of perceiving and sensing that shape how people know and interact with the world around them. We believe that non-Western research about bodily perceiving sheds light on the limitations of the mind-body dichotomy that pervades Western traditions of culture and philosophy. For example, there is a linguistic reference in the Anlo-Ewe language (in Ghana) that refers to embodied knowing, equivalent to "feel-feel-at-flesh-inside" (Geurts, 2003). Perhaps this is similar to Ressler and Kleinman's (Chapter 20) description of "clinical intuition." Other research has shown how cognition and language are fundamentally shaped by people's subjective, felt experiences in their bodies, which are in dynamic interaction with their environments (Gibbs, 2017). Further research is needed that addresses the connection between cognition and the body as it relates to disordered eating. Another disciplinary perspective that is needed in this area of research is literary studies. Women's bodies as a site of political struggle emerges thematically in a wide variety of English literature, dating back far earlier than eating disorders were recognized as a psychiatric diagnosis (Silver, 2002). We suggest that this body of literature be brought into the academic discourse about eating disorders and embodiment and believe seeing the liberation of women through embodiment represented in literature, can be drawn on to change the current cultural narrative of femininity.

Transformative Research Paradigms

We envision a greater inclusion of transformative research paradigms to engage questions about embodiment and eating disorders with an aim to be part of societal change. As mentioned before, research from the post-positive paradigm is criticized by researchers doing feminist and transformative research for imposing assumptions on participants and restricting their ability to describe experiences as they are lived and understood by the participants themselves. Transformative research is designed to facilitate the dissolving of power hierarchies and the promotion of social justice. It is possible that by conducting research from a certain framework, the research community may facilitate further oppression of marginalization of certain people groups by leaving people feeling used, as though they have had their experiences or knowledge taken from them. This style of research honors the knowledge and experiences of the participants and invites them to join with the researchers to build meaning and understanding. As it has been framed in this book, the body is often the site of oppression for women, where because of complex systems, they are often disembodied. This includes the further silencing through reductive research endeavors. In the research community, we have a duty to find ways to minimize the disembodiment, using research to foster, not impair, the integration of self and body.

Emphasis on health and thriving. Although there is ample research addressing eating disorders, their development, and the consequences, there is still a paucity of research exploring embodied health and thriving. This includes more research about simply what embodiment is like for people who experience it. More research is needed, and then needs to be made available, about what families, communities, partners, care providers, and peers can do to support the development of embodiment, health, and thriving in individuals.

Outcome Research of Holistic Embodiment-Focused Eating Disorder Interventions

Given the importance of, yet relatively new interest in examining the relevance of embodiment to eating disorders in research (Underwood, 2013), outcome research of holistic embodiment-focused eating disorder interventions is immensely needed. Contributors to this book are suggesting that individuals who suffer from eating disorders need to be more themselves and more in their bodies. We largely reject the paradigm in eating disorder treatment of managing and controlling the body as a material object separate from the self. Consistent with our vision to see more embodied research strategies incorporated into this area, we recognize the need to shift research outcome questions from external body characteristics and behaviors to existential embodied questions of being an embodied self. Research that examines interventions with a holistic embodiment focus for eating disorder prevention and treatment needs to compare recidivism and relapse rates in eating disorders and also ask questions about participants' experience of personal agency, ability to "take up space" physically and relationally, and experience of "voice."

Men's Experiences of Eating Disorders

Most of the chapters in this book focus specifically on women's experiences of their bodies, eating disorders in women, and the social construction of women and femininity. However, rates of eating disorders among boys and men are rising (Anderson, 2014), and the patriarchal construction of men and masculinity is also harmful and limiting for males. Although the masculine body ideals are different from the feminine body ideals, they are similarly unattainable and dangerous. More research must be done to explore how eating disorders develop in boys and men, and how factors at every level of the ecological systems model facilitate the development, prevention, and treatment of disordered eating among men.

Prevention and Treatment

The exclusive focus on evaluating external characteristics of the body and behaviors, including weight, shape, and eating, promotes the disconnect between mind and body and perpetuates the split that has led to the problem of eating disorders in the first place. Contributors to the section on prevention and treatment have offered several alternatives of embodied intervention approaches, including (a) yoga; (b) various emotion-based psychotherapies including Emotion-Focused Therapy, Emotion-Focused Family Therapy, and Advanced Experiential Dynamic Psychotherapy; (c) "Free To Be talks" as a school-based health promotion program; (d) Lifespan Integration therapy; and (e) dance and movement therapy. As we move into the future of eating disorder prevention and treatment, we hope to see more health promotion and prevention, a stronger movement of social change and activism, and embodied treatment approaches becoming the gold standard in eating disorder best practice.

More Health Promotion

Health promotion can take many forms and occurs at the level of broad societal views, as well as in individual and community practices. Here, we discuss the need for health promotion programs and identify the protective role of spirituality in promoting healthy experiences of embodiment.

Program development. It is important that there are programs like Free To Be as part of health curriculums in schools and that these programs are understood by teachers and school administrators who support the vision and engage in becoming embodied themselves. Workplace health promotion programs also need to be developed. For many people, work is a relatively disembodied place where people sit still all day at a computer or a desk. Workplaces need to develop body-centered policies. This may include things like work-sponsored yoga or walks during lunch breaks, or permission to use standing desks, or to take walking meetings.

Spirituality. Spirituality is an important resource for the development embodiment and the prevention of eating disorders across the lifespan. Spirituality can be more readily integrated into all levels of treatment as an additional resource to support eating disorder recovery. When individuals struggling with eating disorders identify with spiritual practices which are supportive of their recovery, individuals will likely benefit from having clinicians honor those spiritual practices, perhaps integrating them into treatment when appropriate.

Social Change and Activism

As exemplified in the chapter of Shaw Nevins and Brown (Chapter 15), we can engage in cultural political resistance through whatever mediums we have available to influence levels of the ecosystem. This can include participating in political actions, refusing to purchase certain products, making visible different kinds of bodies in our personal and professional endeavors (for example, following body positivity accounts on social media), and communicating publicly about our resistance to invite others to think critically. This may also include critical conversations with men and boys about the harmful nature both for men and women of masculinity and its associated appearance pressures.

Embodied Treatment Approaches

The return of agency and experience within the body must be a priority for treatment in eating disorders facilities. When individuals are medically stable to engage in therapy, embodied therapies must not be peripheral or secondary, but must be a primary and standard approach to the treatment of eating disorders. This includes the uses of body-focused therapies including those described in this book as well as others such as Hakomi Body-Centered Therapy (Kurtz, 1990), Sensorimotor Psychotherapy (Ogden, Minton, & Pain, 2006), and Somatic Experiencing (Payne, Levine, & Crane-Godreau, 2015). Treatment facilities, outpatient programs, and individual therapists need to find ways to incorporate a variety of body-based activities to enhance the lived experience of embodiment in their clients. This could include things like yoga, dance, authentic movement, music and art, and martial arts.

Embodied clinicians. To most fully engender this paradigm shift in eating disorder work, clinicians must prioritize their own development as embodied beings in life and in clinical practice. To promote embodiment in others, clinicians must show up in their body-self unity, thus valuing and practicing themselves the embodiment they desire to take root in others. This models embodiment for clients as it is made visible for them in session and enhances the therapist's own capacity to feel presence within themselves and to make therapeutic use of their somatic awareness.

Concluding Comments

The seriousness of eating disorders, and the problematic context within which they develop, demands an informed response. This response needs to involve multiple approaches from multiple disciplines, which target different levels of the social ecological system to promote embodiment among girls and women, boys and men. These efforts should be focused on prevention, promotion of health and well-being, and effective treatment of disordered eating. Incorporating a holistic lens of embodiment which acknowledges the sociopolitical context of eating disorders impacts various aspects of our work, including (a) how we write and theorize about embodiment and eating disorders; (b) our research questions and methods; and (c) our lived action in programs for prevention, therapeutic intervention, and social and political activism. Combined multidisciplinary efforts in these areas will ultimately influence all levels of our social ecology, from the personal existential experience of embodiment that we have as individuals to changes in the sociocultural landscape. The scope of the challenges associated with eating disorders requires a multidisciplinary effort aimed at decreasing human suffering, increasing human flourishing, and promoting healing within a society that has perpetuated body objectification and the proliferation of disordered eating.

References

Allan, H. T. (2005). Gender and embodiment in nursing: The role of the female chaperone in the infertility clinic. *Nursing Inquiry, 12*, 175–183.

Anderson, A. (2014). A brief history of eating disorders in males. In L. Cohn & R. Lemberg (Eds.), *Current findings on males with eating disorders*. New York, NY: Routledge.

Arcelus, J., Mitchell, A. J., Wales, J., & Nielsen, S. (2011). Mortality rates in patients with anorexia nervosa and other eating disorders: A meta-analysis of 36 studies. *Archives of General Psychiatry, 68*(7), 724–731. doi:10.1001/archgenpsychiatry.2011.74

Bordo, S. (1993). *Unberable weight*. Los Angeles, CA: University of California Press.

Franko, D. L. (2007). Race, ethnicity, and eating disorders: Considerations for DSM-V. *International Journal of Eating Disorders, 40*(Suppl.), S31–S34. doi:10.1002/eat.20455Geurts, K. L. (2003). *Culture and the senses: Bodily ways of knowing in an African community*. Berkeley: University of California Press. doi:10.1525/j.ctt1pnrfv

Gibbs, R. W. (2017). *Metaphor wars: Conceptual metaphors in human life*. New York, NY: Cambridge University Press.

Jáuregui-Garrido, B., & Jáuregui-Lobera, I. (2012). Sudden death in eating disorders. *Vascular Health and Risk Management, 8*, 91–98. doi:10.2147/VHRM. S28652

Kurtz, R. (1990). *Body-centered psychotherapy: The hakomi method: The integrated use of mindfulness, nonviolence and the body*. Mendocino, CA: LifeRhythm.

Levine, M. P., & Piran, N. (2004). The role of body image in the prevention of eating disorders. *Body Image: An International Journal of Research, 1*, 57–70. doi:10.1016/S1740-1445(03)00006-8

Ogden, P., Minton, K., & Pain, C. (2006). *Trauma and the body: A sensorimotor approach to psychotherapy*. New York, NY: W.W. Norton.

Payne, P., Levine, P. A., & Crane-Godreau, M. A. (2015). Somatic experiencing: Using interoception and proprioception as core elements of trauma therapy. *Frontiers in Psychology, 6*, 93. doi:10.3389/fpsyg.2015.00093

Pike, K. M., & Dunne, P. E. (2015). The rise of eating disorders in Asia: A review. *Journal of Eating Disorders, 3*(1), 33.

Piran, N., & Cormier, H. C. (2005). The social construction of women and disordered eating patterns. *Journal of Counseling Psychology, 52*, 549–558.

Piran, N., & Teall, T. (2012). *The developmental theory of embodiment. Preventing eating-related and weight-related disorders: Collaborative research, advocacy, and policy change* (pp. 169–198). Waterloo, ON: Wilfred Laurier University Press.

Silver, A. K. (2002). *Victorian literature and the anorexic body.* Cambridge, UK: Cambridge University Press.

Stanghellini, G., Castellini, G., Brogna, P., Faravelli, C., & Ricca, V. (2012). Identity and eating disorders (IDEA): A questionnaire evaluating identity and embodiment in eating disorder patients. *Psychopathology, 45*(3), 147–158. doi:10.1159/000330258

Underwood, M. (2013). Body as choice or body as compulsion: An experiential perspective on body-self relations and the boundary between normal and pathological. *Health Sociology Review, 22*, 377–388.

Wilson, G. T., Becker, C. B., & Heffernan, K. (2003). Eating disorders. In E. J. Mash & R. A. Barkley (Eds.), *Child psychopathology* (2nd ed.). New York, NY: Guilford Press.

Wilson, G. T., Grilo, C. M., & Vitousek, K. M. (2007). Psychological treatment of eating disorders. *American Psychologist, 62*(3), 199–216. doi:10.1037/0003-066X.62.3.199

Index

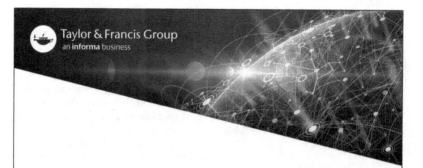